THE EMC Write-In READER
The American Tradition

Reading Strategies and Test Practice

PINE LEVEL

EMCParadigm Publishing Company

Staff Credits

Editorial

Laurie Skiba
Managing Editor

Brenda Owens
Editor

Becky Palmer
Reading Specialist

Nichola Torbett
Associate Editor

Jennifer Joline Anderson
Associate Editor

Diana Moen
Associate Editor

Mary Curfman
Editorial Consultant

Paul Spencer
Art and Photo Researcher

Design and Production

Shelley Clubb
Production Manager

Matthias Frasch
Cover Designer and Production Specialist

Jennifer Wreisner
Text Designer

Erica Tava
Production Specialist

Lisa Beller
Production Specialist

Sharon O'Donnell
Proofreader

ISBN 0-8219-2918-6
© 2005 EMC Corporation

All rights reserved. No part of this publication may be adapted, reproduced, stored in a retrieval system, or transmitted in any form or by any means, electronic, mechanical, photocopying, recording, or otherwise without permission from the publisher.

Published by EMC/Paradigm Publishing
875 Montreal Way
St. Paul, Minnesota 55102
www.emcp.com
E-mail: educate@emcp.com

Printed in the United States of America
10 9 8 7 6 5 4   XXX 10 09 08 07

Consultants and Contributors

Maria Callis
Reading Specialist/Department Chair
Trafalgar Middle School
Cape Coral, Florida

Shari Carlson
English/Reading Instructor
Fridley Middle School
Fridley, Minnesota

T. Carolyn Coleman
Language Arts/Reading Instructor
Gwinnett County Schools
Lawrenceville, Georgia

Dr. Edmund J. Farrell
Emeritus Professor of English Education
University of Texas at Austin
Austin, Texas

Sharon Kremer
Language Arts Instructor
Denton High School
Denton, Texas

Lisa Larnerd
English Department Chairperson
Basic High School
Henderson, Nevada

Beth Lee
Language Arts Instructor
Heritage Middle School
Longmont, Colorado

Cecilia Lewis
Language Arts Instructor
Mariner High School
Cape Coral, Florida

John Oricchio
Educational Consultant
Port Washington, New York

John Owens
Literacy Specialist
Heritage Middle School
Longmont, Colorado

Mary Spychalla
English/Reading Instructor
Valley Middle School
Apple Valley, Minnesota

Contents

Overview of Skills	viii
Overview of Features	xi
How to Use This Book	xii

UNIT 1 INTRODUCTION TO READING

PURPOSES OF READING	1
Reading for Experience	1
Reading to Learn	1
Reading for Information	2
THE READING PROCESS	2
Before Reading	2
During Reading	3
After Reading	3
USING ACTIVE READING STRATEGIES	4
1 Read with a Purpose	4
2 Connect to Prior Knowledge	6
3 Write Things Down	7
4 Make Predictions	10
5 Visualize	12
6 Use Text Organization	12
7 Tackle Difficult Vocabulary	13
8 Monitor Your Reading Progress	14
UNIT 1 READING REVIEW	16

UNIT 2 ESSENTIAL READING SKILLS

READING SKILLS	17
Identify the Author's Purpose	18
Find the Main Idea	19
Make Inferences	20
Use Context Clues	20
Analyze Text Organization	22
Identify Sequence of Events	23
Compare and Contrast	24
Evaluate Cause and Effect	25
Classify and Reorganize Information	26
Distinguish Fact from Opinion	27
Interpret Visual Aids	28
Understand Literary Elements	30
Draw Conclusions	31
UNIT 2 READING REVIEW	33

UNIT 3 READING FICTION

FICTION			35
Forms of Fiction			35
Elements of Fiction			36
USING READING STRATEGIES WITH FICTION			39
Ambrose Bierce	"An Occurrence at Owl Creek Bridge"	Make Predictions	42
Mark Twain	"The Notorious Jumping Frog of Calaveras County"	Tackle Difficult Vocabulary	57
Kate Chopin	"The Story of an Hour"	Write Things Down	69
Katherine Anne Porter	"The Jilting of Granny Weatherall"	Write Things Down	77
Eudora Welty	"A Worn Path"	Visualize	92
Tim O'Brien	"Ambush"	Visualize	106
UNIT 3 READING REVIEW			114

THE EMC WRITE-IN READER

Unit 4 Reading Poetry

Poetry			117
Forms of Poetry			117
Techniques of Poetry: Imagery			118
Techniques of Poetry: Shape			118
Techniques of Poetry: Rhythm			119
Techniques of Poetry: Sound			120
Using Reading Strategies with Poetry			120
Anne Bradstreet	"To My Dear and Loving Husband"	Tackle Difficult Vocabulary	124
Emily Dickinson	"This is my letter to the World," "Because I could not stop for Death—," and "I heard a Fly buzz—when I died—"	Connect to Prior Knowledge	129
Edgar Allan Poe	"The Raven"	Tackle Difficult Vocabulary	137
Walt Whitman	from "Song of Myself"	Read with a Purpose	147
Robert Frost	"Mending Wall"	Write Things Down	158
Langston Hughes	"I, too, sing America" and "The Negro Speaks of Rivers"	Connect to Prior Knowledge	164
E. E. Cummings	"somewhere i have never travelled, gladly beyond" and "anyone lived in a pretty how town"	Use Text Organization	170
Unit 4 Reading Review			178

Unit 5 Reading Folk Literature

Folk Literature			181
Types of Folk Literature			181
Using Reading Strategies with Folk Literature			182
Tewa Tribal Song	"Song of the Sky Loom"	Write Things Down	186
African-American Folk Song	"Follow the Drinking Gourd"	Visualize	191
Anonymus African-American Spiritual	"Swing Low, Sweet Chariot"	Connect to Prior Knowledge	197
Stephen C. Foster	"My Old Kentucky Home"	Use Text Organization	202
Julia Ward Howe	"The Battle Hymn of the Republic"	Read with a Purpose	208
Unit 5 Reading Review			215

Unit 6 Reading Drama

Drama			219
Types of Drama			219
Elements of Drama			219
Using Reading Strategies with Drama			221
Arthur Miller	from *The Crucible*, Act 3	Visualize	225
Tennessee Williams	from *The Glass Menagerie*, Act 1, Scenes 1–3	Write Things Down	235
Unit 6 Reading Review			259

Unit 7 Reading Nonfiction

Nonfiction			263
Forms of Nonfiction			263
Purposes and Methods of Writing in Nonfiction			264
Types of Nonfiction Writing			265
Using Reading Strategies with Nonfiction			266
Jonathan Edwards	from "Sinners in the Hands of an Angry God"	Read with a Purpose	270
Patrick Henry	Speech to the Virginia Convention	Read with a Purpose	278
Ralph Waldo Emerson	from "Self-Reliance"	Write Things Down	286
Henry David Thoreau	from *Walden*	Use Text Organization	293
Abraham Lincoln	The Gettysburg Address	Use Text Organization	312

Chief Joseph	"I will fight no more forever"	Connect to Prior Knowledge	317
John Hersey	"A Noiseless Flash"	Write Things Down	322
UNIT 7 READING REVIEW			342

UNIT 8 READING INFORMATIONAL AND VISUAL MEDIA

INFORMATIONAL AND VISUAL MEDIA			345
Informational Media			345
Elements of Informatioal Media			346
Electronic Media			346
Elements of Electronic Media			346
Visual Media			347
Elements of Visual Media			347
Bartolome de las Casas	from *The Very Brief Relation of the Devastation of the Indies*	Tackle Difficult Vocabulary	352
Anonymous	from *The New England Primer*	Connect to Prior Knowledge	361
Thomas Jefferson	Declaration of Independence	Read with a Purpose	367
from *Literature and the Language Arts: The American Tradition*	"The Susan B. Anthony Dollar"	Write Things Down	377
John Dos Passos	from *The Big Money*, "Newsreel LXVII"	Use Text Organization	383
UNIT 8 READING REVIEW			393

UNIT 9 DEVELOPING VOCABULARY SKILLS

TACKLING DIFFICULT VOCABULARY AS YOU READ	397
Using Definitions, Footnotes, Endnotes, and Glossaries	397
Using Context Clues	398
Using Your Prior Knowledge	399
Common Prefixes Chart	400
Common Suffixes Chart	401
Common Word Roots Chart	402
Combining Forms Chart	406
Exploring Word Origins and Word Families	407
Using a Dictionary	408
Understanding Multiple Meanings	409
Understanding Denotation and Connotation	409
IMPROVING YOUR ACTIVE VOCABULARY	409
Keeping a Word Study Notebook	409
Using Mnemonic Devices	411
Categorizing and Classifying Words	411
Learning Synonyms, Antonyms, and Homonyms	412
UNIT 9 VOCABULARY REVIEW	414

UNIT 10 TEST-TAKING STRATEGIES

PREPARING FOR TESTS IN YOUR CLASSES	417
Answering Objective Questions	418
Answering Essay Questions	419
TAKING STANDARDIZED TESTS	421
Answering Multiple-Choice Questions	421
Answering Reading Comprehension Questions	422
Answering Analogy Questions	423
Answering Synonym and Antonym Questions	424
Answering Sentence Completion Questions	424
Answering Constructed-Response Questions	425
UNIT 10 TEST-TAKING REVIEW	427

APPENDICES

| APPENDIX A: BUILDING READING FLUENCY | A-1 |
| WORD RECOGNITION SKILLS | A-2 |

Increase Your Automaticity	A-2
Crossword Puzzle	A-3
Word Race	A-4
Word Matrix	A-5
SILENT READING SKILLS	A-6
Increase the Amount You Read	A-6
How Much Can You Learn in 10 Minutes?	A-6
Free Reading Log	A-7
Pages-per-Minute Graph	A-8
Minutes-per-Section Graph	A-8
ORAL READING SKILLS	A-9
Perform Rereading Activities	A-9
Repeated Reading Exercise	A-11
Repeated Reading Record	A-12
Passages for Fluency Practice	A-13

APPENDIX B: GRAPHIC ORGANIZERS FOR READING STRATEGIES	**B-1**
READING STRATEGIES CHECKLIST	B-2
READ WITH A PURPOSE	B-3
Author's Purpose Chart	B-3
Reader's Purpose Chart	B-4
CONNECT TO PRIOR KNOWLEDGE	B-5
K-W-L Chart	B-5
Reactions Chart	B-5
WRITE THINGS DOWN	B-6
Note Taking Chart	B-6
Pro and Con Chart	B-6
Venn Diagram	B-7
Cluster Chart	B-7
MAKE PREDICTIONS	B-8
Prediction Chart	B-8
Character Chart	B-8
VISUALIZE	B-9
Sensory Details Chart	B-9
Figurative Language Chart	B-9
USE TEXT ORGANIZATION	B-10
Story Strip	B-10
Time Line	B-10
Plot Diagram	B-11
Cause-and-Effect Chart	B-12
Summary Chart	B-12
Drawing Conclusions Log	B-13
Main Idea Map	B-13
TACKLE DIFFICULT VOCABULARY	B-14
Word Sort	B-14
Word Study Notebook	B-15
Word Map	B-15
MONITOR YOUR READING PROGRESS	B-16
Fix-Up Ideas Log	B-16
Your Own Graphic Organizer	B-16

APPENDIX C: ACKNOWLEDGMENTS	
Literary Acknowledgments	C-1
Art Acknowledgments	C-2

Overview of Skills

READING STRATEGIES
Read with a Purpose 4, 39, 120, 147, 182, 208, 221, 266, 270, 279, 348, 367
Connect to Prior Knowledge 6, 39, 121, 129, 164, 183, 197, 221, 266, 317, 349, 361
Write Things Down 7, 39, 69, 77, 121, 158, 183, 186, 222, 235, 266, 286, 322, 349, 377
Make Predictions 10, 39, 42, 121, 183, 222, 267, 349
Visualize 12, 40, 92, 106, 121, 183, 191, 222, 225, 267, 349
Use Text Organization 12, 40, 122, 170, 184, 202, 222, 267, 293, 312, 350, 383
Tackle Difficult Vocabulary 13, 40, 57, 122, 124, 137, 184, 223, 267, 350, 352
Monitor Your Reading Progress 14, 40, 122, 184, 223, 268, 350

READING SKILLS AND TEST-TAKING PRACTICE
Identify Plot Elements 54
Use Context Clues 66, 126, 144, 358
Analyze Plot 74, 111
Analyze Character 89
Analyze Literary Elements 103, 232
Synthesize and Draw Conclusions 134, 290
Compare and Contrast Symbols 155
Compare and Contrast 161, 167
Identify Main Ideas 175, 299, 380
Identify Metaphors 188
Identify the Author's Purpose 194, 212, 275, 283, 309, 319, 339, 364, 374
Make Inferences 205
Analyze Literary Techniques 256
Identify Cause and Effect 314
Identify a Theme 390
Answering Objective Questions 468
Answering Essay Questions 469
Answering Multiple-Choice Questions 471
Answering Reading Comprehension Questions 472
Answering Analogy Questions 473
Answering Synonym and Antonym Questions 474
Answering Sentence Completion Questions 474
Answering Constructed-Response Questions 475

VOCABULARY SKILLS
Vocabulary Cards 56, 176
Denotation and Connotation 68, 459
Synonyms 76, 321, 462
Exploring Word Knowledge 91, 284, 310
Contextual Sentences 105
Word Sort 113
Archaic Language 128, 214
Using Context Clues 135, 145, 360, 366, 448, 234
Categorize and Use New Words 156, 461
Word Clusters 163
Antonyms 168, 462
Figurative Language 190
Word Meanings 196
Semantic Feature Analysis 201, 376
Dialect 207
Words with Multiple Meanings 277, 316, 459
Using Vocabulary in Aphorisms 291
Roots and Affixes 341
Prefixes 258, 382
Vocabulary Collage 391
Using Definitions, Footnotes, Endnotes, and Glossaries 447
Using Your Prior Knowledge 449
Using a Dictionary 458
Keeping a Word Study Notebook 459
Using Mnemonic Devices 393, 461
Learning Synonyms, Antonyms, and Homonyms 462

LITERARY TOOLS
Act 220
Alliteration 120
Allusion 280
Analogy 272, 276
Antithesis 312, 315
Aphorism 286, 308, 310
Article 263
Aside 220
Assonance 120

viii THE EMC WRITE-IN READER

Autobiography 263
Biographical Criticism 76
Biography 263
Blank Verse 158
Character 30, 36, 96, 104, 160, 162, 226
Character Chart 30
Character Sketch 89
Characterization 30, 36, 160, 162
Climax 38
Comedy 219
Concrete or Shape Poem 119
Conflict 37, 250, 257
Consonance 120
Dénouement 38
Dialect 57
Dialogue 220, 226
Documentary Writing 263
Drama 219
Dramatic Irony 73, 75, 329, 340
Dramatic Poem 117
Draw Conclusions 31
Drawing Conclusions Log 32
Elaboration 150, 157
End Rhyme 120, 139, 145
Essay 263, 287, 292
Exposition 38
Expressionism 236
Extended Metaphor 132
External Conflict 37, 250, 257
Fable 182
Fairy Tale 181
Falling Action 38
Fiction 35
Figure of Speech 118
Flashback 47, 55
Folk Literature 181
Folk Song 182, 206
Folk Tale 181
Foot 119
Frame Tale 59, 67
Historical Fiction 35
History 264
How-To Writing 264
Hymn 213
Hyperbole 125, 127
Image 118
Imagery 118

Inciting Incident 38
Internal Conflict 37, 250, 257
Internal Rhyme 120, 139, 145
Inversion 158
Irony 73, 75, 248, 327, 340
Irony of Situation 340
Legend 182
Lyric Poem 117
Melodrama 219
Memoir 264
Metaphor 118, 281
Meter 119, 130, 136
Modern Drama 219
Monologue 220
Mood 30, 37
Motivation 36
Myth 181, 187, 189
Narrative Poem 117
Nonfiction 263
Novel 35
Novella 35
Onomatopoeia 120
Oral Tradition 320
Parable 182
Paradox 171, 177
Parallelism 312, 315
Personification 118
Playwright 220
Plot 31, 37
Plot Diagram 31, 38
Point of View 30, 37
Purpose or Aim 264, 338
Realism 44, 108, 112
Realist Theater 219
Repetition 170
Resolution 38
Reversal 69
Rhetorical Question 278, 284
Rhyme 120, 139, 145
Rhyme Scheme 120
Rhythm 119
Romance 35
Scene 220
Science Fiction 35
Script 220
Setting 36
Short Story 35

Sight Rhyme 120
Simile 118
Soliloquy 220
Spectacle 221
Speech 264
Spiritual 192, 195
Stage Directions 220, 227, 233, 237
Stream-of-Consciousness Writing 77, 81, 90
Symbol 147, 159, 255
Tall Tale 57, 59, 67, 181
Theme 200, 287, 291
Tone 30, 37, 165, 169
Tragedy 219
Verbal Irony 328, 340
Writing Style 30

INFORMATIONAL AND VISUAL MEDIA TOOLS
Article 379, 381
Bulletin Board System 347
Collage 385, 391
Commentary 346
Computer News Services 346
Couplet 363, 365
Digital Photography 348
Editorial 346
Electronic Mail or E-Mail 346
Electronic Media 346
Essay 346
Graphic Aids 347
Information Services or News Services 347
Internet 346
Interview 346
Media 345
Multimedia 346
News Articles 346
Newsgroups 347
Newspapers 345
Parallelism 370, 375
Periodicals 345
Photographs 347
Photojournalism 348
Point of View 356, 359
Review or Critique 346
Technical Writing 345
Visual Arts 347, 348
Web Page 347
Web-Based Newspapers 346
Webzines or E-Zines 346, 347

Overview of Features

The EMC Write-In Reader helps you to interact with reading selections as never before! This portable anthology guides you in using reading strategies—reading tools that help you get more meaning from what you read. Questions and tips in the margins prompt you to record your thoughts and notes as you read. Using selections from the *Literature and the Language Arts* textbook, *The EMC Write-In Reader* gives you an opportunity to complete rich reading tasks, expand your reading skills, and increase your test-taking abilities.

The EMC Write-In Reader shows you how to use reading strategies before, during, and after reading and includes activities that develop your comprehension, fluency, and vocabulary skills.

The EMC Write-In Reader helps you learn how reading strategies work, how to combine them, and how to apply them to any reading task. These eight active reading strategies help you interact with a text to create meaning.

1. Read with a Purpose
2. Connect to Prior Knowledge
3. Write Things Down
4. Make Predictions
5. Visualize
6. Use Text Organization
7. Tackle Difficult Vocabulary
8. Monitor Your Reading Progress

Detailed instruction on one reading strategy is carried through the before, during, and after stages of the reading process for each selection.

The EMC Write-In Reader offers a unique text organization, including

- an **introduction to reading** unit that defines and explains the reading process, eight active reading strategies, and fix-up ideas to use when you have trouble
- a unit focusing on **essential reading skills** and tasks evaluated on standardized tests
- a unit for each **genre,** or kind of text, with an introduction on how to apply reading strategies to that genre
- a unit on **vocabulary development** to help you unlock word meaning
- a unit on **standardized test practice** to help you prepare for state and national tests
- an appendix of **fluency activities** to build word recognition skills, silent reading fluency, and oral reading fluency
- an appendix containing a multitude of **reading strategy graphic organizers**

Become a successful, active reader with *The EMC Write-In Reader!*

How to use this book

These pages from the short story "A Worn Path" show you how to get the most from your reading experience.

BEFORE READING

1 Reader's Resource provides background information to help you **set a purpose** for reading.

2 The **Active Reading Strategy** gives you step-by-step instruction on how to use the reading strategy **before reading**.

3 A **Graphic Organizer** for each selection helps you to **visualize** and **understand text organization** as you read.

CONNECT

1 Reader's resource

"A Worn Path" explores the intricacies of the inner life and the small heroisms of an ordinary character. In the story, Phoenix Jackson makes an archetypal journey. The story of the journey in which someone sets out on a path, experiences adventures, and emerges wiser, is considered archetypal in that it recurs throughout history and literature. On her journey, Phoenix Jackson demonstrates determination, generosity, and resourcefulness. "A Worn Path" is one of Eudora Welty's most popular stories.

4 Word watch

PREVIEW VOCABULARY

limber   quivering
pendulum   ravine
pullet   rouse

5 Reader's journal

What journey have you taken that held personal significance for you?

_____
_____
_____
_____

"A Worn Path"
by Eudora Welty

2 *Active* READING STRATEGY

VISUALIZE

Before Reading ➤ BEGIN TO PICTURE WHAT MAY HAPPEN

❑ Read the Reader's Resource and answer the Reader's Journal question.
❑ Begin to imagine what might happen in the story.
❑ As you read, you will sketch or jot down ideas from your mind movies in the graphic organizer below.

Graphic Organizer: Visualization Sketches **3**

[Four blank boxes for sketches]

---

92 THE EMC WRITE-IN READER

4 WordWatch gives you the opportunity to **preview** the vocabulary Words for Everyday Use for the selection.

5 Reader's Journal helps you to **connect** with what you know and to your own life.

xii   THE EMC WRITE-IN READER

DURING READING

During Reading

CREATE A MIND MOVIE

- Listen as your teacher reads the first three paragraphs of the story. Begin to create a mind movie as you listen. Involve all of your senses in the mind movie. Then make quick sketches that show what you saw, heard, and felt.
- Continue reading on your own. As you read, continue making a mind movie. Use the graphic organizer to make quick sketches or write a brief summary to explain what you imagined in your mind movie.

NOTE THE FACTS

When does Phoenix Jackson make her journey?

an early morning in

December

6 During Reading instruction in the margin tells you how to apply the reading strategy as you read.

7 Note the Facts questions give you the space to **make notes** about factual information as you read (see example).

It was December—a bright frozen day in the early morning. Far out in the country there was an old Negro woman with her head tied in a red rag, coming along a path through the pinewoods. Her name was Phoenix Jackson. She was very old and small and she walked slowly in the dark pine shadows, moving a little from side to side in her steps, with the balanced heaviness and lightness of a <u>pendulum</u> in a grandfather clock. She carried a thin, small cane made from an umbrella, and with this she kept tapping the frozen earth in front of her. This made a grave and persistent noise in the still air, that seemed meditative like the chirping of a solitary little bird.

She wore a dark striped dress reaching down to her shoe tops, and an equally long apron of bleached sugar sacks, with a full pocket: all neat and tidy, but every time she took

words for everyday use 8 pen • du • lum (pen' jə ləm) n., body suspended from a fixed point so as to swing freely to and fro under the action of gravity and commonly used to regulate movements (as of clockwork). *The sharp, descending <u>pendulum</u> threatened the narrator's life in the Edgar Allan Poe story "The Pit and the Pendulum."*

UNIT 3 / READING FICTION   93

8 Words for Everyday Use includes the definition and pronunciation for new vocabulary. A sample sentence demonstrates the use of the word in context.

How to use this book

DURING READING

9 Fix-Up Ideas help you get back on track if you encounter problems or lose focus.

10 Mark the Text activities ask you to **underline or highlight** information in the text to help you read actively and organize your thoughts (see example).

11 Literary Tools explain **literary techniques and concepts** and help you recognize these elements as you read.

---

they were caught in another. It was not possible to allow the dress to tear. "I in the thorny bush," she said. "Thorns, you doing your appointed work. Never want to let folks pass, no sir. Old eyes thought you was a pretty little *green* bush."

Finally, trembling all over, she stood free, and after a moment dared to stoop for her cane.

"Sun so high!" she cried, leaning back and looking, while the thick tears went over her eyes. "The time getting all gone here."

At the foot of this hill was a place where a log was laid across the creek.

"Now comes the trial," said Phoenix.

Putting her right foot out, she mounted the log and shut her eyes. Lifting her skirt, leveling her cane fiercely before her, like a festival figure in some parade, she began to march across. Then she opened her eyes and she was safe on the other side.

"I wasn't as old as I thought," she said.

But she sat down to rest. She spread her skirts on the bank around her and folded her hands over her knees. Up above her was a tree in a pearly cloud of mistletoe. She did not dare to close her eyes, and when a little boy brought her a plate with a slice of marble-cake on it she spoke to him. "That would be acceptable," she said. But when she went to take it there was just her own hand in the air.

So she left that tree, and had to go through a barbed-wire fence. There she had to creep and crawl, spreading her knees and stretching her fingers like a baby trying to climb the steps. But she talked loudly to herself: she could not let her dress be torn now, so late in the day, and she could not pay for having her arm or her leg sawed off if she got caught fast where she was.

At last she was safe through the fence and risen up out in the clearing. Big dead trees, like black men with one arm, were standing in the purple stalks of the withered cotton field. There sat a buzzard.

"Who you watching?"

In the furrow she made her way along.

"Glad this not the season for bulls," she said, looking sideways, "and the good Lord made his snakes to curl up and sleep in the winter. A pleasure I don't see no two-

---

9 FIX-UP IDEA

Write Things Down
To better understand the story, make a list of the obstacles Phoenix encounters on her journey. For example, she has already encountered the thorn bush at the bottom of the hill. List two obstacles on this page. Then continue listing obstacles in the margins as you read.

_____
_____

10 MARK THE TEXT
Underline or highlight how Phoenix crosses the log over the creek.

11 Literary TOOLS

CHARACTER. A **character** is a person who figures in the action of a literary work. Phoenix Jackson is the main character in this story. You learn about her from description of her appearance. As you read, think about what you learn about her through her words, actions, and motivations.

DURING READING

12 READ ALOUD

With a partner read aloud the dialogue between the hunter and Phoenix. One person should read the hunter's lines, the other should read Phoenix's lines. How does the hunter treat Phoenix?

_____
_____
_____

13 THINK AND REFLECT

Why does Phoenix divert the man's attention to the dog? (Infer)

_____
_____

14

USE THE STRATEGY

VISUALIZE. Sketch in your graphic organizer the images that come to mind as you read.

"Where do you live, Granny?" he asked, while the two dogs were growling at each other.

"Away back yonder, sir, behind the ridge. You can't even see it from here."

"On your way home?"

"No sir, I going to town."

"Why, that's too far! That's as far as I walk when I come out myself, and I get something for my trouble." He patted the stuffed bag he carried, and there hung down a little closed claw. It was one of the bob-whites, with its beak hooked bitterly to show it was dead. "Now you go on home, Granny!"

"I bound to go to town, mister," said Phoenix. "The time come around."

He gave another laugh, filling the whole landscape. "I know you old colored people! Wouldn't miss going to town to see Santa Claus!"

But something held old Phoenix very still. The deep lines in her face went into a fierce and different radiation. Without warning, she had seen with her own eyes a flashing nickel fall out of the man's pocket onto the ground.

"How old are you, Granny?" he was saying.

"There is no telling, mister," she said, "no telling."

Then she gave a little cry and clapped her hands and said, "Git on away from here, dog! Look! Look at that dog!" She laughed as if in admiration. "He ain't scared of nobody. He a big black dog." She whispered, "Sic him!"

"Watch me get rid of that cur," said the man. "Sic him, Pete! Sic him!"

Phoenix heard the dogs fighting, and heard the man running and throwing sticks. She even heard a gunshot. But she was slowly bending forward by that time, further and further forward, the lids stretched down over her eyes, as if she were doing this in her sleep. Her chin was lowered almost to her knees. The yellow palm of her hand came out from the fold of her apron. Her fingers slid down and along the ground under the piece of money with the grace and care they would have in lifting an egg from under a setting hen. Then she slowly straightened up, she stood erect, and the nickel was in

---

12 Read Aloud activities in the margins help you to **build fluency** by giving you the chance to speak and listen to ideas you are trying to understand.

13 Think and Reflect questions deepen your understanding of what you are reading.

14 Use the Strategy reminds you to use the strategy to read actively.

How to use this book

AFTER READING

15 After Reading activities follow up on the reading strategy and help you to summarize, synthesize, and reflect on the material you have read.

16 Reading Skills and Test Practice develops essential reading skills assessed on standardized tests.

17 Think-Aloud Notes help you organize your discussion ideas in writing.

15 Reflect ON YOUR READING

After Reading ➤ SHARE YOUR MIND MOVIE

- With a few of your classmates, share your sketches or summary of your mind movie.
- Talk about which events or images in the story were the most prominent or meaningful to you.

Reading Skills and Test Practice 16

ANALYZE LITERARY ELEMENTS
READ, THINK, AND EXPLAIN. Describe the journey taken by Phoenix Jackson and explain why it is archetypal. Use details and information from the story to support your answer. Jot down your ideas using the Think-Aloud Notes in the margin.

_____
_____
_____
_____
_____
_____
_____
_____
_____

REFLECT ON YOUR RESPONSE. Compare your response to that of your partner and talk about how your visualizations helped form your response.

_____
_____
_____
_____

17 THINK-ALOUD NOTES

AFTER READING

Investigate, Inquire, and Imagine

RECALL: GATHER FACTS
1a. When does Phoenix begin her journey?

INTERPRET: FIND MEANING
1b. How old is Phoenix? How do you know?

ANALYZE: TAKE THINGS APART
2a. Identify the obstacles that Phoenix runs into during her journey. Describe how she overcomes each one.

SYNTHESIZE: BRING THINGS TOGETHER
2b. Why does Welty wait until the end of the story to reveal why the journey was made?

EVALUATE: MAKE JUDGEMENTS
3a. When a work of literature is ambiguous, it can be interpreted in more than one way. Is Phoenix's grandson dead or alive? Cite examples from the text to support your viewpoint.

EXTEND: CONNECT IDEAS
3b. Compare and contrast the journey in this story to a journey in another work of literature or in a film.

Literary Tools

CHARACTER. A **character** is a person who figures in the action of a literary work. A *one-dimensional character* is one who exhibits a single dominant quality. A *three-dimensional character* is one who exhibits the complexity of traits associated with actual human beings. Fill in the chart that follows with details of Phoenix's character.

Physical Appearance	Dress	Habits/ Mannerisms/ Behaviors	Relationships with Other People	Other
	long, dark striped dress			

What do you learn about Phoenix's character from each of the following encounters?

bramblebush _____

the scarecrow _____

the hunter _____

the woman who ties her shoe _____

What character trait does Phoenix demonstrate by getting the medicine and a paper windmill for her grandson? Is Phoenix a three-dimensional or one-dimensional character?

104 THE EMC WRITE-IN READER

---

18 Investigate, Inquire, and Imagine critical thinking questions further your understanding of the reading, from basic recall and interpret questions to those that ask you to analyze, synthesize, evaluate, and extend your ideas. Some questions also ask you to look at a specific point of view or a different perspective.

19 Literary Tools follows up on the literary techniques and concepts introduced during reading and asks you to apply your understanding.

How to use this book

AFTER READING

20 WordWorkshop activities apply vocabulary development concepts to the words from the selection.

21 Read-Write Connection gives you the opportunity to write about your responses to the selection.

22 Beyond the Reading activities extend the ideas, topics, and themes from the selection.

WordWorkshop

CONTEXTUAL SENTENCES. Write a sentence that shows the meaning of each Word for Everyday Use from this story.

1. limber _____
2. pendulum _____
3. pullet _____
4. quivering _____
5. ravine _____
6. rouse _____

Read-Write Connection

Imagine that you are Phoenix. What would you tell people you live for?

_____
_____
_____
_____

Beyond the Reading

RESEARCH AN AUTHOR. Use the library and the Internet to find information about Eudora Welty. Look for adaptations and reviews of her work, interviews with her, and awards she has received. Then work with a few of your classmates to lay out a page of a newsletter honoring Welty. You might want to include your own review of "A Worn Path."

GO ONLINE. To find links and additional activities for this selection, visit the EMC Internet Resource Center at **emcp.com/languagearts** and click on Write-In Reader.

Unit ONE

Introduction to Reading

PURPOSES OF READING

As a reader, you read for different purposes. You might **read for experience**—for insights into ideas, other people, and the world around you. You can also **read to learn**. This is the kind of reading done most often in school. When you read to learn, you may read textbooks, newspapers and newsmagazines, and visual "texts" such as art and photographs. The purpose of this type of reading is to gain knowledge. Third, you can **read for information**. When you read in this way, you are looking for specific data in sources such as reference materials, tables, databases, and diagrams.

Reading for Experience
READING LITERATURE
The most important reason to read literature is to educate your imagination. Reading literary works, which include fiction, nonfiction, poetry, and drama, will train you to think and feel in new ways. In the process of reading literary works and thinking about your own and others' responses to them, you will exercise your imagination as you encounter characters and situations that you would otherwise never know.

Reading to Learn
READING TEXTBOOKS AND NONFICTION
When you are reading to learn, you have two main goals: to expand your knowledge on a particular topic and to remember the information later. When you read to learn, you will often work with textbooks; reference books; periodicals such as newspapers, journals, and newsmagazines; and related art and photographs.

   Textbooks provide a broad overview of a course of study in an objective, factual way. Other types of nonfiction works provide information about people, places, things, events, and ideas. Types of

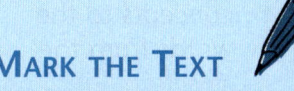
MARK THE TEXT
Underline or highlight three purposes for reading.

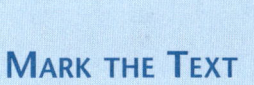
MARK THE TEXT
Underline or highlight goals you have when you are reading for experience and reading to learn.

nonfiction include histories, biographies, autobiographies, and memoirs. Periodicals such as newspapers, journals, and newsmagazines contain an enormous amount of information about current events around the world. While few people have time to read everything that appears in news periodicals, it is important to stay aware of what is going on in the world around you.

Reading for Information
READING INTERNET, REFERENCE, AND VISUAL MATERIALS

When you are reading for information, you are looking for information that answers a specific, immediate question; that helps you learn how to do something; or that helps you make a decision or draw a conclusion about something. One of the most important things for you to learn in school is how to find, process, and think about the vast amount of information available to you in online and printed reference works, graphic aids, and other visual materials.

THE READING PROCESS

The reading process begins before you actually start to read. Before reading, you begin to develop your own purpose and expectations for what you are about to read. These are related to what you already know and what you have experienced. During reading, you use your natural habits and responses to help you understand what you are reading, perhaps by adjusting your initial purpose and expectations. After reading, you think and reflect on what you have read. All readers use a reading process, even if they don't think about it. By becoming aware of this process, you can become a more effective reader. The reading process can be broken down into three stages: before reading, during reading, and after reading.

Before Reading

Have a plan for reading actively. Before you begin to read, establish a plan for reading actively by setting a purpose, previewing the material, and connecting with what you already know.

- ❑ **Set a purpose** for reading. Know why you are reading and what information you seek. Are you reading for experience or enjoyment, reading to learn, or reading for specific information?
- ❑ **Preview** the organization of the material. Glance at any visuals and think about how they add to the meaning of the text. Skim headings and introductory paragraphs.
- ❑ **Connect** with what you know. Think about how what you are reading connects to your own life and to your prior experience.

Before Reading

ASK YOURSELF

- What's my purpose for reading this?
- What is this going to be about?
- How is this information organized?
- What do I already know about the topic?
- How can I apply this information to my life?

During Reading

Use reading strategies to read actively. **Reading strategies** are actions you can take on paper, in your head, or aloud that help you understand what you are reading. During reading, you will use reading strategies to read actively. Keep in mind that you will often use a combination of these strategies to read a single text.

- **Read aloud** to build reading fluency and give oral emphasis to ideas you are trying to understand. Hearing words aloud may help you untangle difficult ideas. Listen to your teacher read passages aloud, or read aloud by yourself or with a partner.
- **Write things down** to note your responses to what you are reading. Methods such as highlighting and marking a text, taking or making notes, and creating graphic organizers help you read actively and organize your thoughts. Underline or copy to your notebook the main points. Note unusual or interesting ideas or things you don't understand. Jot down words you need to define. Write your reactions to what you read.
- **Think and reflect** by asking questions to further your understanding of what you are reading. Asking questions helps you to pinpoint parts of the text that are confusing. You can ask questions in your head, or you may write them down.

Check your reading and use fix-up ideas. Monitor your reading comprehension by paying attention to how well you understand what you are reading. If you find yourself reading the words but not actually understanding what you are reading, get back on track by using a **fix-up idea** such as rereading, reading in shorter chunks, changing your reading rate, or trying a new reading strategy. A fix-up idea will be presented with each reading strategy accompanying the selections in this text. (For more information on fix-up ideas, see pages 14–15.)

After Reading

Reflect on your reading. After you finish reading, summarize, synthesize, and reflect on the material you have read.

- **Summarize** what you have read to help identify, understand, and remember the main and supporting ideas in the text.
- **Synthesize** different ideas in the material by pulling the ideas together and drawing conclusions about them. Reread any sections you don't remember clearly. Answer any questions you had.
- **Extend** your reading by examining how your knowledge has grown and identifying questions you still have about the material.

During Reading

ASK YOURSELF
- What is the best way to accomplish my purpose for reading?
- What do I want or need to find out while I'm reading?
- What is the essential information presented here?
- What is the importance of what I am reading?

CHECK YOUR READING
- Do I understand what I just read? Can I summarize it?
- What can I do to make the meaning more clear?

After Reading

ASK YOURSELF
- What did I learn from what I have read?
- What is still confusing?
- What do I need to remember from my reading?
- What effect did this text have on my thinking?
- What else do I want to know about this topic?

NOTE THE FACTS

What does it mean to read actively?

_____

_____

_____

THE READING PROCESS

BEFORE READING
Have a plan for reading
 ❑ Set a purpose
 ❑ Preview
 ❑ Connect

DURING READING
Use reading strategies
 ❑ Read aloud
 ❑ Write things down
 ❑ Think and reflect
 ❑ Check your reading and use fix-up ideas

AFTER READING
Reflect on your reading
 ❑ Summarize
 ❑ Synthesize
 ❑ Extend

USING ACTIVE READING STRATEGIES

Reading actively means thinking about what you are reading as you read. A reading strategy, or plan, helps you read actively and search for meaning in what you are reading. As a reader, you are in charge of unlocking the meaning of each text you read. This book will introduce you to eight excellent strategies that develop active reading. The following strategies can be applied at each stage of the reading process: before, during, and after reading.

Active Reading Strategies

1. Read with a Purpose
2. Connect to Prior Knowledge
3. Write Things Down
4. Make Predictions
5. Visualize
6. Use Text Organization
7. Tackle Difficult Vocabulary
8. Monitor Your Reading Progress

As you become experienced with each of the reading strategies, you will be able to use two or three strategies at a time, instead of just one. By using multiple strategies, you will become a thoughtful, active, and successful reader—not only in your English language arts classes but also in other content areas, during testing situations, and beyond the classroom. You will learn which strategies work best for you and use these strategies in every reading task you encounter.

1 Read with a Purpose

Before you begin reading, think about your reason for reading the material. You might be reading from a textbook to complete a homework assignment, skimming a magazine for information about one of your hobbies, or reading a novel for your own personal enjoyment. Know why you are reading and what information you seek. Decide on your purpose for reading as clearly as you can. Be aware that your purpose may change as you read.

Read with a Purpose

Before Reading	Establish a purpose for reading
During Reading	Read with this purpose in mind
After Reading	Reflect on how the purpose affected the reading experience

After you determine your purpose for reading, you can choose a method of reading that fits that purpose. Scanning, skimming, and close reading are three different ways of reading.

SCANNING. When you **scan**, you look through written material quickly to locate particular information. Scanning is useful when, for example, you want to find an entry in an index or a definition in a textbook chapter. To scan, simply run your eye down the page, looking for a key word or words. When you find the key words, slow down and read carefully.

SKIMMING. When you **skim,** you glance through material quickly to get a general idea of what it is about. Skimming is an excellent way to get a quick overview of material. It is useful for previewing a chapter in a textbook, for surveying material to see if it contains information that will be useful to you, and for reviewing material for a test or essay. When skimming, look at titles, headings, and words that appear in boldface or colored type. Also read topic sentences of paragraphs, first and last paragraphs of sections, and any summaries or conclusions. In addition, glance at illustrations, photographs, charts, maps, or other graphics.

READING CLOSELY. When you **read closely**, you read slowly and carefully, looking at each sentence and taking the time to absorb its meaning before going on. Close reading is appropriate, for example, when you are reading some poems for pleasure or studying a textbook chapter for the first time. If you encounter words that you do not understand, try to figure them out from context or look them up in a dictionary. You may want to record such words in a word study notebook. The act of writing a word will help you to remember it later. When reading for school, take notes using a rough outline form or other note-taking format. Outlining the material will help you to learn it.

Setting a purpose gives you something to focus on as you read. For example, you might read the user's manual for your new phone to find out how to program speed-dial numbers. Or, you might read a mystery novel to find out which character committed the crime.

A few of the purposes you might have for reading "The Battle Hymn of the Republic" by Julia Ward Howe in Unit 5, page 208, might be to find out why the hymn is so popular, to learn what the speaker has to say, or to look for images and themes in the hymn. Read the

NOTE THE FACTS

List three different ways to read printed material.

_____

_____

_____

NOTE THE FACTS

When should you **read closely?**

_____

_____

_____

MARK THE TEXT

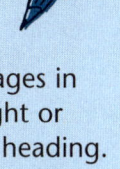

Go back over the pages in this unit and highlight or underline a colored heading. Then underline the boldface headings beneath the colored heading. Marking the text in this way helps you keep track of key ideas.

following background information from the Reader's Resource for "The Battle Hymn of the Republic." When you finish reading, complete the **Think and Reflect** activity in the margin.

> After visiting a Union camp near Washington, DC in November 1861, where she saw soldiers marching off to battle, Julia Ward Howe was inspired to write "The Battle Hymn of the Republic." Some sources maintain that she was compelled to write the hymn after hearing Union troops sing "John Brown's body lies a-mouldering in the grave," a reference to farmer and abolitionist John Brown (1800–1859), who was hanged in Charlestown, Virginia (now West Virginia), for his fight against slavery. Howe's song was published in *The Atlantic Monthly* in February 1862 and soon became the Civil War anthem of the North. A patriotic hymn, "The Battle Hymn of the Republic" justifies the Union cause and celebrates heroic self-sacrifice.

THINK AND REFLECT

Write a purpose for reading "The Battle Hymn of the Republic." (Connect)

_____

_____

_____

2 Connect to Prior Knowledge

Prior knowledge is what you already know or have already experienced before reading something. Before and during reading, think about what you already know about the topic or subject matter. By connecting to your prior knowledge, you can increase your interest in and understanding of what you read. The Reader's Journal activities that come before each selection in this book provide an opportunity to connect to experiences in your own life. Information in the Reader's Resource expands your knowledge of what you are about to read.

Connect to Prior Knowledge	
Before Reading	Think about what you already know about the topic
During Reading	Use what you already know about the topic to make inferences and predictions
After Reading	Describe how the reading experience expanded your knowledge of the topic

Read the following information from the Reader's Resource for Patrick Henry's Speech in the Virginia Convention in Unit 7, page 278. As you read, connect to what you already know about Henry's speech by underlining ideas you have read before.

The Speech in the Virginia Convention, probably Patrick Henry's best-known oration, was not written down until years after its delivery on March 23, 1775. It had so captured the attention of its listeners that they were able to recall it for Henry's biographer, William Wirt. This speech against the Stamp Act in 1765 is considered one of his finest and is the one in which he uttered the famous words: "I know not what course others may take, but as for me, give me liberty or give me death!" The speech was delivered to the Virginia Convention during a time of growing political unrest. Less than a month after Henry's speech, his prediction of open battle in the North was fulfilled in the opening skirmishes of the American Revolution at Lexington and Concord on April 19, 1775.

THINK AND REFLECT

What new information did you learn abut Henry's speech? (**Connect**)

_____

③ Write Things Down

Writing things down helps you pay attention to the words on a page. It is an excellent way to remember important ideas. Methods such as highlighting and marking or coding a text, taking or making notes, and creating graphic organizers help you read actively and organize your thoughts.

NOTE THE FACTS

Why is writing things down important?

_____

Write Things Down	
Before Reading	Have a plan for writing things down: sticky notes, handwritten notes, highlighters, or charts to fill in
During Reading	Use a method for writing things down; ask questions; respond
After Reading	Summarize things written down

Highlighting and marking a text helps you locate key ideas. Mark important ideas, things you would like to come back to, things that are confusing, things you like or dislike, and things with which you agree or disagree. In this *Write-In Reader* or a book you own, you may highlight the text itself. With other books you may need to use sticky notes and bookmarks to keep track of your thoughts.

As you read, find a way to connect to what you are reading by **coding** your reactions. Use the following system to keep track of your reactions in the margins or on sticky notes. Create additional notations for reactions you have that are not listed.

MARK THE TEXT

Underline or highlight what you should do before, during, and after reading when you use the Write Things Down strategy.

UNIT 1 / INTRODUCTION TO READING 7

Reading TIP

Additional ways to take notes:
- Outline
- Make lists
- Create a chart or diagram
- Write down main ideas and your responses
- Use a tape recorder

YES	I agree with this
NO	I disagree with this
?	I do not understand this
W	I wonder . . .
+	I like this part
−	I do not like this part
!	This is like something else I know
√	This seems important
∞	I need to come back and look at this
___	_____
___	_____

If you do not have sticky notes, keep track of your reactions in a chart like the one below.

Reactions Chart

Page, Column, or Line Number:	Short Note about My Reactions
Ex: page 107	I had to reread this part. I see now that there is a jump back in time.

After reading, summarize your reactions and compare them to those of your classmates.

Reading TIP

As you read the selections in this book, write down important ideas and your thoughts about them. The more things you write down in the margins, the more you will understand and remember.

Here is a summary of my reactions: <u>The story really kept my attention. It created vivid pictures in my mind of what it must be like to be a soldier on guard duty at night.</u>

Here is how my reactions were the same as those of my classmates: <u>Most of my classmates were riveted by the storyline.</u>

Here is how my reactions were different from those of my classmates: <u>A few of my classmates had trouble with the narrator's actions. They thought the narrator should have let the enemy soldier keep on walking.</u>

Taking or making notes helps you select ideas you consider important. *Paraphrase*, or write in your own words, what you have read and put it into notes you can read later. Taking or making notes is also a quick way for you to retell what you have just read. Since you cannot write in, mark up, or highlight information in a textbook or library book, make a response bookmark like the following and use it to record your thoughts and reactions. As you read, ask yourself questions, make predictions, react to ideas, identify key points, and/or write down unfamiliar words.

Response Bookmark

Page #	Questions, Predictions, Reactions, Key Points, and Unfamiliar Words
108	The narrator is on guard duty. I predict that he will see the enemy approaching.
108	This description of the narrator's fear is excellent.
109	This part isn't as gory as I would have expected.

MARK THE TEXT

Underline or highlight what you should record on a response bookmark.

Graphic organizers help you organize ideas as you read. For instance, if you are reading an essay that compares two authors, you might use a Venn diagram or a cluster chart to collect information about each author. If you are reading about an author's life, you may construct a time line. As you read a selection, create your own method for gathering and organizing information. You might use your own version of a common graphic organizer or invent a new way to show what the selection describes. Signal words in the text can help you construct an organizer. (See Appendix B for examples of these and other graphic organizers.)

Signal Words	Common Graphic Organizer
descriptive words: *also, for instance, for example, in the beginning, in addition, the main reason, one point*	Character Chart, page B-8 Sensory Details Chart, page B-9 Summary Chart, page B-12
sequence words: *after, as before, next, now, on, first, second, finally*	Time Line, page B-10 Story Strip, page B-10 Plot Diagram, page B-11

NOTE THE FACTS

List graphic organizers you might use to gather information when you read stories that use sequence words like *next, now,* and *finally.*

_____

_____

_____

comparison-and-contrast words: *as well as, but, either/or, likewise, on the other hand, similarly, not only/but*	Pro and Con Chart, page B-6 Cluster Chart, page B-7 Venn Diagram, page B-7
cause-and-effect words: *as a result, because, if/then, since, therefore, this led to*	Note Taking Chart, page B-6 Cause-and-Effect Chart, page B-12 Drawing Conclusions Log, page B-13

After reading the following excerpt from "A Worn Path," Unit 3, page 92, answer the question in the margin. Underline or highlight signal words in the excerpt that direct you to the answer.

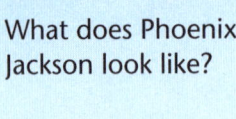

NOTE THE FACTS

What does Phoenix Jackson look like?

_____
_____
_____
_____

> It was December—a bright frozen day in the early morning. Far out in the country there was an old Negro woman with her head tied in a red rag, coming along a path through the pinewoods. Her name was Phoenix Jackson. She was very old and small and she walked slowly in the dark pine shadows, moving a little from side to side in her steps, with the balanced heaviness and lightness of a pendulum in a grandfather clock. She carried a thin, small cane made from an umbrella, and with this she kept tapping the frozen earth in front of her. This made a grave and persistent noise in the still air, that seemed meditative like the chirping of a solitary little bird.
>
> She wore a dark striped dress reaching down to her shoe tops, and an equally long apron of bleached sugar sacks, with a full pocket: all neat and tidy, but every time she took a step she might have fallen over her shoelaces, which dragged from her unlaced shoes. She looked straight ahead. Her eyes were blue with age. Her skin had a pattern all its own of numberless branching wrinkles and as though a whole little tree stood in the middle of her forehead, but a golden color ran underneath, and the two knobs of her cheeks were illumined by a yellow burning under the dark. Under the red rag her hair came down on her neck in the frailest of ringlets, still black, and with an odor like copper.

4 Make Predictions

When you **make predictions** during reading, you are making guesses about what the reading is going to be about or what might happen next. Before reading, make predictions based on clues from the page

10   THE EMC WRITE-IN READER

and from what you already know about the topic. Continue making predictions as you read. Remember, your predictions do not have to be correct. Pause during reading to gather information that helps you make more predictions and check predictions you have already made.

Make Predictions

Before Reading	Gather information and make preliminary predictions
During Reading	Continue making predictions
After Reading	Analyze and verify predictions

Read an excerpt from the short story "An Occurrence at Owl Creek Bridge" by Ambrose Bierce, Unit 3, page 42. Look for clues that suggest what might happen next.

> A man stood upon a railroad bridge in northern Alabama, looking down into the swift water twenty feet below. The man's hands were behind his back, the wrists bound with a cord. A rope closely encircled his neck. It was attached to a stout cross timber above his head and the slack fell to the level of his knees. Some loose boards laid upon the sleepers [wooden ties that support railroad tracks] supporting the metals of the railway supplied a footing for him and his executioners—two private soldiers of the Federal army, directed by a sergeant who in civil life may have been a deputy sheriff. At a short remove upon the same temporary platform was an officer in the uniform of his rank, armed. He was a captain.

Prediction Chart

Predictions	Clues	What Really Happens
A man will be hanged above the railroad tracks.	"A rope closely encircled his neck."	

Reading TIP

By learning to make predictions while you read, you become more engaged in what you're reading and you remember more information.

THINK AND REFLECT

Based on the clues in the excerpt, make a **prediction** about what might happen later in the story. Record your prediction in the first column of the chart. In the second column, tell what clues led you to make this prediction. After you read the rest of the story, you would be able to record what really happened in the story and to compare that to your original predictions. **(Predict)**

5 Visualize

Reading is more than simply sounding out words. It is an active process that requires you to use your imagination. When you **visualize,** you form a picture or an image in your mind of what the text describes. Each reader's images will be different based on his or her prior knowledge and experience. Keep in mind that there are no "right" or "wrong" visualizations.

Visualize	
Before Reading	Begin to picture what may happen
During Reading	Create mind pictures as you read
After Reading	Draw or summarize what you saw in your mind pictures

Read the following excerpt from "Sinners in the Hands of an Angry God" by Jonathan Edwards, Unit 7, page 270. As you read, imagine what the speaker is describing.

> The bow of God's wrath is bent, and the arrow made ready on the string, and justice bends the arrow at your heart, and strains the bow, and it is nothing but the mere pleasure of God, and that of an angry God, without any promise or obligation at all, that keeps the arrow one moment from being made drunk with your blood.

6 Use Text Organization

Text organization refers to the different ways a text may be presented or organized. If you are aware of the ways different texts are organized, you will find it easier to understand what you read. For example, knowing about typical plot elements—the exposition, rising action, climax, falling action, and resolution—is important for understanding the events in a short story or novel. Focusing on signal words and text patterns is important for understanding nonfiction and informational text. For instance, transition words, such as *first*, *second*, *next*, *then*, and *finally*, might indicate that an essay is written in chronological, or time, order.

DRAW A PICTURE

Draw a picture that shows what you picture as you read Edwards's words.

Use Text Organization

Before Reading	Preview organizational features (look over headings, pictures, format)
During Reading	Be aware of organizational features as you read
After Reading	Discuss how the text organization affected your reading experience

In "Newsreel LXVIII" by John Dos Passos, Unit 8, page 383, italicized lyrics from a folk song, "The Wreck of the Old 97," are interspersed with newspaper headlines and clips from news reports.

> here is the most dangerous example of how at the decisive moment the bourgeois ideology liquidates class solidarity and turns a friend of the workingclass of yesterday into a most miserable propagandist for imperialism today
>
> RED PICKETS FINED FOR PROTEST HERE
>
> *We leave our home in the morning*
>
> *We kiss our children goodbye*
>
> OFFICIALS STILL HOPE FOR RESCUE OF MEN
>
> *He was goin' downgrade makin' ninety miles an hour*
>
> *When his whistle broke into a scream*
>
> *He was found in the wreck with his hand on the throttle*
>
> *An' was scalded to death with the steam*

THINK AND REFLECT

How does Dos Passos's text structure affect your understanding? What can a reader do to understand these lines better? **(Analyze)**

_____
_____
_____

7 Tackle Difficult Vocabulary

How do you deal with new or unfamiliar words as you read? Learning how to tackle difficult vocabulary on your own leads to improved reading comprehension. In some cases, you may want to identify and define new vocabulary before reading. Use context clues to guess meanings, find definitions in the dictionary, and decode words by recognizing common word parts.

Reading TIP

If you take the time to learn new words, you increase your ability to understand what you read in class and on standardized tests. One of the best ways to learn new words is to associate an image with the meaning of a new word. For instance, you might associate the word *importunity* with an image of someone knocking persistently at a door because *importunity* means "persistent demand." What image could you associate with the word *tumultuously*, meaning "wildly"? Draw that image here.

THINK AND REFLECT

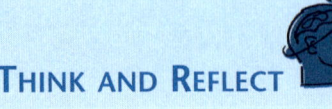

Using context clues, what might *append* mean? (Analyze)

_____

_____

Tackle Difficult Vocabulary	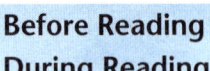
Before Reading	Have a plan for tackling difficult words
During Reading	Use context, word structure, footnotes, or a dictionary; ask for help
After Reading	Describe how vocabulary affected your reading experience

Read the following excerpt from "The Notorious Jumping Frog of Calaveras County" by Mark Twain, Unit 3, page 57. As you read, record unfamiliar words in the margin or in your notebook. After you finish, go back to each word you recorded. Using both context clues (words nearby that provide hints about the meaning) and word parts, unlock the meaning of each unfamiliar word. Consult a dictionary if context clues or word parts do not help.

> In compliance with the request of a friend of mine, who wrote me from the East, I called on good-natured, garrulous old Simon Wheeler, and inquired after my friend's friend, Leonidas W. Smiley, as requested to do, and I hereunto append the result. I have a lurking suspicion that *Leonidas W.* Smiley is a myth; that my friend never knew such a personage; and that he only conjectured that if I asked old Wheeler about him, it would remind him of his infamous *Jim* Smiley, and he would go to work and bore me to death with some exasperating reminiscence of him as long and as tedious as it should be useless to me. If that was the design, it succeeded.

8 Monitor Your Reading Progress

All readers occasionally have difficulty as they read. The key to reading success is being aware of these difficulties. As you read, **monitor**, or pay attention to, your progress, stopping frequently to check how well you are understanding what you are reading. If you encounter problems or lose focus, use a **fix-up idea** to regain understanding. Readers who know how to apply fix-up ideas are well on the way to reading independence. They know when they are having a problem and are able to adjust and get back on track.

USING FIX-UP IDEAS

The following **fix-up ideas** can help you "fix up" any confusion or lack of attention you experience as you read. You probably use many of these already.

- **Reread.** If you don't understand a sentence, paragraph, or section the first time through, go back and reread it. Each time you reread a text, you understand and remember more.

- **Read in shorter chunks.** Break a long text into shorter chunks. Read through each "chunk." Then go back and make sure you understand that section before moving on.

- **Read aloud.** If you are having trouble keeping your focus, try reading aloud to yourself. Go somewhere private and read aloud, putting emphasis and expression in your voice. Reading aloud may help you to untangle difficult text by talking your way through it.

- **Ask questions.** As you read, stop and ask yourself questions about the text. These questions help you pinpoint things that are confusing or things you want to come back to later. You can ask questions in your head, or jot them down in the margins or on a piece of paper.

- **Change your reading rate.** Your reading rate is how fast or slow you read. Good readers adjust their rate to fit the situation. Read quickly, when you just need an overview, or if the reading task is easy. Slow down and read carefully when a text is difficult or contains a lot of description.

- **Create a mnemonic device.** A mnemonic (ni mä′ nik) device is a memory trick that helps you memorize specific information in a text. One memory trick is to make up an acronym, or abbreviation, to help you remember items in a list. For example, the acronym *HOMES* can help you remember the names of the five great lakes, Huron, Ontario, Michigan, Erie, and Superior. Another memory trick is to create a short sentence or rhyme. For instance, if you need to remember that in the eardrum, the anvil comes before the stirrup, remember "the letter *a* comes before the letter *s*."

Monitor Your Reading Progress

Before Reading	Be aware of fix-up ideas that ease reading problems
During Reading	Use fix-up ideas
After Reading	Evaluate the fix-up ideas used

READ ALOUD

Reading fluency is your ability to read something quickly and easily. Increase your reading fluency by rereading a 100–150-word passage aloud several times. Reread the passage until you are able to read through it in less than a minute without making any mistakes. Read the passage to a partner and have your partner track your errors, or read the passage into a tape recorder, play back your recording, and keep track of your own errors. For additional fluency practice, see Appendix A.

Reading TIP

As you read, use your classmates as resources to help you uncover the meaning in a selection. Working with a partner or a small group can increase your understanding of what you read.

THINK ALOUD. When you **think aloud**, you communicate your thoughts aloud to your classmates about what you are reading. Thinking aloud helps you share ideas about the text and ways in which to read it.

SHARE FIX-UP IDEAS. When you **share fix-up ideas**, you and your classmates can figure out ways to deal with difficult sections of a text.

Unit 1 READING Review

Choose and Use Reading Strategies

Before reading the excerpt below, review with a partner how to use each of these reading strategies (see pages 4–15).

1. Read with a Purpose
2. Connect to Prior Knowledge
3. Write Things Down
4. Make Predictions
5. Visualize
6. Use Text Organization
7. Tackle Difficult Vocabulary
8. Monitor Your Reading Progress

Now apply at least two reading strategies to an excerpt from "The Outcasts of Poker Flat" by Bret Harte. When you finish reading, summarize the excerpt in two to three sentences.

> In point of fact, Poker Flat was "after somebody." It had lately suffered the loss of several thousand dollars, two valuable horses, and a prominent citizen. It was experiencing a spasm of virtuous reaction, quite as lawless and ungovernable as any of the acts that had provoked it. A secret committee had determined to rid the town of all improper persons. This was done permanently in regard of two men who were then hanging from the boughs of a sycamore in the gulch, and temporarily in the banishment of certain other objectionable characters. I regret to say that some of these were ladies. It is but due to the sex, however, to state that their impropriety was professional, and it was only in such easily established standards of evil that Poker Flat ventured to sit in judgment.

On Your Own

Select a 100–150-word passage from your favorite book, magazine, or newspaper, and try one of the following activities.

FLUENTLY SPEAKING. Rehearse reading your passage aloud several times. Have a partner track your errors, or read the passage into a tape recorder, play back your recording, and keep track of your own errors. Reread the passage until you are able to read it aloud without making any mistakes. Then create a short introduction to your passage and read the passage aloud to your class. Use an appropriate tone, pace, and volume in your oral interpretation of the passage.

PICTURE THIS. Create a drawing, painting, sculpture, graph, or other visual representation that will help others understand your passage. Use artistic tools, colors, objects, or shapes that communicate the passage's ideas.

PUT IT IN WRITING. Create a graphic organizer that organizes ideas in your passage. Pages B-2–B-16 in Appendix B contain graphic organizers you can use or modify. Then write a brief summary of your passage.

Unit TWO

ESSENTIAL READING SKILLS

READING SKILLS

Each of the reading strategies we've discussed in Unit 1 helps you learn to think, question, and respond while you read. By using the eight active reading strategies, you will be able to demonstrate your mastery of the following reading skills:

- **Identify the Author's Purpose**
- **Find the Main Idea**
- **Make Inferences**
- **Use Context Clues**
- **Analyze Text Organization**
- **Identify Sequence of Events**
- **Compare and Contrast**
- **Evaluate Cause and Effect**
- **Classify and Reorganize Information**
- **Distinguish Fact from Opinion**
- **Interpret Visual Aids**
- **Understand Literary Elements**
- **Draw Conclusions**

Using these skills as you read helps you to become an independent, thoughtful, and active reader who can accomplish tasks evaluated on tests, particularly standardized tests. Standardized test practice connected to these skills follows each selection in this book.

NOTE THE FACTS

How does using reading strategies help you?

_____

_____

_____

Reading TIP

For more practice on test-taking skills, see Unit 10, Test-Taking Strategies, pages 417–430.

Identify the Author's Purpose

A writer's **purpose** is his or her aim or goal. Being able to figure out an author's purpose, or purposes, is an important reading skill. An author may write with one or more of the purposes listed in the following chart. A writer's purpose corresponds to a specific mode, or type, of writing. A writer can choose from a variety of forms while working within a mode.

Reading TIP

To **identify the author's purpose**, ask yourself

- Why did the author create this piece of writing?
- Is the author simply sharing information or trying to convince me of something?
- Is he or she writing to entertain or trying to make a point?

Purposes of Writing

Purpose	Mode	Writing Forms
to reflect	personal/ expressive writing	diary entry, personal letter, autobiography, personal essay
to entertain, to describe, to enrich, and to enlighten	imaginative/ descriptive writing	poem, character sketch, play
to tell a story, to narrate a series of events	narrative writing	short story, biography, legend, myth, history
to inform, to explain	informative/ expository writing	news article, research report, expository essay, book review
to persuade	persuasive/ argumentative writing	editorial, petition, political speech, persuasive essay

Once you identify what the author is trying to do, you can evaluate, or judge, how well the author achieved that purpose. For example, you may judge that the author of a persuasive essay made a good and convincing argument. Or, you may decide that the novel you are reading has a boring plot. In other words, the author has done a bad job of entertaining you!

Read the following lines from Ralph Waldo Emerson's essay "Self-Reliance," Unit 7, page 286. Think about Emerson's purpose for writing. Is he trying to entertain, persuade, inform, or express his feelings?

> There is a time in every man's education when he arrives at the conviction that envy is ignorance; that imitation is suicide; that he must take himself for better, for worse, as his portion; that though the wide universe is full of good, no kernel of nourishing corn can come to him but through his toil bestowed on that plot of ground which is given to him to till.

THINK AND REFLECT

Which words or phrases in the paragraph help you determine the author's purpose? (Infer)

_____

_____

_____

Find the Main Idea

The **main idea** is a brief statement of what you think the author wants you to know, think, or feel after reading the text. In some cases, the main idea will actually be stated. Check the first and last paragraphs for a sentence that sums up the entire passage. Usually, the author will not tell you what the main idea is, and you will have to infer it.

In general, nonfiction texts have main ideas; literary texts (poems, short stories, novels, plays, and personal essays) have themes. Sometimes, however, the term *main idea* is used to refer to the theme of a literary work, especially an essay or poem. Both deal with the central idea in a written work.

A good way to find the main or overall idea of a whole selection (or part of a selection) is to gather important details into a Main Idea Map like the one below. Use the details to determine the main or overall thought or message. This will help you to draw conclusions about the main idea when you finish reading.

Reading TIP

To **infer the main idea,** ask yourself

- Who or what is this passage about?
- What does the author want me to know, think, feel, or do about this "who" or "what"?
- If I had to tell someone in one sentence what this passage is about, what would I say?

Main Idea Map

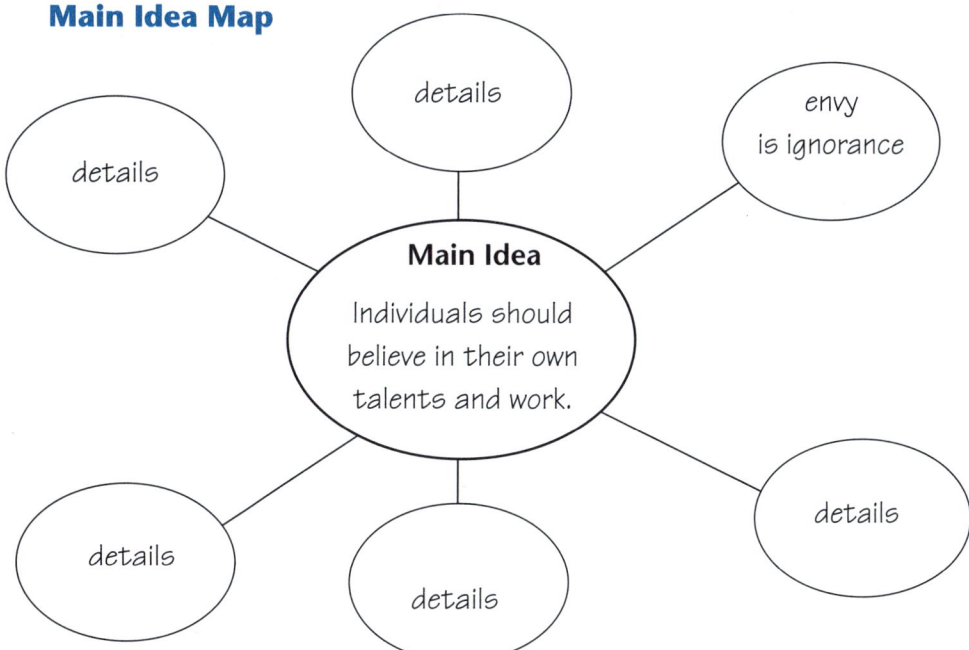

UNIT 2 / ESSENTIAL READING SKILLS

Make Inferences

By paying close attention to what you read, you will be able to make inferences about what the writer is trying to communicate. **Making an inference** means putting together the clues given in the text with your own prior knowledge.

Reading TIP

As you make inferences, remember that each inference needs to fit with all of the clues in the text and with your prior knowledge.

Inference Chart

Text	What I Infer
"There was a feverish triumph in her eyes, and she carried herself unwittingly like a goddess of Victory."	The woman is excited and happy.

Use Context Clues

You can often figure out the meaning of an unfamiliar word by using context clues. **Context clues** are words and phrases near a difficult word that provide hints about its meaning. The context in which a word is used may help you guess what it means without having to look it up in the dictionary.

The following table explains different kinds of context clues and includes words that signal each type of clue. Look for these words in the sentences around an unfamiliar word to see if they signal a context clue.

Reading TIP

Sometimes you can determine the meaning of a word by using the context as a clue. For example, the word choice or mood of a passage in general may help you determine the meaning of a particular word.

Context Clues

comparison clue	shows a comparison, or how the unfamiliar word is like something that might be familiar to you
signal words	*and, like, as, just as, as if, as though*

EXAMPLE
"ABIGAIL. (now staring full front as though *hypnotized*, and mimicking the exact tone of Mary Warren's cry)"—stage directions from *The Crucible* by Arthur Miller. (The context shows that someone who is *hypnotized* is someone who stares straight ahead and talks like someone else.)

contrast clue	shows that something contrasts, or differs in meaning, from something else
signal words	*but, nevertheless, on the other hand, however, although, though, in spite of*

EXAMPLE

"You will hardly know who I am or what I mean, / But I shall be good health to you *nevertheless*, / And filter and fibre your blood."—from "Song of Myself" by Walt Whitman. (The word *nevertheless* signals that *fibre* refers to something that is good for one's health.)

restatement clue	uses different words to express the same idea
signal words	*that is, in other words, or, namely*

EXAMPLE

"A sentinel at each end of the bridge stood with his rifle in the position known as '*support*,' that is to say, vertical in front of the left shoulder, the hammer resting on the forearm thrown straight across the chest"—from "An Occurrence at Owl Creek Bridge" by Ambrose Bierce. (The phrase *that is to say* signals that the soldier's *support* position is one in which he holds the rifle vertically in front of his left shoulder.)

examples clue	gives examples of other items to illustrate the meaning of something
signal words	*including, such as, for example, for instance, especially, particularly*

EXAMPLE

"TOM fishes in his pockets for door-key, removing a *motley assortment* of articles in the search, including a perfect shower of movie-ticket stubs and an empty bottle."—from stage directions for *The Glass Menagerie* by Tennessee Williams. (The word *including* shows that the *motley assortment* is a "mixture of different things.")

cause-and-effect clue	tells you that something happened as a result of something else
signal words	*if/then, when/then, thus, therefore, because, so, as a result of, consequently, since*

EXAMPLE

". . . and if the pearl diver shows signs of wanting to rest, he is *showered with blows,* his hair is pulled, and he is thrown back into the water, obliged to continue the hard work of tearing out the oysters and bringing them again to the surface."—from *The Very Brief Relation of the Devastation of the Indies* by Bartolomé de las Casas. (In this sentence, the context shows that the phrase *showered with blows* describes one of the bad things that happens to a pearl diver "wanting to rest"—the diver is beaten.)

MARK THE TEXT

Underline or highlight five kinds of context clues listed on pages 20 and 21.

NOTE THE FACTS

What words signal a cause-and-effect relationship?

_____

_____

_____

Analyze Text Organization

Writing can be organized in different ways. To be an effective reader you need to know how to analyze how the text is organized. When you analyze something, you break it down into parts and then think about how the parts are related to each other and to the whole.

Transition words connect ideas. They indicate how a text is organized. Look for words that
- describe main points (descriptive words)
- show sequence (sequence words)
- show comparison and contrast (comparison-and-contrast words)
- show cause and effect (cause-and-effect words)

Chronological or Time Order

Events are given in the order in which they happen or should be done. Events are connected by transition words such as *first, second, next, then, furthermore,* and *finally*. Chronological order is often used to relate a narrative, as in a short story; to write a how-to article on a topic like building a bird feeder; or to describe a process, such as what happens when a volcano erupts.

Spatial or Location Order

Parts are described in order of their location in space, for example, from back to front, left to right, or top to bottom. Descriptions are connected by transition words or phrases such as *next to, beside, above, below, beyond,* and *around*. Spatial order could be used for an article that discusses a project's physical aspects, such as describing the remodeling of a kitchen, or for a descriptive passage in literature, as in establishing the setting of a science fiction story set in a space station.

Order of Importance

Details are listed from least important to most important or from most important to least important; transition phrases are used such as *more important, less important, most important,* and *least important*. For example, a speech telling voters why they should elect you class president could build from the least important reason to the most important reason.

Comparison-and-Contrast Order

Details of two subjects are presented in one of two ways. In the first method, the characteristics of one subject are presented, followed by the characteristics of the second subject. This method could be used to organize an essay that compares and contrasts two fast-food chains, and to tell why one is superior to the other.

In the second method, both subjects are compared and contrasted with regard to one quality, then with regard to a second quality, and so on. An essay organized according to this method could compare the platforms of two political parties issue by issue: the environment, the economy, and so forth. Ideas are connected by transition words and phrases that indicate similarities or differences, such as *likewise, similarly, in contrast, a different kind, on the other hand,* and *another difference.*

Cause-and-Effect Order

One or more causes are followed by one or more effects, or one or more effects are followed by one or more causes. Transition words and phrases that indicate cause and effect include *one cause, another effect, as a result, consequently,* and *therefore.* Cause-and-effect organization might be used for a public health announcement warning about the dangers of playing with fire or an essay discussing the outbreak of World War I and the events that led up to it.

Classification or Sorting Order

Items are classified, or grouped, in categories to show how one group is similar to or different from another. Items in the same category should share one or more characteristics. For example, Edgar Allan Poe, Agatha Christie, and Stephen King can be classified together as mystery writers. Transition words that indicate classification order are the same words that indicate comparison-and-contrast order, words such as *likewise, similarly, in contrast, a different kind,* and *another difference.*

Identify Sequence of Events

Sequence refers to the order in which things happen. When you read certain types of writing, such as a short story, a novel, a biography of a person's life, or a history book, keep track of the sequence of events. You might do this by making a time line or a sequence map.

Time Line

To make a time line, draw a line and divide it into equal parts like the one on the next page. Label each part with a date or a time. Then add key events at the right places along the time line.

MARK THE TEXT

Underline or highlight the six methods of text organization listed on pages 22 and 23.

NOTE THE FACTS

What are two ways to keep track of the sequence of events?

_____
_____
_____

NOTE THE FACTS

What happened in 1929?

_____
_____
_____

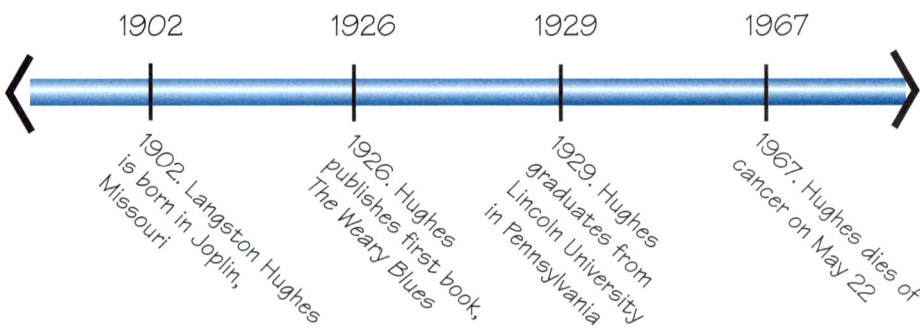

Sequence Map

In each box, draw pictures that represent key events in a selection. Then write a caption under each box that explains each event. Draw the events in the order in which they occur.

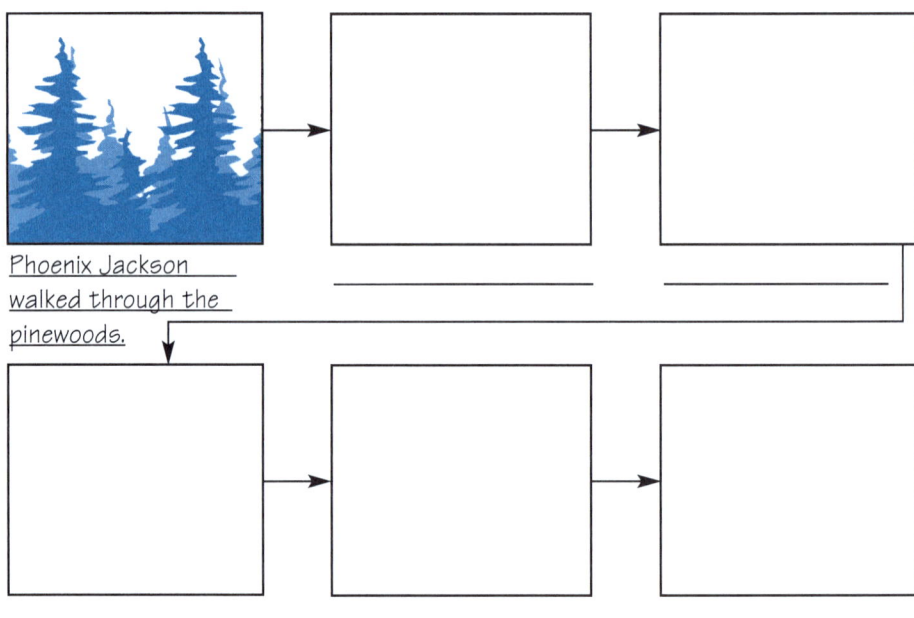

Phoenix Jackson walked through the pinewoods.

Compare and Contrast

Comparing and contrasting are closely related processes. When you **compare** one thing to another, you describe similarities between the two things; when you **contrast** two things, you describe their differences. To compare and contrast, begin by listing the features of each subject. Then go down both lists and check whether each feature is shared or not. You can also show similarities and differences in a Venn diagram. A Venn diagram uses two slightly overlapping circles. The outer part of each circle shows what aspects of two things are different from each other. The inner, or shared, part of each circle shows what aspects the two things share.

MARK THE TEXT

Underline or highlight the definitions of *compare* and *contrast*.

Venn Diagram

Write down ideas about Topic 1 in the first circle and ideas about Topic 2 in the second circle. The area in which the circles overlap should contain ideas common to both topics.

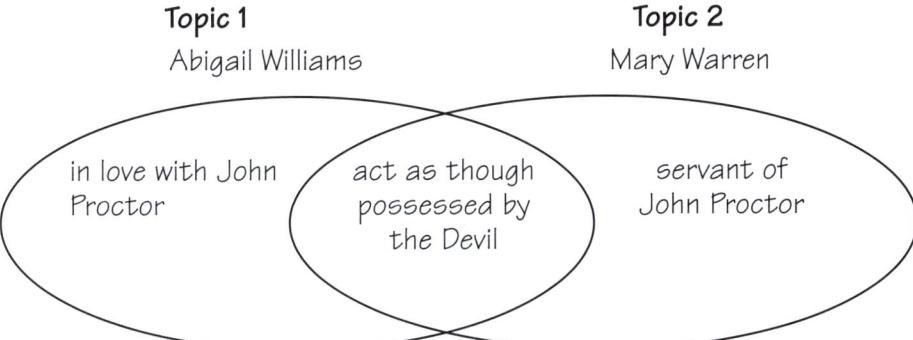

Evaluate Cause and Effect

When you evaluate **cause and effect**, you are looking for a logical relationship between a cause or causes and one or more effects. A writer may present one or more causes followed by one or more effects, or one or more effects followed by one or more causes. Transitional, or signal, words and phrases that indicate cause and effect include *one cause, another effect, as a result, because, since, consequently,* and *therefore*. As a reader, you determine whether the causes and effects in a text are reasonable. A graphic organizer like the one below will help you to recognize relationships between causes and effects.

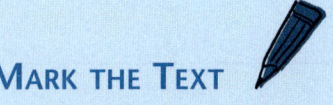

MARK THE TEXT

Underline or highlight words that signal cause and effect.

Cause-and-Effect Chart

Keep track of what happens in a story and why in a chart like the one below. Use cause-and-effect signal words to help you identify causes and their effects.

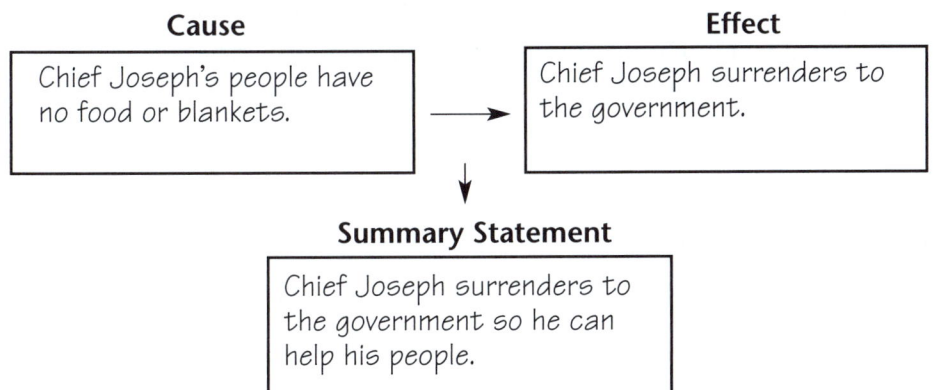

Classify and Reorganize Information

To **classify** is to put into classes or categories. Items in the same category should share one or more characteristics. A writer may group, or categorize, things to show similarities and name the categories to clarify how one group is similar or different from another. For example, whales can be classified by their method of eating as *baleen* or *toothed*, or by their types such as *orca* or *blue*. Classifying or reorganizing the information into categories as you read increases your understanding. The key step in classifying is choosing categories that fit your purpose. Take classification notes in a chart like the one below to help you organize separate types or groups and sort their characteristics.

Note the Facts

What do you do when you classify information?

_____

_____

_____

Classification Chart

Category 1 Northern Boreal Forest	Category 2 Temperate Forest	Category 3 Tropical Forest
Items in Category spruce fir hemlock	**Items in Category** maple beech birch	**Items in Category** teak cinchona kapok
Details and Characteristics Band of coniferous trees in North America, Europe, and Asia	**Details and Characteristics** Mixture of deciduous and coniferous trees just south of the northern boreal forest	**Details and Characteristics** Band of trees near the equator; most are evergreen

Distinguish Fact from Opinion

A **fact** is a statement that could be proven by direct observation or a reliable reference guide. Every statement of fact is either true or false. The following statement is an example of a fact:

> Abraham Lincoln delivered The Gettysburg Address on November 19, 1863. (This statement is a fact that can be proven by checking historical records from that day.)

An **opinion** is a statement that expresses an attitude or desire, not a fact about the world. One common type of opinion statement is a *value statement*. A value statement expresses an attitude toward something.

> The Gettysburg Address is Lincoln's most powerful speech. (This statement expresses an opinion that can be supported but not proved.)

Mark the Text

Underline or highlight the definitions of *fact* and *opinion*.

Value statements often include judgment words such as the following:

attractive	honest	ugly
awesome	junk	unattractive
beautiful	kind	valuable
cheap	mean	wonderful
dishonest	nice	worthless
excellent	petty	
good	treasure	

A **policy statement** is an opinion that tells not what is but what someone believes should be. Such statements usually include words like *should, should not, ought, ought not, must,* or *must not.*

> You **should** wear a seat belt when riding in a car.
> You **must not** ignore the signs urging you to buckle up.

A **prediction** makes a statement about the future. Because the future is unpredictable, most predictions can be considered opinions.

> New research will show that seat belts should be mandatory. Automobile computers may soon be able to prevent a car from operating if the driver is not wearing a seat belt.

When evaluating a fact, ask yourself whether it can be proven through direct observation or by checking a reliable source such as a reference book or an unbiased expert. An opinion is only as good as the facts that support it. When reading or listening, be critical about the statements that you encounter. It may be helpful to make a chart like the one below to help distinguish fact from opinion as you read.

Fact or Opinion Chart

Fact: Henry David Thoreau lived for two years in a cabin on Walden Pond.	**Opinion:** "Simplicity, simplicity, simplicity! I say, let your affairs be as two or three, and not a hundred or a thousand."
Proof: Thoreau wrote about his experience in his book *Walden*, which was published in 1854.	**Support:** Thoreau lived a simplified life at Walden that was very satisfying; however, others may not want to live this kind of life.
Fact:	**Opinion:**
Proof:	**Support:**

THINK AND REFLECT

What are three judgment words you could add to the chart on the left? **(Apply)**

_____
_____
_____
_____

Reading TIP

Facts can be proven by direct observation or by checking a reliable source. **Opinions** are supported by facts, but there is no actual proof. Use a Fact or Opinion Chart to determine whether you have proof or support.

NOTE THE FACTS

What are visual aids?

_____
_____
_____

Interpret Visual Aids

Visual aids are charts, graphs, pictures, illustrations, photos, maps, diagrams, spreadsheets, and other materials that present information. Many writers use visual aids to present data in understandable ways. Information visually presented in tables, charts, and graphs can help you find information, see trends, discover facts, and uncover patterns.

Reading Graphics

Before Reading	■ Determine the subject of the graphic by reading the title, headings, and other textual clues.
	■ Determine how the data are organized, classified, or divided by reading the labels along rows or columns.
During Reading	■ Survey the data and look for trends by comparing columns and rows, noting changes among information fields, looking for patterns, or studying map sections.
	■ Use legends, keys, and other helpful sections in the graphic.
After Reading	■ Check footnotes or references for additional information about the data and their sources.
	■ List conclusions or summarize the data.

Pie Chart

A **pie chart** is a circle that stands for a whole group or set. The circle is divided into parts to show the divisions of the whole. When you look at a pie chart, you can see the relationships of the parts to one another and to the whole.

NOTE THE FACTS

What percentage of students have more than two pets?

_____
_____
_____

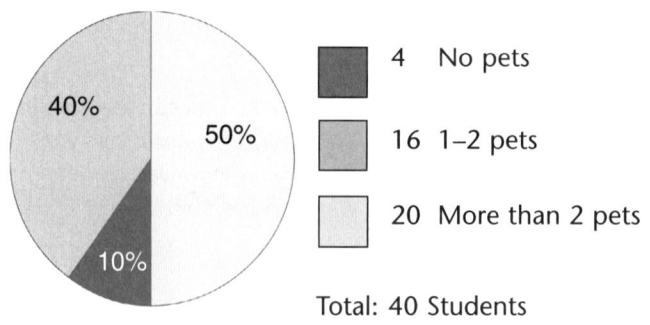

Total: 40 Students

NUMBER OF PETS STUDENTS HAVE

Bar Graph

A **bar graph** compares amounts of something by representing the amounts as bars of different lengths. In the bar graph below, each bar represents the number of common ravens sighted and reported to the Great Backyard Bird Count in 2004. To read the graph, simply imagine a line drawn from the edge of the bar to the bottom of the graph. Then read the number. For example, the bar graph below shows that birdwatchers in Ajo, Arizona, reported sighting nearly 500 common ravens in 2004.

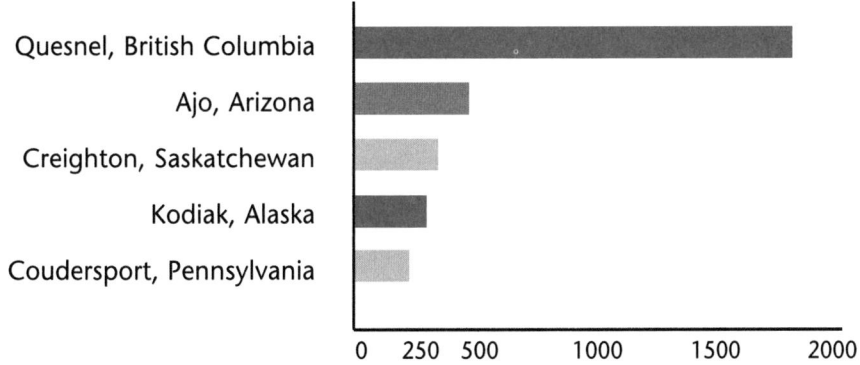

TOP FIVE TOWNS REPORTING SIGHTINGS OF THE COMMON RAVEN IN 2004

NOTE THE FACTS

How many common ravens were sighted in Kodiak, Alaska, in 2004?

_____

_____

Map

A **map** is a representation, usually on a surface such as paper or a sheet of plastic, of a geographic area showing various significant features of that area.

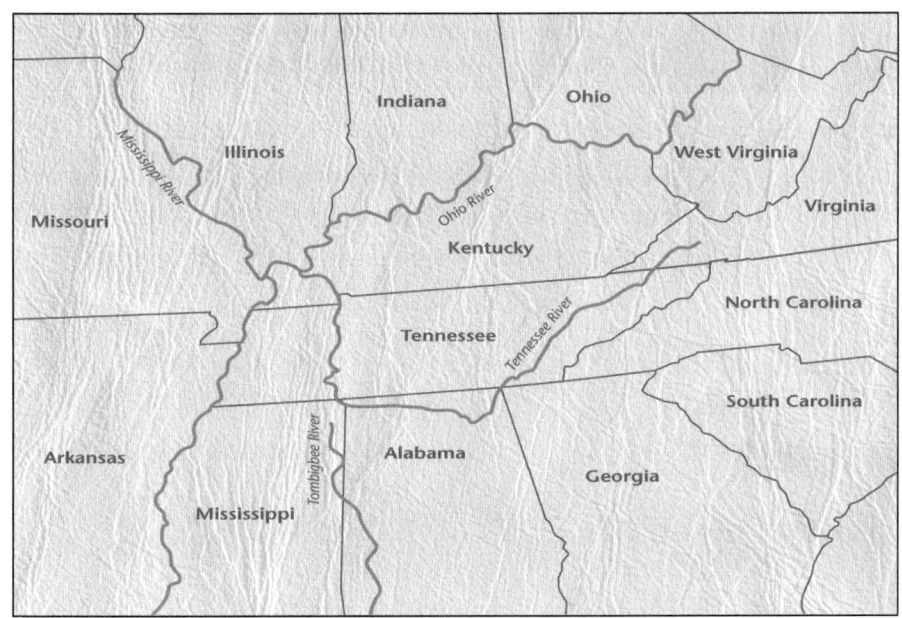

MAP OF THE SOUTHEASTERN STATES

NOTE THE FACTS

Through which states does the Tennessee River flow?

_____

_____

_____

Understand Literary Elements

Literary elements are the terms and techniques that are used in literature. When you read literature, you need to be familiar with the literary terms and reading skills listed below. These literary elements are explained in more detail in Unit 3, Reading Fiction, pages 36–38. Other literary elements are described in Units 4–7. Here are descriptions of the reading skills needed for some of the most common literary elements.

- **RECOGNIZE MOOD AND TONE. Mood** is the atmosphere or emotion conveyed by a literary work. A writer creates mood by using concrete details to describe the setting, characters, or events. The writer can evoke in the reader an emotional response—such as fear, discomfort, longing, or anticipation—by working carefully with descriptive language and sensory details. The mood of a work might be dark, mysterious, gloomy, cheerful, inspiring, or peaceful. **Tone** is the writer's attitude toward the subject or toward the reader of a work. Examples of different tones that a work may have include familiar, ironic, playful, sarcastic, serious, and sincere.

> *Reading* TIP
>
> An author's **writing style** can affect tone and mood. For example, sentence length, sentence variety, vocabulary difficulty (the number of mono-, bi-, and polysyllabic words), and the connotations (the associations a word has in addition to its literal meaning) of words help determine the tone and mood.

- **UNDERSTAND POINT OF VIEW. Point of view** is the vantage point, or perspective, from which a story or narrative is told. Stories are typically written from the following points of view:

first-person point of view	narrator uses words such as *I* and *we*
second-person point of view	narrator uses *you*
third-person point of view	narrator uses words such as *he, she, it,* and *they*

- **ANALYZE CHARACTER AND CHARACTERIZATION.** A **character** is a person (or sometimes an animal) who takes part in the action of a story. **Characterization** is the literary techniques writers use to create characters and make them come alive. Writers use the following techniques to create characters:

> *Reading* TIP
>
> A **character chart** can be used as a graphic organizer to keep track of character development as you read. See the example in Appendix B, page B-8.

direct description	describing the physical features, dress, and personality of the character
behavior	showing what characters say, do, or think
interaction with others	showing what other characters say or think about them
internal state	revealing the character's private thoughts and emotions

- **EXAMINE PLOT DEVELOPMENT.** The plot is basically what happens in a story. A **plot** is a series of events related to a *central conflict*, or struggle. A typical plot involves the introduction of a conflict, its development, and its eventual resolution. The elements of plot include the following:

exposition	sets the tone or mood, introduces the characters and setting, and provides necessary background information
inciting incident	introduces a central conflict with or within one or more characters
rising action	develops a central conflict with or within one or more characters and develops toward a high point of intensity
climax	marks the highest point of interest or suspense in the plot at which something decisive happens
falling action	details the events that follow the climax
resolution	marks the point at which the central conflict is ended or resolved
dénouement	includes any material that follows the resolution and that ties up loose ends

Reading TIP

A graphic organizer called a **plot diagram** can be used to chart the plot of a literature selection. Refer to the example in Appendix B, page B-11.

Draw Conclusions

When you **draw conclusions,** you are gathering pieces of information and then deciding what that information means.

This passage from "A Noiseless Flash" by John Hersey, Unit 7, page 322, describes what one of the survivors of the atomic bombing of Hiroshima, Japan, saw immediately after the blast.

> In the street, the first thing he saw was a squad of soldiers who had been burrowing into the hillside opposite, making one of the thousands of dugouts in which the Japanese apparently intended to resist invasion, hill by hill, life for life; the soldiers were coming out of the hole, where they should have been safe, and blood was running from their heads, chests, and backs. They were silent and dazed.

NOTE THE FACTS

Reread the excerpt from "A Noiseless Flash." What does one survivor see?

_____
_____
_____

NOTE THE FACTS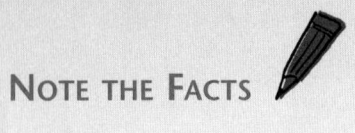

How can a drawing conclusions log help you?

_____

_____

_____

Drawing conclusions is an essential part of reading. As you read, it may be helpful to use a graphic organizer such as a chart or log to keep track of the information you find and the conclusions you draw.

Drawing Conclusions Log

Key Idea	Key Idea	Key Idea
Japanese soldiers were building dugouts meant to keep people safe.		
Supporting Points "soldiers who had been burrowing into the hillside" "making . . . dugouts in which the Japanese apparently intended to resist invasion" "the soldiers were coming out of the hole, where they should have been safe, and blood was running from their heads, chests, and backs"	**Supporting Points**	**Supporting Points**
Overall Conclusion No place in Hiroshima was safe from the atomic bomb.	**Overall Conclusion**	**Overall Conclusion**

32 THE EMC WRITE-IN READER

Unit 2 READING Review

Choose and Use Reading Skills

Before reading the excerpt below, review with a partner how to use each of these essential reading skills.

- Identify the Author's Purpose
- Find the Main Idea
- Make Inferences
- Use Context Clues
- Analyze Text Organization
- Identify Sequence of Events
- Compare and Contrast
- Evaluate Cause and Effect
- Classify and Reorganize Information
- Distinguish Fact from Opinion
- Interpret Visual Aids
- Understand Literary Elements
- Draw Conclusions

Read an excerpt from Sarah Orne Jewett's short story "A White Heron." In the story a young girl who lives on a farm with her grandmother brings a stranger home. The excerpt below is a discussion between the grandmother and the stranger. As you read, note how you can use some of the reading skills discussed in this unit. After you finish reading, summarize the excerpt in two or three sentences. Then answer the questions that follow.

> "There ain't a foot o' ground she [Sylvy] don't know her way over, and the wild creaturs counts her one o' themselves. Squer'ls she'll tame to come an' feed right out o' her hands, and all sorts o' birds. Last winter she got the jay-birds to bangeing[1] . . . here, and I believe she'd 'a' scanted herself[2] . . . of her own meals to have plenty to throw out amongst 'em, if I hadn't kep' watch. Anything but crows, I tell her. . . .
>
> "So Sylvy knows all about birds, does she?" he exclaimed, as he looked round at the little girl who sat, very demure but increasingly sleepy, in the moonlight. "I am making a collection of birds myself. I have been at it ever since I was a boy." (Mrs. Tilley smiled.) "There are two or three very rare ones I have been hunting for these five years. I mean to get them on my own ground if they can be found."
>
> "Do you cage 'em up?" asked Mrs. Tilley doubtfully, in response to this enthusiastic announcement.
>
> "Oh, no, they're stuffed and preserved, dozens and dozens of them," said the ornithologist, "and I have shot or snared every one myself. I caught a glimpse of a white heron three miles from here on Saturday, and I have followed it in this direction. They have never been found in this district at all. The little white heron, it is,"

> and he turned again to look at Sylvia with the hope of discovering that the rare bird was one of her acquaintances.

1. **bangeing.** Hanging around
2. **she'd 'a' scanted herself.** Would have deprived herself

1. What is the stranger interested in?

2. How does the stranger think Sylvy might help?

3. What context clues or word parts help you guess the meaning of *demure?* of *ornithologist?*

4. Do you think the stranger will be able to accomplish his task?

5. What clues in the excerpt make you think this?

On Your Own

FLUENTLY SPEAKING. Select a 100–150-word passage from a book, magazine, or newspaper that you are currently reading. Working with a partner, take turns reading the passage aloud several times. Break it down into shorter sections and alternate reading paragraphs or sentences. Use the Oral Reading Skills: Repeated Reading Record in Appendix A, page A-12, to chart your progress.

PICTURE THIS. Find an article that contains data. Think about how this data can be presented using a visual aid, such as a table, chart, or graph. Do you notice any trends or patterns? Draw a visual aid, such as a pie chart or bar graph, to present the information in a more understandable way.

PUT IT IN WRITING. Read a short article from a magazine or newspaper. Now go back and reread the first and last paragraphs. Write a summary of the main idea. What is it that the author wants you to know, think, feel, or do after reading this text? Is the main idea stated, or did you have to infer it?

Unit THREE
Reading Fiction

FICTION

Fiction is prose writing that tells an invented or imaginary story. *Prose* is writing that uses straightforward language and differs from poetry in that it doesn't have a rhythmic pattern. Some fiction, such as the historical novel, is based on fact. Other forms of fiction, such as the fantasy tale, are highly unrealistic. Fictional works also vary in structure and length.

Forms of Fiction

The oldest form of fiction is the stories told in the oral, or folk, tradition, which include myths, legends, and fables. The most common forms of fiction are short stories, novels, and novellas.

THE SHORT STORY. A **short story** is a brief work of fiction that tells a story. It usually focuses on a single episode or scene and involves a limited number of characters. Although a short story contains all the main elements of fiction—character, setting, plot, and theme—it may not fully develop each element. The selections in this unit are examples of short stories.

THE NOVEL AND NOVELLA. A **novel** is a long work of fiction that usually has more complex elements than a short story. Its longer format allows the elements of fiction to be more fully developed. A **novella** is a work of fiction that is longer than a typical short story but shorter than a typical novel.

Other types of fiction include romances, historical fiction, and science fiction. **Romances** are tales that feature the adventures of legendary figures such as Alexander the Great and King Arthur. **Historical fiction** is partly based on actual historical events and is partly made up. **Science fiction** is imaginative literature based on scientific principles, discoveries, or laws; it often deals with the future, the distant past, or worlds other than our own.

THINK AND REFLECT

Based on the definition of *fiction*, define *nonfiction*. **(Infer)**

_____

_____

THINK AND REFLECT

What characteristics of a short story make it different from a novel? **(Compare and Contrast)**

_____

_____

MARK THE TEXT

Highlight or underline the typical subjects of romance, historical fiction, and science fiction.

Elements of Fiction

CHARACTER. A **character** is a person (or sometimes an animal or thing) who takes part in the action of a story. The following are some useful terms for describing characters.

protagonist (main character)	central figure in a story
antagonist	character who struggles against the protagonist
major character	character with a significant role in the action of the story
minor character	character who plays a lesser role
one-dimensional character (flat character)	character who exhibits a single dominant quality (character trait)
three-dimensional character (full or rounded character)	character who exhibits the complexity of traits of a human being
static character	character who does not change during the course of the story
dynamic character	character who does change during the course of the story
stock character	character found again and again in different literary works

CHARACTERIZATION. **Characterization** is the use of literary techniques to create characters and make them come alive. Writers use the following techniques to create characters:

direct description	describing the physical features, dress, and personality of the character
behavior	showing what the character says or does
interaction with others	showing what other characters say or think about the character
internal state	revealing the character's private thoughts and emotions

SETTING. The **setting** of a work of fiction is the time and place in which the events take place. In fiction, setting is most often revealed by description of landscape, scenery, buildings, weather, and season. Setting reveals important information about the time period, geographical location, cultural environment, and physical conditions in which the characters live.

THINK AND REFLECT

Give an example of an antagonist. **(Extend)**

_____

_____

_____

Reading TIP

Motivation is the force that moves a character to think, feel, or behave in a certain way. For example, a character may be motivated by greed, love, or friendship.

MOOD AND TONE. Mood is the atmosphere or emotion created by a literary work. A writer creates mood by using concrete details to describe the setting, characters, or events. The mood of a work might be dark, mysterious, gloomy, cheerful, inspiring, or peaceful.

Tone is the writer's attitude toward the subject or toward the reader of a work. The tone of a work may be familiar, ironic, playful, sarcastic, serious, or sincere.

POINT OF VIEW. Point of view is the vantage point from which a story is told. You need to consider point of view to understand the perspective from which the events in the story are being told. Stories are typically written from the following points of view:

first-person point of view	narrator uses words such as *I* and *we*
second-person point of view	narrator uses *you*
third-person point of view	narrator uses words such as *he, she, it,* and *they*

Most of the literature you read will be told from either the first-person or third-person point of view. In stories written from a first-person point of view, the narrator may be a participant or a witness of the action. In stories told from a third-person point of view, the narrator generally stands outside the action. In some stories, the narrator's point of view is *limited*. In this case, the narrator can reveal only his or her private, internal thoughts or those of a single character. In other stories, the narrator's point of view is *omniscient*. In such stories the narrator can reveal the private, internal thoughts of any character.

CONFLICT. A **conflict** is a struggle between two forces in a literary work. A plot involves the introduction, development, and eventual resolution of a conflict. A struggle that takes place between a character and some outside force is called an **external conflict**. A struggle that takes place within a character is called an **internal conflict**.

PLOT. When you read short stories or novels, it helps to know the parts of a plot. The plot is basically what happens in a story. A **plot** is a series of events related to a central conflict, or struggle. A typical plot involves the introduction of a conflict, its development, and its eventual resolution. The elements of plot include the following:

Reading TIP

Writers often work carefully with descriptive language and sensory details to create an emotional response, such as fear or longing, in the reader. Sensory details appeal to any of the five senses—sight, hearing, smell, taste, and touch.

THINK AND REFLECT

What is the benefit of using an omniscient narrator? **(Infer)**

_____

_____

Reading TIP

In a work of fiction, the main character often takes one side of the central conflict. That character may struggle against an outside force, such as another character, the forces of nature, society or social norms, or fate. This is called an *external conflict*. A character may struggle against some elements within himself or herself. This is called an *internal conflict*.

NOTE THE FACTS

What do all plots center around?

_____

_____

exposition	sets the tone or mood, introduces the characters and setting, and provides necessary background information
inciting incident	event that introduces a central conflict
rising action	develops a central conflict and rises toward a high point of intensity
climax	the high point of interest or suspense in the plot where something decisive happens
falling action	the events that follow the climax
resolution	the point at which the central conflict is ended or resolved
dénouement	any material that follows the resolution and that ties up loose ends

Use a **plot diagram** like the one that follows to chart the plot of a literature selection.

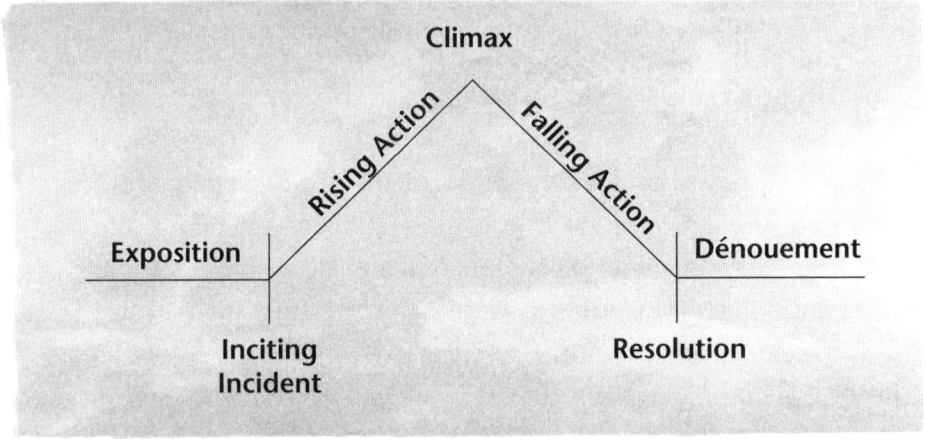

Reading TIP

Plots rarely contain all these elements in this exact order. Elements of exposition may be introduced at any time in the course of a work. Plots can have many variations. If you understand the purpose of each element, you will be able to identify them whenever they appear.

Become an Active Reader

Active reading strategy instruction in this unit gives you an in-depth look at how to use one active reading strategy for each story. Margin notes guide your use of this strategy and show you how to combine it with other strategies. Using just one reading strategy increases your chances of reading success. Learning how to use several strategies in combination increases your chances of success even more. Use the questions and tips in the margins to keep your attention focused on reading actively. Use the space in the margins to jot down responses to your reading. For further information about the active reading strategies, see Unit 1, pages 4–15.

USING READING STRATEGIES WITH FICTION

Active Reading Strategy Checklists

When reading fiction, you need to be aware of the plot (or what happens), the characters, and the setting. The following checklists offer things to consider as you read fiction.

1 READ WITH A PURPOSE. Before reading about imagined events and characters, give yourself a purpose, or something to look for, as you read. Say to yourself
- ❏ I want to look for . . .
- ❏ I need to learn what happens to . . .
- ❏ I want to experience what it is like in . . .
- ❏ I want to understand . . .

2 CONNECT TO PRIOR KNOWLEDGE. Being aware of what you already know and thinking about it as you read can help you keep track of what's happening and will increase your knowledge. As you read, say to yourself
- ❏ I already know this about the story . . .
- ❏ This part of the story reminds me of . . .
- ❏ I think this part of the story is like . . .
- ❏ My experience tells me that . . .
- ❏ I like this description because . . .

3 WRITE THINGS DOWN. As you read short stories or novels, writing things down is very important. Possible ways to write things down include
- ❏ Underline characters' names.
- ❏ Write messages on sticky notes.
- ❏ Highlight the setting.
- ❏ Create a graphic organizer to keep track of plot elements.
- ❏ Use a code in the margin that shows how you respond to the characters, setting, or events. For instance, you can mark a description you like with a "+."

4 MAKE PREDICTIONS. Make predictions about characters, settings, and events in a story. Your predictions will help you think about what lies ahead. Make predictions like the following:
- ❏ I predict that this character will . . .
- ❏ The setting of this story makes me think that . . .
- ❏ I bet there will be a conflict between . . .
- ❏ This event in the story makes me guess that . . .

Reading **TIP**

Sometimes your teacher will set a purpose for reading: "Compare the narrator's experience to your own life." Other times you can set your own purpose. To set a purpose, preview the title, the opening paragraphs, and instructional information for the story. Think about what you want to get out of the reading.

Reading **TIP**

Instead of writing down a short response, use a symbol or a short word to indicate your response. Use codes like the ones listed below.

+	I like this.
–	I don't like this.
√	This is important.
Yes	I agree with this.
No	I disagree with this.
?	I don't understand this.
!	This is like something I know.
↶	I need to come back to this later.

Reading TIP

Other tips for visualizing:
- Say to yourself, "If this were a movie, I'd see and hear . . ."
- Make quick sketches of what you imagine.
- Fill in gaps with details based on your experience or personal knowledge.
- Think about how things would sound, smell, and feel if you were in the scene.

Reading TIP

Keep a vocabulary notebook as you read. Jot down new words and their meanings. After you finish reading, practice using the words in sentences, word sorts, and daily conversation.

Fix-Up Ideas

- Reread
- Ask a question
- Read in shorter chunks
- Read aloud
- Retell
- Work with a partner
- Unlock difficult words
- Vary your reading rate
- Choose a new reading strategy
- Create a mnemonic device

---

5 **VISUALIZE.** Visualizing, or allowing the words on the page to create images in your mind, is one of the most important things to do while reading fiction. Become part of the action. "See" what the author describes. Make statements like
- ❑ I imagine the setting to look like . . .
- ❑ This description of the main character makes me . . .
- ❑ I picture that this is what happens in this section . . .
- ❑ I envision myself in the action by . . .

6 **USE TEXT ORGANIZATION.** Fiction writing has a plot that you can follow. Use the plot, or the series of events, to keep track of what is happening. Say to yourself
- ❑ The exposition, or introduction, tells me . . .
- ❑ The central conflict centers on . . .
- ❑ The climax, or high point of interest, occurs when . . .
- ❑ The resolution, or the outcome, of this story lets me know . . .
- ❑ Signal words like *first*, *then*, and *finally* explain . . .

7 **TACKLE DIFFICULT VOCABULARY.** Difficult words in a story can get in the way of your ability to follow the events in a work of fiction. Use aids that a text provides, consult a dictionary, or ask someone about words you do not understand. When you come across a word you do not know, say to yourself
- ❑ The context tells me that this word means . . .
- ❑ A dictionary definition provided in the story shows that the word means . . .
- ❑ My work with the word before class helps me know that the word means . . .
- ❑ A classmate said that the word means . . .
- ❑ I can skip knowing the exact meaning of this word because . . .

8 **MONITOR YOUR READING PROGRESS.** All readers encounter difficulty when they read, especially if they don't choose the reading material themselves. When you have to read something, take note of problems you are having and fix them. The key to reading success is knowing when you are having difficulty. To fix problems, say to yourself
- ❑ Because I do not understand this part, I will . . .
- ❑ Because I am having trouble staying interested in the story, I will . . .
- ❑ Because the words are too hard, I will . . .
- ❑ Because the story is very long, I will . . .
- ❑ Because I cannot remember what I have just read, I will . . .

How to Use Reading Strategies with Fiction

Read the following excerpts to discover how you might use reading strategies as you read fiction.

Excerpt 1. Note how a reader uses active reading strategies while reading this excerpt from "Sophistication" from *Winesburg, Ohio* by Sherwood Anderson.

READ WITH A PURPOSE
I want to find out what is going to happen at the fair.

WRITE THINGS DOWN
I'll make a sensory details chart to note what I visualize and what the author describes.

It was early evening of a day in the late fall and the Winesburg County Fair had brought crowds of country people into town. The day had been clear and the night came on warm and pleasant. On the Trunton Pike, where the road after it left town stretched away between berry fields now covered with dry brown leaves, the dust from passing wagons arose in clouds. Children, curled into little balls, slept on the straw scattered on wagon beds. Their hair was full of dust and their fingers black and sticky. The dust rolled away over the fields and the departing sun set it ablaze with colors.

In the main street of Winesburg, crowds filled the stores and the sidewalks. Night came on, horses whinnied, the clerks in the stores ran madly about, children became lost and cried lustily, an American town worked terribly at the task of amusing itself.

CONNECT TO PRIOR KNOWLEDGE
I've been to the fair before, so I picture vegetable displays, cotton candy, people, and rides.

VISUALIZE
I can see the dust rising along the road as the sky turns red streaked with orange.

Excerpt 2. Note how a reader uses active reading strategies while reading this excerpt from "The Outcasts of Poker Flat" by Bret Harte.

MONITOR YOUR READING PROGRESS
I'm not really sure what the trouble is yet. I'll read a few more paragraphs. If I'm still unsure, I'll reread this section.

MAKE A PREDICTION
I predict that Mr. Oakhurst will get in trouble for gambling.

As Mr. John Oakhurst, gambler, stepped into the main street of Poker Flat on the morning of the twenty-third of November, 1850, he was conscious of a change in its moral atmosphere from the preceding night. Two or three men, conversing earnestly together, ceased as he approached, and exchanged significant glances. There was a Sabbath lull in the air, which, in a settlement unused to Sabbath influences, looked ominous.

Mr. Oakhurst's calm, handsome face betrayed small concern of these indications. Whether he was conscious of any predisposing cause, was another question. "I reckon they're after somebody," he reflected; "likely it's me."

TACKLE DIFFICULT VOCABULARY
The word *ominous* must be something negative because the narrator seems surprised that Mr. Oakhurst betrayed small concern.

USE TEXT ORGANIZATION
This seems to be the beginning of a conflict between Mr. Oakhurst and the townsmen.

CONNECT

Reader's resource

Ambrose Bierce uses details about military customs and regulations to lend authenticity to **"An Occurrence at Owl Creek Bridge."** The story, set during the American Civil War, is an example of American Realism. It is also an example of Naturalism, a type of writing that reveals the forces beyond people's control that determine not only their circumstances and fate but also their characters, personalities, and experiences. The story is filled with twists and turns to keep the reader guessing until the last sentence.

Word watch

PREVIEW VOCABULARY

acclivity
aspirated
efface
embrasure
gesticulate
ludicrous
malign
oscillation
sentinel

Reader's journal

If you knew you were about to die, what would you think about?

___
___
___

"An Occurrence at Owl Creek Bridge"
by Ambrose Bierce

Active READING STRATEGY

MAKE PREDICTIONS

Before Reading ➤ GATHER INFORMATION

❑ Read the Reader's Resource carefully and think about the story's title. Think also about the Reader's Journal question.
❑ What do you think will happen in this story? Using information you have gathered, make one or more preliminary predictions in the Prediction Chart below.

Graphic Organizer: Prediction Chart

Clues	Predictions	Adjustments

An Occurrence at Owl Creek Bridge

Ambrose Bierce

A man stood upon a railroad bridge in northern Alabama, looking down into the swift water twenty feet below. The man's hands were behind his back, the wrists bound with a cord. A rope closely encircled his neck. It was attached to a stout cross timber above his head and the slack fell to the level of his knees. Some loose boards laid upon the sleepers[1] supporting the metals of the railway supplied a footing for him and his executioners—two private soldiers of the Federal army, directed by a sergeant who in civil life may have been a deputy sheriff. At a short remove upon the same temporary platform was an officer in the uniform of his rank, armed. He was a captain. A <u>sentinel</u> at each end of the bridge stood with his rifle in the position known as "support," that is to say, vertical in front of the left shoulder, the hammer resting on the forearm thrown straight across the chest—a formal and unnatural position, enforcing an

---

1. **sleepers.** Ties that support railroad tracks

words for everyday use

sen • ti • nel (sen´ti nəl) *n.*, person acting as a guard. *The <u>sentinel</u> stood watch on the ramparts.*

During Reading

MAKE PREDICTIONS

❑ Listen as your teacher reads the first three paragraphs. Did anything in the opening paragraphs fit your previous prediction? Did anything make you change your ideas? Write your new ideas in the Adjustments column. What do you think will happen next? Write down new predictions in the Predictions column of your chart.

❑ Read the rest of the story on your own. Stop occasionally to make new predictions and write them in your chart.

THINK AND REFLECT

What is about to happen to the man? **(Infer)**

_____
_____

DRAW A PICTURE

Draw a sketch of the opening scene. Use details in the first paragraph.

Reading TIP

Realism is the attempt to create an accurate portrayal of reality. As you read, look for descriptions and parts of the plot that are realistic.

NOTE THE FACTS

What is Death, according to the narrator? How should Death be received?

_____
_____
_____

MARK THE TEXT

Highlight or underline the physical characteristics of the man who is about to be hanged. Try to picture him in your mind.

---

erect carriage of the body. It did not appear to be the duty of these two men to know what was occurring at the center of the bridge; they merely blockaded the two ends of the foot planking that traversed it.

Beyond one of the sentinels nobody was in sight; the railroad ran straight away into a forest for a hundred yards, then, curving, was lost to view. Doubtless there was an outpost farther along. The other bank of the stream was open ground—a gentle <u>acclivity</u> topped with a stockade of vertical tree trunks, loopholed for rifles with a single <u>embrasure</u> through which protruded the muzzle of a brass cannon commanding the bridge. Midway of the slope between bridge and fort were the spectators—a single company of infantry in line, at "parade rest," the butts of the rifles on the ground, the barrels inclining slightly backward against the right shoulder, the hands crossed upon the stock. A lieutenant stood at the right of the line, the point of his sword upon the ground, his left hand resting upon his right. Excepting the group of four at the center of the bridge, not a man moved. The company faced the bridge, staring stonily, motionless. The sentinels, facing the banks of the stream, might have been statues to adorn the bridge. The captain stood with folded arms, silent, observing the work of his subordinates, but making no sign. Death is a dignitary who when he comes announced is to be received with formal manifestations of respect, even by those most familiar with him. In the code of military etiquette silence and fixity are forms of deference.

The man who was engaged in being hanged was apparently about thirty-five years of age. He was a civilian, if one might judge from his habit, which was that of a planter. His features were good—a straight nose, firm mouth, broad forehead, from which his long, dark hair was combed straight back, falling behind his ears to the collar of his well-fitting frock coat. He wore a mustache and pointed beard, but no whiskers; his eyes were large and

---

words for everyday use

ac • cliv • i • ty (ə klivˊə tē) *n.*, upward slope. *Due to the <u>acclivity</u> of the land their house stood on, the Nelsons dreaded mowing the lawn.*

em • bra • sure (em brāˊzhər) *n.*, slanted opening in a wall that increases the firing angle of a gun. *Firing through the <u>embrasure</u>, the police were protected from the criminals' bullets.*

dark gray, and had a kindly expression which one would hardly have expected in one whose neck was in the hemp.[2] Evidently this was no vulgar assassin. The liberal military code makes provision for hanging many kinds of persons, and gentlemen are not excluded.

The preparations being complete, the two private soldiers stepped aside and each drew away the plank upon which he had been standing. The sergeant turned to the captain, saluted and placed himself immediately behind that officer, who in turn moved apart one pace. These movements left the condemned man and the sergeant standing on the two ends of the same plank, which spanned three of the crossties of the bridge. The end upon which the civilian stood almost, but not quite, reached a fourth. This plank had been held in place by the weight of the captain; it was now held by that of the sergeant. At a signal from the former the latter would step aside, the plank would tilt and the condemned man go down between two ties. The arrangement commended itself to his judgment as simple and effective. His face had not been covered nor his eyes bandaged. He looked a moment at his "unsteadfast footing," then let his gaze wander to the swirling water of the stream racing madly beneath his feet. A piece of dancing driftwood caught his attention and his eyes followed it down the current. How slowly it appeared to move! What a sluggish stream!

He closed his eyes in order to fix his last thoughts upon his wife and children. The water, touched to gold by the early sun, the brooding mists under the banks at some distance down the stream, the fort, the soldiers, the piece of drift—all had distracted him. And now he became conscious of a new disturbance. Striking through the thought of his dear ones was a sound which he could neither ignore nor understand, a sharp, distinct, metallic percussion like the stroke of a blacksmith's hammer upon the anvil; it had the same ringing quality. He wondered what it was, and whether immeasurably distant or near by—it seemed both. Its recurrence was regular, but as slow as the tolling of a death knell. He awaited each stroke with

---

2. **hemp.** Rope made of hemp

MARK THE TEXT

Highlight or underline what the man was really hearing.

Use THE STRATEGY

MAKE A PREDICTION. Read the last paragraph of section I again. What do you think will happen next? Write this prediction in your Prediction Chart.

FIX-UP IDEA

Read Short Sections
If you have trouble staying focused while reading this story, try reading smaller sections. Use the natural breaks in the story, marked by Roman numerals. Stop more frequently if you need to. For example, stop after every paragraph and answer any margin questions in that section. Try to summarize the paragraph or section you have just read. Then move on to the next paragraph.

impatience and—he knew not why—apprehension. The intervals of silence grew progressively longer; the delays became maddening. With their greater infrequency the sounds increased in strength and sharpness. They hurt his ear like the thrust of a knife; he feared he would shriek. What he heard was the ticking of his watch.

He unclosed his eyes and saw again the water below him. "If I could free my hands," he thought, "I might throw off the noose and spring into the stream. By diving I could evade the bullets and, swimming vigorously, reach the bank, take to the woods and get away home. My home, thank God, is as yet outside their lines; my wife and little ones are still beyond the invader's farthest advance."

As these thoughts, which have here to be set down in words, were flashed into the doomed man's brain rather than evolved from it the captain nodded to the sergeant. The sergeant stepped aside.

II

Peyton Farquhar was a well-to-do planter, of an old and highly respected Alabama family. Being a slave owner and like other slave owners a politician he was naturally an original secessionist and ardently devoted to the Southern cause. Circumstances of an imperious nature, which it is unnecessary to relate here, had prevented him from taking service with the gallant army that had fought the disastrous campaigns ending with the fall of Corinth, and he chafed under the inglorious restraint, longing for the release of his energies, the larger life of the soldier, the opportunity for distinction. That opportunity, he felt, would come, as it comes to all in war time. Meanwhile he did what he could. No service was too humble for him to perform in aid of the South, no adventure too perilous for him to undertake if consistent with the character of a civilian who was at heart a soldier, and who in good faith and without too much qualification assented to at least a part of the frankly villainous dictum that all is fair in love and war.

One evening while Farquhar and his wife were sitting on a rustic bench near the entrance to his grounds, a gray-clad soldier rode up to the gate and asked for a drink of water. Mrs. Farquhar was only too happy to serve him with her own white hands. While she was fetching the water her husband approached the dusty horseman and inquired eagerly for news from the front.

"The Yanks are repairing the railroads," said the man, "and are getting ready for another advance. They have reached the Owl Creek bridge, put it in order and built a stockade on the north bank. The commandant has issued an order, which is posted everywhere, declaring that any civilian caught interfering with the railroad, its bridges, tunnels or trains will be summarily hanged. I saw the order."

"How far is it to the Owl Creek bridge?" Farquhar asked.

"About thirty miles."

"Is there no force on this side the creek?"

"Only a picket post[3] half a mile out, on the railroad, and a single sentinel at this end of the bridge."

"Suppose a man—a civilian and student of hanging—should elude the picket post and perhaps get the better of the sentinel," said Farquhar, smiling, "what could he accomplish?"

The soldier reflected. "I was there a month ago," he replied. "I observed that the flood of last winter had lodged a great quantity of driftwood against the wooden pier at this end of the bridge. It is now dry and would burn like tow."[4]

The lady had now brought the water, which the soldier drank. He thanked her ceremoniously, bowed to her husband and rode away. An hour later, after nightfall, he repassed the plantation, going northward in the direction from which he had come. He was a Federal scout.

III

As Peyton Farquhar fell straight downward through the bridge he lost consciousness and was as one already dead. From this state he was awakened—ages later, it seemed to him—by the pain of a sharp pressure upon his throat, followed by a sense of suffocation. Keen, poignant agonies seemed to shoot from his neck downward through every

---

3. **picket post.** Troops that protect an army from a surprise attack
4. **tow.** Flammable fibers of hemp or flax

Literary TOOLS

FLASHBACK. A **flashback** is a section of a literary work that presents an event or series of events that occurred earlier than the current time in the work. As you read, try to determine the chronological order of events. You might make a time line to show when each event happened.

THINK AND REFLECT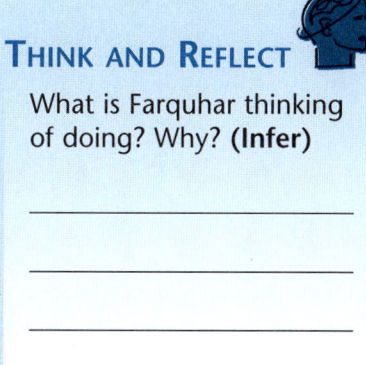

What is Farquhar thinking of doing? Why? **(Infer)**

_____
_____
_____

Use THE STRATEGY

MAKE A PREDICTION. Read the last paragraph of section II again. What do you think will happen next? Write this prediction in your Prediction Chart.

MARK THE TEXT

Read lines 168–190. Highlight or underline the things Farquhar feels, sees, and hears.

170 fiber of his body and limbs. These pains appeared to flash along well defined lines of ramification and to beat with an inconceivably rapid periodicity. They seemed like streams of pulsating fire heating him to an intolerable temperature. As to his head, he was conscious of nothing but a feeling of fullness—of congestion. These sensations were unaccompanied by thought. The intellectual part of his nature was already <u>effaced</u>; he had power only to feel, and feeling was torment. He was conscious of motion. Encompassed in a luminous cloud, of which he was now merely the fiery heart, without material substance, he swung through unthinkable arcs of <u>oscillation</u>, like a vast pendulum. Then
180 all at once, with terrible suddenness, the light about him shot upward with the noise of a loud splash; a frightful roaring was in his ears, and all was cold and dark. The power of thought was restored; he knew that the rope had broken and he had fallen into the stream. There was no additional strangulation; the noose about his neck was already suffocating him and kept the water from his lungs. To die of hanging at the bottom of a river!—the idea seemed to him <u>ludicrous</u>. He opened his eyes in the darkness and saw above him a gleam of light, but how
190 distant, how inaccessible! He was still sinking, for the light became fainter and fainter until it was a mere glimmer. Then it began to grow and brighten, and he knew that he was rising toward the surface—knew it with reluctance, for he was now very comfortable. "To be hanged and drowned," he thought, "that is not so bad; but I do not wish to be shot. No; I will not be shot; that is not fair."

  He was not conscious of an effort, but a sharp pain in his wrist apprised him that he was trying to free his hands. He gave the struggle his attention, as an idler might observe
200 the feat of a juggler, without interest in the outcome. What splendid effort!—what magnificent, what superhuman strength! Ah, that was a fine endeavor! Bravo! The cord fell away; his arms parted and floated upward, the hands dimly

NOTE THE FACTS

What thought does Farquhar have as he rises to the surface of the water?

_____
_____
_____

words for everyday use

ef • face (ə fās´) vt., erase, wipe out. *The thick coat of paint <u>effaced</u> the graffiti on the bathroom wall.*
os • cil • la • tion (äs´ə lā´shən) n., act of swinging back and forth. *The <u>oscillation</u> of the hypnotist's watch soon put the audience volunteer in a trance.*
lu • di • crous (lü´di krəs) adj., absurd, ridiculous. *It was <u>ludicrous</u> how the elephant in the cartoon was afraid of a tiny mouse.*

seen on each side in the growing light. He watched them with a new interest as first one and then the other pounced upon the noose at his neck. They tore it away and thrust it fiercely aside, its undulations resembling those of a watersnake. "Put it back, put it back!" He thought he shouted these words to his hands, for the undoing of the noose had been succeeded by the direst pang that he had yet experienced. His neck ached horribly; his brain was on fire; his heart, which had been fluttering faintly, gave a great leap, trying to force itself out at his mouth. His whole body was racked and wrenched with an insupportable anguish! But his disobedient hands gave no heed to the command. They beat the water vigorously with quick, downward strokes, forcing him to the surface. He felt his head emerge; his eyes were blinded by the sunlight; his chest expanded convulsively, and with a supreme and crowning agony his lungs engulfed a great draft of air, which instantly he expelled in a shriek!

He was now in full possession of his physical senses. They were, indeed, preternaturally[5] keen and alert. Something in the awful disturbance of his organic system had so exalted and refined them that they made record of things never before perceived. He felt the ripples upon his face and heard their separate sounds as they struck. He looked at the forest on the bank of the stream, saw the individual trees, the leaves and the veining of each leaf—saw the very insects upon them: the locusts, the brilliant-bodied flies, the gray spiders stretching their webs from twig to twig. He noted the prismatic colors in all the dewdrops upon a million blades of grass. The humming of the gnats that danced above the eddies of the stream, the beating of the dragonflies' wings, the strokes of the water spiders' legs, like oars which had lifted their boat—all these made audible music. A fish slid along beneath his eyes and he heard the rush of its body parting the water.

He had come to the surface facing down the stream; in a moment the visible world seemed to wheel slowly round, himself the pivotal point, and he saw the bridge, the fort, the soldiers upon the bridge, the captain, the sergeant, the

---

5. **preternaturally.** Inexplicably

NOTE THE FACTS

What effect does taking off the noose have?

_____
_____
_____

NOTE THE FACTS

In what state are Farquhar's senses? What sensory details does he notice?

_____
_____
_____

two privates, his executioners. They were in silhouette against the blue sky. They shouted and gesticulated, pointing at him. The captain had drawn his pistol, but did not fire; the others were unarmed. Their movements were grotesque and horrible, their forms gigantic.

Suddenly he heard a sharp report and something struck the water smartly within a few inches of his head, spattering his face with spray. He heard a second report, and saw one of the sentinels with his rifle at his shoulder, a light cloud of blue smoke rising from the muzzle. The man in the water saw the eye of the man on the bridge gazing into his own through the sights of the rifle. He observed that it was a gray eye and remembered having read that gray eyes were keenest, and that all famous marksmen had them. Nevertheless, this one had missed.

A counterswirl had caught Farquhar and turned him half round; he was again looking into the forest on the bank opposite the fort. The sound of a clear, high voice in a monotonous singsong now rang out behind him and came across the water with a distinctness that pierced and subdued all other sounds, even the beating of the ripples in his ears. Although no soldier, he had frequented camps enough to know the dread significance of that deliberate, drawling, aspirated chant; the lieutenant on shore was taking a part in the morning's work. How coldly and pitilessly—with what an even, calm intonation, presaging, and enforcing tranquillity in the men—with what accurately measured intervals fell those cruel words:

"Attention, company! . . . Shoulder arms! . . . Ready! . . . Aim! . . . fire!"

Farquhar dived—dived as deeply as he could. The water roared in his ears like the voice of Niagara, yet he heard the dulled thunder of the volley and, rising again toward the surface, met shining bits of metal, singularly flattened, oscillating slowly downward. Some of them touched him on the face and hands, then fell away, continuing their descent.

NOTE THE FACTS

What does Farquhar notice about the marksman? What does he fear this means?

_____

_____

_____

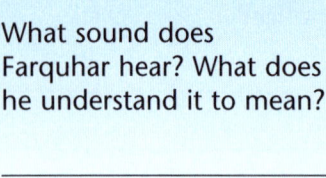

NOTE THE FACTS

What sound does Farquhar hear? What does he understand it to mean?

_____

_____

_____

words for everyday use

ges • tic • u • late (jes tik´yü lāt´) vi., make gestures with hands or arms. *Late for her appointment, the woman wildly gesticulated to the taxi driver to stop.*
as • pi • rat • ed (as´pə rāt´əd) adj., articulated with a puff of breath before or after. *The choir director made sure the singers warmed up with aspirated vocalizing before the concert.*

One lodged between his collar and neck; it was uncomfortably warm and he snatched it out.

As he rose to the surface, gasping for breath, he saw that he had been a long time under water; he was perceptibly farther down stream—nearer to safety. The soldiers had almost finished reloading; the metal ramrods flashed all at once in the sunshine as they were drawn from the barrels, turned in the air, and thrust into their sockets. The two sentinels fired again, independently and ineffectually.

The hunted man saw all this over his shoulder; he was now swimming vigorously with the current. His brain was as energetic as his arms and legs; he thought with the rapidity of lightning.

"The officer," he reasoned, "will not make that martinet's[6] error a second time. It is as easy to dodge a volley as a single shot. He has probably already given the command to fire at will. God help me, I cannot dodge them all!"

An appalling splash within two yards of him was followed by a loud, rushing sound, *diminuendo*,[7] which seemed to travel back through the air to the fort and died in an explosion which stirred the very river to its deeps! A rising sheet of water curved over him, fell down upon him, blinded him, strangled him! The cannon had taken a hand in the game. As he shook his head free from the commotion of the smitten water he heard the deflected shot humming through the air ahead, and in an instant it was cracking and smashing the branches in the forest beyond.

"They will not do that again," he thought; "the next time they will use a charge of grape.[8] I must keep my eye upon the gun; the smoke will apprise me—the report arrives too late; it lags behind the missile. That is a good gun."

Suddenly he felt himself whirled round and round—spinning like a top. The water, the banks, the forests, the now distant bridge, fort and men—all were commingled and blurred. Objects were represented by their colors only; circular horizontal streaks of color—that was all he saw. He

---

6. **martinet.** Strict disciplinarian
7. ***diminuendo.*** Musical term meaning a reduction in volume
8. **grape.** Cluster of small iron balls fired from a cannon

Reading STRATEGY REVIEW

VISUALIZE. Review visualizing on page 40. As you read this scene, put yourself in Farquhar's place. Think about what you would notice with all your senses.

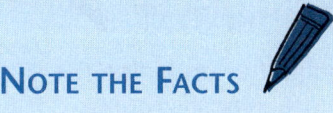

NOTE THE FACTS

Why does Farquhar focus on the smoke of the gun?

_____

_____

NOTE THE FACTS

What causes Farquhar delight and contentment?

_____
_____
_____

had been caught in a vortex and was being whirled on with a velocity of advance and gyration that made him giddy and sick. In a few moments he was flung upon the gravel at the foot of the left bank of the stream—the southern bank— and behind a projecting point which concealed him from his enemies. The sudden arrest of his motion, the abrasion of one of his hands on the gravel, restored him, and he wept with delight. He dug his fingers into the sand, threw it over himself in handfuls and audibly blessed it. It looked like diamonds, rubies, emeralds; he could think of nothing beautiful which it did not resemble. The trees upon the bank were giant garden plants; he noted a definite order in their arrangement, inhaled the fragrance of their blooms. A strange, roseate light shone through the spaces among their trunks and the wind made in their branches the music of aeolian harps.[9] He had no wish to perfect his escape—was content to remain in that enchanting spot until retaken.

A whiz and rattle of grapeshot among the branches high above his head roused him from his dream. The baffled cannoneer had fired him a random farewell. He sprang to his feet, rushed up the sloping bank, and plunged into the forest.

All that day he traveled, laying his course by the rounding sun. The forest seemed interminable; nowhere did he discover a break in it, not even a woodman's road. He had not known that he lived in so wild a region. There was something uncanny in the revelation.

By night fall he was fatigued, footsore, famishing. The thought of his wife and children urged him on. At last he found a road which led him in what he knew to be the right direction. It was as wide and straight as a city street, yet it seemed untraveled. No fields bordered it, no dwelling anywhere. Not so much as the barking of a dog suggested human habitation. The black bodies of the trees formed a straight wall on both sides, terminating on the horizon in a point, like a diagram in a lesson in perspective. Overhead, as he looked up through this rift in the wood, shone great golden stars looking unfamiliar and grouped in strange constellations. He was sure they were arranged in some

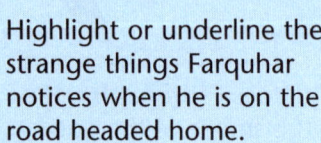

MARK THE TEXT

Highlight or underline the strange things Farquhar notices when he is on the road headed home.

---

9. **aeolian harps.** Harps that produce music when air blows over the strings

order which had a secret and <u>malign</u> significance. The wood on either side was full of singular noises, among which—once, twice, and again, he distinctly heard whispers in an unknown tongue.

His neck was in pain and lifting his hand to it he found it horribly swollen. He knew that it had a circle of black where the rope had bruised it. His eyes felt congested; he could no longer close them. His tongue was swollen with thirst; he relieved its fever by thrusting it forward from between his teeth into the cold air. How softly the turf had carpeted the untraveled avenue—he could no longer feel the roadway beneath his feet!

Doubtless, despite his suffering, he had fallen asleep while walking, for now he sees another scene—perhaps he has merely recovered from a delirium. He stands at the gate of his own home. All is as he left it, and all bright and beautiful in the morning sunshine. He must have traveled the entire night. As he pushes open the gate and passes up the wide white walk, he sees a flutter of female garments; his wife, looking fresh and cool and sweet, steps down from the veranda to meet him. At the bottom of the steps she stands waiting, with a smile of ineffable joy, an attitude of matchless grace and dignity. Ah, how beautiful she is! He springs forward with extended arms. As he is about to clasp her he feels a stunning blow upon the back of the neck; a blinding white light blazes all about him with a sound like the shock of a cannon—then all is darkness and silence!

Peyton Farquhar was dead; his body, with a broken neck, swung gently from side to side beneath the timbers of the Owl Creek bridge. ■

THINK AND REFLECT

What image does this description of Farquhar suggest? **(Infer)**

_____
_____
_____

NOTE THE FACTS

What is revealed in the last paragraph about Farquhar's actions?

_____
_____
_____

words for everyday use

ma • lign (mə līn´) *adj.*, malicious, evil. *The wolf's <u>malign</u> intention was to eat Little Red Riding Hood.*

Reflect ON YOUR READING

After Reading → ANALYZE AND VERIFY PREDICTIONS

- ❏ Go through the list of predictions in your Prediction Chart. Put a star next to every prediction that you were right about. Put a check next to every prediction where you changed your ideas from a previous prediction.
- ❏ Share your predictions with a partner. Talk about what clues in the story led you to make the predictions.

Reading Skills and Test Practice

IDENTIFY PLOT ELEMENTS

Discuss with your partner how best to answer these questions about plot elements in the story. Use the Think-Aloud Notes to write down your reasons for eliminating incorrect answers.

_____ 1. What is the resolution of the story?
   a. Farquhar escapes into the river and forest.
   b. Farquhar imagines escaping.
   c. Farquhar tries to destroy the Owl Creek bridge and is caught.
   d. Farquhar is hanged.

_____ 2. Why is the flashback important to the plot?
   a. It reveals Farquhar's motivations and lets the reader know why he was hanged.
   b. It reveals that Farquhar is actually dead.
   c. It reveals that Farquhar is actually a Federal scout.
   d. It details what Farquhar accomplished before he was caught and why he was hanged.

How did using the reading strategy help you to answer the questions?

_____
_____
_____
_____

THINK-ALOUD NOTES

Investigate, Inquire, and Imagine

RECALL: GATHER FACTS
1a. What does the soldier in gray tell Farquhar and his wife when he stops by their home?

ANALYZE: TAKE THINGS APART
2a. How are Farquhar's experiences after his escape realistic? How are they unrealistic?

EVALUATE: MAKE JUDGMENTS
3a. How effectively has the author depicted Farquhar's psychological trauma? Use examples from the text to justify your response.

INTERPRET: FIND MEANING
1b. Who is the soldier in gray in reality? How do you know?

SYNTHESIZE: BRING THINGS TOGETHER
2b. Overall, is this story realistic? Think about the plot and about the descriptions in the story.

EXTEND: CONNECT IDEAS
3b. If this story were a movie, what techniques would the director use to show Farquhar's psychological trauma? What techniques would the director use to create suspense and to show the differences in time?

Literary Tools

FLASHBACK. A **flashback** is a section of a literary work that presents an event or series of events that occurred earlier than the current time in the work. Fill in the chart that follows. Put the story's events in the order you read about them on the left. On the right, list the events in chronological order. How does the flashback in this story affect the plot?

Reading Order	Chronological Order
A man stands with a noose around his neck on a railroad bridge.	Farquhar sits outside on the grounds of his home with his wife.

WordWorkshop

VOCABULARY CARDS. A good way to learn and remember new words is to create vocabulary cards. Create a separate note card or notebook page for each word. Write the word in the center. In the top left corner write the definition. In the top right corner, write a synonym (a word with the same or nearly the same meaning). In the bottom left corner, write a sentence using the word. In the bottom right corner, draw a picture to help you remember the word. Look at the sample that follows. Then create your own vocabulary cards for the Words for Everyday Use for this story.

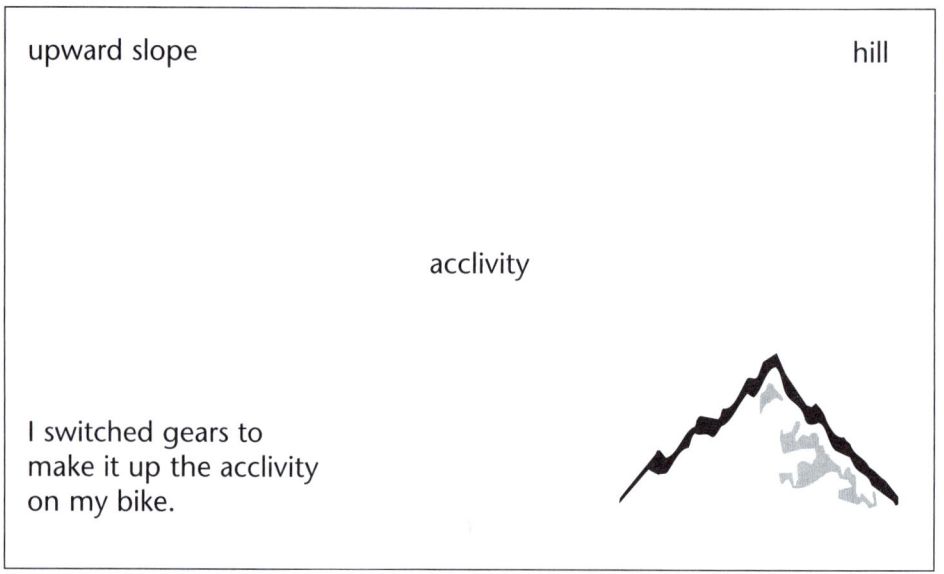

Read-Write Connection

If you were Farquhar, would you regret your decision to try to destroy the railroad bridge? Why, or why not?

_____

_____

_____

Beyond the Reading

WRITE A SCREENPLAY. Write a screenplay for section III of the selection. Describe Farquhar's actions. Use parentheses to identify special effects, such as lighting and music.

GO ONLINE. To find links and additional activities for this selection, visit the EMC Internet Resource Center at **emcp.com/languagearts** and click on Write-In Reader.

The Notorious Jumping Frog of Calaveras County

by Mark Twain

Active READING STRATEGY

TACKLE DIFFICULT VOCABULARY

Before Reading ▶ **PREVIEW VOCABULARY**

- ❏ Begin by previewing the Words for Everyday Use at the bottom of the pages of the selection. Read each word, its definition, and the sentence in which it is used. Copy the words and their definitions into your notebook.
- ❏ **Dialect** is a version of a language spoken by the people of a particular place, time, or social group. This story uses the regional dialect of California frontiersmen during the mid-1800s. Some words may look unfamiliar at first, but you will find that many of them are similar to standard English words.
- ❏ As you read, keep track of unfamiliar and dialectical words in the graphic organizer.

Graphic Organizer: Vocabulary Chart

Unfamiliar Word	Standard English or Dialect	Meaning

CONNECT

Reader's resource

Mark Twain, the pen name of Samuel Langhorne Clemens, is perhaps best known for his novels *The Adventures of Tom Sawyer* and *Adventures of Huckleberry Finn*. "**The Notorious Jumping Frog of Calaveras County**" is Twain's retelling of a popular nineteenth-century tall tale. A **tall tale** is a lighthearted and humorous story that contains highly exaggerated and unrealistic events. The story, which was first published in 1865, portrays the entertainments of simple men living in a frontier mining camp in California. To commemorate Twain's story, a frog-jumping contest is still held in Calaveras County today.

Word watch

PREVIEW VOCABULARY

afflicted	exhorter
append	garrulous
cavort	interminable
conjecture	ornery
dilapidated	vagabond

Reader's journal

What story have you exaggerated to impress your listeners?

_____
_____
_____

UNIT 3 / READING FICTION 57

During Reading

USE VOCABULARY STRATEGIES

❑ Follow along in your text as your teacher reads the first four paragraphs aloud. Write unfamiliar words in the graphic organizer.
❑ Review the words you listed, and determine if they are part of the regional dialect. Use context clues to help you find the meaning of unfamiliar words.
❑ Continue reading the selection on your own. Jot down unfamiliar words, and define them by using context clues.

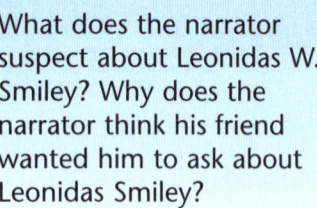

NOTE THE FACTS

What does the narrator suspect about Leonidas W. Smiley? Why does the narrator think his friend wanted him to ask about Leonidas Smiley?

_____
_____
_____

Reading TIP

Many unfamiliar words that contain apostrophes are dialectical. The apostrophe shows where a letter has been removed. Try reading the word aloud. The word will probably sound familiar.

The Notorious Jumping Frog of Calaveras County

Mark Twain

In compliance with the request of a friend of mine, who wrote me from the East, I called on good-natured, <u>garrulous</u> old Simon Wheeler, and inquired after my friend's friend, Leonidas W. Smiley, as requested to do, and I 10 hereunto <u>append</u> the result. I have a lurking suspicion that *Leonidas W.* Smiley is a myth; that my friend never knew such a personage; and that he only <u>conjectured</u> that if I asked old Wheeler about him, it would remind him of his infamous *Jim* Smiley, and he would go to work and bore me to death with some exasperating reminiscence of him as long and as tedious as it should be useless to me. If that was the design, it succeeded.

20 I found Simon Wheeler dozing comfortably by the barroom stove of the <u>dilapidated</u> tavern in the decayed mining camp of Angel's, and I noticed that he was fat and bald-headed, and had an expression of winning gentleness and simplicity upon his tranquil countenance. He roused up, and gave me good-day. I told him a friend of mine had commissioned me to make some inquiries about a cherished

words for everyday use

gar • ru • lous (gar´ə ləs) *adj.*, talking much or too much. *The <u>garrulous</u> shopkeeper told us his entire life story.*
ap • pend (ə pend´) *vt.*, attach or affix. *My mother <u>appended</u> a note to the refrigerator, telling me to start dinner.*
con • jec • ture (kən jek´chər) *vi.*, guess. *I <u>conjecture</u> that the magician will pull a rabbit out of his hat.*
di • lap • i • dat • ed (də lap´ ə dāt´ id) *adj.*, falling to pieces or into disrepair. *The <u>dilapidated</u> fishing shack was finally torn down.*

companion of his boyhood named *Leonidas W.* Smiley—
Rev. Leonidas W. Smiley, a young minister of the Gospel,
who he had heard was at one time a resident of Angel's
Camp. I added that if Mr. Wheeler could tell me anything
about this Rev. Leonidas W. Smiley, I would feel under
many obligations to him.

   Simon Wheeler backed me into a corner and blockaded
me there with his chair, and then sat down and reeled off
the monotonous narrative which follows this paragraph. He
never smiled, he never frowned, he never changed his voice
from the gentle-flowing key to which he tuned his initial
sentence, he never betrayed the slightest suspicion of
enthusiasm; but all through the interminable narrative
there ran a vein of impressive earnestness and sincerity,
which showed me plainly that, so far from his imagining
that there was anything ridiculous or funny about his story,
he regarded it as a really important matter, and admired its
two heroes as men of transcendent genius in *finesse*.[1] I let
him go on in his own way, and never interrupted him once.

   Rev. Leonidas W. H'm, Reverend Le—well, there was a
feller here once by the name of *Jim* Smiley, in the winter of
'49—or maybe it was the spring of '50—I don't recollect
exactly, somehow, though what makes me think it was one
or the other is because I remember the big flume[2] warn't
finished when he first come to the camp; but any way, he
was the curiousest man about always betting on anything
that turned up you ever see, if he could get anybody to bet
on the other side; and if he couldn't he'd change sides. Any
way that suited the other man would suit *him*—any way just
so's he got a bet, *he* was satisfied. But still he was lucky,
uncommon lucky; he most always come out winner. He was
always ready and laying for a chance; there couldn't be no
solit'ry thing mentioned but that feller'd offer to bet on it,

---

1. **transcendent . . . finesse.** Extraordinary skill, cunning, or artfulness
2. **flume.** Artificial channel for carrying water to furnish power or transport objects

words for everyday use
in • ter • mi • na • ble (in tur´mi nə bəl) *adj.*, without, or apparently without, end. *The <u>interminable</u> lecture on genetics bored Julian to tears.*

Literary TOOLS

FRAME TALE AND TALL TALE. A **frame tale** is a story that provides a vehicle for the telling of other stories. This story contains a frame tale. Within the story, one of the characters tells a **tall tale**, or a humorous story containing highly exaggerated events.

NOTE THE FACTS

What is curious about Jim Smiley?

_____
_____
_____

FIX-UP IDEA

Use Text Organization
As you read, determine which part of the story is the frame and which part is the story told within the frame. This story also contains elements of a tall tale. What features of a tall tale can you look for as you read?

_____
_____

MARK THE TEXT

Highlight or underline examples of Jim Smiley's betting on this page.

USE THE STRATEGY

TACKLE DIFFICULT VOCABULARY. In addition to words with apostrophes, many examples of dialect in this story are similar in spelling to a standard word. For example, the work *resk* is used instead of *risk* and *thish-yer* is used instead of *this here*. Reading aloud may help you find the meaning of these words.

60 and take ary side you please, as I was just telling you. If there was a horse-race, you'd find him flush[3] or you'd find him busted[4] at the end of it; if there was a dog-fight, he'd bet on it; if there was a cat-fight, he'd bet on it; if there was a chicken-fight, he'd bet on it; why, if there was two birds setting on a fence, he would bet you which one would fly first, or if there was a camp-meeting,[5] he would be there reg'lar to bet on Parson Walker, which he judged to be the best <u>exhorter</u> about here, and so he was too, and a good man. If he even see a straddle-bug[6] start to go anywheres,
70 he would bet you how long it would take him to get to—to wherever he was going to, and if you took him up, he would foller that straddle-bug to Mexico but what he would find out where he was bound for and how long he was on the road. Lots of the boys here has seen that Smiley, and can tell you about him. Why, it never made no difference to *him*—he'd bet on *any* thing—the dangdest feller. Parson Walker's wife laid very sick once, for a good while, and it seemed as if they warn't going to save her; but one morning he come in, and Smiley up and asked him how she was, and he said she
80 was considable better—thank the Lord for his inf'nite mercy—and coming on so smart that with the blessing of Prov'dence she'd get well yet; and Smiley, before he thought says, "Well, I'll resk two-and-a-half she don't anyway."

Thish-yer Smiley had a mare—the boys called her the fifteen-minute nag, but that was only in fun, you know, because of course she was faster than that—and he used to win money on that horse, for all she was so slow and always had the asthma, or the distemper, or the consumption, or something of that kind. They used to give her two or three
90 hundred yards start, and then pass her under way; but always at the fag end[7] of the race she'd get excited and

---

3. **flush.** Well supplied with money
4. **busted.** Penniless
5. **camp-meeting.** Religious gathering at a camp or mining community
6. **straddle-bug.** Long-legged insect
7. **fag end.** Last part

words for everyday use

ex • hor • ter (eg zôrt´ər) *n.,* one who urges earnestly, by advice or warning. *Dad is an <u>exhorter</u> who wants to steer us away from mistakes.*

desperate-like, and come <u>cavorting</u> and straddling up, and scattering her legs around limber, sometimes in the air, and sometimes out to one side among the fences, and kicking up m-o-r-e dust and raising m-o-r-e racket with her coughing and sneezing and blowing her nose—and *always* fetch up at the stand just about a neck ahead, as near as you could cipher it down.

And he had a little small bull-pup, that to look at him you'd think he warn't worth a cent but to set around and look <u>ornery</u> and lay for a chance to steal something. But as soon as money was up on him he was a different dog; his underjaw'd begin to stick out like the fo'castle[8] of a steamboat, and his teeth would uncover and shine like the furnaces. And a dog might tackle him and bully-rag him, and bite him, and throw him over his shoulder two or three times, and Andrew Jackson—which was the name of the pup—Andrew Jackson would never let on but what *he* was satisfied, and hadn't expected nothing else—and the bets being doubled and doubled on the other side all the time, till the money was all up; and then all of a sudden he would grab that other dog jest by the j'int of his hind leg and freeze to it—not chaw, you understand, but only just grip and hang on till they throwed up the sponge, if it was a year. Smiley always come out winner on that pup, till he harnessed a dog once that didn't have no hind legs, because they'd been sawed off in a circular saw, and when the thing had gone along far enough, and the money was all up, and he come to make a snatch for his pet holt[9] he see in a minute how he's been imposed on, and how the other dog had him in the door, so to speak, and he 'peared surprised, and then he looked sorter discouraged-like, and didn't try no more to win the fight, and so he got shucked out bad. He give Smiley a look, as much as to say his heart was broke, and it was *his* fault, for putting up a dog that hadn't

THINK AND REFLECT

What do Smiley's horse and pup have in common? **(Compare and Contrast)**

_____
_____
_____

NOTE THE FACTS

Why does the dog without hind legs have an advantage over Andrew Jackson?

_____
_____
_____

---

8. **fo'castle.** Upper deck of a boat; part of a bow that protrudes
9. **pet holt.** Favorite hold

words for everyday use
ca • vort (kə vȯrt′) *vi.*, leap about, prance. *Full of energy, the filly <u>cavorted</u> in the meadow.*
or • ner • y (ȯr′nər ē) *adj.*, having an ugly or mean disposition. *It was difficult for Chris to get along with a teacher as <u>ornery</u> as Mr. Kellett.*

Use THE STRATEGY

TACKLE DIFFICULT VOCABULARY. If the context clues do not provide the meaning, try analyzing word parts—prefixes, roots, and suffixes—to determine meanings. If that strategy fails, consult a dictionary. Record the definitions in your Vocabulary Chart.

NOTE THE FACTS

What does Smiley teach the frog to do?

_____
_____
_____

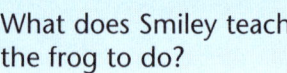

THINK AND REFLECT

Why is it humorous or ironic to call the frog modest and gifted? (Analyze)

_____
_____
_____

no hind legs for him to take holt of, which was his main dependence in a fight, and then he limped off a piece and laid down and died. It was a good pup, was that Andrew Jackson, and would have made a name for hisself if he'd lived, for the stuff was in him and he had genius—I know it, because he hadn't no opportunities to speak of, and it don't stand to reason that a dog could make such a fight as he could under them circumstances if he hadn't no talent. It always makes me feel sorry when I think of that last fight of his'n, and the way it turned out.

    Well, thish-yer Smiley had rat-terriers[10] and chicken cocks,[11] and tomcats and all them kind of things, till you couldn't rest, and you couldn't fetch nothing for him to bet on but he'd match you. He ketched a frog one day, and took him home, and said he cal'lated to educate him; and so he never done nothing for three months but set in his back yard and learn that frog to jump. And you bet you he *did* learn him, too. He'd give him a little punch behind, and the next minute you'd see that frog whirling in the air like a doughnut—see him turn one summerset, or maybe a couple, if he got a good start, and come down flat-footed and all right, like a cat. He got him up so in the matter of ketching flies, and kep' him in practice so constant, that he'd nail a fly every time as fur as he could see him. Smiley said all a frog wanted was education, and he could do 'most anything—and I believe him. Why, I've seen him set Dan'l Webster down here on this floor—Dan'l Webster was the name of the frog—and sing out, "Flies, Dan'l, flies!" and quicker'n you could wink he'd spring straight up and snake a fly off'n the counter there, and flop down on the floor ag'in as solid as a gob of mud, and fall to scratching the side of his head with his hind foot as indifferent as if he hadn't no idea he'd been doin' any more'n any frog might do. You never see a frog so modest and straightfor'ard as he was, for all he was so gifted. And when it come to fair and square jumping on a dead level, he could get over more ground at one straddle than any animal of his breed you ever see. Jumping on a dead level was his strong suit, you understand; and when it

---

10. **rat-terriers.** Small, aggressive dogs
11. **chicken cocks.** Roosters trained to fight each other

come to that, Smiley would ante up money on him as long as he had a red.[12] Smiley was monstrous proud of his frog, and well he might be, for fellers that had traveled and been everywheres all said he laid over any frog that ever *they* see.

Well, Smiley kep' the beast in a little lattice box, and he used to fetch him down-town sometimes and lay for a bet. One day a feller—a stranger in the camp, he was—come acrost him with his box, and says:

"What might it be that you've got in the box?"

And Smiley says, sorter indifferent-like, "It might be a parrot, or it might be a canary, maybe, but it ain't—it's only just a frog."

And the feller took it, and looked at it careful, and turned it round this way and that, and says, "H'm—so 'tis. Well, what's *he* good for?"

"Well," Smiley says, easy and careless, "he's good enough for *one* thing, I should judge—he can outjump any frog in Calaveras county."

The feller took the box again, and took another long, particular look, and give it back to Smiley, and says, very deliberate, "Well," he says, "I don't see no p'ints about that frog that's any better'n any other frog."

"Maybe you don't," Smiley says. "Maybe you understand frogs and maybe you don't understand em; maybe you've had experience, and maybe you ain't only a amature, as it were. Anyways, I've got *my* opinion, and I'll resk forty dollars that he can outjump any frog in Calaveras county."

And the feller studied a minute, and then says, kinder sad like, "Well, I'm only a stranger here, and I ain't got no frog; but if I had a frog, I'd bet you."

And then Smiley says. "That's all right—that's all right—if you'll hold my box a minute, I'll go and get you a frog." And so the feller took the box and put up his forty dollars along with Smiley's, and set down to wait.

So he set there a good while thinking and thinking to hisself, and then he got the frog out and prized his mouth open and took a teaspoon and filled him full of quailshot[13]—filled him pretty near up to his chin—and set him on the

---

12. **red.** Red cent; a very small amount of money
13. **quailshot.** Lead pellets used for hunting quail

MARK THE TEXT

Highlight or underline the boast Smiley makes about Dan'l Webster, the frog.

Reading **STRATEGY REVIEW**

MAKE PREDICTIONS. Review making predictions on page 39. Then predict whether Smiley will win his bet.

_____

_____

_____

floor. Smiley he went to the swamp and slopped around in the mud for a long time, and finally he ketched a frog, and fetched him in, and give him to this feller, and says:

"Now, if you're ready, set him alongside of Dan'l, with his forepaws just even with Dan'l's, and I'll give the word." Then he says, "One—two—three—*git!*" and him and the feller touched up the frogs from behind, and the new frog hopped off lively, but Dan'l give a heave, and hysted up his shoulders—so—like a Frenchman, but it warn't no use—he couldn't budge; he was planted as solid as a church, and he couldn't no more stir than if he was anchored out. Smiley was a good deal surprised, and he was disgusted too, but he didn't have no idea what the matter was, of course.

The feller took the money and started away; and when he was going out at the door, he sorter jerked his thumb over his shoulder—so—at Dan'l, and says, again very deliberate, "Well," he says, "*I* don't see no p'ints about that frog that's any better'n any other frog."

Smiley he stood scratching his head and looking down at Dan'l a long time, and at last he says, "I do wonder what in the nation that frog throw'd off for—I wonder if there ain't something the matter with him—he 'pears to look mighty baggy, somehow." And he ketched Dan'l by the nap of the neck, and hefted him, and says, "Why blame my cats if he don't weigh five pound!" and turned him upside down and he belched out a double handful of shot. And then he see how it was, and he was the maddest man—he set the frog down and took out after that feller, but he never ketched him. And—

Here Simon Wheeler heard his name called from the front yard, and got up to see what was wanted. And turning to me as he moved away, he said: "Just set where you are, stranger, and rest easy—I ain't going to be gone a second."

But, by your leave, I did not think that a continuation of the history of the enterprising <u>vagabond</u> *Jim* Smiley would be likely to afford me much information concerning the

NOTE THE FACTS

Why didn't Dan'l Webster win the contest? How did Smiley feel when he figured out why his frog lost?

_____
_____
_____

MARK THE TEXT

Highlight or underline why the narrator left.

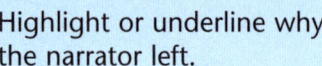

vag • a • bond (vag´ ə bänd´) *n.*, wandering, idle, disreputable, or shiftless person. The <u>vagabond</u> slept on a park bench.

64   THE EMC WRITE-IN READER

Rev. Leonidas W. Smiley, and so I started away.

At the door I met the sociable Wheeler returning, and he button-holed[14] me and recommenced:

"Well, thish-yer Smiley had a yaller one-eyed cow that didn't have no tail, only jest a short stump like a bannanner, and—"

However, lacking both time and inclination, I did not wait to hear about the <u>afflicted</u> cow, but took my leave. ∎

---

14. **button-holed.** Made a person listen to one, as if by grabbing his or her coat by a buttonhole

THINK AND REFLECT

How does the narrator feel about Simon Wheeler? Did he enjoy his visit? **(Infer)**

_____
_____
_____

words for everyday use

af • flic • ted (ə flikt′ əd) *adj.,* having a physical condition, usually painful or distressing. *Nicole's grandmother is <u>afflicted</u> with painful arthritis.*

Reflect ON YOUR READING

After Reading → **PRACTICE USING NEW WORDS**

❏ Share your list of standard English words with a partner. Work together to write two sentences of your own for each of the listed words. Make sure your sentences show that you understand the definition of the word.

❏ Then talk about some examples of dialect you found. Why do you think Twain used this dialect?

_____
_____
_____
_____

Reading Skills and Test Practice

USE CONTEXT CLUES

Discuss with your partner how to answer the following questions about words in context. Use the Think-Aloud Notes to write down your reasons for eliminating the incorrect answers.

____1. What is the best synonym for *deteriorate* in the statement below?

   If man could be crossed with the cat it would improve the man, but it would deteriorate the cat.

   a. strengthen
   b. disgust
   c. satisfy
   d. worsen

____2. Read the passage below.

   <u>Garrulous</u> Simon Wheeler cornered the narrator and talked his ear off.

   What is the best antonym of the underlined word in the passage?
   a. old
   b. talkative
   c. silent
   d. boring

How did using the reading strategy help you to answer the questions?

_____
_____

THINK-ALOUD NOTES

Investigate, Inquire, and Imagine

RECALL: GATHER FACTS
1a. What bets involving animals does Jim Smiley make?

INTERPRET: FIND MEANING
1b. Why do Jim Smiley's animals almost always win? Why does Dan'l Webster lose the contest?

ANALYZE: TAKE THINGS APART
2a. What elements make this story humorous?

SYNTHESIZE: BRING THINGS TOGETHER
2b. What tale do you think Simon Wheeler would have told about the cow if he had been given the chance?

EVALUATE: MAKE JUDGMENTS
3a. Evaluate the role gambling plays in this story. How does betting affect Jim Smiley?

EXTEND: CONNECT IDEAS
3b. Compare this story to "An Occurrence at Owl Creek Bridge." Which story is more realistic? Why?

Literary Tools

FRAME TALE AND TALL TALE. A **frame tale** is a story that provides a vehicle for the telling of other stories. This story contains a frame tale. Within the story, one of the characters tells a **tall tale**, or a humorous story containing highly exaggerated events. What is the frame in "The Notorious Jumping Frog of Calaveras County"? What is the tall tale? Summarize each part in the chart below. In the margin, note how these two stories work together.

Frame

Tall Tale

UNIT 3 / READING FICTION

WordWorkshop

DENOTATION AND CONNOTATION. When you learn a new word, it is important to pay attention to the **denotation**, or its dictionary definition, and to its **connotations**, or emotional associations or implications. Several of the Words for Everyday Use have somewhat negative connotations. For each word below, write a contextual sentence, keeping in mind the word's connotations.

1. interminable

   _____

2. vagabond

   _____

3. garrulous

   _____

4. notorious

   _____

Next, try to identify a word that has a similar denotation as each word but more positive connotations. If necessary, use a thesaurus to identify these words.

Read-Write Connection

If you were the narrator, would you be bored or interested by Simon Wheeler's story? Explain.

_____

_____

Beyond the Reading

PRESENT A TALL TALE. Tall tales are excellent stories to tell aloud. Use the library or the Internet to find a tall tale, or write a tall tale of your own. Remember that tall tales are humorous and highly exaggerated. Practice reading the story aloud. Try varying your tone, volume, and pace to make your story interesting. Share your tall tale with a group of your classmates.

GO ONLINE. To find links and additional activities for this selection, visit the EMC Internet Resource Center at **emcp.com/languagearts** and click on Write-In Reader.

"The Story of an Hour"
by Kate Chopin

Active READING STRATEGY

WRITE THINGS DOWN

Before Reading ➤ START A SEQUENCE CHART

- A **reversal** is a dramatic change in the direction of events in a story. In "The Story of an Hour," two reversals occur. These changes dramatically affect the emotions of Mrs. Mallard, the main character.
- A Sequence Chart can help you track the sequence of events and the reactions of the characters to these events. As you read, use the Sequence Chart that follows to track Mrs. Mallard's changing feelings.

Graphic Organizer: Sequence Chart

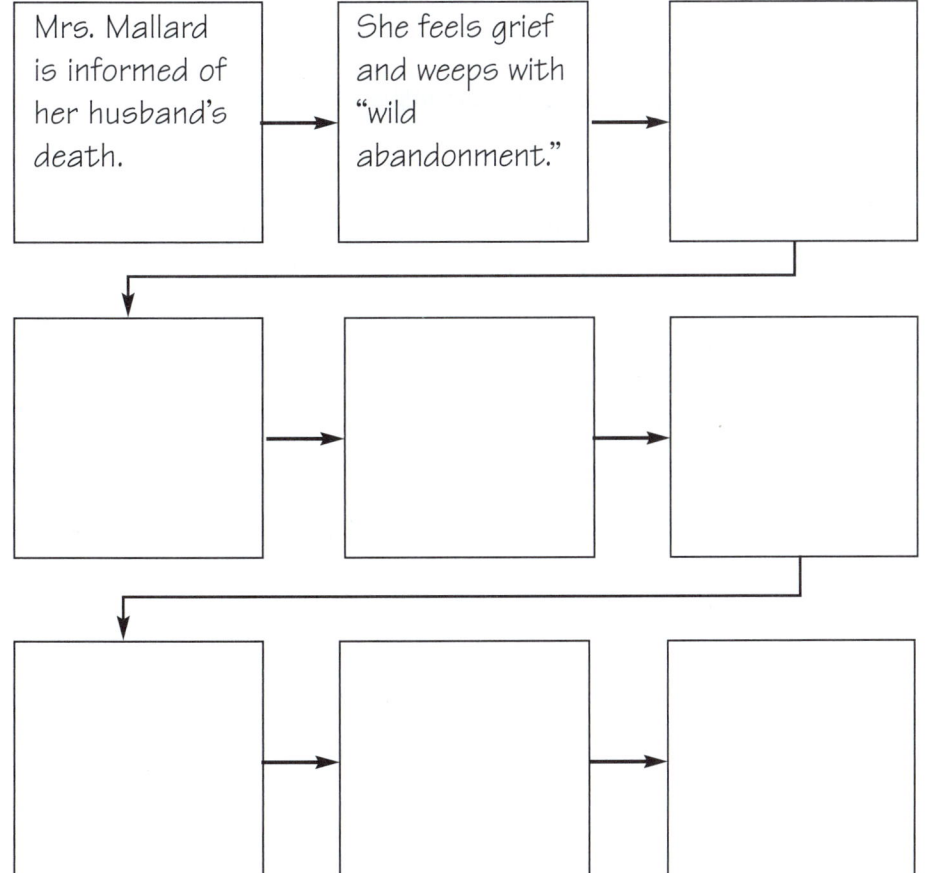

CONNECT

Reader's resource

Kate Chopin was a Regionalist who portrayed the landscape of the Gulf Islands and the people of Louisiana. She was also a pioneering feminist writer. **"The Story of an Hour"** is an example of Chopin's feminist fiction. The story is set in the nineteenth century when women's lives were quite restricted. In the story, Mrs. Mallard briefly finds and cherishes freedom from such restrictions.

Word watch

PREVIEW VOCABULARY

importunity
tumultuously

Reader's journal

When have you experienced an emotion that was considered inappropriate by your friends or family?

_____
_____
_____
_____
_____

UNIT 3 / READING FICTION 69

During Reading

NOTE SEQUENCE OF EVENTS

- Listen as your teacher reads the first three paragraphs of the story. Write in your Sequence Chart the most important things that happen. Include Mrs. Mallard's reaction.
- Continue reading on your own, and keep adding to your Sequence Chart as you read. The margin questions may help you identify some of the key elements in the story. If necessary, continue the Sequence Chart on your own paper.

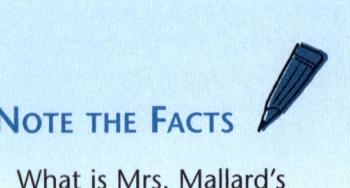

NOTE THE FACTS

What is Mrs. Mallard's immediate reaction to the death of her husband?

_____

_____

Kate Chopin

Knowing that Mrs. Mallard was afflicted with a heart trouble, great care was taken to break to her as gently as possible the news of her husband's death.

It was her sister Josephine who told her, in broken sentences; veiled hints that revealed in half concealing. Her husband's friend Richards was there, too, near her. It was he who had been in the newspaper office when intelligence of the railroad disaster was received, with Brently Mallard's name leading the list of "killed." He had only taken the time to assure himself of its truth by a second telegram, and had hastened to forestall any less careful, less tender friend in bearing the sad message.

She did not hear the story as many women have heard the same, with a paralyzed inability to accept its significance. She wept at once, with sudden, wild abandonment, in her sister's arms. When the storm of grief had spent itself she went away to her room alone. She would have no one follow her.

There stood, facing the open window, a comfortable, roomy armchair. Into this she sank, pressed down by a

70 THE EMC WRITE-IN READER

physical exhaustion that haunted her body and seemed to reach into her soul.

She could see in the open square before her house the tops of trees that were all aquiver with the new spring life. The delicious breath of rain was in the air. In the street below a peddler was crying his wares. The notes of a distant song which someone was singing reached her faintly, and countless sparrows were twittering in the eaves.

There were patches of blue sky showing here and there through the clouds that had met and piled one above the other in the west facing her window.

She sat with her head thrown back upon the cushion of the chair, quite motionless except when a sob came up into her throat and shook her, as a child who has cried itself to sleep continues to sob in its dreams.

She was young, with a fair, calm face, whose lines bespoke repression and even a certain strength. But now there was a dull stare in her eyes, whose gaze was fixed away off yonder on one of those patches of blue sky. It was not a glance of reflection but rather indicated a suspension of intelligent thought.

There was something coming to her and she was waiting for it, fearfully. What was it? She did not know: it was too subtle and elusive to name. But she felt it, creeping out of the sky, reaching toward her through the sounds, the scents, the color that filled the air.

Now her bosom rose and fell <u>tumultuously</u>. She was beginning to recognize this thing that was approaching to possess her, and she was striving to beat it back with her will— as powerless as her two white slender hands would have been.

When she abandoned herself, a little whispered word escaped her slightly parted lips. She said it over and over under her breath: "free, free, free!" The vacant stare and the look of terror that had followed it went from her eyes. They stayed keen and bright. Her pulses beat fast, and the coursing blood warmed and relaxed every inch of her body.

FIX-UP IDEA

Visualize
If you are having trouble following the story or identifying Mrs. Mallard's reactions, try visualizing as you read. As you read a sentence or paragraph, form a picture in your mind. Imagine yourself in Mrs. Mallard's place. What do you see, hear, feel, and do?

_____

_____

_____

NOTE THE FACTS

What thought possesses Mrs. Mallard?

_____

_____

_____

words for everyday use

tu • mul • tu • ous • ly (tü mul´ chü əs lē) adv., wildly. *The hurricane made the sea rage <u>tumultuously</u>.*

READ ALOUD

Read aloud the highlighted text. How have Mrs. Mallard's feelings changed?

_____

_____

_____

THINK AND REFLECT

How does Mrs. Mallard define freedom? **(Infer)**

_____

_____

_____

Use **THE STRATEGY**

WRITE THINGS DOWN. How does Mrs. Mallard's attitude about living a long life change?

_____

_____

_____

> She did not stop to ask if it were or were not a monstrous joy that held her. A clear and exalted perception enabled her to dismiss the suggestion as trivial.
> She knew that she would weep again when she saw the kind, tender hands folded in death; the face that had never looked save with love upon her, fixed and gray and dead. But she saw beyond that bitter moment a long procession of years to come that would belong to her absolutely. And she opened and spread her arms out to them in welcome.
> There would be no one to live for her during those coming years; she would live for herself. There would be no powerful will bending hers in that blind persistence with which men and women believe they have a right to impose a private will upon a fellow creature. A kind intention or a cruel intention made the act seem no less a crime as she looked upon it in that brief moment of illumination.
> And yet she had loved him—sometimes. Often she had not. What did it matter! What could love, the unsolved mystery, count for in face of this possession of self-assertion which she suddenly recognized as the strongest impulse of her being!

"Free! Body and soul free!" she kept whispering.

Josephine was kneeling before the closed door with her lips to the keyhole, imploring for admission. "Louise, open the door! I beg; open the door—you will make yourself ill. What are you doing, Louise? For heaven's sake open the door."

"Go away. I am not making myself ill." No; she was drinking in a very elixir of life[1] through that open window. Her fancy was running riot along those days ahead of her. Spring days, and summer days, and all sorts of days that would be her own. She breathed a quick prayer that life might be long. It was only yesterday she had thought with a shudder that life might be long.

She arose at length and opened the door to her sister's <u>importunities</u>. There was a feverish triumph in her eyes,

---

1. **elixir of life.** Substance sought by medieval alchemists to prolong life indefinitely

> **words for everyday use**
>
> **im • por • tu • ni • ty** (im´pər tün´ i tē) *n.*, persistent demand. *The child's <u>importunity</u> persuaded her parents to stay at the park.*

and she carried herself unwittingly like a goddess of Victory. She clasped her sister's waist, and together they descended the stairs. Richards stood waiting for them at the bottom.

Someone was opening the front door with a latchkey. It was Brently Mallard who entered, a little travel-stained, composedly carrying his gripsack[2] and umbrella. He had been far from the scene of accident, and did not know there had been one. He stood amazed at Josephine's piercing cry; at Richards's quick motion to screen him from the view of his wife.

But Richards was too late. When the doctors came they said she had died of heart disease—of joy that kills. ∎

---

2. **gripsack.** Small bag for traveling clothes

> **Literary TOOLS**
>
> **IRONY. Irony** is a difference between appearance and reality. *Dramatic irony* occurs when a situation appears one way to the reader and another way to the characters. Note the ironic ending to the story.

Reflect ON YOUR READING

After Reading → SUMMARIZE CHARACTER DEVELOPMENT

❏ Compare your Sequence Chart with a partner. Examine the changes in Mrs. Mallard's emotional state throughout the story.
❏ Write a brief summary or graph the ups and downs of her emotions. What are the two reversals in the story?

_____
_____
_____
_____

Reading Skills and Test Practice

ANALYZE PLOT

Discuss with your partner how to answer the following questions about the plot. Use the Think-Aloud Notes to write down your reasons for eliminating the incorrect answers.

____1. Which sequence best reflects Mrs. Mallard's changing emotions throughout the hour?
  a. disbelief, despair, acceptance
  b. grief, acceptance, joy
  c. grief, joy, despair
  d. joy, excitement, anger

____2. Why is the last line of the story ironic?
  a. Mrs. Mallard was so happy to see that her husband was alive that she died.
  b. People thought Mrs. Mallard died of joy, but it was the loss of her newfound freedom that killed her.
  c. Mrs. Mallard was not happy to see her husband.
  d. Mrs. Mallard did not get to enjoy the freedom she was beginning to cherish.

How did using the reading strategy help you to answer the questions?

_____
_____
_____
_____

THINK-ALOUD NOTES

Investigate, Inquire, and Imagine

RECALL: GATHER FACTS
1a. What news does Josephine deliver to Mrs. Mallard at the beginning of the story? Who enters the house as Josephine and Mrs. Mallard are coming down the stairs?

INTERPRET: FIND MEANING
1b. Why does Josephine have to break this news gently? Why does the doctor think joy is the cause of Mrs. Mallard's death?

ANALYZE: TAKE THINGS APART
2a. List the emotions Mrs. Mallard experiences as she responds to the news of her husband's death.

SYNTHESIZE: BRING THINGS TOGETHER
2b. Why is the story called "The Story of an Hour"? What happens in an hour?

PERSPECTIVE: LOOK AT OTHER VIEWS
3a. In the context of nineteenth-century marriage, is Mrs. Mallard's joy at her husband's death understandable? What circumstances in today's society might make such a response acceptable?

EMPATHY: SEE FROM INSIDE
3b. If you were Mrs. Mallard, would you tell your sister how you really felt about your husband's death?

Literary Tools

IRONY. **Irony** is a difference between appearance and reality. *Dramatic irony* occurs when a situation appears one way to the reader and another way to the characters. At the end of the story, the doctor says that Mrs. Mallard died of "joy that kills." What actually caused her death? How is this ending an example of dramatic irony?

_____
_____
_____
_____
_____

WordWorkshop

SYNONYMS. Synonyms are words that mean the same or nearly the same. Find synonyms for each of the following words from "The Story of an Hour." If you can, come up with a synonym from words that you know. Use a dictionary or thesaurus if necessary. Write a sentence using each pair of synonyms.

1. **afflicted** _____

    Sentence _____

2. **importunity** _____

    Sentence _____

3. **composedly** _____

    Sentence _____

4. **tumultuously** _____

    Sentence _____

5. **unwittingly** _____

    Sentence _____

Read-Write Connection

If you were Mrs. Mallard, what would be your first act of freedom?

_____

_____

_____

_____

Beyond the Reading

WRITE BIOGRAPHICAL CRITICISM. Biographical criticism attempts to analyze elements of literary works by relating them to events in the lives of their authors. Research the life of Kate Chopin. Then write a short paper discussing the ways in which Chopin's life experience affected her fiction.

GO ONLINE. To find links and additional activities for this selection, visit the EMC Internet Resource Center at **emcp.com/languagearts** and click on Write-In Reader.

"The Jilting of Granny Weatherall"

by Katherine Anne Porter

Active READING STRATEGY

WRITE THINGS DOWN

Before Reading ➤ MAKE A PLAN

- ❑ Read about stream-of-consciousness writing in the Reader's Resource.
- ❑ As you read, try to understand Granny Weatherall's stream of consciousness. Make notes in the margins or use the first column of the following Stream-of-Consciousness Chart to keep track of her thoughts.
- ❑ Then write your reactions or what you think her thoughts mean in the second column.

Graphic Organizer: Stream-of-Consciousness Chart

Stream of Consciousness	Explanation
"It was Hapsy she really wanted. . . . They leaned forward to kiss. . . ."	Granny remembers her dead daughter; in her confused mind she is also Hapsy and Hapsy's baby is Hapsy.

CONNECT

Reader's resource

"The Jilting of Granny Weatherall" uses stream of consciousness to explore the flow of ideas of Granny Weatherall as she draws close to death. **Stream-of-consciousness writing** attempts to render the flow of feelings, thoughts, and impressions within the minds of characters. The story also uses other viewpoints. For example, the first sentence is written from a third-person point of view, while the second sentence shifts to Granny Weatherall's perspective. Such shifts in viewpoints are common in Modernist fiction. Katherine Anne Porter is a Modernist considered a master of the short story form.

Word watch

PREVIEW VOCABULARY

dwindle   rummage
jilt

Reader's journal

What do you think you will be like when you are old?

_____
_____
_____
_____

UNIT 3 / READING FICTION   77

During Reading

WRITE THINGS DOWN AS YOU READ

- Listen as your teacher reads lines 1–48. Which parts of the story are taking place in Granny Weatherall's head? Mark her thoughts in the margins and write your reactions or what you think her thoughts mean in your Stream-of-Consciousness Chart.
- Continue reading on your own. Make notes and use your chart to track Granny Weatherall's stream of consciousness.

THINK AND REFLECT

What does Granny Weatherall think of the doctor? **(Infer)**

_____
_____
_____

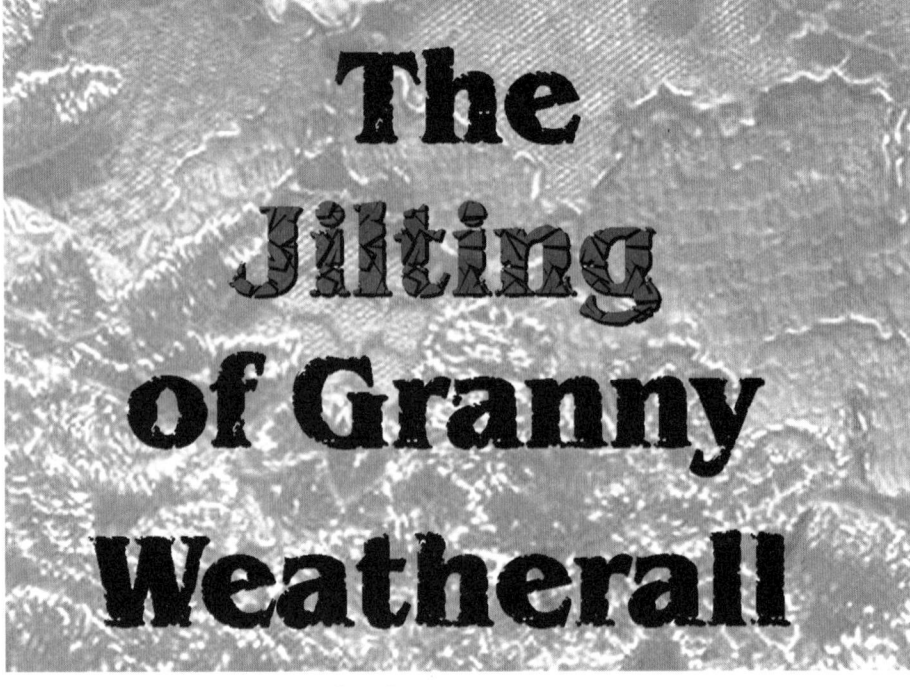

The Jilting of Granny Weatherall

Katherine Anne Porter

She flicked her wrist neatly out of Doctor Harry's pudgy careful fingers and pulled the sheet up to her chin. The brat ought to be in knee breeches. Doctoring around the country with spectacles on his nose! "Get along now, take your schoolbooks and go. There's nothing wrong with me."

Doctor Harry spread a warm paw like a cushion on her forehead where the forked green vein danced and made her eyelids twitch. "Now, now, be a good girl, and we'll have you up in no time."

"That's no way to speak to a woman nearly eighty years old just because she's down. I'd have you respect your elders, young man."

"Well, Missy, excuse me," Doctor Harry patted her cheek. "But I've got to warn you, haven't I? You're a marvel, but you must be careful or you're going to be good and sorry."

"Don't tell me what I'm going to be. I'm on my feet now, morally speaking. It's Cornelia. I had to go to bed to get rid of her."

Her bones felt loose, and floated around in her skin, and Doctor Harry floated like a balloon around the foot of the bed. He floated and pulled down his waistcoat and swung his glasses on a cord. "Well, stay where you are, it certainly can't hurt you."

"Get along and doctor your sick," said Granny Weatherall. "Leave a well woman alone. I'll call for you when I want you. . . . Where were you forty years ago when I pulled through milk leg[1] and double pneumonia? You weren't even born. Don't let Cornelia lead you on," she shouted, because Doctor Harry appeared to float up to the ceiling and out. "I pay my own bills, and I don't throw my money away on nonsense!"

She meant to wave good-bye, but it was too much trouble. Her eyes closed of themselves, it was like a dark curtain drawn around the bed. The pillow rose and floated under her, pleasant as a hammock in a light wind. She listened to the leaves rustling outside the window. No, somebody was swishing newspapers: no, Cornelia and Doctor Harry were whispering together. She leaped broad awake, thinking they whispered in her ear.

"She was never like this, *never* like this!" "Well, what can we expect?" "Yes, eighty years old. . . ."

Well, and what if she was? She still had ears. It was like Cornelia to whisper around doors. She always kept things secret in such a public way. She was always being tactful and kind. Cornelia was dutiful: that was the trouble with her. Dutiful and good: "So good and dutiful," said Granny, "that I'd like to spank her." She saw herself spanking Cornelia and making a fine job of it.

"What'd you say, Mother?"

Granny felt her face tying up in hard knots.

"Can't a body think, I'd like to know?"

"I thought you might want something."

"I do. I want a lot of things. First off, go away and don't whisper."

She lay and drowsed, hoping in her sleep that the children would keep out and let her rest a minute. It had been a long day. Not that she was tired. It was always pleasant to snatch a minute now and then. There was always so much to be done, let me see: tomorrow.

---

1. **milk leg.** Painful swelling of the leg

THINK AND REFLECT

Why does Granny Weatherall think Cornelia is whispering secrets? How does it make her feel? **(Infer)**

Use THE STRATEGY

WRITE THINGS DOWN. Remember to pause during reading to note Granny's thoughts and write your reactions or what you think her thoughts mean in your Stream-of-Consciousness Chart.

READ ALOUD

Read aloud the highlighted text. What does Granny Weatherall have to do tomorrow? Why does she want to do this task?

_____
_____
_____

NOTE THE FACTS

What had Granny Weatherall done when she was sixty?

_____
_____
_____

Tomorrow was far away and there was nothing to trouble about. Things were finished somehow when the time came: thank God there was always a little margin over for peace: then a person could spread out the plan of life and tuck in the edges orderly. It was good to have everything clean and folded away, with the hair brushes and tonic bottles sitting straight on the white embroidered linen: the day started without fuss and the pantry shelves laid out with rows of jelly glasses and brown jugs and white stonechina jars with blue whirligigs and words painted on them: coffee, tea, sugar, ginger, cinnamon, allspice: and the bronze clock with the lion on top nicely dusted off. The dust that lion could collect in twenty-four hours! The box in the attic with all those letters tied up, well, she'd have to go through that tomorrow. All those letters—George's letters and John's letters and her letters to them both—lying around for the children to find afterwards made her uneasy. Yes, that would be tomorrow's business. No use to let them know how silly she had been once.

While she was <u>rummaging</u> around she found death in her mind and it felt clammy and unfamiliar. She had spent so much time preparing for death there was no need for bringing it up again. Let it take care of itself now. When she was sixty she had felt very old, finished, and went around making farewell trips to see her children and grandchildren, with a secret in her mind: This is the very last of your mother, children! Then she made her will and came down with a long fever. That was all just a notion like a lot of other things, but it was lucky too, for she had once for all got over the idea of dying for a long time. Now she couldn't be worried. She hoped she had better sense now. Her father had lived to be one hundred and two years old and had drunk a noggin of strong hot toddy on his last birthday. He told the reporters it was his daily habit, and he owed his long life to that. He had made quite a scandal and

---

words for everyday use

rum • mage (rum´ij) *vt.,* search through thoroughly; ransack. *Mr. Sorenson <u>rummaged</u> around in the garage until he found the drill he had borrowed from his neighbor.*

was very pleased about it. She believed she'd just plague Cornelia a little.

"Cornelia! Cornelia!" No footsteps, but a sudden hand on her cheek. "Bless you, where have you been?"

"Here, mother."

"Well, Cornelia, I want a noggin of hot toddy."

"Are you cold, darling?"

"I'm chilly, Cornelia. Lying in bed stops the circulation. I must have told you that a thousand times."

Well, she could just hear Cornelia telling her husband that Mother was getting a little childish and they'd have to humor her. The thing that most annoyed her was that Cornelia thought she was deaf, dumb, and blind. Little hasty glances and tiny gestures tossed around her and over her head saying, "Don't cross her, let her have her way, she's eighty years old," and she sitting there as if she lived in a thin glass cage. Sometimes Granny almost made up her mind to pack up and move back to her own house where nobody could remind her every minute that she was old. Wait, wait, Cornelia, till your own children whisper behind your back!

In her day she had kept a better house and had got more work done. She wasn't too old yet for Lydia to be driving eighty miles for advice when one of the children jumped the track, and Jimmy still dropped in and talked things over: "Now, Mammy, you've a good business head, I want to know what you think of this? . . ." Old. Cornelia couldn't change the furniture around without asking. Little things, little things! They had been so sweet when they were little. Granny wished the old days were back again with the children young and everything to be done over. It had been a hard pull, but not too much for her. When she thought of all the food she had cooked, and all the clothes she had cut and sewed, and all the gardens she had made—well, the children showed it. There they were, made out of her, and they couldn't get away from that. Sometimes she wanted to see John again and point to them and say, Well, I didn't do so badly, did I? But that would have to wait. That was for tomorrow. She used to think of him as a man, but now all the children were older than their father, and he would be a

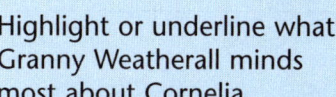

MARK THE TEXT

Highlight or underline what Granny Weatherall minds most about Cornelia.

Literary **TOOLS**

STREAM-OF-CONSCIOUSNESS WRITING. Remember, **stream-of-consciousness writing** attempts to render the flow of feelings, thoughts, and impressions within the minds of characters. As you read, think about why it is important to know Granny Weatherall's thoughts and feelings.

MARK THE TEXT

Highlight or underline what Granny Weatherall wants to say to John.

NOTE THE FACTS

What kinds of things has Granny Weatherall done?

_____
_____
_____

FIX-UP IDEA

Reread

If you are having trouble following the story, try rereading. Remember that some parts of the story are happening inside Granny Weatherall's head. Other times, characters are speaking and acting. Reread a short section. Keep track of whose point of view is being used in each section. If you are unsure, reread sections to find out. Mark passages you are still having trouble with. Reread those sections and discuss the meaning with a partner.

child beside her if she saw him now. It seemed strange and there was something wrong in the idea. Why, he couldn't possibly recognize her. She had fenced in a hundred acres once, digging the post holes herself and clamping the wires with just a negro boy to help. That changed a woman. John would be looking for a young woman with the peaked Spanish comb in her hair and the painted fan. Digging post holes changed a woman. Riding country roads in the winter when women had their babies was another thing: sitting up nights with sick horses and sick children and hardly ever losing one. John, I hardly ever lost one of them! John would see that in a minute, that would be something he could understand, she wouldn't have to explain anything!

It made her feel like rolling up her sleeves and putting the whole place to rights again. No matter if Cornelia was determined to be everywhere at once, there were a great many things left undone on this place. She would start tomorrow and do them. It was good to be strong enough for everything, even if all you made melted and changed and slipped under your hands, so that by the time you finished you almost forgot what you were working for. What was it I set out to do? she asked herself intently, but she could not remember. A fog rose over the valley, she saw it marching across the creek swallowing the trees and moving up the hill like an army of ghosts. Soon it would be at the near edge of the orchard, and then it was time to go in and light the lamps. Come in, children, don't stay out in the night air.

Lighting the lamps had been beautiful. The children huddled up to her and breathed like little calves waiting at the bars in the twilight. Their eyes followed the match and watched the flame rise and settle in a blue curve, then they moved away from her. The lamp was lit, they didn't have to be scared and hang on to mother any more. Never, never, never more. God, for all my life I thank Thee. Without Thee, my God, I could never have done it. Hail Mary, full of grace.

I want you to pick all the fruit this year and see that nothing is wasted. There's always someone who can use it. Don't let good things rot for want of using. You waste life when you waste good food. Don't let things get lost. It's bitter to lose things. Now, don't let me get to thinking, not when I am tired and taking a little nap before supper....

The pillow rose about her shoulders and pressed against her heart and the memory was being squeezed out of it: oh, push down the pillow, somebody: it would smother her if she tried to hold it. Such a fresh breeze blowing and such a green day with no threats in it. But he had not come, just the same. What does a woman do when she has put on the white veil and set out the white cake for a man and he doesn't come? She tried to remember. No, I swear he never harmed me but in that. He never harmed me but in that . . . and what if he did? There was the day, the day, but a whirl of dark smoke rose and covered it, crept up and over into the bright field where everything was planted so carefully in orderly rows. That was hell, she knew hell when she saw it. For sixty years she had prayed against remembering him and against losing her soul in the deep pit of hell, and now the two things were mingled in one and the thought of him was a smoky cloud from hell that moved and crept in her head when she had just got rid of Doctor Harry and was trying to rest a minute. Wounded vanity, Ellen, said a sharp voice in the top of her mind. Don't let your wounded vanity get the upper hand of you. Plenty of girls get <u>jilted</u>. You were jilted, weren't you? Then stand up to it. Her eyelids wavered and let in streamers of blue-gray light like tissue paper over her eyes. She must get up and pull the shades down or she'd never sleep. She was in bed again and the shades were not down. How could that happen? Better turn over, hide from the light, sleeping in the light gave you nightmares. "Mother, how do you feel now?" and a stinging wetness on her forehead. But I don't like having my face washed in cold water!

Hapsy? George? Lydia? Jimmy? No, Cornelia, and her features were swollen and full of little puddles. "They're

---

Use THE STRATEGY

WRITE THINGS DOWN. Read the highlighted lines. What is Granny Weatherall remembering here?

_____
_____

NOTE THE FACTS

What two things mingle together?

_____
_____
_____

---

words for everyday use

jilt (jilt) *vt.*, reject; cast off. *Carol <u>jilted</u> her friends when she ran into Bill at the fair.*

NOTE THE FACTS

When does Granny Weatherall think she saw the doctor? When did she really see him?

_____
_____
_____

THINK AND REFLECT

Who is Hapsy? What has happened to Hapsy? What might Hapsy mean when she says, "I thought you'd never come"? **(Infer)**

_____
_____
_____

210 coming, darling, they'll all be here soon." Go wash your face, child, you look funny.

Instead of obeying, Cornelia knelt down and put her head on the pillow. She seemed to be talking but there was no sound. "Well, are you tongue-tied? Whose birthday is it? Are you going to give a party?"

Cornelia's mouth moved urgently in strange shapes. "Don't do that, you bother me, daughter."

"Oh, no, Mother. Oh, no. . . ."

Nonsense. It was strange about children. They disputed
220 your every word. "No what, Cornelia?"

"Here's Doctor Harry."

"I won't see that boy again. He just left five minutes ago."

"That was this morning, Mother. It's night now. Here's the nurse."

"This is Doctor Harry, Mrs. Weatherall. I never saw you look so young and happy!"

"Ah, I'll never be young again—but I'd be happy if they'd let me lie in peace and get rested."

She thought she spoke up loudly, but no one answered. A
230 warm weight on her forehead, a warm bracelet on her wrist, and a breeze went on whispering, trying to tell her something. A shuffle of leaves in the everlasting hand of God, He blew on them and they danced and rattled. "Mother, don't mind, we're going to give you a little hypodermic."[2]

"Look here, daughter, how do ants get in this bed? I saw sugar ants yesterday." Did you send for Hapsy too?

It was Hapsy she really wanted. She had to go a long way back through a great many rooms to find Hapsy standing with a baby on her arm. She seemed to herself to be Hapsy
240 also, and the baby on Hapsy's arm was Hapsy and himself and herself, all at once, and there was no surprise in the meeting. Then Hapsy melted from within and turned flimsy as gray gauze and the baby was a gauzy shadow, and Hapsy came up close and said, "I thought you'd never come," and looked at her very searchingly and said, "You haven't changed a bit!" They leaned forward to kiss, when Cornelia began whispering from a long way off. "Oh, is

---

2. **hypodermic.** Injection

there anything you want to tell me? Is there anything I can do for you?"

250 Yes, she had changed her mind after sixty years and she would like to see George. I want you to find George. Find him and be sure to tell him I forgot him. I want him to know I had my husband just the same and my children and my house like any other woman. A good house too and a good husband that I loved and fine children out of him. Better than I hoped for even. Tell him I was given back everything he took away and more. Oh, no, oh, God, no, there was something else besides the house and the man and the children. Oh, surely they were not all? What was
260 it? Something not given back.... Her breath crowded down under her ribs and grew into a monstrous frightening shape with cutting edges; it bored up into her head, and the agony was unbelievable: Yes, John, get the Doctor now, no more talk, my time has come.

When this one was born it should be the last. The last. It should have been born first, for it was the one she had truly wanted. Everything came in good time. Nothing left out, left over. She was strong, in three days she would be as well as ever. Better. A woman needed milk in her to have her
270 full health. "Mother, do you hear me?"

"I've been telling you—"

"Mother, Father Connolly's here."

"I went to Holy Communion only last week. Tell him I'm not so sinful as all that."

"Father just wants to speak to you."

He could speak as much as he pleased. It was like him to drop in and inquire about her soul as if it were a teething baby, and then stay on for a cup of tea and a round of cards and gossip. He always had a funny story of some sort, usually
280 about an Irishman who made his little mistakes and confessed them, and the point lay in some absurd thing he would blurt out in the confessional showing his struggles between native piety and original sin. Granny felt easy about her soul. Cornelia, where are your manners? Give Father Connolly a chair. She had her secret comfortable understanding with a few favorite saints who cleared a straight road to God for her. All as surely signed and sealed

THINK AND REFLECT

Has Granny Weatherall's life been complete? **(Evaluate)**

_____
_____
_____

NOTE THE FACTS

What does Granny Weatherall think is happening?

_____
_____
_____

NOTE THE FACTS

Who came to Granny's aid on the day she was jilted?

_____

_____

_____

Reading STRATEGY REVIEW

TACKLE DIFFICULT VOCABULARY. If you encounter words you do not understand, use context clues to try to figure out the meaning. For example, from context you can tell that the word *frippery* refers to something impractical. Underline words you do not recognize as you read. Try to determine the meaning from context. When you are done reading, check the meaning of each word in a dictionary. Practice using each word.

as the papers for the new Forty Acres. Forever . . . heirs and assigns³ forever. Since the day the wedding cake was not cut, but thrown out and wasted. The whole bottom dropped out of the world, and there she was blind and sweating with nothing under her feet and the walls falling away. His hand had caught her under the breast, she had not fallen, there was the freshly polished floor with the green rug on it, just as before. He had cursed like a sailor's parrot and said, "I'll kill him for you." Don't lay a hand on him, for my sake leave something to God. "Now, Ellen, you must believe what I tell you. . . ."

So there was nothing, nothing to worry about any more, except sometimes in the night one of the children screamed in a nightmare, and they both hustled out shaking and hunting for the matches and calling, "There, wait a minute, here we are!" John, get the doctor now. Hapsy's time has come. But there was Hapsy standing by the bed in a white cap. "Cornelia, tell Hapsy to take off her cap. I can't see her plain."

Her eyes opened very wide and the room stood out like a picture she had seen somewhere. Dark colors with the shadows rising towards the ceiling in long angles. The tall black dresser gleamed with nothing on it but John's picture, enlarged from a little one, with John's eyes very black when they should have been blue. You never saw him, so how do you know how he looked? But the man insisted the copy was perfect, it was very rich and handsome. For a picture, yes, but it's not my husband. The table by the bed had a linen cover and a candle and a crucifix. The light was blue from Cornelia's silk lampshades. No sort of light at all, just frippery. You had to live forty years with kerosene lamps to appreciate honest electricity. She felt very strong and she saw Doctor Harry with a rosy nimbus⁴ around him.

"You look like a saint, Doctor Harry, and I vow that's as near as you'll ever come to it."

"She's saying something."

"I heard you, Cornelia. What's all this carrying on?"

"Father Connolly's saying—"

---

3. **assigns.** People to whom property is transferred
4. **nimbus.** Halo; circle of light around the head of a saint or divinity

Cornelia's voice staggered and bumped like a cart in a bad road. It rounded corners and turned back again and arrived nowhere. Granny stepped up in the cart very lightly and reached for the reins, but a man sat beside her and she knew him by his hands, driving the cart. She did not look in his face, for she knew without seeing, but looked instead down the road where the trees leaned over and bowed to each other and a thousand birds were singing a Mass. She felt like singing too, but she put her hand in the bosom of her dress and pulled out a rosary, and Father Connolly murmured Latin in a very solemn voice and tickled her feet.[5] My God, will you stop that nonsense? I'm a married woman. What if he did run away and leave me to face the priest by myself? I found another a whole world better. I wouldn't have exchanged my husband for anybody except St. Michael himself, and you may tell him that for me with a thank you in the bargain.

Light flashed on her closed eyelids, and a deep roaring shook her. Cornelia, is that lightning? I hear thunder. There's going to be a storm. Close all the windows. Call the children in. "Mother, here we are, all of us." "Is that you, Hapsy?" "Oh, no, I'm Lydia. We drove as fast as we could." Their faces drifted above her, drifted away. The rosary fell out of her hands and Lydia put it back. Jimmy tried to help, their hands fumbled together, and Granny closed two fingers around Jimmy's thumb. Beads wouldn't do, it must be something alive. She was so amazed her thoughts ran round and round. So, my dear Lord, this is my death and I wasn't even thinking about it. My children have come to see me die. But I can't, it's not time. Oh, I always hated surprises. I wanted to give Cornelia the amethyst set—Cornelia, you're to have the amethyst set, but Hapsy's to wear it when she wants, and, Doctor Harry, do shut up. Nobody sent for you. Oh, my dear Lord, do wait a minute. I meant to do something about the Forty Acres, Jimmy doesn't need it and Lydia will later on, with that worthless husband of hers. I meant to finish the altar cloth and send six bottles of wine to Sister Borgia for her dyspepsia. I want to send six bottles of

---

5. **murmured . . . feet.** Administered the last rites, a sacrament in the Catholic church for a person who is dying

NOTE THE FACTS

What idea does Granny Weatherall repeat?

_____

_____

_____

THINK AND REFLECT

Is Granny Weatherall ready to die? How do you know? **(Infer)**

_____

_____

_____

wine to Sister Borgia, Father Connolly, now don't let me forget.

Cornelia's voice made short turns and tilted over and crashed. "Oh, Mother, oh, Mother, oh Mother. . . ."

"I'm not going, Cornelia. I'm taken by surprise. I can't go."

You'll see Hapsy again. What about her? "I thought you'd never come." Granny made a long journey outward, looking for Hapsy. What if I don't find her? What then? Her heart sank down and down, there was no bottom to death, she couldn't come to the end of it. The blue light from Cornelia's lampshade drew into a tiny point in the center of her brain, it flickered and winked like an eye, quietly it fluttered and <u>dwindled</u>. Granny lay curled down within herself, amazed and watchful, staring at the point of light that was herself: her body was now only a deeper mass of shadow in an endless darkness and this darkness would curl around the light and swallow it up. God, give a sign!

For the second time there was no sign. Again no bridegroom and the priest in the house. She could not remember any other sorrow because this grief wiped them all away. Oh, no, there's nothing more cruel than this—I'll never forgive it. She stretched herself with a deep breath and blew out the light. ■

words for everyday use

dwin • dle (dwin´dəl) vt., languish; fade. *When the light <u>dwindled</u> at sunset, we lit candles.*

Reflect ON YOUR READING

After Reading → SUMMARIZE YOUR NOTES

- ❏ Look through your margin notes or examine what you wrote in your chart. Share your responses with a few of your classmates.
- ❏ As a group, prepare a character sketch of Granny Weatherall. A **character sketch** is a brief written description of a character.

_____
_____
_____
_____
_____
_____
_____

Reading Skills and Test Practice

ANALYZE CHARACTER

Discuss with your partner how best to answer these questions about character. Use the Think-Aloud Notes to write down your reasons for eliminating the incorrect answers.

____ 1. Why is Granny Weatherall's name appropriate?
   a. She has lived outside in all types of weather.
   b. She loves snow, rain, storms, and other types of weather.
   c. She has lived through many difficulties and tragedies.
   d. Her favorite sayings begin "I wonder whether all. . . ."

____ 2. Who jilted Granny Weatherall?
   a. Hapsy
   b. George and God
   c. George and the doctor
   d. John and George

How did using the reading strategy help you to answer the questions?

_____
_____
_____
_____

THINK-ALOUD NOTES

Investigate, Inquire, and Imagine

RECALL: GATHER FACTS
1a. What explanation for being in bed does Granny Weatherall give to the doctor?

INTERPRET: FIND MEANING
1b. What traits describe Granny Weatherall before she became ill?

ANALYZE: TAKE THINGS APART
2a. Identify two times when Granny Weatherall was jilted. What do the two jiltings have in common? Which jilting is the hardest for her to take?

SYNTHESIZE: BRING THINGS TOGETHER
2b. Why is Granny Weatherall an appropriate name for the character in this story?

EVALUATE: MAKE JUDGMENTS
3a. To what degree do the past and future influence Granny Weatherall's thinking?

EXTEND: CONNECT IDEAS
3b. Compare Granny Weatherall's experiences as she gets close to dying to Peyton Farquhar's experience in "An Occurrence at Owl Creek Bridge."

Literary Tools

STREAM-OF-CONSCIOUSNESS WRITING. Stream-of-consciousness writing attempts to render the flow of feelings, thoughts, and impressions within the minds of characters. Review the notes you made in your graphic organizer while reading. What do you learn about Granny Weatherall from the flow of her thoughts and feelings? Why is this technique important in this story?

_____
_____
_____
_____
_____
_____
_____

WordWorkshop

EXPLORING WORD KNOWLEDGE. Take a closer look at each of the Words for Everyday Use from "The Jilting of Granny Weatherall." On your own paper, answer the questions that follow each word.

dwindle

1. What is the opposite of *dwindle?*
2. Give an example of something dwindling.
3. Draw a picture that shows something dwindling.

jilt

4. How does the meaning of *jilt* differ from the meaning of *reject?*
5. Describe how you would feel if you were jilted.

rummage

6. What is a synonym for *rummage?*
7. Would a thief or an investigator be more likely to rummage through your drawers? Explain.
8. What would you expect to do at a rummage sale?

Read-Write Connection

If you were Granny Weatherall, would you finally forgive George for jilting you on your wedding day? Why, or why not?

Beyond the Reading

RESEARCH IMAGES OF DEATH. Katherine Anne Porter portrays Granny Weatherall's encounter with death using the image of a cart with a man driving it. Emily Dickinson uses a similar image in "Because I could not stop for Death—" (Unit 4, page 131). Use the library and the Internet to find other depictions of death in art and literature. Share the images you find with your classmates. Talk about which images of death are most common and why you think they are widely used.

GO ONLINE. To find links and additional activities for this selection, visit the EMC Internet Resource Center at **emcp.com/languagearts** and click on Write-In Reader.

CONNECT

Reader's resource

"A Worn Path" explores the intricacies of the inner life and the small heroisms of an ordinary character. In the story, Phoenix Jackson makes an archetypal journey. The story of the journey in which someone sets out on a path, experiences adventures, and emerges wiser, is considered archetypal in that it recurs throughout history and literature. On her journey, Phoenix Jackson demonstrates determination, generosity, and resourcefulness. "A Worn Path" is one of Eudora Welty's most popular stories.

Word watch

PREVIEW VOCABULARY

limber
pendulum
pullet
quivering
ravine
rouse

Reader's journal

What journey have you taken that held personal significance for you?

_____
_____
_____
_____

"A Worn Path"

by Eudora Welty

Active READING STRATEGY

VISUALIZE

Before Reading ➔ BEGIN TO PICTURE WHAT MAY HAPPEN

❑ Read the Reader's Resource and answer the Reader's Journal question.
❑ Begin to imagine what might happen in the story.
❑ As you read, you will sketch or jot down ideas from your mind movies in the graphic organizer below.

Graphic Organizer: Visualization Sketches

92   THE EMC WRITE-IN READER

A Worn Path

Eudora Welty

> **During Reading**
>
> ## CREATE A MIND MOVIE
>
> ❏ Listen as your teacher reads the first three paragraphs of the story. Begin to create a mind movie as you listen. Involve all of your senses in the mind movie. Then make quick sketches that show what you saw, heard, and felt.
>
> ❏ Continue reading on your own. As you read, continue making a mind movie. Use the graphic organizer to make quick sketches or write a brief summary to explain what you imagined in your mind movie.

It was December—a bright frozen day in the early morning. Far out in the country there was an old Negro woman with her head tied in a red rag, coming along a path through the pinewoods. Her name was Phoenix Jackson. She was very old and small and she walked slowly in the dark pine shadows, moving a little from side to side in her steps, with the balanced heaviness and lightness of a <u>pendulum</u> in a grandfather clock. She carried a thin, small cane made from an umbrella, and with this she kept tapping the frozen earth in front of her. This made a grave and persistent noise in the still air, that seemed meditative like the chirping of a solitary little bird.

She wore a dark striped dress reaching down to her shoe tops, and an equally long apron of bleached sugar sacks, with a full pocket: all neat and tidy, but every time she took

> **NOTE THE FACTS**
>
> When does Phoenix Jackson make her journey?
>
> _____
> _____

words for everyday use

pen • du • lum (pen′ jə ləm) *n.*, body suspended from a fixed point so as to swing freely to and fro under the action of gravity and commonly used to regulate movements (as of clockwork). *The sharp, descending <u>pendulum</u> threatened the narrator's life in the Edgar Allan Poe story "The Pit and the Pendulum."*

Use the Strategy

VISUALIZE. The second paragraph of the story gives a vivid visual description of Phoenix. Use the details to help you picture this character. Draw a sketch in your graphic organizer.

Note the Facts

To whom is Phoenix speaking?

_____

_____

Mark the Text

Highlight or underline why Phoenix had to stop on her way down the hill.

---

a step she might have fallen over her shoelaces, which dragged from her unlaced shoes. She looked straight ahead. Her eyes were blue with age. Her skin had a pattern all its own of numberless branching wrinkles and as though a whole little tree stood in the middle of her forehead, but a golden color ran underneath, and the two knobs of her cheeks were illumined by a yellow burning under the dark. Under the red rag her hair came down on her neck in the frailest of ringlets, still black, and with an odor like copper.

Now and then there was a <u>quivering</u> in the thicket. Old Phoenix said, "Out of my way, all you foxes, owls, beetles, jack rabbits, coons and wild animals! . . . Keep out from under these feet, little bob-whites. . . . Keep the big wild hogs out of my path. Don't let none of those come running my direction. I got a long way." Under her small black-freckled hand her cane, <u>limber</u> as a buggy whip, would switch at the brush as if to <u>rouse</u> up any hiding things.

On she went. The woods were deep and still. The sun made the pine needles almost too bright to look at, up where the wind rocked. The cones dropped as light as feathers. Down in the hollow was the morning dove—it was not too late for him.

The path ran up a hill. "Seem like there is chains about my feet, time I get this far," she said, in the voice of argument old people keep to use with themselves. "Something always take a hold of me on this hill—pleads I should stay."

After she got to the top she turned and gave a full, severe look behind her where she had come. "Up through pines," she said at length. "Now down through oaks."

Her eyes opened their widest, and she started down gently. But before she got to the bottom of the hill a bush caught her dress.

Her fingers were busy and intent, but her skirts were full and long, so that before she could pull them free in one place

---

words for everyday use

quiv • er • ing (kwiv′ riŋ) *n.*, shaking or moving characterized by a slight trembling motion. *The <u>quivering</u> of Grandpa's hands is due to Parkinson's disease.*

lim • ber (lim′ bər) *adj.*, having a supple and resilient quality. *After a few warm-up exercises, Mr. Hogan felt as <u>limber</u> as a twenty-year-old.*

rouse (rouz) *vi.*, awaken or stir up. *The slamming of the kitchen door <u>roused</u> the birds, and they flew up into the trees.*

50 they were caught in another. It was not possible to allow the dress to tear. "I in the thorny bush," she said. "Thorns, you doing your appointed work. Never want to let folks pass, no sir. Old eyes thought you was a pretty little *green* bush."

Finally, trembling all over, she stood free, and after a moment dared to stoop for her cane.

"Sun so high!" she cried, leaning back and looking, while the thick tears went over her eyes. "The time getting all gone here."

At the foot of this hill was a place where a log was laid
60 across the creek.

"Now comes the trial," said Phoenix.

Putting her right foot out, she mounted the log and shut her eyes. Lifting her skirt, leveling her cane fiercely before her, like a festival figure in some parade, she began to march across. Then she opened her eyes and she was safe on the other side.

"I wasn't as old as I thought," she said.

But she sat down to rest. She spread her skirts on the bank around her and folded her hands over her knees. Up
70 above her was a tree in a pearly cloud of mistletoe. She did not dare to close her eyes, and when a little boy brought her a plate with a slice of marble-cake on it she spoke to him. "That would be acceptable," she said. But when she went to take it there was just her own hand in the air.

So she left that tree, and had to go through a barbed-wire fence. There she had to creep and crawl, spreading her knees and stretching her fingers like a baby trying to climb the steps. But she talked loudly to herself: she could not let her dress be torn now, so late in the day, and she could not
80 pay for having her arm or her leg sawed off if she got caught fast where she was.

At last she was safe through the fence and risen up out in the clearing. Big dead trees, like black men with one arm, were standing in the purple stalks of the withered cotton field. There sat a buzzard.

"Who you watching?"

In the furrow she made her way along.

"Glad this not the season for bulls," she said, looking sideways, "and the good Lord made his snakes to curl up
90 and sleep in the winter. A pleasure I don't see no two-

FIX-UP IDEA

Write Things Down
To better understand the story, make a list of the obstacles Phoenix encounters on her journey. For example, she has already encountered the thorn bush at the bottom of the hill. List two obstacles on this page. Then continue listing obstacles in the margins as you read.

_____

_____

MARK THE TEXT

Underline or highlight how Phoenix crosses the log over the creek.

NOTE THE FACTS

Why does Phoenix take such care in crossing through the barbed-wire fence?

_____

_____

_____

headed snake coming around that tree, where it come once. It took a while to get by him, back in the summer."

She passed through the old cotton and went into a field of dead corn. It whispered and shook and was taller than her head. "Through the maze now," she said, for there was no path.

Then there was something tall, black, and skinny there, moving before her.

At first she took it for a man. It could have been a man dancing in the field. But she stood still and listened, and it did not make a sound. It was as silent as a ghost.

"Ghost," she said sharply, "who be you the ghost of? For I have heard of nary death close by."

But there was no answer—only the ragged dancing in the wind.

She shut her eyes, reached out her hand, and touched a sleeve. She found a coat and inside that an emptiness, cold as ice.

"You scarecrow," she said. Her face lighted. "I ought to be shut up for good," she said with laughter. "My senses is gone. I too old. I the oldest people I ever know. Dance, old scarecrow," she said, "while I dancing with you."

She kicked her foot over the furrow, and with mouth drawn down, shook her head once or twice in a little strutting way. Some husks blew down and whirled in streamers about her skirts.

Then she went on, parting her way from side to side with the cane, through the whispering field. At last she came to the end, to a wagon track where the silver grass blew between the red ruts. The quail were walking around like <u>pullets</u>, seeming all dainty and unseen.

"Walk pretty," she said. "This the easy place. This the easy going."

She followed the track, swaying through the quiet bare fields, through the little strings of trees silver in their dead

NOTE THE FACTS

What does Phoenix think is in the cornfield? What does it turn out to be?

_____

_____

_____

Literary **TOOLS**

CHARACTER. A **character** is a person who figures in the action of a literary work. Phoenix Jackson is the main character in this story. You learn about her from description of her appearance. As you read, think about what you learn about her through her words, actions, and motivations.

words for everyday use

pul • let (pu̇´ lət) *n.*, young hen. *The farmer put the* pullets *in the chicken coop for safety.*

leaves, past cabins silver from weather, with the doors and windows boarded shut, all like old women under a spell sitting there. "I walking in their sleep," she said, nodding her head vigorously.

130   In a <u>ravine</u> she went where a spring was silently flowing through a hollow log. Old Phoenix bent and drank. "Sweetgum makes the water sweet," she said, and drank more. "Nobody know who made this well, for it was here when I was born."

The track crossed a swampy part where the moss hung as white as lace from every limb. "Sleep on, alligators, and blow your bubbles." Then the track went into the road.

Deep, deep the road went down between the high green-colored banks. Overhead the live-oaks met, and it was as
140   dark as a cave.

A black dog with a lolling tongue came up out of the weeds by the ditch. She was meditating, and not ready, and when he came at her she only hit him a little with her cane. Over she went in the ditch, like a little puff of milkweed.

Down there, her senses drifted away. A dream visited her, and she reached her hand up, but nothing reached down and gave her a pull. So she lay there and presently went to talking. "Old woman," she said to herself, "that black dog come up out of the weeds to stall you off, and now there he
150   sitting on his fine tail, smiling at you."

A white man finally came along and found her—a hunter, a young man, with his dog on a chain.

"Well, Granny!" he laughed. "What are you doing there?"

"Lying on my back like a June-bug waiting to be turned over, mister," she said, reaching up her hand.

He lifted her up, gave her a swing in the air, and set her down. "Anything broken, Granny?"

"No sir, them old dead weeds is springy enough," said Phoenix, when she had got her breath. "I thank you for
160   your trouble."

Use THE STRATEGY

VISUALIZE. Read the highlighted text. What images come to mind? In your graphic organizer, describe what you pictured.

_____

_____

_____

Reading STRATEGY REVIEW

WRITE THINGS DOWN. As you read, keep a chart of Phoenix Jackson's character traits. You can use the chart in Literary Tools on page 104.

---

words for everyday use

ra • vine (rə vēn') *n.,* small, narrow, steep-sided valley larger than a gully and smaller than a canyon. *The wheel fell off the carriage and tumbled down into the* <u>ravine</u>.

READ ALOUD

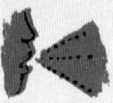

With a partner read aloud the dialogue between the hunter and Phoenix. One person should read the hunter's lines, the other should read Phoenix's lines. How does the hunter treat Phoenix?

_____
_____
_____

MARK THE TEXT

Highlight or underline what Phoenix spots on the ground.

"Where do you live, Granny?" he asked, while the two dogs were growling at each other.

"Away back yonder, sir, behind the ridge. You can't even see it from here."

"On your way home?"

"No sir, I going to town."

"Why, that's too far! That's as far as I walk when I come out myself, and I get something for my trouble." He patted the stuffed bag he carried, and there hung down a little closed claw. It was one of the bob-whites, with its beak hooked bitterly to show it was dead. "Now you go on home, Granny!"

"I bound to go to town, mister," said Phoenix. "The time come around."

He gave another laugh, filling the whole landscape. "I know you old colored people! Wouldn't miss going to town to see Santa Claus!"

But something held old Phoenix very still. The deep lines in her face went into a fierce and different radiation. Without warning, she had seen with her own eyes a flashing nickel fall out of the man's pocket onto the ground.

"How old are you, Granny?" he was saying.

"There is no telling, mister," she said, "no telling."

Then she gave a little cry and clapped her hands and said, "Git on away from here, dog! Look! Look at that dog!" She laughed as if in admiration. "He ain't scared of nobody. He a big black dog." She whispered, "Sic him!"

"Watch me get rid of that cur," said the man. "Sic him, Pete! Sic him!"

Phoenix heard the dogs fighting, and heard the man running and throwing sticks. She even heard a gunshot. But she was slowly bending forward by that time, further and further forward, the lids stretched down over her eyes, as if she were doing this in her sleep. Her chin was lowered almost to her knees. The yellow palm of her hand came out from the fold of her apron. Her fingers slid down and along the ground under the piece of money with the grace and care they would have in lifting an egg from under a setting hen. Then she slowly straightened up, she stood erect, and the nickel was in her apron pocket. A bird flew by. Her lips moved: "God watching me the whole time. I come to stealing."

The man came back, and his own dog panted about them. "Well, I scared him off that time," he said, and then he laughed and lifted his gun and pointed it at Phoenix.

She stood straight and faced him.

"Doesn't the gun scare you?" he said, still pointing it.

"No, sir, I seen plenty go off closer by, in my day, and for less than what I done," she said, holding utterly still.

He smiled, and shouldered the gun. "Well, Granny," he said, "you must be a hundred years old, and scared of nothing. I'd give you a dime if I had any money with me. But you take my advice and stay home, and nothing will happen to you."

"I bound to go on my way, mister," said Phoenix. She inclined her head in the red rag. Then they went in different directions, but she could hear the gun shooting again and again over the hill.

She walked on. The shadows hung from the oak trees to the road like curtains. Then she smelled wood-smoke, and smelled the river, and she saw a steeple and the cabins on their steep steps. Dozens of little black children whirled around her. There ahead was Natchez shining. Bells were ringing. She walked on.

In the paved city it was Christmas time. There were red and green electric lights strung and criss-crossed everywhere, and all turned on in the daytime. Old Phoenix would have been lost if she had not distrusted her eyesight and depended on her feet to know where to take her.

She paused quietly on the sidewalk where people were passing by. A lady came along in the crowd, carrying an armful of red-, green- and silver-wrapped presents; she gave off perfume like the red roses in hot summer, and Phoenix stopped her.

"Please, missy, will you lace up my shoe?" She held up her foot.

"What do you want, Grandma?"

"See my shoe," said Phoenix. "Do all right for out in the country, but wouldn't look right to go in a big building."

NOTE THE FACTS

Of what action is Phoenix ashamed?

_____
_____
_____

THINK AND REFLECT

What do you learn about Phoenix from her reaction when the hunter points his gun at her? Why doesn't she take his advice? **(Infer)**

_____
_____
_____

MARK THE TEXT

Highlight or underline what Phoenix wants the woman on the street to do.

NOTE THE FACTS

How does Phoenix know she's reached the right location?

---

240 "Stand still then, Grandma," said the lady. She put her packages down on the sidewalk beside her and laced and tied both shoes tightly.

"Can't lace 'em with a cane," said Phoenix. "Thank you, missy. I doesn't mind asking a nice lady to tie up my shoe, when I gets out on the street."

Moving slowly and from side to side, she went into the big building, and into a tower of steps, where she walked up and around and around until her feet knew to stop.

She entered a door, and there she saw nailed up on the wall the document that had been stamped with the gold seal and 250 framed in the gold frame, which matched the dream that was hung up in her head.

"Here I be," she said. There was a fixed and ceremonial stiffness over her body.

"A charity case, I suppose," said an attendant who sat at the desk before her.

But Phoenix only looked above her head. There was sweat on her face, the wrinkles in her skin shone like a bright net.

"Speak up, Grandma," the woman said. "What's your name? We must have your history, you know. Have you 260 been here before? What seems to be the trouble with you?"

Old Phoenix only gave a twitch to her face as if a fly were bothering her.

"Are you deaf?" cried the attendant.

But then the nurse came in.

"Oh, that's just old Aunt Phoenix," she said. "She doesn't come for herself—she has a little grandson. She makes these trips just as regular as clockwork. She lives away back off the Old Natchez Trace." She bent down. "Well, Aunt Phoenix, why don't you just take a seat? We won't keep you 270 standing after your long trip." She pointed.

The old woman sat down, bolt upright in the chair.

"Now, how is the boy?" asked the nurse.

Old Phoenix did not speak.

"I said, how is the boy?"

But Phoenix only waited and stared straight ahead, her face very solemn and withdrawn into rigidity.

NOTE THE FACTS

Why has Phoenix come? What do you learn about her journey?

"Is his throat any better?" asked the nurse. "Aunt Phoenix, don't you hear me? Is your grandson's throat any better since the last time you came for the medicine?"

With her hands on her knees, the old woman waited, silent, erect and motionless, just as if she were in armor.

"You mustn't take up our time this way, Aunt Phoenix," the nurse said. "Tell us quickly about your grandson, and get it over. He isn't dead, is he?"

At last there came a flicker and then a flame of comprehension across her face, and she spoke.

"My grandson. It was my memory had left me. There I sat and forgot why I made my long trip."

"Forgot?" The nurse frowned. "After you came so far?"

Then Phoenix was like an old woman begging a dignified forgiveness for waking up frightened in the night. "I never did go to school, I was too old at the Surrender,"[1] she said in a soft voice. "I'm an old woman without an education. It was my memory fail me. My little grandson, he is just the same, and I forgot it in the coming."

"Throat never heals, does it?" said the nurse, speaking in a loud, sure voice to old Phoenix. By now she had a card with something written on it, a little list. "Yes. Swallowed lye. When was it?—January—two-three years ago—"

Phoenix spoke unasked now. "No, missy, he not dead, he just the same. Every little while his throat begin to close up again, and he not able to swallow. He not get his breath. He not able to help himself. So the time come around, and I go on another trip for the soothing medicine."

"All right. The doctor said as long as you came to get it, you could have it," said the nurse. "But it's an obstinate case."

"My little grandson, he sit up there in the house all wrapped up, waiting by himself," Phoenix went on. "We is the only two left in the world. He suffer and it don't seem to put him back at all. He got a sweet look. He going to last. He wear a little patch quilt and peep out holding his mouth open like a little bird. I remembers so plain now. I not going to forget him again, no, the whole enduring time. I could tell him from all the others in creation."

---

1. **Surrender.** Surrender of the South to the North at the end of the Civil War in 1865

THINK AND REFLECT

Why does Phoenix take so long to answer the nurse's questions? (Infer)

_____

_____

_____

NOTE THE FACTS

What is wrong with Phoenix's grandson?

_____

_____

_____

NOTE THE FACTS

Why does the attendant offer Phoenix a few pennies?

_____
_____
_____

NOTE THE FACTS

What does Phoenix decide to do with her two nickels?

_____
_____
_____

"All right." The nurse was trying to hush her now. She brought her a bottle of medicine. "Charity," she said, making a check mark in a book.

Old Phoenix held the bottle close to her eyes, and then carefully put it into her pocket.

320 "I thank you," she said.

"It's Christmas time, Grandma," said the attendant. "Could I give you a few pennies out of my purse?"

"Five pennies is a nickel," said Phoenix stiffly.

"Here's a nickel," said the attendant.

Phoenix rose carefully and held out her hand. She received the nickel and then fished the other nickel out of her pocket and laid it beside the new one. She stared at her palm closely, with her head on one side.

Then she gave a tap with her cane on the floor.

330 "This is what come to me to do," she said. "I going to the store and buy my child a little windmill they sells, made out of paper. He going to find it hard to believe there such a thing in the world. I'll march myself back where he waiting, holding it straight up in this hand."

She lifted her free hand, gave a little nod, turned around, and walked out of the doctor's office. Then her slow step began on the stairs, going down. ■

Reflect ON YOUR READING

After Reading → **SHARE YOUR MIND MOVIE**

❏ With a few of your classmates, share your sketches or summary of your mind movie.
❏ Talk about which events or images in the story were the most prominent or meaningful to you.

Reading Skills and Test Practice

ANALYZE LITERARY ELEMENTS

READ, THINK, AND EXPLAIN. Describe the journey taken by Phoenix Jackson and explain why it is archetypal. Use details and information from the story to support your answer. Jot down your ideas using the Think-Aloud Notes in the margin.

THINK-ALOUD NOTES

_____
_____
_____
_____
_____
_____
_____
_____
_____
_____

REFLECT ON YOUR RESPONSE. Compare your response to that of your partner and talk about how your visualizations helped form your response.

_____
_____
_____
_____

Investigate, Inquire, and Imagine

RECALL: GATHER FACTS
1a. When does Phoenix begin her journey?

INTERPRET: FIND MEANING
1b. How old is Phoenix? How do you know?

ANALYZE: TAKE THINGS APART
2a. Identify the obstacles that Phoenix runs into during her journey. Describe how she overcomes each one.

SYNTHESIZE: BRING THINGS TOGETHER
2b. Why does Welty wait until the end of the story to reveal why the journey was made?

EVALUATE: MAKE JUDGMENTS
3a. When a work of literature is ambiguous, it can be interpreted in more than one way. Is Phoenix's grandson dead or alive? Cite examples from the text to support your viewpoint.

EXTEND: CONNECT IDEAS
3b. Compare and contrast the journey in this story to a journey in another work of literature or in a film.

Literary Tools

CHARACTER. A **character** is a person who figures in the action of a literary work. A *one-dimensional character* is one who exhibits a single dominant quality. A *three-dimensional character* is one who exhibits the complexity of traits associated with actual human beings. Fill in the chart that follows with details of Phoenix's character.

Physical Appearance	Dress	Habits/ Mannerisms/ Behaviors	Relationships with Other People	Other
	long, dark striped dress			

What do you learn about Phoenix's character from each of the following encounters?

bramblebush _____

the scarecrow _____

the hunter _____

the woman who ties her shoe _____

What character trait does Phoenix demonstrate by getting the medicine and a paper windmill for her grandson? Is Phoenix a three-dimensional or one-dimensional character?

WordWorkshop

CONTEXTUAL SENTENCES. Write a sentence that shows the meaning of each Word for Everyday Use from this story.

1. limber _____

2. pendulum _____

3. pullet _____

4. quivering _____

5. ravine _____

6. rouse _____

Read-Write Connection

Imagine that you are Phoenix. What would you tell people you live for?

_____
_____
_____
_____

Beyond the Reading

RESEARCH AN AUTHOR. Use the library and the Internet to find information about Eudora Welty. Look for adaptations and reviews of her work, interviews with her, and awards she has received. Then work with a few of your classmates to lay out a page of a newsletter honoring Welty. You might want to include your own review of "A Worn Path."

GO ONLINE. To find links and additional activities for this selection, visit the EMC Internet Resource Center at **emcp.com/languagearts** and click on Write-In Reader.

"AMBUSH"

by Tim O'Brien

CONNECT

Reader's resource

Tim O'Brien is a veteran of the Vietnam War, and he is best known for his fiction about the wartime experiences of American soldiers in Vietnam. His short story collection *The Things They Carried* was nominated for a Pulitzer Prize. "**Ambush**" is from this collection. In "Ambush," the narrator relives a moment of the Vietnam War that has haunted him for many years.

Word watch

PREVIEW VOCABULARY

ambush	muzzle
gape	peril
grenade	platoon
lob	swivel
morality	watch

Reader's journal

When have you told a lie to protect someone?

_____
_____
_____
_____
_____
_____

Active READING STRATEGY

VISUALIZE

Before Reading → BEGIN TO PICTURE WHAT MAY HAPPEN

- ❑ Read the Reader's Resource carefully and look at the background picture on page 107.
- ❑ Begin to imagine what might happen in the story.
- ❑ Preview the Sensory Details Chart below. As you read, you will sketch or jot down sensory details from the mind movies you create during reading.

Graphic Organizer: Sensory Details Chart

Sight	Sound	Touch	Taste	Smell

106 THE EMC WRITE-IN READER

AMBUSH

Tim O'Brien

When she was nine, my daughter Kathleen asked if I had ever killed anyone. She knew about the war; she knew I'd been a soldier. "You keep writing these war stories," she said, "so I guess you must've killed somebody." It was a difficult moment, but I did what seemed right, which was to say, "Of course not," and then to take her onto my lap and hold her for a while. Someday, I hope, she'll ask again. But here I want to pretend she's a grown-up. I want to tell her exactly what happened, or what I remember happening, and then I want to say to her that as a little girl she was absolutely right. This is why I keep writing war stories:

He was a short, slender young man of about twenty. I was afraid of him—afraid of something—and as he passed me on the trail I threw a <u>grenade</u> that exploded at his feet and killed him.

words for everyday use

gre • nade (grə nād′) *n.*, small missile that contains an explosive or a chemical agent and that is thrown by hand or projected. *When the <u>grenade</u> exploded, tear gas was emitted, driving the student protesters outside.*

During Reading

CREATE A MIND MOVIE

☐ Listen as your teacher reads the first two paragraphs of the story. Begin to create a mind movie as you listen. Involve all of your senses in the mind movie. Make quick sketches that show what you see, hear, and feel.

☐ Write down sensory details from your mind movies in your Sensory Details Chart.

☐ Continue reading and making your mind movie. When you are finished with the short story, create quick sketches or write a brief summary that explains what you saw in your mind movie.

MARK THE TEXT

Highlight or underline the narrator's response to his daughter.

FIX-UP IDEA

Connect to Personal Experience
Discuss your response to the Reader's Journal with a partner. Think about why the speaker lies to his daughter.

UNIT 3 / READING FICTION

Literary TOOLS

REALISM. Realism is the attempt to render in art an accurate portrayal of reality. As you read, look for realistic details.

Reading STRATEGY REVIEW

WRITE THINGS DOWN. Try writing things down to help you examine the realism of "Ambush." As you read, make a cluster chart that lists the realistic details of the story. You can use the cluster chart in Literary Tools on page 112.

Use THE STRATEGY

VISUALIZE. Read the highlighted text. What images come to mind? In your own words, describe what you pictured.

_____
_____
_____

---

20 Or to go back:

Shortly after midnight we moved into the <u>ambush</u> site outside My Khe.[1] The whole <u>platoon</u> was there, spread out in the dense brush along the trail, and for five hours nothing at all happened. We were working in two-man teams—one man on guard while the other slept, switching off every two hours—and I remember it was still dark when Kiowa shook me awake for the final <u>watch</u>. The night was foggy and hot. For the first few moments I felt lost, not sure about directions, groping for my helmet and weapon. I
30 reached out and found three grenades and lined them up in front of me; the pins had already been straightened for quick throwing. And then for maybe half an hour I kneeled there and waited. Very gradually, in tiny slivers, dawn began to break through the fog, and from my position in the brush I could see ten or fifteen meters up the trail. The mosquitoes were fierce. I remember slapping at them, wondering if I should wake up Kiowa and ask for some repellent, then thinking it was a bad idea, then looking up and seeing the young man come out of the fog. He wore
40 black clothing and rubber sandals and a gray ammunition belt. His shoulders were slightly stooped, his head cocked to the side as if listening for something. He seemed at ease. He carried his weapon in one hand, <u>muzzle</u> down, moving without any hurry up the center of the trail. There was no sound at all—none that I can remember. In a way, it seemed, he was part of the morning fog, or my own imagination, but there was also the reality of what was happening in my stomach. I had already pulled the pin on a grenade. I had come up to a crouch. It was entirely

---

1. **My Khe.** Village in Vietnam

words for everyday use

am • bush (am' bush) *n.*, trap in which a concealed person or persons lie in wait to attack by surprise. *The <u>ambush</u> surprised the stagecoach, and the robbers took all the passengers' money and jewelry.*

pla • toon (plə tün') *n.*, subdivision of a company-size military unit normally consisting of two or more squads or sections. *The <u>platoon</u> ran two miles every day as part of its training.*

watch (wäch) *n.*, act of keeping awake to guard or protect. *Private Johnson was reprimanded for falling asleep during his <u>watch</u>.*

muz • zle (mə' zəl) *n.*, discharging end of a weapon. *The <u>muzzle</u> of the rifle was aimed at the deer.*

50 automatic. I did not hate the young man; I did not see him as the enemy; I did not ponder issues of <u>morality</u> or politics or military duty. I crouched and kept my head low. I tried to swallow whatever was rising from my stomach, which tasted like lemonade, something fruity and sour. I was terrified. There were no thoughts about killing. The grenade was to make him go away—just evaporate—and I leaned back and felt my mind go empty and then felt it fill up again. I had already thrown the grenade before telling myself to throw it. The brush was thick and I had to <u>lob</u> it
60 high, not aiming, and I remember the grenade seeming to freeze above me for an instant, as if a camera had clicked, and I remember ducking down and holding my breath and seeing little wisps of fog rise from the earth. The grenade bounced once and rolled across the trail. I did not hear it, but there must've been a sound, because the young man dropped his weapon and began to run, just two or three quick steps, then he hesitated, <u>swiveling</u> to his right, and he glanced down at the grenade and tried to cover his head but never did. It occurred to me then that he was about to
70 die. I wanted to warn him. The grenade made a popping noise—not soft but not loud either—not what I'd expected—and there was a puff of dust and smoke—a small white puff—and the young man seemed to jerk upward as if pulled by invisible wires. He fell on his back. His rubber sandals had been blown off. There was no wind. He lay at the center of the trail, his right leg bent beneath him, his one eye shut, his other eye a huge star-shaped hole.

It was not a matter of live or die. There was no real <u>peril</u>. Almost certainly the young man would have passed by.
80 And it will always be that way.

Later, I remember, Kiowa tried to tell me that the man would've died anyway. He told me that it was a good kill,

NOTE THE FACTS

What prompts the narrator to throw the grenade?

_____

_____

_____

Use THE STRATEGY

VISUALIZE. Read the highlighted text. What sounds do you imagine? What would you see or feel if you were there? Write these details in your Sensory Details Chart.

NOTE THE FACTS

What does Kiowa tell the narrator about the kill?

_____

_____

_____

words for everyday use
mo • ral • i • ty (mə ra' lə tē) *n.*, doctrine or system of moral conduct. *The governor's speech about <u>morality</u> strengthened his support from the conservatives within his party.*
lob (läb) *vt.*, throw, hit, or propel easily or in a high arc. *Jamal <u>lobbed</u> the tennis ball over the net.*
swiv • el (swi' vəl) *vi.*, swing or turn or pivot freely. *The child got dizzy when the chair <u>swiveled</u>.*
per • il (per' əl) *n.*, exposure to the risk of being injured, destroyed, or lost. *The fire in the apartment building put the residents in <u>peril</u>.*

that I was a soldier and this was a war, that I should shape up and stop staring and ask myself what the dead man would've done if things were reversed.

None of it mattered. The words seemed far too complicated. All I could do was <u>gape</u> at the fact of the young man's body.

Even now I haven't finished sorting it out. Sometimes I forgive myself, other times I don't. In the ordinary hours of life I try not to dwell on it, but now and then, when I'm reading a newspaper or just sitting alone in a room, I'll look up and see the young man coming out of the morning fog. I'll watch him walk toward me, his shoulders slightly stooped, his head cocked to the side, and he'll pass within a few yards of me and suddenly smile at some secret thought and then continue up the trail to where it bends back into the fog. ■

> **THINK AND REFLECT**
>
> How does the narrator feel about killing the young man? (Infer)
>
> _____
> _____

words for everyday use

gape (gāp) *vi.*, gaze stupidly or in openmouthed surprise or wonder. *The students <u>gaped</u> at their teacher when he walked into the classroom wearing a Halloween costume.*

Reflect ON YOUR READING

After Reading → SHARE YOUR MIND MOVIE

- ❑ With a few of your classmates, share your sketches or a summary of your mind movie.
- ❑ Review your Sensory Details Chart. Talk about what events or images in the story were the most prominent or meaningful to you.

Reading Skills and Test Practice

ANALYZE ELEMENTS OF PLOT

Discuss with your partner how best to answer these questions about plot elements in the story. Use the Think-Aloud Notes to write down your reasons for eliminating the incorrect answers.

____1. What conflict does the narrator face in the introduction to the story?
   a. He must decide whether or not to kill a man.
   b. He struggles with having killed a man.
   c. He is not sure what to tell his daughter about what he did in the war.
   d. He has a conflict about whether to tell the truth in the stories he writes.

____2. Which of the following marks the crisis of "Ambush"?
   a. the narrator's decision to lie to his daughter
   b. the narrator's decision to throw the grenade
   c. the narrator's efforts to sort out what happened
   d. the narrator's vision of the man walking away

How did using the reading strategy help you to answer the questions?

_____
_____
_____
_____

THINK-ALOUD NOTES

Investigate, Inquire, and Imagine

RECALL: GATHER FACTS
1a. What sound does the grenade make when it goes off?

INTERPRET: FIND MEANING
1b. What do the narrator's comments about the sound of the grenade going off tell you about the length of his combat experience?

ANALYZE: TAKE THINGS APART
2a. Analyze the thoughts and emotions of the narrator when he throws the grenade.

SYNTHESIZE: BRING THINGS TOGETHER
2b. How does the narrator feel now about having thrown the grenade? Do you agree with Kiowa's defense of the narrator's action? Explain.

EVALUATE: MAKE JUDGMENTS
3a. Evaluate the effectiveness of the story as an antiwar message.

EXTEND: CONNECT IDEAS
3b. Compare and contrast the attitude toward war expressed in "Ambush" with the attitude toward war expressed in another work you have read.

Literary Tools

REALISM. **Realism** is the attempt to render in art an accurate portrayal of reality. If you did not fill in the cluster chart while reading, review the story and add realistic details to the chart below. What realistic details does the story give about the man who is killed? Is he portrayed as the enemy?

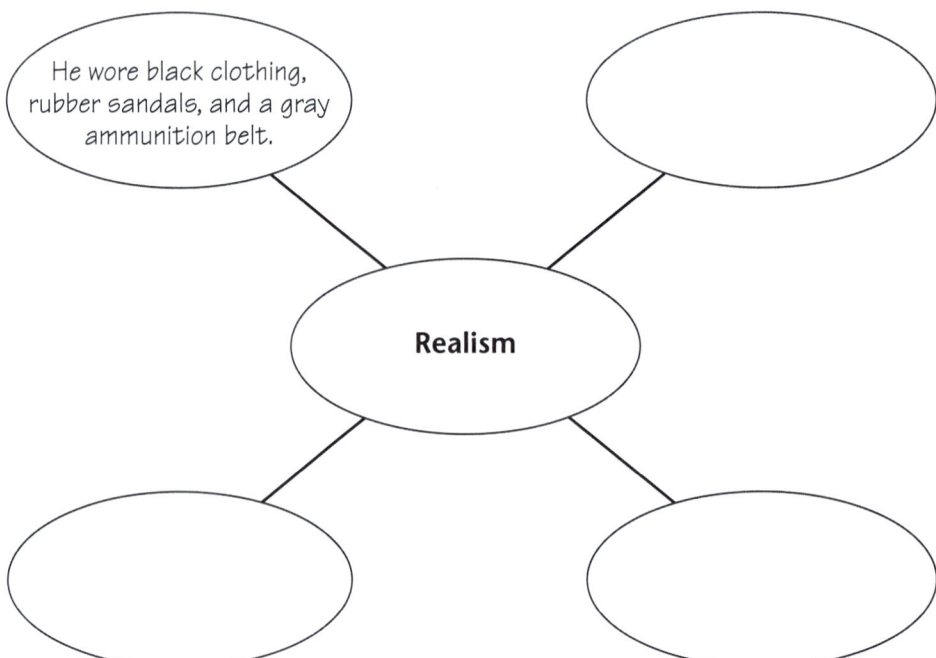

WordWorkshop

WORD SORT. Choose categories, such as "Related to War" or "Actions." Sort the Words for Everyday Use into these categories. Try using different categories to sort the words. If you found other new words as you read, add them to your word sort.

Category:	Category:	Category:	Category:
Words:	Words:	Words:	Words:

Read-Write Connection

What kind of soldier was the speaker?

_____
_____
_____
_____
_____

Beyond the Reading

CREATE A MULTIMEDIA SHOW. Work with a group to create a multimedia show about war. Choose a topic, such as a patriotic look at war, the justification of warfare, or the tragedy of war. Then select media to demonstrate your point of view. Your show can include live demonstrations, such as skits, dance, or poetry readings; audio- or video-recordings; and other visual media, such as photography or painting. Include commentary and transitional material to hold the elements of your show together.

GO ONLINE. To find links and additional activities for this selection, visit the EMC Internet Resource Center at **emcp.com/languagearts** and click on Write-In Reader.

Unit 3 READING Review

Choose and Use Reading Strategies

Before reading the selection below, review with a partner how to use each of these reading strategies.

1. Read with a Purpose
2. Connect to Prior Knowledge
3. Write Things Down
4. Make Predictions
5. Visualize
6. Use Text Organization
7. Tackle Difficult Vocabulary
8. Monitor Your Reading Progress

Now apply at least two of these reading strategies as you read the excerpt from "The Pit and the Pendulum" by Edgar Allan Poe. Use the margins and mark up the text to show how you are using the reading strategies to read actively. You may find it helpful to choose a graphic organizer from Appendix B to gather information as you read the excerpt, or use the Summary Chart on page B-12 to create a graphic organizer that summarizes the excerpt.

> I was sick—sick unto death with that long agony; and when they at length unbound me, and I was permitted to sit, I felt that my senses were leaving me. The sentence—the dread sentence of death—was the last of distinct accentuation which reached my ears. After that, the sound of the inquisitorial voices seemed merged in one dreamy indeterminate hum. It conveyed to my soul the idea of *revolution*—perhaps from its association in fancy with the burr of a mill wheel. This only for a brief period: for presently I heard no more. Yet for a while I saw; but with how terrible an exaggeration! I saw the lips of the black-robed judges. They appeared to me white—whiter than the sheet upon which I trace these words—and thin even to grotesqueness; thin with the intensity of their expression of firmness—of immovable resolution—of stern contempt of human torture. I saw that the decrees of what to me was Fate were still issuing from those lips.

WordWorkshop

UNIT 3 WORDS FOR EVERYDAY USE

acclivity, 44
afflicted, 65
ambush, 108
append, 58
aspirated, 50
cavort, 61
conjecture, 58
dilapidated, 58
dwindle, 88
efface, 48
embrasure, 44
exhorter, 60
gape, 110
garrulous, 58
gesticulate, 50
grenade, 107
importunity, 72
interminable, 59
jilt, 83
limber, 94
lob, 109
ludicrous, 48
malign, 53
morality, 109
muzzle, 108
ornery, 61
oscillation, 48
pendulum, 93
peril, 109
platoon, 108
pullet, 96
quivering, 94
ravine, 97
rouse, 94
rummage, 80
sentinel, 43
swivel, 109
tumultuously, 71
vagabond, 64
watch, 108

WORD SORT. Choose some of the Words for Everyday Use from Unit 3. Write one word in each of the boxes below. Then write its definition and part of speech. You may refer to the page number listed to review the definition and part of speech. Then sort the words using one of the following methods:

- Same part of speech
- Words with similar or opposite meanings
- Words with prefixes and suffixes
- Words that can be used together
- Other sorting method: _____

Word: Definition: Part of Speech:	Word: Definition: Part of Speech:	Word: Definition: Part of Speech:
Word: Definition: Part of Speech:	Word: Definition: Part of Speech:	Word: Definition: Part of Speech:
Word: Definition: Part of Speech:	Word: Definition: Part of Speech:	Word: Definition: Part of Speech:

Literary Tools

Select the best literary element on the right to complete each sentence on the left. Write the correct letter in the blank.

1. _____ "The Notorious Jumping Frog of Calaveras County" is an example of a(n) ____ because it is a story that serves to tell another story.
2. _____ The narrator in "Ambush" is a(n) ____ because he has the complexity of a real person.
3. _____ Part of "An Occurrence at Owl Creek Bridge" is told in _____.
4. _____ A person in a story is a(n) ____.
5. _____ A(n) ____ often contains exaggeration.
6. _____ The ending of "The Story of an Hour" is an example of ____.
7. _____ Simon Wheeler is a(n) _____.
8. _____ Tim O'Brien tries to capture how things really are in his writing; this style is called ____.
9. _____ The reader knows Granny Weatherall's thoughts and feelings through the author's use of ____.

a. character, 36, 96, 104
b. flashback, 47, 55
c. frame tale, 59, 67
d. irony, page 73, 75
e. one-dimensional character, 36, 104
f. Realism, 44, 108, 112
g. stream-of-consciousness writing, 77, 81, 90
h. tall tale, 57, 59, 67
i. three-dimensional character, 36, 104

On Your Own

FLUENTLY SPEAKING. Research one of the authors from this unit. Give a brief oral presentation about the author. Consider including excerpts from the works of the author in your presentation.

PICTURE THIS. Choose one of the stories from this unit. Create a graphic version representing the main plot of the story. Use illustrations, captions, and speech bubbles.

PUT IT IN WRITING. Choose one of the stories from this unit. Write a review of the story. In your review, try to convince your peers to read the story. Consider submitting your review to the school paper, uploading it to an online book review site, or asking to display your review with those of your classmates at a library.

Unit FOUR

Reading Poetry

POETRY

Defining the word *poetry* is difficult because poems take so many different forms. Poems do not have to be written down; some are chanted or sung. Some poems rhyme and have a consistent rhythm, but others do not.

Poetry differs from prose in that it packs more meaning into fewer words and often uses meter, rhyme, and rhythm more obviously. One thing that all poems have in common is that they use imaginative language carefully chosen and arranged to communicate experiences, thoughts, or emotions.

There are many different kinds of poetry. Some common kinds are listed below. The most common techniques of poetry involve imagery, shape, sound, and meaning. Each of these techniques is also discussed below.

Forms of Poetry

NARRATIVE POETRY. A **narrative poem** is a poem that tells a story. Edgar Allan Poe's "The Raven" in this unit is an example of a narrative poem.

DRAMATIC POETRY. A **dramatic poem** is a poem that relies heavily on dramatic elements such as monologue (speech by a single character) or dialogue (conversation involving two or more characters). Often dramatic poems tell stories like narrative poems.

LYRIC POETRY. A **lyric poem** is a highly musical verse that expresses the emotions of a speaker. Many of the poems in this unit are lyric poems, including "I heard a Fly buzz—when I died—" by Emily Dickinson and "somewhere i have never travelled,gladly beyond" by E. E. Cummings. **Sonnets, odes, free verse, elegies, haiku**, and **imagist poems** are all forms of lyric poetry.

NOTE THE FACTS

What do all poems have in common?

_____
_____
_____

THINK AND REFLECT

What is the difference between a lyric and a narrative poem? (Compare and Contrast)

_____
_____
_____

Techniques of Poetry: Imagery

An **image** is language that creates a concrete representation of an object or experience. An image is also the vivid mental picture created in the reader's mind by that language. For example, in "I heard a Fly buzz—when I died—," Emily Dickinson writes "I heard a Fly buzz—when I died— / The Stillness in the Room / Was like the Stillness in the Air— / Between the Heaves of Storm." The picture created in your mind of a fly flitting about a hot, still room is an image. When considered in a group, images are called **imagery**. Poets use colorful, vivid language and figures of speech to create imagery. A **figure of speech** is language meant to be understood imaginatively instead of literally. The following are common figures of speech:

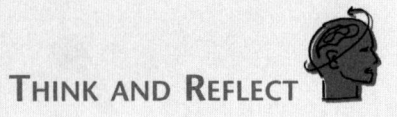

THINK AND REFLECT

Write an example of personification. (**Apply**)

_____
_____
_____

Figure of Speech	Definition	Example
metaphor	figure of speech in which one thing is written about as if it were another	"My heart is a flower opening to the warmth of your love"
simile	comparison using *like* or *as*	"My soul has grown deep like the rivers"
personification	figure of speech in which an idea, animal, or thing is described as if it were a person	"Because I could not stop for Death— / He kindly stopped for me—"

Techniques of Poetry: Shape

The shape of a poem is how it looks on the page. Poems are often divided into stanzas, or groups of lines. The following are some common types of stanzas:

Stanza Name	Number of Lines
couplet	two
triplet or tercet	three
quatrain	four
quintain	five
sestet	six
heptastich	seven
octave	eight

A **concrete poem**, or **shape poem**, is one with a shape that suggests its subject. A poem about a cloud, for example, might be written in the shape of a cloud.

Techniques of Poetry: Rhythm

The **rhythm** is the pattern of beats or stresses in a line. A regular rhythmic pattern is called a **meter**. Units of rhythm are called **feet**. A **foot** consists of some combination of weakly stressed (˘) and strongly stressed (/) syllables, as follows:

Type of Foot	Pattern	Example
iamb, or **iambic foot**	˘ /	a**fraid**
trochee, or **trochaic foot**	/ ˘	**free**dom
anapest, or **anapestic foot**	˘ ˘ /	in a **flash**
dactyl, or **dactylic foot**	/ ˘ ˘	**fe**verish
spondee, or **spondaic foot**	/ /	**baseball**

READ ALOUD

First read the examples in the chart aloud. Make sure you stress the correct syllable. Then read the examples in the next chart aloud. Again, practice stressing the correct syllables.

The following terms are used to describe the number of feet in a line of poetry:

Term	# of Feet	Example
monometer	one foot	˘ / To**day** ˘ / We **play**
dimeter	two feet	/ ˘ ˘ / ˘ **Fol**lowing | **close**ly
trimeter	three feet	˘ / ˘ / ˘ / God **shed** | His **light** | on **thee**
tetrameter	four feet	/ ˘ / ˘ / ˘ / ˘ **In** the | **green**est | **of** our | **val**leys
pentameter	five feet	˘ / ˘ / ˘ / A **vast** | re **pub** | lic **famed** | ˘ / ˘ / through **ev** | ry **clime**
hexameter or **Alexandrine**	six feet	˘ / ˘ / ˘ / In **o** | ther's **eyes** | we **see** | ˘ / ˘ / ˘ / our**selves** | the **truth** | to **tell**

MARK THE TEXT

Underline or highlight the rhyming words in the following lines from "The Raven" by Edgar Allan Poe:

While I nodded, nearly napping, suddenly there came a tapping,
As of some one gently rapping, rapping at my chamber door.
" 'Tis some visitor," I muttered, "tapping at my chamber door—
          Only this, and nothing more.

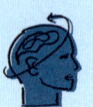

THINK AND REFLECT

Write a sentence that contains alliteration. (Apply)

_____

_____

_____

THINK AND REFLECT

Give another example of consonance. (Apply)

_____

_____

_____

Techniques of Poetry: Sound

RHYME. Rhyme is the repetition of sounds at the ends of words. **End rhyme** is rhyme that occurs at the ends of lines. **Internal rhyme** occurs within lines as in "Once upon a midnight *dreary*, while I pondered, weak and *weary*." **Sight rhyme** occurs when two words are spelled similarly but pronounced differently. **Rhyme scheme** is a pattern of end rhymes.

ALLITERATION. Alliteration is the repetition of initial consonant sounds. The following lines from Walt Whitman's "Song of Myself" contains alliteration: "*F*ailing to *f*etch me at *f*irst keep encouraged."

ASSONANCE. Assonance is the repetition of vowel sounds in stressed syllables that end with different consonant sounds as in this line from Emily Dickinson's "Because I could not stop for Death—":

   We passed the Fields of G*a*zing Gr*a*in—

CONSONANCE. Consonance is a kind of slant rhyme in which the ending consonant sounds match, but the preceding vowel sound does not, as in *wind* and *found*.

ONOMATOPOEIA. Onomatopoeia is the use of words or phrases that sound like the things to which they refer, like *meow*, *buzz*, and *murmur*.

USING READING STRATEGIES WITH POETRY

Active Reading Strategy Checklists

The following checklists offer strategies for reading poetry.

1 READ WITH A PURPOSE. Before reading a poem, give yourself a purpose, or something to look for, as you read. Sometimes a purpose will be a directive from a teacher: "Pay attention to symbols in the poem." Other times you can set your own purpose by previewing the title, the opening lines, and other information presented with the poem. Say to yourself

- ❏ I want to look for . . .
- ❏ I want to experience . . .
- ❏ I want to enjoy . . .
- ❏ I wonder . . .
- ❏ I want to see if . . .

2 CONNECT TO PRIOR KNOWLEDGE. Being aware of what you already know and thinking about it as you read can help you keep track of what's happening and will increase your knowledge. As you read, say to yourself

- ❑ I already know this about the poem's subject matter . . .
- ❑ This part of the poem reminds me of . . .
- ❑ I think this part of the poem is like . . .
- ❑ My experience tells me that . . .
- ❑ If I were the speaker, I would feel . . .
- ❑ I associate this image with . . .

3 WRITE THINGS DOWN. As you read poetry, write down how the poem helps you "see" what is described. Possible ways to write things down include:

- ❑ Underline words and phrases that appeal to your five senses.
- ❑ Write down your questions and comments.
- ❑ Highlight figures of speech and phrases you enjoy.
- ❑ Create a graphic organizer to keep track of your responses.

4 MAKE PREDICTIONS. Before you read a poem, use information about the author, the subject matter, and the title to make a guess about what a poem may describe. As you read, confirm or deny your predictions, and make new ones based on how the poem develops. Make predictions like the following

- ❑ The title tells me that . . .
- ❑ I predict that this poem will be about . . .
- ❑ This poet usually writes about . . .
- ❑ I think the poet will repeat . . .
- ❑ These lines in the poem make me guess that . . .

5 VISUALIZE. Visualizing, or allowing the words on the page to create images in your mind, is extremely important while reading poetry. In order to visualize the words, change your reading pace and savor the words. Allow the words to affect all of your senses. Make statements such as

- ❑ The words help me see . . .
- ❑ The words help me hear . . .
- ❑ The words help me feel . . .
- ❑ The words help me taste . . .
- ❑ The words help me smell . . .

Reading **TIP**

Remember that lyric poems express the emotions of the speaker. You can draw on your experience with certain emotions as you read.

Reading **TIP**

A simple code can help you remember your reactions to a poem. You can use
- ! for "This is like something I have experienced"
- ? for "I don't understand this"
- ✓ for "This seems important"

Reading **TIP**

Remember that narrative poems tell a story. You can make a plot chart as you would for any other story.

Reading **TIP**

Try visualizing as a partner reads the poem aloud.

Reading TIP

Look for repetition. It often signals a key idea that the writer wants to emphasize.

Reading TIP

If a poem has unfamiliar words, read the poem, tackle the vocabulary you don't understand, and then reread the poem.

Fix-Up Ideas

- Reread
- Read in shorter chunks
- Read aloud
- Ask questions
- Change your reading rate
- Try a different reading strategy

6 USE TEXT ORGANIZATION. When you read a poem, pay attention to punctuation and line breaks. Learn to chunk the lines in a poem so they make sense. Try reading all the way to the end of the sentence rather than stopping at each line break. Punctuation, rhythm, repetition, and line length offer clues that help you vary your reading rate and word emphasis. Say to yourself

- ❏ The punctuation in these lines helps me . . .
- ❏ The writer started a new stanza here because . . .
- ❏ The writer repeats this line because . . .
- ❏ The rhythm of this poem makes me think of . . .
- ❏ These short lines affect my reading speed by . . .

7 TACKLE DIFFICULT VOCABULARY. Difficult words in a poem can get in the way of your ability to respond to the poet's words and ideas. Use context clues that the lines provide, consult a dictionary, or ask someone about words you do not understand. When you come across a difficult word in a poem, say to yourself

- ❏ The lines near this word tell me that this word means . . .
- ❏ A definition provided with the poem shows that the word means . . .
- ❏ My work with the word before reading helps me know that the word means . . .
- ❏ A classmate said that the word means . . .

8 MONITOR YOUR READING PROGRESS. All readers encounter difficulty when they read, especially if the reading material is not self-selected. When you have to read something, take note of problems you are having and fix them. The key to reading success is knowing when you are having difficulty. To fix problems, say to yourself

- ❏ Because I don't understand this part, I will . . .
- ❏ Because I'm having trouble staying connected to the ideas in the poem, I will . . .
- ❏ Because the words in the poem are too hard, I will . . .
- ❏ Because the poem is long, I will . . .
- ❏ Because I can't retell what the poem was about, I will . . .

Become an Active Reader

Each poem in this unit gives you an in-depth look at how to use one reading strategy. Learn how to use several strategies in combination to ensure your complete understanding. When you have difficulty, use fix-up ideas. For further information about active reading strategies, see Unit 1, pages 4–15.

How to Use Reading Strategies with Poetry

To see how readers use active reading strategies, look over one reader's response to reading poetry. Underline or highlight responses that demonstrate that the reader is reading actively.

Excerpt 1. Note how a reader uses active reading strategies while reading this excerpt from "Do not weep, maiden, for war is kind" by Stephen Crane.

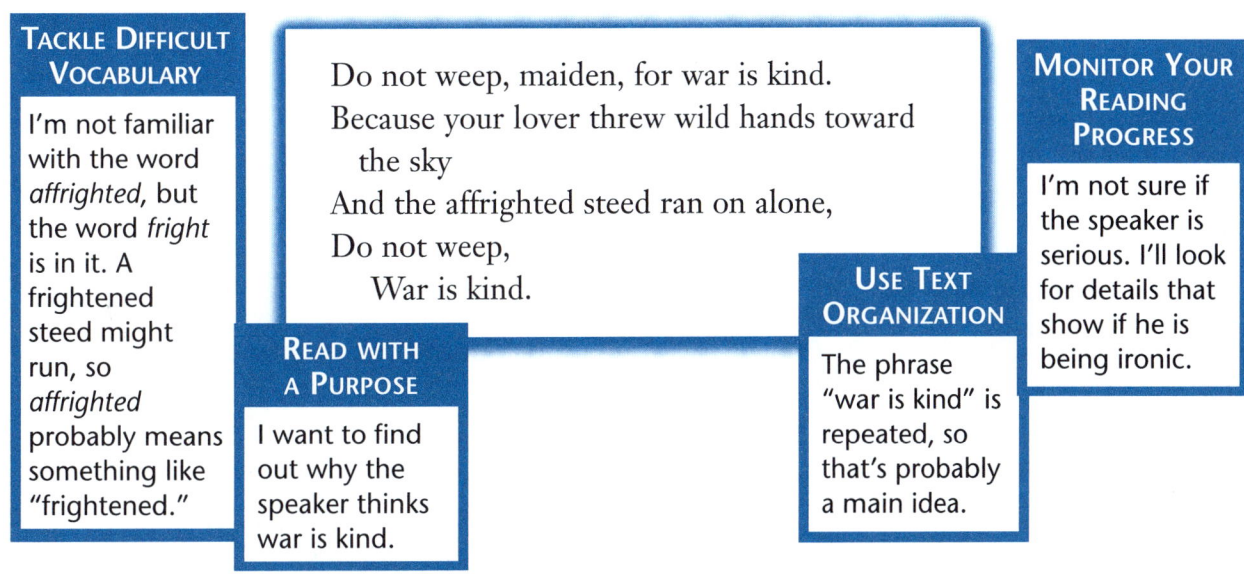

TACKLE DIFFICULT VOCABULARY
I'm not familiar with the word *affrighted*, but the word *fright* is in it. A frightened steed might run, so *affrighted* probably means something like "frightened."

> Do not weep, maiden, for war is kind.
> Because your lover threw wild hands toward
>   the sky
> And the affrighted steed ran on alone,
> Do not weep,
>   War is kind.

MONITOR YOUR READING PROGRESS
I'm not sure if the speaker is serious. I'll look for details that show if he is being ironic.

READ WITH A PURPOSE
I want to find out why the speaker thinks war is kind.

USE TEXT ORGANIZATION
The phrase "war is kind" is repeated, so that's probably a main idea.

Excerpt 2. Note how a reader uses active reading strategies while reading this excerpt from "The Village Blacksmith" by Henry Wadsworth Longfellow.

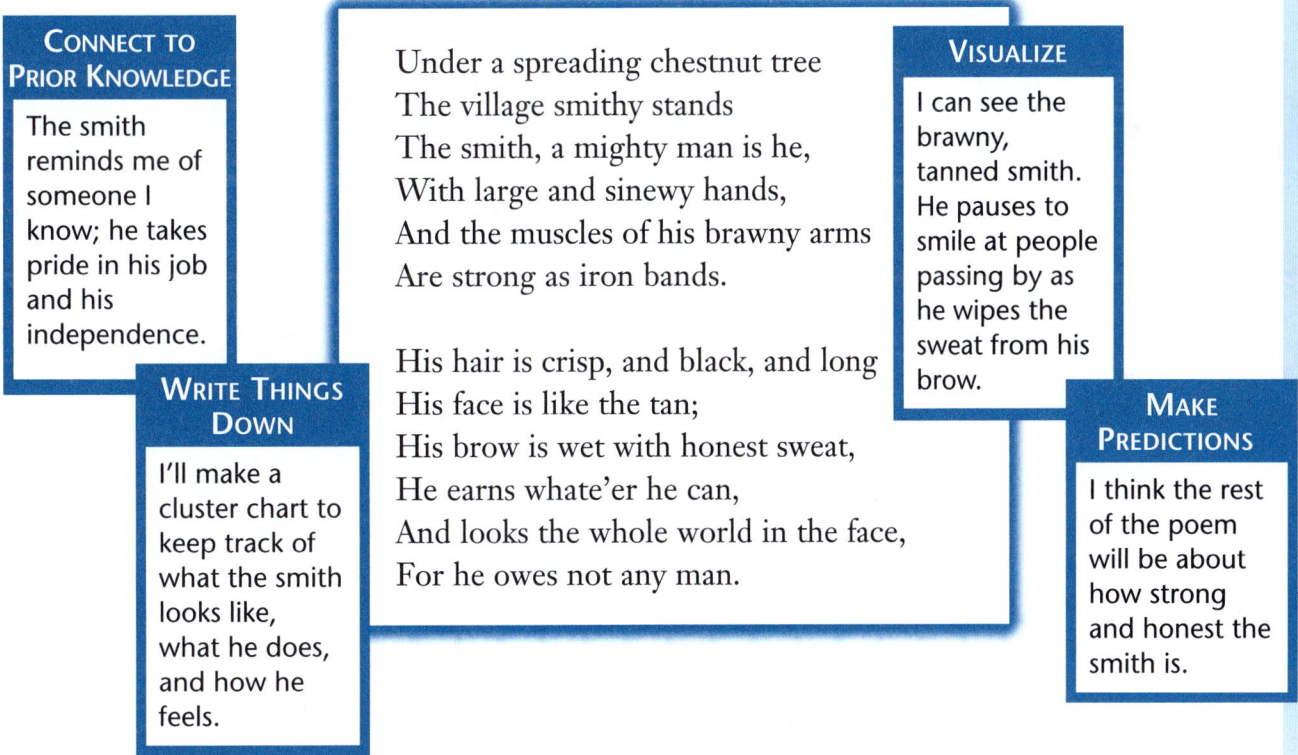

CONNECT TO PRIOR KNOWLEDGE
The smith reminds me of someone I know; he takes pride in his job and his independence.

> Under a spreading chestnut tree
> The village smithy stands
> The smith, a mighty man is he,
> With large and sinewy hands,
> And the muscles of his brawny arms
> Are strong as iron bands.
>
> His hair is crisp, and black, and long
> His face is like the tan;
> His brow is wet with honest sweat,
> He earns whate'er he can,
> And looks the whole world in the face,
> For he owes not any man.

VISUALIZE
I can see the brawny, tanned smith. He pauses to smile at people passing by as he wipes the sweat from his brow.

WRITE THINGS DOWN
I'll make a cluster chart to keep track of what the smith looks like, what he does, and how he feels.

MAKE PREDICTIONS
I think the rest of the poem will be about how strong and honest the smith is.

UNIT 4 / READING POETRY   **123**

CONNECT

Reader's resource

Anne Bradstreet had the advantage of an education, unusual for women of her time, and began writing poetry as a child. She married Simon Bradstreet when she was sixteen. A year later, Simon was appointed to assist in the preparations of the Massachusetts Bay Company, and they sailed to the New World. There she continued writing poetry. **"To My Dear and Loving Husband"** is a noble expression of the sustaining and transforming power of love. It appeared in the second edition of a volume of her poetry.

Word watch

PREVIEW VOCABULARY

manifold
persevere
recompense

Reader's journal

When you choose greeting cards, what sort of messages do you prefer? For whom might you buy a card and for what occasion?

_____
_____
_____

"To My Dear and Loving Husband"
by Anne Bradstreet

Active READING STRATEGY

TACKLE DIFFICULT VOCABULARY

Before Reading ➤ PREVIEW WORDS

❏ With a partner, preview the Words for Everyday Use at the bottom of the selection. Read each word, its definition, and the sentence in which it is used.
❏ Copy the words and their definitions into the Vocabulary Chart below. Skim the poem for other words you do not recognize.

Graphic Organizer: Vocabulary Chart

Word	Meaning	Sentence

To My Dear and Loving Husband

Anne Bradstreet

If ever two were one, then surely we.
If ever man were loved by wife, then thee;
If ever wife was happy in a man,
Compare with me, ye women, if you can.
I prize thy love more than whole mines of gold
Or all the riches that the East doth hold.
My love is such that rivers cannot quench,
Nor ought but love from thee, give recompense.
Thy love is such I can no way repay,
10   The heavens reward thee manifold, I pray.
Then while we live, in love let's so persevere
That when we live no more, we may live ever.

words for everyday use

rec • om • pense (rek´əm pens´) *n.*, reward; compensation, payment. *The only recompense the volunteers received was the thanks of the people they helped.*
man • i • fold (man´ə fōld´) *adv.*, in many forms or ways. *Their parents hoped that the marriage would increase the newlyweds' blessings manifold.*
per • se • vere (pʉr´sə vir´) *vi.*, continue in spite of difficulty; persist. *After the battle, the general shouted, "We must persevere! Onward, troops!"*

During Reading

UNLOCK MEANING

- Follow along as your teacher reads the first three lines aloud. Add any unfamiliar words to your Vocabulary Chart.
- Review the words you listed and try to determine their meanings by using context clues.
- Continue reading on your own. Try to define them by using context clues. If that strategy fails, consult a dictionary. Record the definitions in your Vocabulary Chart.

Literary TOOLS

HYPERBOLE. A **hyperbole** is an exaggeration made for rhetorical effect. As you read, look for hyperbole in this poem.

FIX-UP IDEA

Reread
If you have trouble applying the reading strategy, reread the poem, focusing first on the meaning of each line or sentence. Use context clues and, if necessary, a dictionary to find the meanings of any words that you do not understand. Once you understand the words, reread again, paying attention to the meaning of the poem as a whole.

Reflect ON YOUR READING

After Reading ➤ **PRACTICE USING NEW WORDS**

❑ Share your word list with your partner. Put a checkmark next to words that are archaic, or no longer in use.
❑ Work together to write sentences for all of the words that are checked.

Reading Skills and Test Practice

USE CONTEXT CLUES

Discuss with your partner how best to answer these questions involving context clues. Use the Think-Aloud Notes to write down your reasons for eliminating the incorrect answers.

THINK-ALOUD NOTES

_____ 1. Which word is the best synonym for *persevered?*

Bradstreet <u>persevered</u>, despite the difficulty of life in the New World, and even found time to write poetry.

a. struggled
b. withered
c. persisted
d. succumbed

_____ 2. Based on the following quotation, choose the best definition for *paradox.*

"That when we live no more, we may live ever " is an example of <u>paradox</u>.

a. an exaggeration made for effect
b. a common saying
c. a repetition of ideas
d. a seemingly contradictory statement

How did using the reading strategy help you to answer the questions?

_____
_____
_____
_____

Investigate, Inquire, and Imagine

RECALL: GATHER FACTS
1a. *Recompense* means "payment." What is the one thing that can be recompense for the speaker's love?

INTERPRET: FIND MEANING
1b. Restate line 10 in your own words.

ANALYZE: TAKE THINGS APART
2a. Is there any objective proof that Anne Bradstreet's husband reciprocates her love, or are all the statements subjective? Support your answer with examples from the poem.

SYNTHESIZE: BRING THINGS TOGETHER
2b. What does the speaker believe about the afterlife and about the consequences of being someone who perseveres in love despite its difficulties?

EVALUATE: MAKE JUDGMENTS
3a. In your own words, how would you describe the relationship between the speaker and her husband? Do you think the poem is an accurate or idealized picture of the relationship they have? Explain your response.

EXTEND: CONNECT IDEAS
3b. Describe a loving relationship of people you know. How is it similar to or different from the relationship described in the poem?

Literary Tools

HYPERBOLE. A **hyperbole** is an exaggeration made for rhetorical effect. What hyperbole can you find in this poem? What is the effect of this hyperbole?

_____
_____
_____

WordWorkshop

ARCHAIC LANGUAGE. "To My Dear and Loving Husband," which was written during the seventeenth century, uses several archaic words, or words no longer used, such as *thee, thy,* and *ye.* These pronouns are now rarely used. In addition, the poem uses *doth,* an archaic form of the verb *do.* These words illustrate how language changes over the course of time.

Different variations of words may develop as well. For example, the word *ought* in line 8 of the poem is a variation of the word *aught.* Several meanings of the word *aught,* including that intended in the poem, are still in current use, while the adverb form of the word, meaning "at all," and one of the definitions of the noun form are considered archaic. Archaic words that you encounter in your reading can be challenging, especially if the word has a contemporary meaning that is quite different. Approach archaic terms as you would any other. Use context clues, footnotes, or a glossary as applicable. If you cannot come to an understanding that makes sense, use a dictionary.

On your own paper, rewrite "To My Dear and Loving Husband," replacing any archaic language with contemporary language.

Read-Write Connection

What is special about the relationship that Anne Bradstreet describes? What enables people to develop this sort of relationship?

_____
_____
_____
_____
_____
_____
_____

Beyond the Reading

CREATE A GREETING CARD. Create a greeting card expressing love. It might be a card expressing romantic love or a card expressing love between family members or friends. Create a verse and image for the card. Consider sending the card to somebody you love when you are done.

GO ONLINE. To find links and additional activities for this selection, visit the EMC Internet Resource Center at **emcp.com/languagearts** and click on Write-In Reader.

"This is my letter to the World"
"Because I could not stop for Death—"
"I heard a Fly buzz—when I died—" by Emily Dickinson

Active READING STRATEGY

CONNECT TO PRIOR KNOWLEDGE

Before Reading ➤ THINK ABOUT WHAT YOU KNOW

- ❑ Respond to the Reader's Journal question. Think about how you view others, how others view you, and how you feel when your work or actions are judged.
- ❑ Discuss these ideas with a partner. Jot your ideas in the My Experience column of the Connections Chart below.

Graphic Organizer: Connections Chart

Speaker's Experience	My Experience

CONNECT

Reader's resource

Emily Dickinson lived a private life. She rarely ventured from her home and her close circle of family and friends. Her life was filled with observation and reflection, expressed in her poetry. **"This is my letter to the World"** deals with fears of being judged. **"Because I could not stop for Death—"** uses vivid imagery to explore death. **"I heard a Fly buzz—when I died—"** is an ironic look at the speaker's fears about the transition from this life to the afterlife.

Word watch

PREVIEW VOCABULARY

civility

Reader's journal

Write a letter to the world. What do you want people to know about you? How do you want them to treat you?

_____
_____
_____
_____

UNIT 4 / READING POETRY   **129**

During Reading

NOTE YOUR REACTIONS

- Listen as your teacher reads the first poem aloud.
- How does the speaker feel about being judged? Jot your ideas in your Connections Chart.
- Mark important points and vivid images as you read the other two poems on your own. Then note your reaction to each stanza in the chart.

NOTE THE FACTS

Where does the poet find her subject matter?

_____

_____

Literary TOOLS

METER. The **meter** of a poem is its rhythmical pattern. Look over the examples of stress patterns on page 119 in the introduction to this unit. Reread "This is my letter to the World," and mark the stressed and unstressed syllables.

This is my letter to the World

Emily Dickinson

This is my letter to the World
That never wrote to Me—
The simple News that Nature told—
With tender Majesty

Her Message is committed
To Hands I cannot see—
For love of Her—Sweet—countrymen—
Judge tenderly—of Me ■

130   THE EMC WRITE-IN READER

Because I could not stop for Death—

Emily Dickinson

Because I could not stop for Death—
He kindly stopped for me—
The Carriage held but just Ourselves—
And Immortality.

We slowly drove—He knew no haste
And I had put away
My labor and my leisure too,
For His Civility—

We passed the School, where Children strove
10   At recess—in the Ring—
We passed the Fields of Gazing Grain—
We passed the Setting Sun—

Or rather—He passed Us—
The Dews drew quivering and Chill—
For only Gossamer, my Gown—
My Tippet[1]—only Tulle[2]—

---

1. **Tippet.** Short cape worn over the shoulders
2. **Tulle.** Thin netting

words for everyday use

ci • vil • i • ty (sə vil´ə tē) n., gentleness; a civilized manner. *She longed for a world of civility in which gentleness, cooperation, and manners would be prized.*

Reading STRATEGY REVIEW

WRITE THINGS DOWN. Make notes to keep track of your ideas and reactions to the poem. Underline key ideas, circle vivid images, and write notes in the margin.

FIX-UP IDEA

Think Aloud
Work with a partner to read one stanza aloud. Then pause and do a think aloud about what you have read. Say which images stick out in your mind, what you think they might mean, what questions you have, and how certain words or images make you feel. Have your partner read the next stanza. Again, stop and think aloud. Do this until you have read the whole poem.

NOTE THE FACTS

What three things does the carriage pass?

_____

_____

_____

Reading TIP

An **extended metaphor** is a point-by-point presentation of one thing as though it were another. As you read, examine the metaphor the poet uses for death.

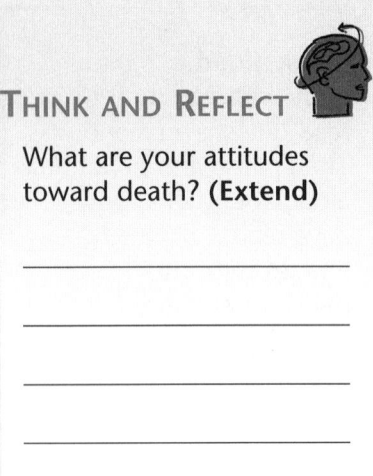

THINK AND REFLECT

What are your attitudes toward death? **(Extend)**

_____
_____
_____

> We paused before a House that seemed
> A Swelling of the Ground—
> The Roof was scarcely visible—
> The Cornice[3]—in the Ground
>
> 20 Since then—'tis Centuries—and yet
> Feels shorter than the Day
> I first surmised the Horses Heads
> Were toward Eternity— ∎

---
3. **Cornice.** Molded projection at the top of a building

I heard a Fly buzz—when I died—

Emily Dickinson

I heard a Fly buzz—when I died—
The Stillness in the Room
Was like the Stillness in the Air—
Between the Heaves of Storm—

The Eyes around—had wrung them dry—
and Breaths were gathering firm
For that last Onset—when the King
Be witnessed—in the Room

I willed my Keepsakes[1]—Signed away
What portion of me be
Assignable—and then it was
There interposed[2] a Fly—

With Blue—uncertain stumbling Buzz—
Between the light—and me—
And then the Windows failed—and then
I could not see to see— ■

---

1. **Keepsakes.** Personal items that are treasured
2. **interposed.** Appeared suddenly

Use the Strategy

CONNECT TO PRIOR KNOWLEDGE. Mark key ideas and vivid images. Note your reactions to different parts of the poem in your Connections chart.

Note the Facts

Who else is in the room besides the speaker?

_____

_____

Use the Strategy

CONNECT TO PRIOR KNOWLEDGE. When you are very sick, what senses are the strongest? How does your experience compare to the experience of the speaker in this poem? Write your answers in the Connections Chart.

Reflect ON YOUR READING

After Reading → **COMPARE YOUR IDEAS**

- With your partner, compare the ideas you wrote down in your Connections Chart and in the margins while you were reading.
- What images do you connect with death? What do you expect to happen when somebody dies? Discuss these questions with your classmates and compare your associations with the images in the poems.

Reading Skills and Test Practice

SYNTHESIZE AND DRAW CONCLUSIONS

READ, THINK, AND EXPLAIN. Describe Emily Dickinson's attitudes toward the world in this life and the afterlife. What things does she fear? Use information from the Reader's Resource and from the poems to support your response.

_____
_____
_____
_____
_____
_____
_____
_____

REFLECT ON YOUR RESPONSE. How did using the reading strategy help you to answer the questions?

_____
_____
_____
_____

THINK-ALOUD NOTES

Investigate, Inquire, and Imagine

RECALL: GATHER FACTS
1a. What does the speaker call the first poem?

➤ **INTERPRET: FIND MEANING**
1b. How does the speaker feel about having a reader for her poetry?

ANALYZE: TAKE THINGS APART
2a. What images does the poet use for death in "Because I could not stop for Death—" and "I heard a Fly buzz—when I died—"?

➤ **SYNTHESIZE: BRING THINGS TOGETHER**
2b. What attitudes toward death do these images convey?

EVALUATE: MAKE JUDGMENTS
3a. Which description of death seems more realistic? Why?

➤ **EXTEND: CONNECT IDEAS**
3b. Compare one of the poems about death to another story or poem you have read about death.

WordWorkshop

USING CONTEXT CLUES. Use context clues in the poems to find the meaning of each of the following words. Write down what you think the word means. Then use a dictionary to check your response. Finally, write a sentence for each word that contains a context clue to its meaning.

from "This is my letter to the World"

1. **majesty**
   I think this word means: _____
   Dictionary definition: _____
   Contextual sentence: _____
   _____

2. **committed**
   I think this word means: _____
   Dictionary definition: _____
   Contextual sentence: _____
   _____

from "Because I could not stop for Death—"

3. **immortality**
   I think this word means: _____
   Dictionary definition: _____
   Contextual sentence: _____
   _____

4. **surmised**
   I think this word means: _____
   Dictionary definition: _____
   Contextual sentence: _____
   _____

from "I head a Fly buzz—when I died—"

5. **assignable**
   I think this word means: _____
   Dictionary definition: _____
   Contextual sentence: _____
   _____

6. **interposed**
   I think this word means: _____
   Dictionary definition: _____
   Contextual sentence: _____
   _____

Literary Tools

METER. The **meter** of a poem is its rhythmical pattern. Review the stresses you marked in "This is my letter to the World." Go back and mark the stresses in the other two poems. If needed, refer to the examples of stress patterns on page 119 in the introduction to this unit.

Read-Write Connection

If you were the speaker of either poem about death, what would you fear most? What do you fear most about dying?

_____
_____
_____
_____

Beyond the Reading

RESEARCH WOMEN OF THE 1800S. With a few classmates, research and report on famous women of the 1800s. Some women to consider are Emily Dickinson, Nelly Bly, Amelia Bloomer, Elizabeth Cady Stanton, Margaret Fuller, Susan B. Anthony, Harriet Tubman, Sojourner Truth, and Florence Nightingale. Use the Internet and library resources to find information about the women you choose. Then prepare a report and visual display to share with your class.

GO ONLINE. To find links and additional activities for this selection, visit the EMC Internet Resource Center at **emcp.com/languagearts** and click on Write-In Reader.

"The Raven"

by Edgar Allan Poe

Active READING STRATEGY

TACKLE DIFFICULT VOCABULARY

Before Reading ➤ PREVIEW WORDS

- ❑ With a partner, preview the Words for Everyday Use at the bottom of the selection's pages. Read each word, its definition, and the sentence in which it is used. Then write your own sentence for each word.
- ❑ Choose a word, and have your partner use it in a sentence of his or her own. Then have your partner choose a word, and you use it in a sentence of your own. Continue taking turns until you have covered all of the words.
- ❑ Preview the Word Map below. As you read, you will use Word Maps to help you remember the meanings of new words.

Graphic Organizer: Word Map

A Challenging Word or Phrase

Definition

Word Parts I Recognize	Synonyms

A Sentence That Contains the Word or Phrase

A Picture That Illustrates the Word or Phrase

CONNECT

Reader's resource

Edgar Allan Poe is considered one of the creators of the modern short story. He also wrote detective fiction, psychological fiction, and lyric poetry. **"The Raven"** is one of Poe's lyric poems. It was his first international success and has been read and reread by critics, poets, and students all over the world.

Word watch

PREVIEW VOCABULARY

adjure	obeisance
beguile	ominous
censer	plume
craven	quaff
entreat	surcease
lattice	tempest
mien	undaunted

Reader's journal

Choose an animal. What might that animal say if it could talk?

_____
_____
_____
_____
_____

UNIT 4 / READING POETRY 137

During Reading

USE VOCABULARY STRATEGIES

❏ Follow along in your text as your teacher reads the first three stanzas aloud. As you read along, start a list of unfamiliar words.

❏ When your teacher has finished reading, review the words you listed and try to determine their meanings by using context clues.

❏ As you continue reading, add unfamiliar words to your list. Complete a Word Map for each word. First try using context clues. If the context clues do not provide the meaning, try analyzing word parts—prefixes, roots, and suffixes. If that strategy fails, consult a dictionary. After completing the Word Maps, reread the poem, using your new word knowledge.

NOTE THE FACTS

What is the cause of the speaker's sorrow?

_____
_____
_____

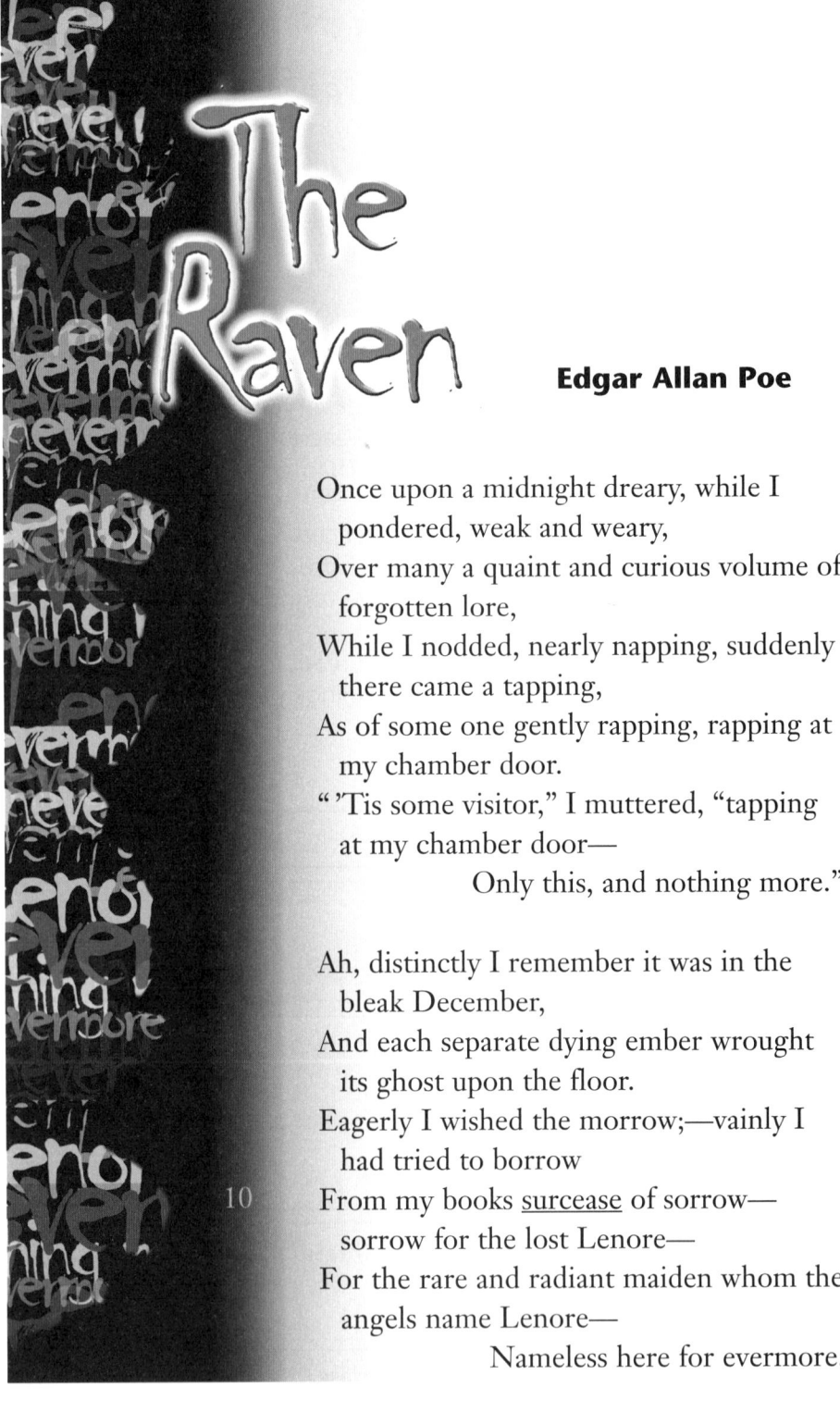

The Raven

Edgar Allan Poe

Once upon a midnight dreary, while I pondered, weak and weary,
Over many a quaint and curious volume of forgotten lore,
While I nodded, nearly napping, suddenly there came a tapping,
As of some one gently rapping, rapping at my chamber door.
" 'Tis some visitor," I muttered, "tapping at my chamber door—
      Only this, and nothing more."

Ah, distinctly I remember it was in the bleak December,
And each separate dying ember wrought its ghost upon the floor.
Eagerly I wished the morrow;—vainly I had tried to borrow
From my books <u>surcease</u> of sorrow— 10
sorrow for the lost Lenore—
For the rare and radiant maiden whom the angels name Lenore—
      Nameless here for evermore.

words for everyday use

sur • cease (sʉr sēsˊ) *n.,* respite; end. *The winning lottery ticket brought him <u>surcease</u> from his financial problems.*

And the silken sad uncertain rustling of each purple curtain
Thrilled me—filled me with fantastic terrors never felt before;
So that now, to still the beating of my heart, I stood repeating
"'Tis some visitor <u>entreating</u> entrance at my chamber door—
Some late visitor entreating entrance at my chamber door;—
          This it is, and nothing more."

Presently my soul grew stronger; hesitating then no longer,
"Sir," said I, "or Madam, truly your forgiveness I implore;
20   But the fact is I was napping, and so gently you came rapping,
And so faintly you came tapping, tapping at my chamber door,
That I scarce was sure I heard you"—here I opened wide the door,—
          Darkness there, and nothing more.

Deep into that darkness peering, long I stood there wondering, fearing,
Doubting dreaming dreams no mortal ever dared to dream before;
But the silence was unbroken, and the darkness gave no token,
And the only word there spoken was the whispered word, "Lenore!"
This *I* whispered, and an echo murmured back the word, "Lenore!"
          Merely this, and nothing more.

30

Then into the chamber turning, all my soul within me burning,
Soon I heard again a tapping somewhat louder than before.
"Surely," said I, "surely that is something at my window <u>lattice</u>;

---

words for everyday use

en • treat (en trēt´) *vt.*, beg; implore; ask earnestly. *The employee <u>entreated</u> his boss for another chance.*

lat • tice (lat´is) *n.*, shutter; openwork structure used as a screen. *In the garden there was a lovely <u>lattice</u> of crossed wood strips.*

Literary TOOLS

RHYME. Rhyme is the repetition of sounds at the ends of words. Patterns of rhyming words that appear at the ends of lines are called *end rhymes*. *Internal rhymes* are rhymes within a line of poetry. As you read, circle rhyming words in the poem.

THINK AND REFLECT

What does the speaker hope to see or hear when he opens the door? (Infer)

_____
_____
_____

READ ALOUD

Try reading the poem aloud to help you hear the rhyme and repetition.

Let me see, then, what thereat is, and this mystery explore—
Let my heart be still a moment and this mystery explore;—
'Tis the wind, and nothing more!"

Open here I flung the shutter, when, with many a flirt and flutter,
In there stepped a stately raven of the saintly days of yore;
Not the least obeisance made he; not an instant stopped or stayed he;
But, with mien of lord or lady, perched above my chamber door—
40 Perched upon a bust of Pallas¹ just above my chamber door—
Perched, and sat, and nothing more.

Then this ebony bird beguiling my sad fancy into smiling,
By the grave and stern decorum of the countenance it wore,
"Though thy crest be shorn and shaven, thou," I said, "art sure no craven,
Ghastly grim and ancient raven wandering from the Nightly shore—
Tell me what thy lordly name is on the Night's Plutonian² shore!"
Quoth the raven, "Nevermore."

Much I marvelled this ungainly fowl to hear discourse so plainly,
Though its answer little meaning—little relevancy bore;
50 For we cannot help agreeing that no sublunary³ being
Ever yet was blessed with seeing bird above his chamber door—

---

1. **Pallas.** Greek goddess of wisdom
2. **Plutonian.** Black; relating to the underworld
3. **sublunary.** Earthly

> **words for everyday use**
>
> o • bei • sance (ō bā´səns) *n.*, gesture of respect. *The servant made a slight bow of obeisance to his master.*
>
> mien (mēn) *n.*, manner; appearance. *The attending royalty gave an aristocratic mien to the affair.*
>
> cra • ven (krā´vən) *n.*, coward. *His failure to try to stop the thief made him appear to be a craven.*

MARK THE TEXT

Highlight or underline what enters through the window.

NOTE THE FACTS

What does the speaker think of the raven's response?

_____
_____

Bird or beast upon the sculptured bust above his chamber door,

      With such name as "Nevermore."

But the raven, sitting lonely on the placid bust, spoke only
That one word, as if his soul in that one word he did outpour.
Nothing farther then he uttered—not a feather then he fluttered—
Till I scarcely more than muttered, "Other friends have flown before—
On the morrow *he* will leave me, as my hopes have flown before."

      Quoth the raven, "Nevermore."

Wondering at the stillness broken by reply so aptly spoken,
"Doubtless," said I, "what it utters is its only stock and store,
Caught from some unhappy master whom unmerciful Disaster
Followed fast and followed faster—so, when Hope he would <u>adjure</u>,
Stern Despair returned, instead of the sweet Hope he dared adjure—

      That sad answer, "Nevermore!"

But the raven still <u>beguiling</u> all my sad soul into smiling,
Straight I wheeled a cushioned seat in front of bird, and bust, and door;
Then upon the velvet sinking, I betook myself to linking
Fancy unto fancy thinking what this <u>ominous</u> bird of yore—

What this grim, ungainly, ghastly, gaunt, and ominous bird of yore

      Meant in croaking "Nevermore."

FIX-UP IDEA

Visualize
Listen to somebody read the poem. As you listen, create a mind movie. Use visual images and sounds in your mind movie. When you are done, draw pictures and add commentary to show what you pictured in your mind movie.

MARK THE TEXT
Highlight or underline the only word the raven ever says.

---

words for everyday use

ad • jure (ə jer´) *vt.*, urge; beg. *I <u>adjure</u> you not to walk home alone after dark.*
be • guile (bē gīl´) *vt.*, charm; lead by deception. *The salesperson <u>beguiled</u> customers into buying useless items.*
om • i • nous (äm´ə nəs) *adj.*, forewarning evil. *The dark cloud was <u>ominous</u> of the storm on the horizon.*

This I sat engaged in guessing, but no syllable expressing
To the fowl whose fiery eyes now burned into my bosom's core;
This and more I sat divining, with my head at ease reclining
On the cushion's velvet lining that the lamplight gloated o'er,
But whose velvet violet lining with the lamplight gloating o'er,
        She shall press, ah, nevermore!

Then, methought, the air grew denser, perfumed from an unseen censer
Swung by angels whose faint foot-falls tinkled on the tufted floor.
"Wretch," I cried, "thy God hath lent thee—by these angels he hath sent thee
Respite—respite and Nepenthe[4] from thy memories of Lenore!
Let me quaff this kind Nepenthe and forget this lost Lenore!"
        Quoth the raven, "Nevermore."

"Prophet!" said I, "thing of evil!—prophet still, if bird or devil!—
Whether Tempter sent, or whether tempest tossed thee here ashore,
Desolate, yet all undaunted, on this desert land enchanted—
On this home by Horror haunted—tell me truly, I implore—
Is there—*is* there balm in Gilead?[5]—tell me—tell me, I implore!"
        Quoth the raven, "Nevermore."

---

4. **Nepenthe.** Potion used to induce forgetfulness of pain or sorrow
5. **balm in Gilead.** Gilead is a mountainous area in the Middle East where evergreens provide medicinal resins. The question echoes Jeremiah 8:22, "Is there no balm in Gilead?"

THINK AND REFLECT
Of whom is the speaker thinking? (Infer)

Reading STRATEGY REVIEW

WRITE THINGS DOWN. As you read, make notes about the speaker's emotions in the margins next to each stanza.

words for everyday use

cen • ser (sen´sər) *n.*, container for burning incense. *The monks chanted and swung the censer, causing fragrant incense to rise toward the heavens.*

quaff (kwäf) *vi.*, drink deeply. *In his great thirst he quaffed the glass of water entirely.*

tem • pest (tem´pəst) *n.*, violent storm. *The boat was lost at sea in the severe tempest.*

un • daunt • ed (ən dônt´əd) *adj.*, resolute in the face of danger. *The brave man's courage was undaunted.*

"Prophet!" said I, "thing of evil!—prophet still, if bird or devil!
By that Heaven that bends above us—by that God we both adore—
Tell this soul with sorrow laden if, within the distant Aidenn,[6]
It shall clasp a sainted maiden whom the angels name Lenore—
Clasp a rare and radiant maiden whom the angels name Lenore."
      Quoth the raven, "Nevermore."

"Be that word our sign of parting, bird or fiend!" I shrieked, upstarting—
Get thee back into the tempest and the Night's Plutonian shore!
Leave no black <u>plume</u> as a token of that lie thy soul hath spoken!
Leave my loneliness unbroken—quit the bust above my door!
100 Take thy beak from out my heart, and take thy form from off my door!"
      Quoth the raven, "Nevermore."

And the raven, never flitting, still is sitting, still is sitting
On the pallid bust of Pallas just above my chamber door;
And his eyes have all the seeming of a demon that is dreaming,
And the lamp-light o'er him streaming throws his shadow on the floor;
And my soul from out that shadow that lies floating on the floor
      Shall be lifted—nevermore! ■

---

6. **Aidenn.** Name created by Poe to suggest Eden

THINK AND REFLECT

How has the speaker's attitude toward the raven's answer changed? (Compare)

NOTE THE FACTS

What does the speaker want the raven to do? How does the raven respond?

words for everyday use

plume (plüm) *n.*, feather. *The peacock is known for its beautiful tail <u>plumes</u>.*

Reflect ON YOUR READING

After Reading → **PRACTICE USING NEW WORDS**

- Share your list of words with your partner from the Before Reading activity. Work together to complete your Word Maps and to reread the poem.
- Then write two additional sentences of your own for each of the listed words. Make sure your sentences show that you understand the definitions of the words.

Reading Skills and Test Practice

USE CONTEXT CLUES

Discuss with your partner how best to answer these questions about word meanings. Use the Think-Aloud Notes to write down your reasons for eliminating the incorrect answers.

____ 1. Read these lines from the poem.

> Once upon a midnight dreary, while I pondered, weak and weary,
> Over many a quaint and curious volume of forgotten lore

What does the word *pondered* mean?

a. slept
b. yawned
c. thought
d. worried

____ 2. Which of the following words would be the best synonym for the word *gaunt* as used in the line "this grim, ungainly, ghastly, gaunt, and ominous bird of yore"?

a. glorious
b. skeletal
c. heavenly
d. giant

How did using the reading strategy help you to answer the questions?

_____
_____
_____
_____

THINK-ALOUD NOTES

Investigate, Inquire, and Imagine

RECALL: GATHER FACTS
1a. What is the raven's single-word answer to every question?

INTERPRET: FIND MEANING
1b. Describe the raven. How is it different from normal birds?

ANALYZE: TAKE THINGS APART
2a. What are the stages of the speaker's developing anger?

SYNTHESIZE: BRING THINGS TOGETHER
2b. What does the speaker's anger have to do with the lost Lenore?

EVALUATE: MAKE JUDGMENTS
3a. Other birds, such as the parrot, also can be trained to speak. Evaluate whether Poe's choice of the raven achieves his desired effect in this poem.

EXTEND: CONNECT IDEAS
3b. What other animal could Poe have chosen? How would a different animal have changed the poem?

Literary Tools

RHYME. **Rhyme** is the repetition of sounds at the ends of words. Patterns of rhyming words that appear at the ends of lines are called *end rhymes*. *Internal rhymes* are rhymes within a line of poetry. The pattern of end rhymes in a poem is called its *rhyme scheme.* Identify six examples of internal rhyme in the poem.

_____

_____

_____

_____

_____

WordWorkshop

CONTEXT CLUES. Context clues may use comparison or contrast. Comparison clues may use words such as *like* or *as* or forms of the verb *to be*. Contrast clues may use words such as *but, yet, however, not*, or *although*. Each of the following sentences below contains a context clue for one of the vocabulary words for "The Raven." Write the correct word in the blank for each sentence. You may need to change the tense of some verbs.

1. Peacock feathers are the most highly prized _____.

2. The meteorologist predicted a calm day for sailing, but we found ourselves in an unexpected _____.

3. Some people think that breaking a mirror is a(n) _____ sign because they believe it brings seven years of bad luck.

4. Rona _____ Jan to help her with the project, but despite her begging, he refused.

5. A storm was pending and we were out of supplies, but Tyrone was _____ in his quest to reach the summit.

6. Many advertisements feature _____ promises that are too good to be true.

7. Julio's _____ was quite charming, while Roberto's manner was shockingly rude.

8. Tonya was still thirsty after finishing her lemonade, so she _____ the rest of the iced tea as well.

9. The Cowardly Lion is a famous _____.

10. The vacation brought Nina respite from her troubles and _____ of her worries.

Read-Write Connection

How does the appearance of the raven affect the speaker's mood? Do you think that the raven is real? Why, or why not?

_____
_____
_____
_____
_____

Beyond the Reading

RESEARCH RAVENS. Research the following questions about ravens: What do ravens look like? What do ravens sound like? What do they eat? How are ravens described in literature? After you answer these questions, discuss why Poe may have chosen a raven for the poem.

GO ONLINE. To find links and additional activities for this selection, visit the EMC Internet Resource Center at **emcp.com/languagearts** and click on Write-In Reader.

from "Song of Myself"

by Walt Whitman

Active READING STRATEGY

READ WITH A PURPOSE

Before Reading ➤ START A SYMBOL CHART

- A **symbol** is a thing that represents both itself and something else. A conventional symbol is one with widely recognized associations. An idiosyncratic symbol is one that assumes secondary meaning because of the way it is used by the writer.
- Brainstorm things that grass could represent. Read the Reader's Resource carefully to help you understand what Whitman was trying to do. This may help you interpret his symbols.
- Preview the Symbol Chart that follows. One example has been provided.

Graphic Organizer: Symbol Chart

Quotation	What the Grass Symbolizes
"I lean and loafe at my ease observing a spear of summer grass."	summer, relaxation

CONNECT

Reader's resource

"Song of Myself" is Walt Whitman's effort to describe his personality. This selection from "Song of Myself" exemplifies all the themes for which Whitman is best known: his belief that insignificant, lowly subjects are in fact worthy of poetry; his democratic celebration of the common people; and his love of natural and animal pleasures. All of these themes are summed up in the grass. Grass is the central symbol in *The Leaves of Grass*, the collection that contains "Song of Myself."

Word watch

PREVIEW VOCABULARY

abeyance	impalpable
barbaric	infidel
contender	jag
creed	linguist
disposition	loitering
fissure	quadruped
harbor	suffice

Reader's journal

What insignificant, lowly, or common thing do you value that many others do not?

_____
_____
_____

UNIT 4 / READING POETRY 147

During Reading

FILL IN SYMBOL CHART AS YOU READ

- Listen as your teacher reads the first four stanzas of the poem. Find any references to grass and add them to your chart. What do you think grass symbolizes here? Write your explanation in your Symbol Chart.
- Continue reading the selection on your own. Keep adding references to grass and the meanings of these references to your chart.

NOTE THE FACTS

What does the speaker celebrate? In what way is the speaker connected to the reader?

_____

_____

FROM

Song of Myself

Walt Whitman

1

I celebrate myself, and sing myself,
And what I assume you shall assume,
For every atom belonging to me as good
  belongs to you.

I loafe and invite my soul,
I lean and loafe at my ease observing a spear
  of summer grass.

My tongue, every atom of my blood, form'd
  from this soil, this air,
Born here of parents born here from parents
  the same, and their parents the same,
I, now thirty-seven years old in perfect health
  begin,
Hoping to cease not till death.

10 <u>Creeds</u> and schools in <u>abeyance</u>,
Retiring back a while <u>sufficed</u> at what they
  are, but never forgotten,

---

words for everyday use

creed (krēd) *n.*, statement of belief, principles, or opinions on any subject. *The <u>creed</u> of the organization centered around helping those in need.*

a · bey · ance (ə bā´əns) *n.*, temporary suspension, as of an activity or function. *Work on the highway was put in <u>abeyance</u> until the city could raise funds to finish building it.*

suf · fice (sə fīs´) *vt.*, be enough; be sufficient or adequate. *For the tip, Kim was sure five dollars would <u>suffice</u>.*

I <u>harbor</u> for good or bad, I permit to speak at every hazard,
Nature without check with original energy.
Looks down, is erect, or bends an arm on an <u>impalpable</u> certain rest,
Looking with side-curved head curious what will come next,
Both in and out of the game and watching and wondering at it.

Backward I see in my own days where I sweated through fog with <u>linguists</u> and <u>contenders</u>,
I have no mockings or arguments, I witness and wait.

6

A child said *What is the grass?* fetching it to me with full hands;
20 How could I answer the child? I do not know what it is any more than he.

I guess it must be the flag of my <u>disposition</u>, out of hopeful green stuff woven.

Or I guess it is the handkerchief of the Lord,
A scented gift and remembrancer designedly dropt,
Bearing the owner's name someway in the corners, that we may see and remark, and say *Whose?*

Reading TIP

Walt Whitman is part of the Romantic tradition. Many of his ideals, such as his belief that lowly subjects are worthy of poetry and his love of nature, are key elements of this tradition. Romantics saw the child as the model of the human capacity to experience objects without preconceptions. They try to recapture the innocence of childhood. Notice the role of the child in lines 18–21.

NOTE THE FACTS

What question does the child ask? What is the speaker's first response?

_____
_____

words for everyday use

har • bor (här´bər) *vt.*, serve as, or provide, a place of protection. *He refused to <u>harbor</u> the runaway criminal.*
im • pal • pa • ble (im pal´pə bəl) *adj.*, that which cannot be felt by touching. *She could not explain the <u>impalpable</u> emotion that filled her when she looked at the painting.*
lin • guist (liŋ´gwist) *n.*, specialist in the science of language. *The <u>linguist</u> wrote a book about the origins of Indo-European languages.*
con • tend • er (kən ten´dər) *n.*, one who strives or fights in competition. *The boxer had been a <u>contender</u> for the heavyweight title.*
dis • po • si • tion (dis´pə zi´shən) *n.*, one's customary frame of mind. *Josh's grandmother always says he has a sunny <u>disposition</u>.*

Literary TOOLS

ELABORATION. Elaboration is a writing technique in which a subject is introduced and then expanded upon by means of repetition with slight changes, the addition of details, or similar devices. Underline or highlight examples of elaboration in section 6.

READ ALOUD

Read the highlighted lines aloud. Notice the repetition in these lines. What things does the speaker say may be?

_____
_____
_____

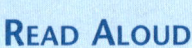

READ WITH A PURPOSE. The speaker tries to explain what the grass is. Look through section 6 and add some quotes and possible meanings to your Symbol Chart.

Or I guess the grass is itself a child, the produced babe of the vegetation.

Or I guess it is a uniform hieroglyphic,[1]
And it means, Sprouting alike in broad zones and narrow zones,
Growing among black folks as among white,
Kanuck, Tuckahoe, Congressman, Cuff,[2] I give them the same, I receive them the same.

30   And now it seems to me the beautiful uncut hair of graves.

Tenderly will I use you curling grass,
It may be you transpire from the breasts of young men,
It may be if I had known them I would have loved them,
It may be you are from old people, or from offspring taken soon out of their mothers' laps,
And here you are the mothers' laps.

This grass is very dark to be from the white heads of old mothers,
Darker than the colorless beards of old men,
Dark to come from under the faint red roofs of mouths.

O I perceive after all so many uttering tongues,
40   And I perceive they do not come from the roofs of mouths for nothing.

I wish I could translate the hints about the dead young men and women,
And the hints about old men and mothers, and the offspring taken soon out of their laps.

What do you think has become of the young and old men?
And what do you think has become of the women and children?

---

1. **hieroglyphic.** Picture or symbol representing a word, syllable, or sound, used by the ancient Egyptians and others instead of alphabetical letters
2. **Kanuck, Tuckahoe, Congressman, Cuff.** *Kanuck*—French Canadian; *Tuckahoe*—Virginian; *Cuff*—from the African word *cuffee*, refers to African Americans

They are alive and well somewhere,
The smallest sprout shows there is really no death,
And if ever there was it led forward life, and does not wait at the end to arrest it,
And ceas'd the moment life appear'd.

All goes onward and outward, nothing collapses,
50 And to die is different from what any one supposed, and luckier.

◆ ◆ ◆

7

Has any one supposed it lucky to be born?
I hasten to inform him or her it is just as lucky to die, and I know it.

I pass death with the dying and birth with the new-wash'd babe, and am not contain'd between my hat and boots,

And peruse manifold objects, no two alike and every one good,
The earth good and the stars good, and their adjuncts all good.

I am not an earth nor an adjunct of an earth,
I am the mate and companion of people, all just as immortal and fathomless as myself,
(They do not know how immortal, but I know.)

Every kind for itself and its own, for me mine male and female,
For me those that have been boys and that love women,
60 For me the man that is proud and feels how it stings to be slighted,
For me the sweet-heart and the old maid, for me mothers and the mothers of mothers,
For me lips that have smiled, eyes that have shed tears,
For me children and the begetters of children.

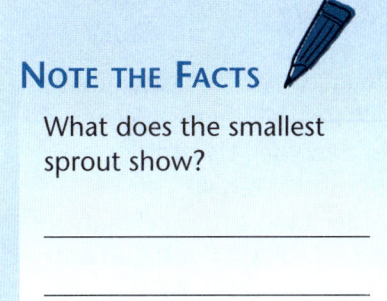

NOTE THE FACTS

What does the smallest sprout show?

_____
_____

FIX-UP IDEA

Identify Difficulties
If you have trouble understanding certain passages in the selection, note the line numbers or mark the section with a sticky note. Then write a specific question about the passage. Try applying a different reading technique, such as using the margin questions or unlocking difficult vocabulary. Then, if you still have questions, try talking with one or more of your classmates.

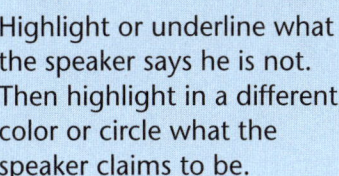

MARK THE TEXT

Highlight or underline what the speaker says he is not. Then highlight in a different color or circle what the speaker claims to be.

Reading Strategy Review

TACKLE DIFFICULT VOCABULARY. Use the definitions of Words for Everyday Use and footnotes to help you understand the vocabulary in the selection. If you find other words you do not know, try using context clues or word parts to find the meanings of the words.

Undrape! you are not guilty to me, nor stale nor discarded,
I see through the broadcloth and gingham[3] whether or no,
And am around, tenacious, acquisitive, tireless, and cannot be shaken away.

◆ ◆ ◆

31

THINK AND REFLECT

Review lines 68–74. Think about the kinds of things the speaker seems to admire. List two other things you think the speaker would respect. (Extend)

_____

_____

I believe a leaf of grass is no less than the journey-work of the stars,
And the pismire[4] is equally perfect, and a grain of sand, and the egg of the wren,
And the tree-toad is a chief-d'oeuvre[5] for the highest,
70　And the running blackberry would adorn the parlors of heaven,
And the narrowest hinge in my hand puts to scorn all machinery,
And the cow crunching with depress'd head surpasses any statue,
And a mouse is miracle enough to stagger sextillions[6] of <u>infidels</u>.

I find I incorporate gneiss,[7] coal, long-threaded moss, fruits, grains, esculent[8] roots,
And am stucco'd with <u>quadrupeds</u> and birds all over,
And have distanced what is behind me for good reasons,
But call any thing back again when I desire it.

---

3. **broadcloth and gingham.** *Broadcloth*—fine wool, cotton, or silk; *gingham*—cotton cloth that is woven in checks or plaids
4. **pismire.** Ant
5. **chief-d'oeuvre.** Master or culminating work
6. **sextillions.** Number represented by one followed by twenty-one zeros
7. **gneiss.** Metamorphic rock with minerals arranged in layers
8. **esculent.** Edible

words for everyday use

in • fi • del (in′fə del′) *n.*, person who does not believe in a particular religion. *The crusaders set off to convert the <u>infidels</u> to Christianity.*

quad • ru • ped (kwä′drü ped′) *n.*, animal, especially a mammal, with four feet. *In science class we studied <u>quadrupeds</u> and bipeds.*

In vain the speeding or shyness,
In vain the plutonic rocks[9] send their old heat against my
    approach,
In vain the mastodon retreats beneath its own powder'd
    bones,
In vain objects stand leagues off and assume manifold shapes,
In vain the ocean settling in hollows and the great monsters
    lying low,
In vain the buzzard houses herself with the sky,
In vain the snake slides through the creepers and logs,
In vain the elk takes to the inner passes of the woods,
In vain the razor-bill'd auk[10] sails far north to Labrador,[11]
I follow quickly, I ascend to the nest in the <u>fissure</u> of the cliff.

♦ ♦ ♦

32

I think I could turn and live with animals, they are so placid
    and self-contain'd,
I stand and look at them long and long.

They do not sweat and whine about their condition,
They do not lie awake in the dark and weep for their sins,
They do not make me sick discussing their duty to God,
Not one is dissatisfied, not one is demented with the mania
    of owning things,
Not one kneels to another, nor to his kind that lived
    thousands of years ago,
Not one is respectable or unhappy over the whole earth.

♦ ♦ ♦

---

9. **plutonic rocks.** Rocks formed far below the surface of the earth
10. **auk.** Shore bird of northern seas with a heavy body, a short tail, and short wings used as paddles
11. **Labrador.** Region along the Atlantic coast of northeastern Canada

words for everyday use

fis • sure (fish´ər) *n.*, long, narrow, deep cleft or crack. *A <u>fissure</u> appeared in the building's foundation after the earthquake.*

> **Reading TIP**
>
> This poem contains may lists. As you read the lists, make sure you know what the speaker is listing. The speaker may state directly or imply the purpose of the list at the beginning or the end of the list.

> **NOTE THE FACTS**
>
> Why would the speaker like to live with animals?

52

The spotted hawk swoops by and accuses me, he complains
   of my gab and my <u>loitering</u>.

I too am not a bit tamed, I too am untranslatable,
I sound my <u>barbaric</u> yawp[12] over the roofs of the world.

The last scud of day holds back for me,
100 It flings my likeness after the rest and true as any on the
        shadow'd wilds,
It coaxes me to the vapor and the dusk.

I depart as air, I shake my white locks at the runaway sun,
I effuse my flesh in eddies, and drift it in lacy <u>jags</u>.

I bequeath myself to the dirt to grow from the grass I love,
If you want me again look for me under your boot-soles.

You will hardly know who I am or what I mean,
But I shall be good health to you nevertheless,
And filter and fibre your blood.

110 Failing to fetch me at first keep encouraged,
Missing me one place search another,
I stop somewhere waiting for you. ■

---
12. **yawp.** Loud, harsh cry or call

NOTE THE FACTS

Where should you look to find the speaker? What will the speaker do for people?

_____

_____

NOTE THE FACTS

Why will the speaker stop?

_____

_____

words for everyday use

loi • ter • ing (loi′tər iŋ) *n.,* lingering in an aimless way. *The convenience store frowns on <u>loitering</u>.*
bar • bar • ic (bär bar′ik) *adj.,* wild, crude, and unrestrained. *Their <u>barbaric</u> treatment of prisoners was chronicled after the war.*
jag (jag) *n.,* sharp, toothlike projection. *The <u>jags</u> on the saw were sharp enough to cut through metal.*

Reflect ON YOUR READING

After Reading → **SUMMARIZE**

- ❑ Share your Symbol Chart with a few of your classmates.
- ❑ Discuss the following questions: How does Whitman answer the question "What is the grass?" Why does he want to treat the grass tenderly? Why is grass the great equalizer?
- ❑ Summarize why Whitman used grass as a recurring symbol.

_____
_____
_____
_____

Reading Skills and Test Practice

COMPARE AND CONTRAST SYMBOLS

Discuss with your partner how best to answer these questions that require you to compare and contrast. Use the Think-Aloud Notes to write down your reasons for eliminating the incorrect answers.

____1. In lines 68–69, what similarity does Whitman see between the grass, the pismire, and the grain of sand?
   a. They are all small and go unnoticed by the speaker.
   b. They are all simple and perfect.
   c. They are all lowly and unimportant.
   d. They are all minor creations of nature.

____2. What contrasting symbolic meanings for grass are found in lines 30 and 105?
   a. innocence and corruption
   b. death and regeneration after death
   c. satisfaction and discontentment
   d. curiosity and love

How did using the reading strategy help you to answer the questions?

_____
_____
_____
_____

THINK-ALOUD NOTES

Investigate, Inquire, and Imagine

RECALL: GATHER FACTS
1a. What are the common and insignificant things Whitman describes in section 31? What is each thing compared to?

INTERPRET: FIND MEANING
1b. What do Whitman's comparisons indicate about his feelings for commonplace things?

ANALYZE: TAKE THINGS APART
2a. A *catalog* is a list of people or things. Identify what Whitman catalogs in this poem.

SYNTHESIZE: BRING THINGS TOGETHER
2b. Why does Whitman catalog these things?

EVALUATE: MAKE JUDGMENTS
3a. Review sections 6 and 7. Do you agree with Whitman that death is a force that unites people with both nature and other human beings? Why?

EXTEND: CONNECT IDEAS
3b. How do Whitman's ideas compare to other ideas about death in this unit?

WordWorkshop

CATEGORIZE AND USE NEW WORDS. Examine the Words for Everyday Use from "Song of Myself." Classify each word into at least one of the following categories.

People	Things	Describes a Thing	Actions

Then write a sentence using each of the following pairs of words.

1. infidel, creed

2. fissure, jag

3. barbaric, disposition

Literary Tools

ELABORATION. **Elaboration** is a writing technique in which a subject is introduced and then expanded upon by means of repetition with slight changes, the addition of details, or similar devices. What does Whitman elaborate on in section 32? What is the purpose of the elaboration?

_____
_____
_____
_____

Read-Write Connection

Whitman says that he could "turn and live with animals." What do you think are the advantages and disadvantages to this proposition?

_____
_____
_____
_____
_____
_____

Beyond the Reading

WRITE A SONG OF YOURSELF. Whitman's aim in writing "Song of Myself" was to express, as he put it, "one man's—the author's—identity, ardors, observations, faiths, and thoughts." Do some freewriting about yourself. What things are most important to you? What qualities do you possess? What beliefs are most central to your life? Then write your own "Song of Myself."

GO ONLINE. To find links and additional activities for this selection, visit the EMC Internet Resource Center at **emcp.com/languagearts** and click on Write-In Reader.

CONNECT

Reader's resource

Many of Robert Frost's poems are set in or include the imagery of New England, the area he called home for most of his life. Frost uses careful local observations and simple details that often have deeper symbolic meanings. In "Mending Wall," Frost uses the activity of mending a wall in the spring to explore relationships. Like many of Frost's poems, "Mending Wall" uses **blank verse**, or unrhymed iambic pentameter. A line of iambic pentameter has ten alternating weakly stressed and strongly stressed syllables.

Reading TIP

Robert Frost often uses **inversions**, or sentences in which the usual sentence order is switched. "Something there is that doesn't love a wall" is an inversion. The usual order of the sentence would be "There is something that doesn't love a wall."

Reader's journal

Why do you think people build walls between themselves and others?

_____
_____
_____

by Robert Frost

Active READING STRATEGY

WRITE THINGS DOWN

Before Reading → COMPARE AND CONTRAST

❑ Write a response to the Reader's Journal question.
❑ Discuss your response with a partner. In your discussion, compare and contrast the positive and negative effects such walls can have.

Graphic Organizer: Cluster Chart

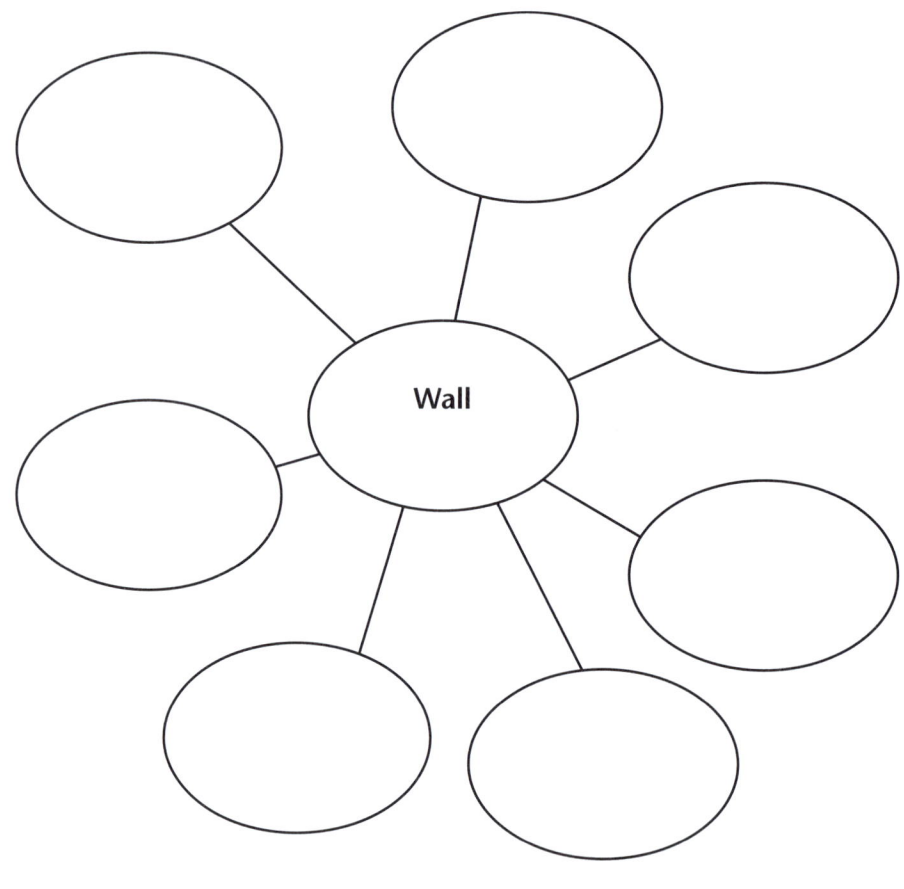

158   THE EMC WRITE-IN READER

MENDING WALL

Robert Frost

Something there is that doesn't love a wall,
That sends the frozen-ground-swell[1] under it,
And spills the upper boulders in the sun,
And makes gaps even two can pass abreast.
The work of hunters is another thing:
I have come after them and made repair
Where they have left not one stone on a stone,
But they would have the rabbit out of hiding,
To please the yelping dogs. The gaps I mean,
10   No one has seen them made or heard them made,
But spring mending-time we find them there.
I let my neighbor know beyond the hill;
And on a day we meet to walk the line
And set the wall between us once again.
We keep the wall between us as we go.
To each the boulders that have fallen to each.
And some are loaves and some so nearly balls
We have to use a spell to make them balance:
"Stay where you are until our backs are turned!"
20   We wear our fingers rough with handling them.
Oh, just another kind of outdoor game.
One on a side. It comes to little more;

---

1. **frozen-ground-swell.** Expansion of frozen ground

Literary TOOLS

CHARACTER AND CHARACTERIZATION. A **character** is a figure who participates in the action of a literary work. **Characterization** is the use of literary techniques to create a character. As you read, look for details about the appearance, actions, and attitudes of the speaker's neighbor.

Reading STRATEGY REVIEW

WRITE THINGS DOWN. Underline or highlight details about the speaker's neighbor. Write notes in the margin about your thoughts and reactions to him.

FIX-UP IDEA

Think Aloud
Practice reading the selection aloud with a partner. Read until you come to a period. Then stop and think aloud with your partner. Here are some questions to discuss: What have you learned about walls? What have you learned about the speaker and his neighbor? Then have your partner read to the next period. Again stop and think aloud. Continue in this way until you have finished the poem.

There where it is we do not need the wall:
He is all pine and I am apple orchard.
My apple trees will never get across
And eat the cones under his pines, I tell him.
He only says, "Good fences make good neighbors."
Spring is the mischief in me, and I wonder
If I could put a notion in his head:
30 "*Why* do they make good neighbors? Isn't it
Where there are cows? But here there are no cows.
Before I built a wall I'd ask to know
What I was walling in or walling out,
And to whom I was like to give offense.
Something there is that doesn't love a wall,
That wants it down." I could say "Elves" to him,
But it's not elves exactly, and I'd rather
He said it for himself. I see him there
Bringing a stone grasped firmly by the top
40 In each hand, like an old-stone savage armed.
He moves in darkness as it seems to me,
Not of woods only and the shade of trees.
He will not go behind his father's saying,
And he likes having thought of it so well
He says again, "Good fences make good neighbors." ■

Reflect ON YOUR READING

After Reading ➤ **SHARE YOUR REACTIONS**

❑ With your partner from the Before Reading activity, share the notes you made during reading.
❑ Then discuss the Read-Write Connection question on page 163.

Reading Skills and Test Practice

COMPARE AND CONTRAST

Discuss with your partner how best to answer these questions that require you to compare and contrast. Use the Think-Aloud Notes to write down your reasons for eliminating the incorrect answers.

____1. How do the speaker's feelings about fences or walls compare with those of his neighbor?
   a. The speaker agrees with the neighbor who says that "good fences make good neighbors."
   b. The speaker thinks there may be times when walls cause harm or offense.
   c. The speaker thinks walls are completely unnecessary.
   d. The speaker's feelings toward walls are not expressed.

____2. Why is it ironic about the neighbors coming together to mend the wall?
   a. The neighbors have different ideas about how to fix the wall.
   b. The neighbors come together to fix something that keeps them apart.
   c. The neighbor loves the wall, but nature doesn't.
   d. The neighbors come together only to fix the wall.

How did using the reading strategy help you to answer the questions?

_____
_____
_____
_____

THINK-ALOUD NOTES

_____
_____
_____
_____
_____
_____
_____
_____
_____
_____

Investigate, Inquire, and Imagine

RECALL: GATHER FACTS
1a. Why do the speaker and his neighbor get together in the spring?

INTERPRET: FIND MEANING
1b. What is ironic about the wall?

ANALYZE: TAKE THINGS APART
2a. Identify the clues that reveal the relationship between the speaker and his neighbor.

SYNTHESIZE: BRING THINGS TOGETHER
2b. Considering the nature of their relationship, who do you think makes a better neighbor, and why?

EVALUATE: MAKE JUDGMENTS
3a. How effective is the speaker in getting the neighbor to consider a new perspective about the wall?

EXTEND: CONNECT IDEAS
3b. Besides walls or fences, what other things keep neighbors apart?

Literary Tools

CHARACTER AND CHARACTERIZATION. A **character** is a figure who participates in the action of a literary work. **Characterization** is the use of literary techniques to create a character. Fill in the chart below with details about the speaker's neighbor.

Physical Appearance	Habits/ Mannerisms/ Behaviors	Relationships with Other People	Other
"an old-stone savage armed"			

WordWorkshop

WORD CLUSTERS. Find the following words in the poem: *abreast, mischief, notion*. Brainstorm one or two other words or phrases that mean the same as each word. Mark them in the cluster charts below.

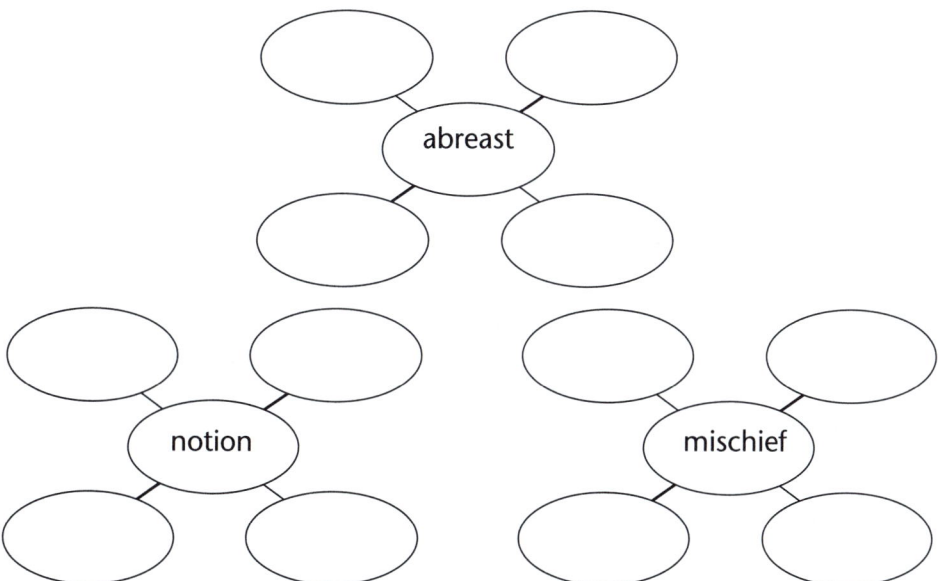

Then use a dictionary or thesaurus to find two additional words or phrases. Write a paragraph or brief story using the three words listed above and at least three words from your word clusters.

Read-Write Connection

Do you agree that good fences make good neighbors? Why, or why not?

_____
_____
_____

Beyond the Reading

ORAL INTERPRETATION. Robert Frost's poems are excellent for reading aloud. Go online or use the library to find other poems by Robert Frost. Choose two or three poems with similar themes. Practice reading the poems aloud. Then prepare a brief introduction to the poems. Deliver your oral presentation to the class.

GO ONLINE. To find links and additional activities for this selection, visit the EMC Internet Resource Center at **emcp.com/languagearts** and click on Write-In Reader.

CONNECT

Reader's resource

Langston Hughes is one of the writers of the Harlem Renaissance, a period of intense creative activity among African-American writers and other artists living in Harlem during the 1920s. Hughes often mixed elements of blues with formal poetry. "I, too, sing America" and "The Negro Speaks of Rivers" were included in Langston Hughes's first collection of poetry, *The Weary Blues*. Both poems explore the black experience in America.

Reader's journal

When were you segregated from a group? How did you react?

_____
_____
_____
_____

"The Negro Speaks of Rivers"
"I, too, sing America"
by Langston Hughes

Active READING STRATEGY

CONNECT TO PRIOR KNOWLEDGE

Before Reading ➤ THINK ABOUT WHAT YOU KNOW

- ❑ Respond to the Reader's Journal questions with your classmates, discuss experiences of segregation and racism and what you know about segregation during the time Hughes was writing.
- ❑ Write some preliminary expectations, predictions, or questions in the Reactions Chart below.

Graphic Organizer: Reactions Chart

Line Numbers	Questions, Predictions, Reactions, Key Points

The Negro Speaks of Rivers

Langston Hughes

I've known rivers:
I've known rivers ancient as the world and older than the
   flow of human blood in human veins.

My soul has grown deep like the rivers.

I bathed in the Euphrates when dawns were young.
I built my hut near the Congo and it lulled me to sleep.
I looked upon the Nile[1] and raised the pyramids above it.
I heard the singing of the Mississippi when Abe Lincoln
   went down to New Orleans, and I've seen its muddy
   bosom turn all golden in the sunset.

I've known rivers:
Ancient, dusky rivers.

My soul has grown deep like the rivers. ■

---

1. **Euphrates . . . Nile.** *Euphrates*—river that flows through Turkey, Syria, and Iraq; *Congo*—river in central Africa; *Nile*—river in northeastern Africa

FIX-UP IDEA

Use Margin Questions
If you are having trouble determining the main ideas or the speaker's feelings in either poem, go back and answer the margin questions. These questions will help you focus on key lines of the poem. What do you learn about the speaker of each poem by answering the margin questions?

NOTE THE FACTS

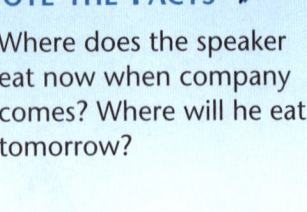

Where does the speaker eat now when company comes? Where will he eat tomorrow?

_____
_____
_____

Reading STRATEGY REVIEW

WRITE THINGS DOWN. Highlight or underline words and phrases that create a strong reaction in you. For example, underline words or phrases that you think convey a central idea of the poem, that remind you of a personal experience, or that create a strong emotional response in you.

I, too, sing America

Langston Hughes

I, too, sing America.

I am the darker brother.
They send me to eat in the kitchen
When company comes,
But I laugh,
And eat well,
And grow strong.

Tomorrow,
I'll be at the table
10 When company comes.
Nobody'll dare
Say to me,
"Eat in the kitchen,"
Then.

Besides,
They'll see how beautiful I am
And be ashamed—

I, too, am America. ■

Reflect ON YOUR READING

After Reading — **SHARE YOUR CONNECTIONS**

- ❑ With your classmates, share the notes you made in your Reactions Chart.
- ❑ Discuss the Read-Write Connection question on page 169.

Reading Skills and Test Practice

COMPARE AND CONTRAST

READ, THINK, AND EXPLAIN. Compare and contrast the speakers' experiences in "The Negro Speaks of Rivers" and "I, too, sing America." What attitude toward these experiences is expressed in each poem?

REFLECT ON YOUR RESPONSE. How did using the reading strategy help you to compare and contrast the speakers' experiences and attitudes?

THINK-ALOUD NOTES

Investigate, Inquire, and Imagine

RECALL: GATHER FACTS
1a. What changes do the speakers mention undergoing in each poem?

INTERPRET: FIND MEANING
1b. What has caused these changes? Are they positive changes? Why?

ANALYZE: TAKE THINGS APART
2a. Identify the details in "I, too, sing America" that suggest that America is one family.

SYNTHESIZE: BRING THINGS TOGETHER
2b. Why does the speaker identify himself with America?

EVALUATE: MAKE JUDGMENTS
3a. Evaluate the vehicles Hughes uses to express the themes of the two poems. Explain whether they are effective, and why.

EXTEND: CONNECT IDEAS
3b. The title of "I, too, sing America" is an allusion to Walt Whitman's "Song of Myself," page 147. Compare and contrast the speakers of the poems by Hughes and Whitman. Why do you think Hughes chose this title for his poem?

WordWorkshop

ANTONYMS. **Antonyms** are opposites. Find an opposite of each of the following words from the selections. Write a contrast sentence to show the meaning of both words.

1. **ancient**

    Meaning _____

    Antonym _____

    Sentence _____

2. **dusky**

    Meaning _____

    Antonym _____

    Sentence _____

3. **lulled**

    Meaning _____

    Antonym _____

    Sentence _____

4. **beautiful**

    Meaning _____

    Antonym _____

    Sentence _____

Literary Tools

TONE. Tone is the emotional attitude toward the reader or toward the subject implied by a literary work. What is the tone of "I, too, sing America"? What is the tone of "The Negro Speaks of Rivers"? How are these tones created?

_____

_____

_____

_____

Read-Write Connection

Imagine the speaker in "I, too, sing America" is alive today. What social progress would he note since the poem was written in the 1920s?

_____

_____

_____

_____

_____

_____

Beyond the Reading

RESEARCH RIVERS. "The Negro Speaks of Rivers" mentions several rivers that have been significant in human civilization. Choose one of these rivers to research. Answer these questions: What countries does the river run through? What cities are located along the river? How do people use the river? What historical or literary allusions have been made to the river? Report on your findings to the class. Then discuss overall why rivers are important to many civilizations.

GO ONLINE. To find links and additional activities for this selection, visit the EMC Internet Resource Center at **emcp.com/languagearts** and click on Write-In Reader.

CONNECT

Reader's resource

E. E. Cummings's work is known for its radical innovations in punctuation, capitalization, spelling, and grammar. Some of his poems seem literally to explode into fragments across the page, for he often arranged letters, words, and phrases in unique ways to make a visual as well as a verbal impact. The two poems "somewhere i have never travelled,gladly beyond" and "anyone lived in a pretty how town" are good examples of Cummings's innovative style.

Reader's journal

Have you ever looked deeply into the eyes of someone else? What did you think you saw in that person's eyes?

_____
_____
_____
_____

"somewhere i have never travelled,gladly beyond"

"anyone lived in a pretty how town"

by E. E. Cummings

Active READING STRATEGY

USE TEXT ORGANIZATION

Before Reading ➤ **START A REPETITION CHART**

- **Repetition** is a writer's conscious reuse of a sound, word, phrase, sentence, or other element.
- Preview the Repetition Chart below. As you read, you will look for different types of repetition in each poem. In the left column, write the quotation containing the repetition. Underline the repeated element. In the right column, paraphrase the meaning of the quotation.

Graphic Organizer: Repetition Chart

Repetition	Meaning
"in your most frail gesture are things which <u>enclose</u> me"	the least action on the part of the subject envelops the speaker

E. E. Cummings

somewhere i have never travelled,gladly beyond
any experience,your eyes have their silence:
in your most frail gesture are things which enclose me,
or which i cannot touch because they are too near

your slightest look easily will unclose me
though i have closed myself as fingers,
you open always petal by petal myself as Spring opens
(touching skilfully,mysteriously)her first rose

or if your wish be to close me,i and
my life will shut very beautifully,suddenly,
as when the heart of this flower imagines
the snow carefully everywhere descending;

nothing which we are to perceive in this world equals
the power of your intense fragility:whose texture

> **USE THE STRATEGY**
>
> **USE TEXT ORGANIZATION.** Note the examples of opening and closing in the last stanza. Make a note in the Repetition Chart.

compels me with the colour of its countries,
rendering death and forever with each breathing

(i do not know what it is about you that closes
and opens; only something in me understands
the voice of your eyes is deeper than all roses)

20   nobody,not even the rain,has such small hands

anyone lived in a pretty how town

E. E. Cummings

anyone lived in a pretty how town
(with up so floating many bells down)
spring summer autumn winter
he sang his didn't he danced his did

Women and men(both little and small)
cared for anyone not at all
they sowed their isn't they reaped their same
sun moon stars rain

children guessed(but only a few
and down they forgot as up they grew
autumn winter spring summer)
that noone loved him more by more

when by now and tree by leaf
she laughed his joy she cried his grief
bird by snow and stir by still
anyone's any was all to her

During Reading

USE THE STRATEGY

USE TEXT ORGANIZATION. As you read "anyone lived in a pretty how town," record words or phrases that are repeated. Think about what the repetition adds to the poem.

Reading TIP

The poem is about a character called "anyone." This naming technique suggests that the poem could be about any person. It is similar to the use of *Everyman* in a medieval morality play.

FIX-UP IDEA

Reread
If you have trouble understanding the poem, try rereading. Read each stanza and try to summarize the meaning. After you have reread the poem, discuss the Read-Write Connection question on page 177 with a partner.

someones married their everyones
laughed their cryings and did their dance
(sleep wake hope and then)they
said their nevers they slept their dream

stars rain sun moon
(and only the snow can begin to explain
how children are apt to forget to remember
with up so floating many bells down)

one day anyone died i guess
(and noone stooped to kiss his face)
busy folk buried them side by side
little by little and was by was

all by all and deep by deep
and more by more they dream their sleep
noone and anyone earth by april
wish by spirit and if by yes.

Women and men(both dong and ding)
summer autumn winter spring
reaped their sowing and went their came
sun moon stars rain ■

NOTE THE FACTS

What happened to "anyone"? How did people react to this event?

Reflect ON YOUR READING

After Reading → **SUMMARIZE**

- ❏ Work with a few of your classmates to review your responses. Compare your completed Repetition Charts, and share the words and phrases you highlighted or underlined.
- ❏ Talk about the meaning or effect of the repetition in both poems.

Reading Skills and Test Practice

IDENTIFY MAIN IDEAS

Discuss with your partner how best to answer these questions that require you to identify main ideas. Use the Think-Aloud Notes to write down your reasons for eliminating the incorrect answers.

____1. What idea is presented by the repetition of things opening and closing in "somewhere i have travelled,gladly beyond"?
   a. the cyclical nature of life
   b. contrasting forces at work in the speaker's relationship
   c. the on-and-off-again nature of the speaker's relationship
   d. the comparison of love to a flower blooming

____2. What idea is stressed by the alternating pattern of the seasons throughout "anyone lived in a pretty how town"?
   a. There is no logic in the world.
   b. The poem could be about anyone.
   c. The order of the seasons is constant.
   d. Life is cyclical and changing.

How did using the reading strategy help you to answer the questions?

_____

_____

_____

THINK-ALOUD NOTES

Investigate, Inquire, and Imagine

RECALL: GATHER FACTS
1a. What will easily unclose the speaker of "somewhere i have never travelled,gladly beyond"? To what is the closing of the speaker compared?

➡ **INTERPRET: FIND MEANING**
1b. Explain the metaphor in lines 7–8. To what does the speaker compare the subject of the poem? To what does he compare himself? What power does the subject of the poem have over the speaker?

ANALYZE: TAKE THINGS APART
2a. List things that are repeated or repeated with variation in "anyone lived in a pretty how town."

➡ **SYNTHESIZE: BRING THINGS TOGETHER**
2b. Why do you think Cummings used varied repetition in this poem?

EVALUATE: MAKE JUDGMENTS
3a. Evaluate the effect the subject of "somewhere I have never travelled,gladly beyond" has on the speaker of that poem.

➡ **EXTEND: CONNECT IDEAS**
3b. Compare and contrast the attitude of the speaker toward the subject of each poem.

WordWorkshop

VOCABULARY CARDS. A good way to learn and remember new words is to create vocabulary cards. Create a separate note card or notebook page for each word. Write the word in the center. In the top left corner, write the definition. In the top right corner, write a synonym. In the bottom left corner, write a sentence using the word. In the bottom right corner, make a mnemonic to help you remember the word. Look at the sample that follows. Then create your own vocabulary cards for *perceive, compels, rendering, sowed,* and *reaped.*

fragile, not strong	weak
frail	
After a long illness, Marta was frail and tired easily.	The fragile rail is frail.

Literary Tools

PARADOX. A **paradox** is a seemingly contradictory statement, idea, or event. Find the ways the speaker describes the subject of the poem. Why is the use of phrases such as "frail gestures" to describe the subject of the poem paradoxical?

_____
_____
_____
_____

Read-Write Connection

Choose one of the two poems. How does the speaker feel about the person he is addressing or describing? Have you felt this way about somebody? Describe your experience.

_____
_____
_____
_____
_____
_____

Beyond the Reading

THINK ALOUD. With a partner, find another poem by E. E. Cummings. Read the poem silently. Then take turns reading the poem aloud. Pause during your reading to think aloud. The partner who begins can free associate about the first half of the poem. He or she might say what the poem is about or what is happening, guess at the meaning of the poem, express a connection or emotional response, or ask a question. The other partner can respond or ask open-ended questions. Continue reading and thinking aloud until you reach the end of the poem. Reread the poem on your own. Then read the poem to your class and lead a discussion of it.

GO ONLINE. To find links and additional activities for this selection, visit the EMC Internet Resource Center at **emcp.com/languagearts** and click on Write-In Reader.

Unit 4 READING Review

Choose and Use Reading Strategies

Before reading the excerpt below, review with a partner how to use each of these reading strategies with poetry, pages 120–122.

1. Read with a Purpose
2. Connect to Prior Knowledge
3. Write Things Down
4. Make Predictions
5. Visualize
6. Use Text Organization
7. Tackle Difficult Vocabulary
8. Monitor Your Reading Progress

Now apply at least two of these reading strategies as you read the excerpt from "Stanzas on Freedom" by James Russell Lowell. Use the margins and mark up the text to show how you are using the reading strategies to read actively. You may find it helpful to choose a graphic organizer from Appendix B to gather information as you read the excerpt, or use the Summary Chart on page B-12 to create a graphic organizer that summarizes the excerpt.

> Men! whose boast it is that ye
> Come of fathers brave and free,
> If there breathe on earth a slave,
> Are ye truly free and brave?
> If ye do not feel the chain,
> When it works a brother's pain,
> Are ye not base slaves indeed,
> Slaves unworthy to be freed?
>
> Women! who shall one day bear
> Sons to breathe New England air,
> If ye hear, without blush,
> Deed to make the roused blood rush
> Like red lava through your veins,
> For your sisters now in chains—
> Answer! Are ye fit to be
> Mothers of the brave and free?

Literary Tools

Select the best literary element on the right to complete each sentence on the left. Write the correct letter in the blank.

___ 1. "Because I could not stop for Death—" uses a(n) ___ to describe death.
___ 2. The line "But the raven still beguiling all my sad soul into smiling" contains an example of ___.
___ 3. "I prize thy love more than whole mines of gold" is an example of ___.
___ 4. "Song of Myself" contains examples of ___, in which the author introduces and expands on an idea.
___ 5. Iambic pentameter is the ___ of "Mending Wall."
___ 6. *Town* and *down* in the lines "anyone lived in a pretty how town / (with up so floating many bells down)" are an example of ___.
___ 7. The line "the power of your intense fragility . . ." contains a(n) ___.
___ 8. The actions of the neighbor in "Mending Wall" help create this ___.
___ 9. The ___ of "I, too, sing America" is optimistic and forgiving.

a. character, 160, 162
b. elaboration, 150, 157
c. end rhyme, 120, 139, 145
d. extended metaphor, 132
e. hyperbole, 125, 127
f. internal rhyme, 120, 139, 145
g. meter, 130, 136
h. paradox, 171, 176
i. tone, 165, 168

WordWorkshop

UNIT 4 WORDS FOR EVERYDAY USE

abeyance, 148	fissure, 153	obeisance, 140
adjure, 141	harbor, 153	ominous, 141
barbaric, 154	impalpable, 149	persevere, 125
beguiling, 141	infidel, 152	plume, 143
censer, 142	jag, 154	quadruped, 152
civility, 131	lattice, 139	quaff, 142
contender, 153	linguist, 149	recompense, 125
craven, 140	loitering, 154	suffice, 148
creed, 148	manifold, 125	surcease, 138
disposition, 149	mien, 140	tempest, 142
entreat, 139		undaunted, 142

MNEMONIC DEVICES. Mnemonic devices help you remember things. For example, you may have heard the spelling rule "*i* before *e* except after *c* and when it sounds like an *a* as in *neighbor* and *weigh*." Mnemonic devices may be rhymes, acronyms, or striking or silly images (see Unit 9, page 411). Choose ten words from the Words for Everyday Use from Unit 4 listed on page 179. Make up mnemonic devices to help you remember the words and their meanings.

On Your Own

FLUENTLY SPEAKING. Prepare a persuasive speech to encourage people to read more poetry. You might include excerpts from poems in your speech. Practice your speech, then deliver it to a few of your classmates. Critique each other's speeches for content and delivery.

PICTURE THIS. Review the themes of the poems in this unit. Choose one of these themes, such as love or death, to represent visually. Make a collage using pictures, color, and words or lines from the poems to express the theme.

PUT IT IN WRITING. Write a letter to one of the poets whose work is represented in this unit. Tell the writer what you thought of his or her poetry. Explain why you connected with the poem. Ask any questions you have about the poet or his or her work.

Unit FIVE

Reading Folk Literature

FOLK LITERATURE

Human beings are storytelling creatures. Long before people invented writing, they were telling stories about the lives of their gods and heroes. The best of their stories were passed by word of mouth from generation to generation, from folk to folk. These early stories were told in the form of poems, songs, and what we would now call prose tales.

Stories, poems, and songs passed by word of mouth from person to person are important elements of a group's culture. Eventually, many of these verbally transmitted stories, poems, and songs were written down. **Folk literature** is the written versions of these stories, poems, and songs. Folk literature is full of literary devices that helped storytellers remember the stories. These devices include the use of repetition, common phrases such as "once upon a time" and "they lived happily ever after," and familiar characters and events. Some common types of folk literature are defined below.

Types of Folk Literature

MYTHS. Myths are stories that explain objects or events in the natural world as resulting from the action of some supernatural force or entity, most often a god. Every early culture around the globe has produced myths. In this unit, "Song of the Sky Loom" is an example of a myth.

FOLK TALES. Folk tales are brief stories passed by word of mouth from generation to generation in a particular culture. **Fairy tales** are folk tales that contain supernatural beings, such as fairies, dragons, ogres, and animals with human qualities. **Tall tales** are colorful stories that depict the exaggerated wild adventures of North American folk heroes. Many of these heroes and stories revolve around the American frontier and the Wild West.

NOTE THE FACTS

What is folk literature?

_____
_____
_____

MARK THE TEXT

Highlight or underline eight types of folk literature. Start here and continue on the next page.

THINK AND REFLECT

Cinderella and Rumpelstiltskin are two fairy tale characters. What others can you think of? (Extend)

_____
_____
_____

PARABLES. Parables are very brief stories told to teach a moral lesson. Some of the most famous parables are those told by Jesus in the Bible.

FABLES. Fables are brief stories, often with animal characters, told to express a moral. Famous fables include those of Æsop and Jean de La Fontaine.

FOLK SONGS. Folk songs are traditional or composed songs typically made up of stanzas, a refrain, and a simple melody. They express commonly shared ideas or feelings and may be narrative (telling a story) or lyrical (expressing an emotion). Traditional folk songs are anonymous songs that have been transmitted orally. In this unit, "My Old Kentucky Home" by Stephen C. Foster is an example of a composed folk song.

LEGENDS. Legends are stories that have been passed down through time. These stories are often believed to be based on history but without evidence that the events occurred.

USING READING STRATEGIES WITH FOLK LITERATURE

Active Reading Strategy Checklists

In the stories, poems, and songs that are a part of folk literature, storytellers want to entertain their audiences and to pass along cultural ideas and beliefs. The following checklists offer strategies for reading folk literature.

1 READ WITH A PURPOSE. Give yourself a purpose, or something to look for, as you read. Often, you can set a purpose for reading by previewing the title, the opening lines, and instructional information. Other times, a teacher may set your purpose: "List the Native American values portrayed in this legend." To read with a purpose, say to yourself

- ❑ I want to look for . . .
- ❑ I will keep track of . . .
- ❑ I want to find out what happens to . . .
- ❑ I want to understand how . . .
- ❑ The message of this selection is . . .

Reading TIP

Listening to a recording of a folk song can help you understand the tone of the lyrics.

NOTE THE FACTS

What is the aim of storytellers?

_____
_____
_____

2 CONNECT TO PRIOR KNOWLEDGE. Connect to what you already know about a particular culture and its storytelling traditions. To connect to prior knowledge, say to yourself

- ❏ I know that this type of folk literature has . . .
- ❏ The events in this selection remind me of . . .
- ❏ Something similar I've read is . . .
- ❏ I like this part of the selection because . . .

3 WRITE THINGS DOWN. Create a written record of the cultural ideas and beliefs that a storyteller passes along. To keep a written record

- ❏ Underline characters' names.
- ❏ Write down your thoughts about the storyteller's ideas and beliefs.
- ❏ Highlight the most exciting, funniest, or most interesting parts of the tale.
- ❏ Create a graphic organizer to keep track of the sequence of events.
- ❏ Use a code to respond to what happens.

Reading **TIP**

Instead of writing down a short response, use a symbol or a short word to indicate your response. Use codes like the ones listed below.

+	I like this.
–	I don't like this.
√	This is important.
Yes	I agree with this.
No	I disagree with this.
?	I don't understand this.
!	This is like something I know.
⌇	I need to come back to this later.

4 MAKE PREDICTIONS. Use information about the title and subject matter to guess what a folk literature selection will be about. Confirm or deny your predictions, and make new ones based on what you learn. To make predictions, say to yourself

- ❏ The title tells me that the selection will be about . . .
- ❏ I predict that this character will . . .
- ❏ Tales from this cultural tradition usually . . .
- ❏ The conflict between the characters will be resolved by . . .
- ❏ I think the selection will end with . . .

5 VISUALIZE. Visualizing, or allowing the words on the page to create images in your mind, helps you understand a storyteller's account. In order to visualize what happens in a folk literature selection, imagine that you are the storyteller. Read the words in your head with the type of expression and feeling that the storyteller might use with an audience. Make statements such as

- ❏ I imagine the characters sound like . . .
- ❏ My sketch of what happens includes . . .
- ❏ I picture this sequence of events . . .
- ❏ I envision the characters as . . .

Reading **TIP**

Sketching story events helps you remember and understand them.

6 **USE TEXT ORGANIZATION.** When you read folk literature, pay attention to transition or signal words such as *first*, *if/then*, and *on the other hand*. These words identify important ideas and text patterns. Stop occasionally to retell what you have read. Say to yourself

- ❏ What happens first is . . .
- ❏ There is a conflict between . . .
- ❏ The high point of interest is . . .
- ❏ I can summarize this section by . . .
- ❏ The message of this selection is that . . .

7 **TACKLE DIFFICULT VOCABULARY.** Difficult words can hinder your ability to understand folk literature. Use context, consult a dictionary, or ask someone about words you do not understand. When you come across a difficult word, say to yourself

- ❏ The words around the difficult word tell me it must mean . . .
- ❏ A dictionary definition shows that the word means . . .
- ❏ My work with the word before reading helps me know that the word means . . .
- ❏ A classmate said that the word means . . .

8 **MONITOR YOUR READING PROGRESS.** All readers encounter difficulty when they read, especially if they are reading assigned material and not something they have chosen on their own. When you are assigned to read folk literature, note the problems you are having and fix them. The key to reading success is knowing when you are having difficulty. To fix problems, say to yourself

- ❏ Because I don't understand this part, I will . . .
- ❏ Because I'm having trouble staying connected, I will . . .
- ❏ Because the words are hard, I will . . .
- ❏ Because this selection is long, I will . . .
- ❏ Because I can't retell what this section was about, I will . . .

Become an Active Reader

The instruction with the folk literature in this unit gives you an in-depth look at how to use one strategy with each folk literature selection. Learn how to combine several strategies to ensure your complete understanding of what you are reading. When you have difficulty, use fix-up ideas to fix a problem. For further information about the active reading strategies, including the fix-up ideas, see Unit 1, pages 4–15.

Reading **TIP**

If the words in a selection are difficult to pronounce, practice saying them aloud before you read.

Fix-Up Ideas

- Reread
- Ask a question
- Read in shorter chunks
- Read aloud
- Retell
- Work with a partner
- Unlock difficult words
- Vary your reading rate
- Choose a new reading strategy
- Create a mnemonic device

How to Use Reading Strategies with Folk Literature

Excerpt 1. Note how a reader uses active reading strategies while reading an excerpt from the African-American spiritual "Swing Low, Sweet Chariot."

CONNECT TO PRIOR KNOWLEDGE
Knowing the melody changes my reading speed.

READ WITH A PURPOSE
I will underline references that allude to a deliverance from slavery.

Swing low, sweet chariot,
Coming for to carry me home,
Swing low, sweet chariot,
Coming for to carry me home.

I looked over Jordan[1] and what did I see
Coming for to carry me home,
A band of angels coming after me,
Coming for to carry me home.

TACKLE DIFFICULT VOCABULARY
The footnote lets me know what *Jordan* refers to.

VISUALIZE
Picturing the workers who might have sung this song helps me understand it.

---
1. **Jordan.** According to a biblical story, the Israelites in exile had to cross the Jordan River to reach the Promised Land of Canaan.

Excerpt 2. Note how a reader uses active reading strategies while reading an excerpt from the African-American folk song "Follow the Drinking Gourd."

USE TEXT ORGANIZATION
The words *when* and *if* signal what the travelers must do.

MAKE A PREDICTION
I predict that each verse will have a message about escape.

When the sun comes back and the first quail calls,
    Follow the drinking gourd,[1]
For the old man is a-waiting for to carry you to freedom
    If you follow the drinking gourd.

Chorus

Follow the drinking gourd,
    Follow the drinking gourd,
For the old man is a-waiting for to carry you to freedom
    If you follow the drinking gourd.

MONITOR YOUR READING PROGRESS
Rereading verses helps me understand unfamiliar phrasing.

WRITE THINGS DOWN
Underlining words in the definition of "drinking gourd" helps me understand the double meaning.

---
1. **drinking gourd.** Dried, hollowed-out shell of a gourd (a hard-rinded inedible fruit similar to a pumpkin) used for dipping water to drink. In this selection, the speaker uses *drinking gourd* as a secret code for the Big Dipper, a constellation that guided escaping slaves.

CONNECT

Reader's resource

"Song of the Sky Loom" is a tribal song. Many words in the song refer to weaving terms. The Tewa, a Pueblo people of the Southwest, are accomplished weavers. They passed on these weaving arts to the Navajo, now renowned weavers of blankets and rugs. In addition to weaving, the Tewa make intricately decorated pottery and elaborate baskets. They live in multi-level, multi-unit adobe structures often built into the hard mesas of the Southwest. Like other Pueblo peoples, the Tewa have a vital interdependence with the natural world, performing various rituals and ceremonies related to nature, often connected to bringing much-needed rain.

Reader's journal

If you could describe yourself only in terms of an art form, such as a painting, a sculpture, or a musical work, which would you choose, and why?

_____
_____
_____

"Song of the Sky Loom"

Tewa Tribal Song

Active READING STRATEGY

WRITE THINGS DOWN

Before Reading — **UNDERSTAND HOW METAPHORS CREATE PICTURES**

❑ Read the Reader's Resource and the Reading Tip on this page, and look over the photograph on page 187.

❑ A **metaphor** is a figure of speech in which one thing is spoken or written about as if it were another, thus encouraging a comparison between features of the two things. The actual subject is called the *tenor* of the metaphor, while the thing to which it is likened is called the *vehicle.* Songs such as the one you are about to read often employ metaphor in order to create pictures in the mind of the reader or listener.

❑ Preview the Metaphor Chart below. As you read, underline or highlight metaphors, or comparison between two things. Mark both the tenor and the vehicle in the comparisons.

Graphic Organizer: Metaphor Chart

Tenor	Vehicle
white light of morning	warp

186   THE EMC WRITE-IN READER

Song of the Sky Loom
Tewa Tribal Song

Navaho Woman Weaving,
1988. David Ryan.

O our Mother the Earth, O our Father the Sky,
Your children are we, and with tired backs
We bring you the gifts you love.
Then weave for us a garment of brightness;
May the warp[1] be the white light of morning,
May the weft[2] be the red light of evening,
May the fringes be the falling rain,
May the border be the standing rainbow.
Thus weave for us a garment of brightness,
10   That we may walk fittingly where birds sing,
That we may walk fittingly where grass is green,
O our Mother the Earth, O our Father the Sky. ∎

---

1. **warp.** Threads in a loom that run lengthwise
2. **weft.** Horizontal threads in a loom. The weft crosses the warp to make a woven fabric.

Reflect ON YOUR READING

After Reading → **SUMMARIZE THE METAPHORS**

- ❑ Go back through the tribal song and add the vehicle and tenor for the metaphors you found to your graphic organizer.
- ❑ Summarize the metaphors you gathered.

_____
_____
_____
_____
_____

Reading Skills and Test Practice

IDENTIFY METAPHORS

Discuss with a partner how best to answer these questions that ask you to identify metaphors. Use the Think-Aloud notes to write down your reasons for eliminating the incorrect answers.

____1. Who are compared to weavers?
    a. the Tewa
    b. the children
    c. Mother Earth and Father Sky
    d. the Navajo

____2. What is compared to weaving in this selection?
    a. the work of the Tewa people
    b. the rain and sunlight
    c. the creation of a beautiful, natural world
    d. a peaceful task

How did using the reading strategy help you to answer the questions?

_____
_____
_____
_____

THINK-ALOUD NOTES

Investigate, Inquire, and Imagine

RECALL: GATHER FACTS
1a. What elements of nature are described in the poem?

INTERPRET: FIND MEANING
1b. What role does each element of nature play in the tapestry woven by Mother Earth and Father Sky? How are the elements linked to one another?

ANALYZE: TAKE THINGS APART
2a. What relationship does the song suggest exists between humans and the divine?

SYNTHESIZE: BRING THINGS TOGETHER
2b. What is the central comparison in "Song of the Sky Loom"?

EVALUATE: MAKE JUDGMENTS
3a. Based on this song, what attitude do you think the Tewa people had toward their gods?

EXTEND: CONNECT IDEAS
3b. How do you think the Tewa people expected their gods to respond to this prayer song?

Literary Tools

MYTH. A **myth** is a story that explains objects or events in the natural world as resulting from the action of some supernatural force or entity. Every early culture around the globe has produced its own myths.

1. What mythical elements appear in "Song of the Sky Loom"?

   _____
   _____
   _____
   _____

2. What can you infer about Tewa religious beliefs and practices based on this song?

   _____
   _____
   _____
   _____

WordWorkshop

FIGURATIVE LANGUAGE. Writers may use language figuratively or literally. *Literal language* presents the actual, or ordinary meaning of words. **Figurative language,** on the other hand, is meant to be understood imaginatively. Many literary techniques, such as simile and metaphor, employ figurative language to help readers see things in new ways. Look at each of the following lines from "Song of the Sky Loom." For each underlined word, identify the literal meaning. Then identify the figurative meaning.

1. "May the warp be the white light of brightness;"
   Literal _____
   Figurative _____

2. "May the weft be the red light of evening,"
   Literal _____
   Figurative _____

Try using language literally and figuratively. First think of two words related to an activity you enjoy. Write a sentence for each word that uses the literal meaning of the word. Then try using the word figuratively.

3. Word _____
   Literal _____
   Figurative _____

4. Word _____
   Literal _____
   Figurative _____

Read-Write Connection

What images does "Song of the Sky Loom" create in your mind?

Beyond the Reading

RESEARCH EARLY NATIVE AMERICAN ART AND ARCHITECTURE. The hundreds of different Native American cultures that existed before the coming of the Europeans created a wide variety of art and architecture. Working in a small group, research the early Native American art and architecture of one cultural group. Your teacher can provide you with a list of groups from which to choose.

GO ONLINE. To find links and additional activities for this selection, visit the EMC Internet Resource Center at **emcp.com/languagearts** and click on Write-In Reader.

"Follow the Drinking Gourd"

African-American Folk Song

Active READING STRATEGY

VISUALIZE

Before Reading ➤ PREVIEW THE SELECTION

❏ Read the Reader's Resource, and look at the map on page 192.
❏ Read the folk song and keep track of details that will help you sketch the path the song describes.
❏ When you finish reading, you will create a sketch of the path in the graphic organizer below.

Graphic Organizer: Path Sketch

The Path Described in "Follow the Drinking Gourd"

CONNECT

Reader's resource

"Follow the Drinking Gourd" is an African-American folk song that describes the Underground Railroad used to help fugitive slaves escape to safety. Although the Underground Railroad was not an actual railroad, it used railroad terminology such as *station* for a stopping place and *conductor* for a person who helped the escaping slaves. The Underground Railroad extended throughout fourteen northern states from Maine to Nebraska with its heaviest concentration of activities in Pennsylvania, Ohio, Indiana, New York, and the New England states. It extended into Canada as well, where fugitive slaves were safe from slave hunters. Estimates of the number of fugitive slaves aided by the Underground Railroad range from forty thousand to one hundred thousand.

Reader's journal

How far would you go to gain freedom?

_____
_____
_____

During Reading

IMAGINE THE PATH DESCRIBED IN THE SONG

- Read the folk song and mark details that help you visualize the path travelers must take.
- Make notes that help you define the path. For instance, you will want to draw the drinking gourd in the sky.

NOTE THE FACTS

Who is waiting to help the travelers to freedom?

_____
_____
_____

Literary TOOLS

SPIRITUAL. A **spiritual** is a folk song of deep religious and emotional character. Spirituals were developed among African Americans in the southern United States during slavery. The words are most often related to biblical passages and frequently reflect patient, profound melancholy, even though the songs seldom refer to slavery itself. Spirituals have influenced blues, jazz, and gospel songs. As you read the selection, determine how "Follow the Drinking Gourd" qualifies as a spiritual.

Follow the Drinking Gourd

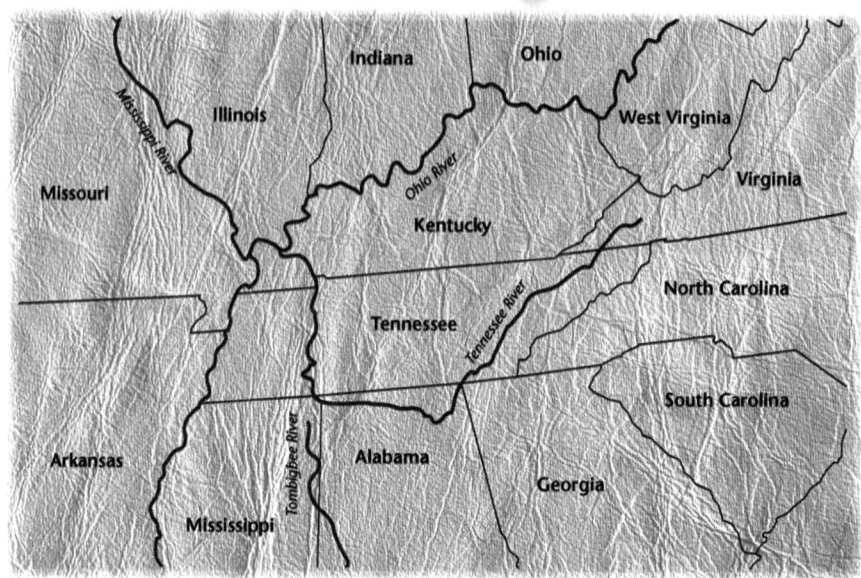

ANONYMOUS AFRICAN-AMERICAN SONG
OF THE UNDERGROUND RAILROAD

When the sun comes back and the first quail calls,
   Follow the drinking gourd,[1]
For the old man is a-waiting for to carry you to freedom
   If you follow the drinking gourd.

Chorus
Follow the drinking gourd,
   Follow the drinking gourd,
For the old man is a-waiting for to carry you to freedom
   If you follow the drinking gourd.

The river bank will make a very good road,
10   The dead trees show you the way,
Left foot, peg foot[2] traveling on
   Follow the drinking gourd.

---

1. **drinking gourd.** Dried, hollowed-out shell of a gourd (a hard-rinded inedible fruit similar to a pumpkin) used for dipping water to drink. In this selection, the speaker uses *drinking gourd* as a secret code word for the Big Dipper, a constellation that served as a guide for escaping slaves.
2. **peg foot.** Wooden foot (replacement for a person's foot)

Repeat Chorus

The river ends between two hills,
   Follow the drinking gourd.
There's another river on the other side,
   Follow the drinking gourd.

Repeat Chorus

Where the little river meets the great big river,
   Follow the drinking gourd.
The old man is a-waiting for to carry you to freedom
20   If you follow the drinking gourd. ■

THINK AND REFLECT

What might "the other side" refer to? **(Interpret)**

_____
_____
_____

THINK AND REFLECT

Who might the old man who "is a-waiting" be? **(Interpret)**

_____
_____
_____

READ ALOUD

To fully experience this song, sing along while someone plays the tune on a piano or a keyboard. Try singing the chorus without looking at the words whenever it is played. It may be necessary to repeat the song two or three times before you can accurately recall the words of the chorus.

Reflect ON YOUR READING

After Reading → SKETCH WHAT THE SONG DESCRIBES

❑ Create a sketch in your graphic organizer that shows how travelers were advised to escape. What key ideas did you include in your sketch?

_____
_____
_____

THINK-ALOUD NOTES

_____
_____
_____
_____
_____
_____
_____
_____
_____

Reading Skills and Test Practice

IDENTIFY THE AUTHOR'S PURPOSE

Discuss with your partner how best to answer the following questions that ask you to identify the author's purpose. Use the Think-Aloud Notes to write down your reasons for eliminating the incorrect answers.

____1. Which of these best describes the purpose of the selection?
    a. to help slave owners find escaping slaves
    b. to state explicitly the route to freedom
    c. to remember the plight of slaves
    d. to provide coded clues to help escaping slaves

____2. The repetition in the song
    a. explains where to buy a ticket for the Underground Railroad.
    b. tells listeners to follow the Big Dipper to get to freedom.
    c. reminds listeners to bring water for the journey.
    d. tells slave owners that slaves are heading north.

How did information you gathered as you read help you eliminate incorrect answers?

_____
_____
_____
_____

194 THE EMC WRITE-IN READER

Investigate, Inquire, and Imagine

RECALL: GATHER FACTS
1a. Who is singing this song? Where are the people going, and why? When are they supposed to travel?

INTERPRET: FIND MEANING
1b. What overriding image is used to guide the travelers toward their destination? Why is the signpost not openly identified? What time of year might be suggested by these natural events?

ANALYZE: TAKE THINGS APART
2a. What can you infer about the challenges facing escaping slaves?

SYNTHESIZE: BRING THINGS TOGETHER
2b. How does the map on page 192 help you visualize the path of the travelers? In what ways do you think seeing the "drinking gourd" in the sky helped them visualize the path to freedom?

EVALUATE: MAKE JUDGMENTS
3a. If you were a slave, how encouraging do you think this song would be in helping you decide whether to escape? Why do you think so?

EXTEND: CONNECT IDEAS
3b. What song, speech, or other inspirational work have you used to encourage yourself to do something difficult? How did it help you?

Literary Tools

SPIRITUAL. A **spiritual** is a folk song of deep religious and emotional character. Spirituals were developed among African Americans in the southern United States during slavery. The words are most often related to biblical passages and frequently reflect patient, profound melancholy, even though the songs seldom refer to slavery itself.

1. In what ways does "Follow the Drinking Gourd" qualify as a spiritual?

   _____
   _____
   _____
   _____

2. Why do you think a song such as "Follow the Drinking Gourd" was part of the oral, rather than written, literary tradition?

   _____
   _____
   _____

WordWorkshop

WORD MEANINGS. Use the definition in footnote 1 on page 192 to write down the two meanings of "drinking gourd." Then draw an illustration for each meaning.

Meaning 1:	Illustration
Meaning 2:	Illustration

Read-Write Connection

What do you think it would be like to run for your freedom and your life?

_____

_____

_____

Beyond the Reading

FIND A FOLK SONG. Find a contemporary popular folk song that you like. In a small group, discuss your song: what story does the song tell, what message is expressed, and whom does the singer address? Summarize information on your songs. Share your summary with the class. If possible, bring in recorded versions of your songs, or try singing them.

GO ONLINE. To find links and additional activities for this selection, visit the EMC Internet Resource Center at **emcp.com/languagearts** and click on Write-In Reader.

"Swing Low, Sweet Chariot"

Anonymous African-American Spiritual

Active READING STRATEGY

CONNECT TO PRIOR KNOWLEDGE

Before Reading ➤ **LEARN ABOUT SPIRITUALS**

- ❑ Read the Reader's Resource. React to what you read by highlighting or underlining the text and asking questions and making comments in the margins.
- ❑ Summarize your reaction to what you read in the Reader's Resource in the Reactions Chart below.

Graphic Organizer: Reactions Chart

Section or Stanza	My Reaction to the Words and Ideas
Reader's Resource	
Stanza 1	
Stanza 2	
Stanza 3	
Stanza 4	

CONNECT

Reader's resource

By the middle of the nineteenth century, more than four million slaves lived in the United States. Most had come from the west coast of Africa, where they had engaged in communal labor accompanied by song. Combining elements of traditional African music, work songs, and Christian hymns, African Americans created a new kind of music known as the spiritual, a forerunner of many modern musical styles, including gospel and blues.

Spirituals often had Christian themes; however, many of the spirituals, such as **"Swing Low, Sweet Chariot,"** were intentionally ambiguous or allegorical, dealing on one level with deliverance from earthly toil into heaven and on another level with deliverance from slavery.

Reader's journal

When you feel a need to escape from reality, of what real or imaginary place do you dream?

_____
_____
_____

UNIT 5 / READING FOLK LITERATURE   **197**

During Reading

NOTE YOUR REACTIONS

- Read the first stanza of the spiritual. Think about what the words *chariot* and *home* mean to you. Then write your ideas in your Reactions Chart.
- Continue reading and reacting to the words and ideas. Look for hidden meanings in each stanza. When you finish, add your reactions to your graphic organizer.

NOTE THE FACTS

Where will the chariot take the speaker?

_____

_____

MARK THE TEXT

Underline or highlight the line that is repeated twice in each stanza.

Fix-Up Idea

Read and Think Aloud
If you have trouble finding hidden meaning in the spiritual, read aloud with a partner. Together, discuss what each stanza means. Then add your reactions to your graphic organizer.

Swing Low, Sweet Chariot

Anonymous African-American Spiritual

Swing low, sweet chariot,
Coming for to carry me home,
Swing low, sweet chariot,
Coming for to carry me home.

I looked over Jordan[1] and what did I see
Coming for to carry me home,
A band of angels coming after me,
Coming for to carry me home.

If you get there before I do,
10   Coming for to carry me home,
Tell all my friends I'm coming too,
Coming for to carry me home.

Swing low, sweet chariot,
Coming for to carry me home,
Swing low, sweet chariot,
Coming for to carry me home. ■

---

1. **Jordan.** According to a biblical story, the Israelites in exile had to cross the Jordan River to reach the Promised Land of Canaan.

Reflect ON YOUR READING

After Reading ➡ **SHARE YOUR REACTIONS**

❑ Share your Reactions Chart with a few of your classmates.
❑ Discuss your reaction to the spiritual. What hidden meanings did you find?

_____
_____
_____

Reading Skills and Test Practice

IDENTIFY MAIN IDEAS

Discuss with your partner how best to answer the following questions that ask you to identify main ideas. Use the Think-Aloud Notes to write down your reasons for eliminating the incorrect answers.

____1. Which answer best describes a main idea of the spiritual "Swing Low, Sweet Chariot"?
   a. The speaker is waiting for a friend with a chariot.
   b. The speaker is trying to get across the Jordan River.
   c. The speaker expresses hope about going to the Promised Land.
   d. The speaker sends a message to friends who are already home.

____2. Which word best describes the speaker's hidden desire?
   a. salvation
   b. comfort
   c. freedom
   d. knowledge

How did using the reading strategy help you to answer the questions?

_____
_____
_____
_____

THINK-ALOUD NOTES

Investigate, Inquire, and Imagine

RECALL: GATHER FACTS
1a. Who, according to stanza 3, is being addressed by the singer?

INTERPRET: FIND MEANING
1b. Why are the singer's friends not with the singer at this time?

ANALYZE: TAKE THINGS APART
2a. Why might this song have been comforting to the person singing it? What feelings does the song express?

SYNTHESIZE: BRING THINGS TOGETHER
2b. Develop an interpretation of the spiritual as a song of hope about earthly freedom, explaining the significance of the chariot, angels, home, and the Jordan River.

EVALUATE: MAKE JUDGMENTS
3a. How relevant is the message of this song today? Explain your answer.

EXTEND: CONNECT IDEAS
3b. Why do you think slaves made Christianity, a religion imposed by their masters, into an expression of their own experience?

Literary Tools

THEME. A **theme** is a central idea in a literary work. Add the theme of "Swing Low, Sweet Chariot" to the center circle below. Add details that support this theme to the outer circles.

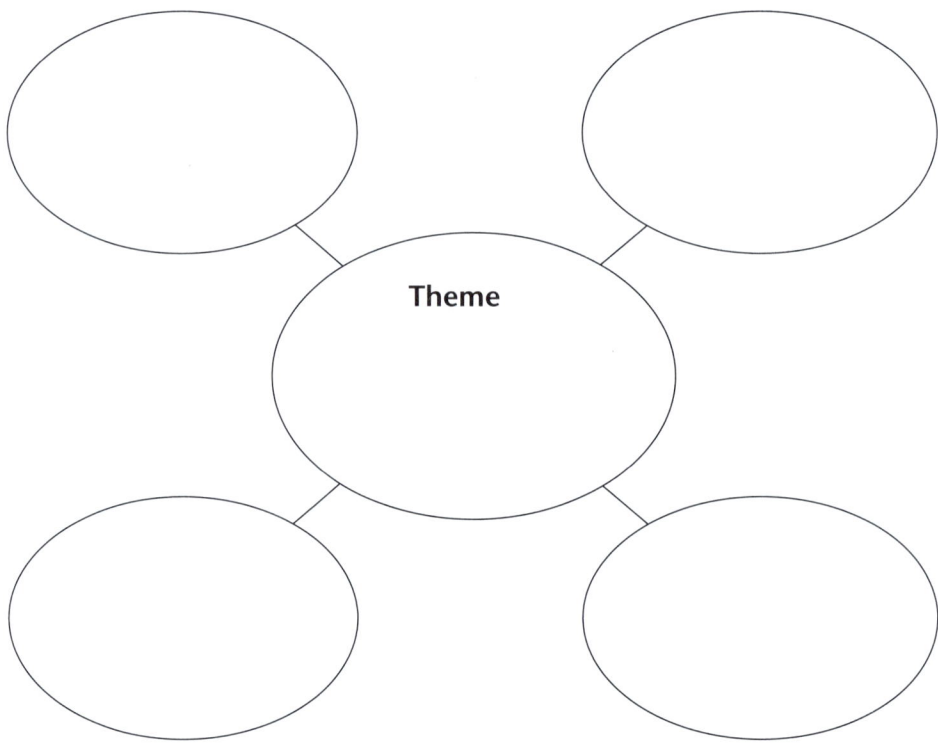

WordWorkshop

SEMANTIC FEATURE ANALYSIS. **Semantic feature analysis** can help you explore how related words differ from one another. To use semantic feature analysis, begin by identifying a topic category to be analyzed. Identify some words related to that category and list them in a column along the left side of the chart. Identify features shared by some of the words and list them in rows across the top of the chart.

Use the chart below for semantic feature analysis. Consider whether each feature applies to each mode of transportation. Put a plus sign (+) for "yes" and a minus sign (–) for "no."

Modes of Transportation	chariot	car	train	bicycle	stage-coach	bus	wagon
not wheeled two-wheeled four-wheeled public private horse-drawn motorized							

On your own paper, summarize the similarities and differences among the modes of transportation.

Read-Write Connection

If you were a slave, what image would console or comfort you?

_____

_____

_____

_____

Beyond the Reading

RESEARCH SPIRITUALS. With several classmates, write a brief report on the history and development of spirituals. At the end of your report, add an appendix with your group's favorite spirituals. Illustrate and lay out the spirituals artistically. If possible, include musical notes for each song.

GO ONLINE. To find links and additional activities for this selection, visit the EMC Internet Resource Center at **emcp.com/languagearts** and click on Write-In Reader.

CONNECT

Reader's resource

"My Old Kentucky Home" was inspired by Harriet Beecher Stowe's abolitionist novel, *Uncle Tom's Cabin,* and expresses deep sympathy for enslaved African Americans. Written in 1858, the first draft of the song in Foster's sketchbook was entitled "Poor Uncle Tom, good night" and was written in black dialect. Prior to publication Foster dropped most of the dialect and removed the references to Uncle Tom, emphasizing the more traditional and common themes of loss of one's family, home, and childhood. "My Old Kentucky Home" is sung on national television every year on the day of the Kentucky Derby and remains the state's official song.

Reader's journal

What was it like the first time you were separated from your family?

_____

_____

_____

"MY OLD KENTUCKY HOME"

by Stephen C. Foster

Active READING STRATEGY

USE TEXT ORGANIZATION

Before Reading ➔ **PREVIEW THE ORGANIZATION**

❑ Read the Reader's Resource.
❑ Skim the song. Note the stanza organization and the refrain.
❑ Preview the graphic organizer below. As you read the song, you will add details in the Cluster Chart.

Graphic Organizer: Cluster Chart

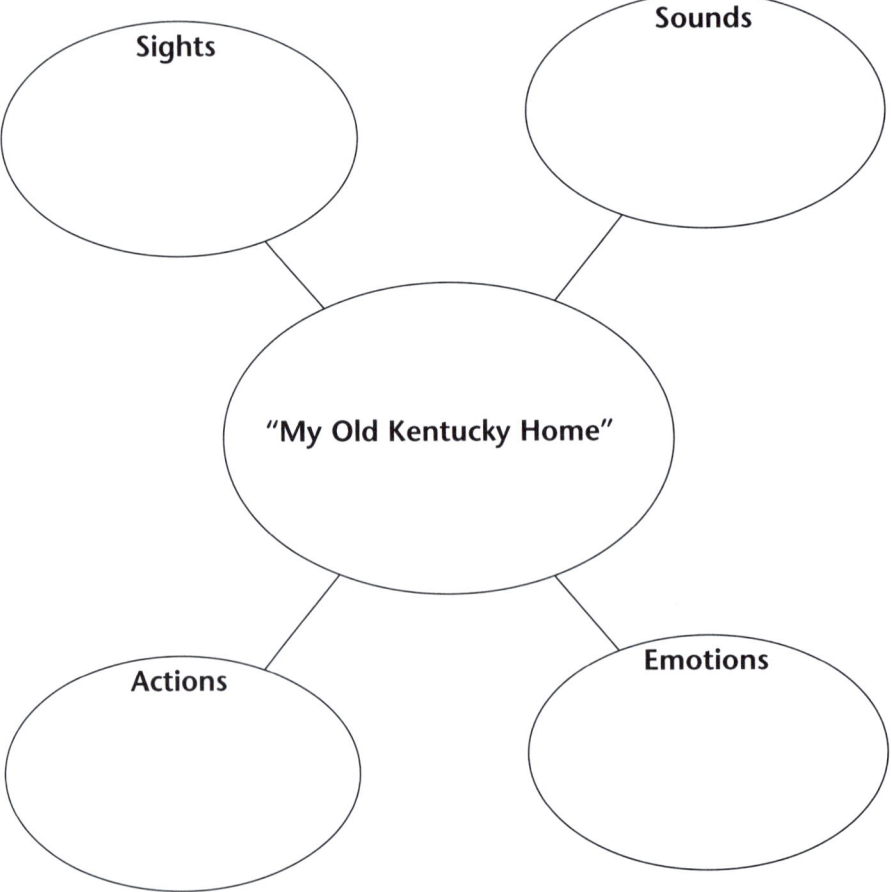

MY OLD KENTUCKY HOME

Stephen C. Foster

1. The sun shines bright in my old Kentucky home
   'tis summer, the folks there are gay.
   The corn top's ripe and the meadow's in the bloom,
   while the birds make music all the day.

2. The young folks roll on the little cabin floor,
   all merry, all happy and bright.
   By'n by, hard times come a-knockin' at the door
   then, my old Kentucky home, good night.

Refrain:
Weep no more, my lady,
oh, weep no more today.
We will sing one song for the old Kentucky home,
for the old Kentucky home far away.

During Reading

USE THE SONG'S ORGANIZATION

- ❑ Read the first stanza of the song and add to your graphic organizer details about the sights, sounds, actions, and emotions expressed in the stanza.
- ❑ Finish reading the song. Stop after each stanza to add information to your graphic organizer.

Fix-Up Idea

Read Aloud
Although Foster dropped much of the dialect in the song, there are still several examples of it. Many of these are in the form of contractions or clipped words. Sometimes hearing dialect can help you unlock the meaning of words that look unfamiliar. Work with a partner to read the selection aloud. Alternate the reading of the stanzas, and read the refrain together.

MARK THE TEXT

Underline or highlight what comes a-knockin' at the door.

WHAT DO YOU WONDER?

Ask a question about the speaker's feelings.

_____
_____
_____

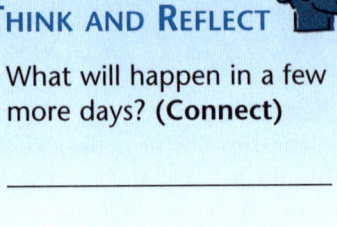

THINK AND REFLECT

What will happen in a few more days? **(Connect)**

_____
_____
_____

3. They hunt no more for the 'possum and the 'coon
   On the meadow, the hill and the shore;
   They sing no more by the glimmer of the moon
   On the bench by that old cabin door.

4. The day goes by like a shadow o'er the heart,
   with sorrow where all was delight.
   The time has come when the old friends have to part,
   Then my old Kentucky home, good night.
   (To Refrain)

5. The head must bow and the back will have to bend
   Wherever the poor folks may go.
   A few more days, and the trouble all will end
   in the field where the sugar canes grow.

6. A few more days for to tote the weary load;
   No matter, 'twill never be light.
   A few more days 'till we totter on the road,
   then my old Kentucky home good night.
   (To Refrain) ■

Reflect ON YOUR READING

After Reading ➤ SUMMARIZE THE IDEAS

- ❑ Review the details you added to your Cluster Chart.
- ❑ Summarize the ideas expressed in the folk song.
- ❑ How does the photograph on page 203 relate to your ideas?

_____
_____
_____

Reading Skills and Test Practice

MAKE INFERENCES

With your partner, discuss how to answer questions that ask you to make inferences. Use the Think-Aloud Notes to write down your reasons for eliminating the incorrect answers.

____ 1. To whom might the lady in the refrain refer?
   a. to a home in Kentucky
   b. to the President's wife
   c. to a woman who has moved away from home
   d. to a woman who is moving back home

____ 2. What emotional effect does Foster create in this song?
   a. nostalgia for his boyhood home in Kentucky
   b. sympathy for people who have to move from place to place to work
   c. pride about living in Kentucky
   d. a yearning for the home he never had

How did using the reading strategy help you to answer the questions?

_____
_____
_____

THINK-ALOUD NOTES

Investigate, Inquire, and Imagine

RECALL: GATHER FACTS
1a. What are the poor folks no longer able to do?

INTERPRET: FIND MEANING
1b. What causes poor folks to have to leave their home?

ANALYZE: TAKE THINGS APART
2a. From the description given of the poor folks and their living conditions, identify to whom Foster might be referring in this song.

SYNTHESIZE: BRING THINGS TOGETHER
2b. Will trouble really end in "a few more days"? Why, or why not?

EVALUATE: MAKE JUDGMENTS
3a. How do you think the poor folks in the song find the strength to continue, considering that they are being forced to do back-breaking work, travel from place to place, and be separated from their friends and family?

EXTEND: CONNECT IDEAS
3b. Has it ever seemed that your life has been ruled by circumstances beyond your control? How did your reaction compare with the way the poor folks in the song deal with their situation?

Literary Tools

FOLK SONG. A **folk song** is a traditional or composed song typically made up of stanzas, a refrain, and a simple melody. A *stanza* is a group of lines in a poem. A *refrain* is a phrase, line, or verse that recurs regularly at intervals throughout a poem or song, especially at the end of each stanza or division. A form of folk literature, folk songs are expressions of commonly shared ideas or feelings. Do you think the ideas and feelings that Foster expressed in this folk song were commonly shared by people of his time period? Why, or why not?

_____

_____

_____

_____

WordWorkshop

DIALECT. Dialect is a version of a language spoken by the people of particular place, time, or social group. Writers often use dialect to give their works a realistic flavor. Regional dialect is spoken by members of a particular social group or class, or of people living in a certain regional area of the country. Fill in the chart below with examples of dialect from "My Old Kentucky Home." Write examples of dialect in the "Dialect" column and explanations of the dialect in the "Explanation" column.

Dialect	Explanation

Read-Write Connection

How would you deal with moving from place to place and never having a place to call home?

_____

_____

_____

Beyond the Reading

CREATE A TIME LINE. Use the Internet or the library to find out more about the life of Stephen Foster. Then create a time line that includes major events in his life.

GO ONLINE. To find links and additional activities for this selection, visit the EMC Internet Resource Center at **emcp.com/languagearts** and click on Write-In Reader.

CONNECT

Reader's resource

After visiting a Union camp near Washington, DC in November 1861, where she saw soldiers marching off to battle, Julia Ward Howe was inspired to write **"The Battle Hymn of the Republic."** Some sources maintain that she was compelled to write the hymn after hearing Union troops sing "John Brown's body lies a-mouldering in the grave," a reference to farmer and abolitionist John Brown (1800–1859), who was hanged in Charlestown, Virginia (now West Virginia), for his fight against slavery. Howe's song was published in *The Atlantic Monthly* in February 1862 and soon became the Civil War anthem of the North. A patriotic hymn, "The Battle Hymn of the Republic" justifies the Union cause and celebrates heroic self-sacrifice.

Word watch

PREVIEW VOCABULARY

burnished   jubilant
fateful   transfigure
flaring   wrath

Reader's journal

If you had to fight in a war, what thoughts would help you feel brave?

"The Battle Hymn of the Republic"

by Julia Ward Howe

Active READING STRATEGY

READ WITH A PURPOSE

Before Reading ➤ ESTABLISH A PURPOSE FOR READING

❑ Read the Reader's Resource and look at the illustration on page 209.
❑ Complete the Reader's Journal question and discuss your response with a few of your classmates.
❑ Set a purpose for reading by looking for references to military terms as you read.

Graphic Organizer: Cluster Chart

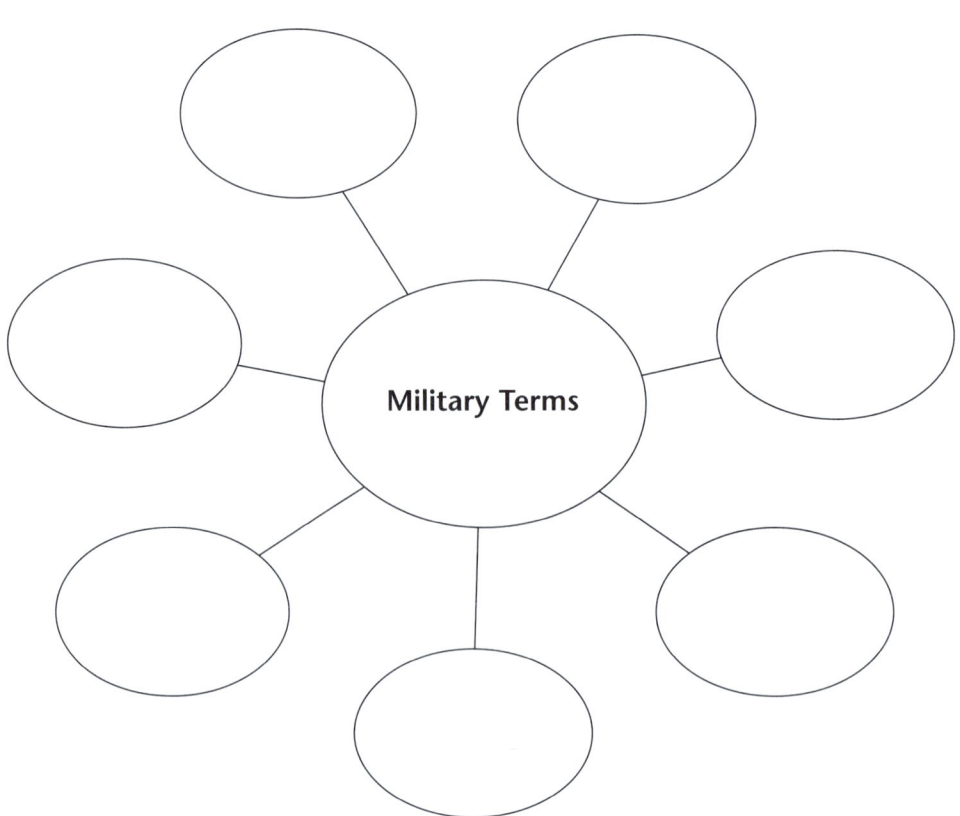

208   THE EMC WRITE-IN READER

During Reading

LOOK FOR MILITARY TERMS

- ❑ As you read, mark military terms.
- ❑ When you finish reading, add these terms to your graphic organizer.

Julia Ward Howe

Mine eyes have seen the glory
of the coming of the Lord,
He is trampling out the vintage[1]
Where the grapes of <u>wrath</u> are stored

READ ALOUD

In a soft voice, read lines 1–12 aloud. According to the speaker, what has the Lord done?

_____
_____
_____

---

1. **vintage.** Season's yield of wine from a vineyard

words for everyday use

wrath (rath) *n.*, strong, vengeful anger. *The captain vented his <u>wrath</u> on the enemy regiment that had killed ten of his men.*

UNIT 5 / READING FOLK LITERATURE **209**

He hath loosed his <u>fateful</u> lightning
of his terrible swift sword,
His truth is marching on.
   Chorus:
10   Glory! Glory! Hallelujah![2]
   Glory! Glory! Hallelujah!
   Glory! Glory! Hallelujah!
   His truth is marching on.

I have seen him in the watchfires[3] of a hundred circling camps,
they have builded Him an altar in the evening dews and damps[4]
I can read his righteous sentence by the dim and <u>flaring</u> lamps;
His day is marching on.
20   *Chorus*

I have read a firey gospel[5]
Writ in <u>burnished</u> rows of steel
As ye deal with my condemners,
So with you my grace will deal;
Let the hero born of woman
Crush the serpent with his heel;
Since God is marching on.
   Chorus

He has sounded forth the trumpet
30 that shall never sound retreat;
He is sifting out the hearts of men

Reading STRATEGY REVIEW

VISUALIZE. Sketch some of the images the speaker creates in lines 13–27.

THINK AND REFLECT

What might the serpent represent? **(Interpret)**

_____
_____

---

2. **Hallelujah!** Interjection of praise, joy, or thanks
3. **watchfires.** Fires lighted as a signal or for the use of a guard
4. **damps.** Mists, fogs
5. **gospel.** Message concerning Jesus, the kingdom of God, and salvation; one of the first four New Testament books in the Bible

words for everyday use

fate • ful (fāt′ fəl) *adj.*, deadly. *The <u>fateful</u> winter storm claimed the lives of many travelers.*
flar • ing (flar′ ing) *adj.*, flaming brightly or unsteadily. *The <u>flaring</u> bonfire cast flickering shadows on our faces.*
bur • nished (bər′nished) *adj.*, polished; made shiny by rubbing. *<u>Burnished</u> silver sparkles like moonlight, but tarnished silver is as black as soot.*

beneath his Judgment Seat.
Oh! Be swift, my soul to answer him,
be <u>jubilant</u>, my feet!
Our God is marching on.
    Chorus

In the beauty of the lilies
Christ was born across the sea
With a glory in his bosom
40   That <u>transfigures</u> you and me;
As he died to make men holy
let us die to make men free,
While God is marching on.
    Chorus ■

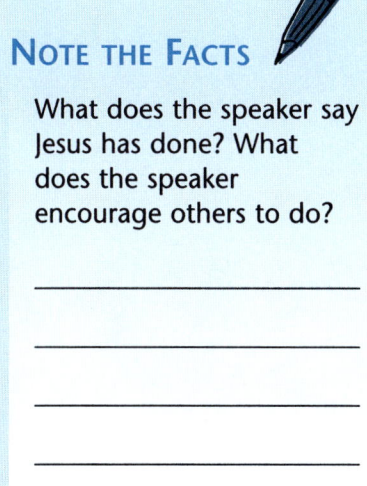

NOTE THE FACTS

What does the speaker say Jesus has done? What does the speaker encourage others to do?

_____
_____
_____
_____

---

words for everyday use

ju • bi • lant (jü′ bə lənt) *adj.,* joyful, triumphant. *When our soccer team won, we let out <u>jubilant</u> shouts of celebration.*

trans • fig • ure (tran[t]s fi′ gyər) *vt.,* give a new and exalted or spiritual appearance to. *According to tradition, Buddha was <u>transfigured</u> while meditating under a tree.*

Reflect ON YOUR READING

After Reading → SUMMARIZE THE MILITARY IDEAS

- ❑ Use your Cluster Chart to summarize ideas that made you think of the military.
- ❑ How did using the reading strategy help you to understand the purpose of the song?

_____
_____
_____
_____

Reading Skills and Test Practice

IDENTIFY THE AUTHOR'S PURPOSE

READ, THINK, AND EXPLAIN. Discuss with a partner how to identify an author's purpose. Use the Think-Aloud Notes to jot down your ideas.

1. Why did Howe write "The Battle Hymn of the Republic"?

_____
_____

2. Did she achieve her purpose? Why, or why not?

_____
_____
_____
_____

REFLECT ON YOUR RESPONSE. Compare your responses with those of a partner. Were your responses similar? How did using the reading strategy help you to answer the questions?

_____
_____

THINK-ALOUD NOTES

Investigate, Inquire, and Imagine

RECALL: GATHER FACTS
1a. In the first stanza of the song, what is the Lord described as doing?

INTERPRET: FIND MEANING
1b. How would you characterize the way the Lord is depicted in this stanza? How might the Lord's action in the vineyard appear?

ANALYZE: TAKE THINGS APART
2a. Analyze the speaker's depiction of God in this song. According to the speaker, is God impartial in matters of war? If so, explain in what way this impartiality is revealed. If not, whose side is God on, according to the speaker, and how can you tell?

SYNTHESIZE: BRING THINGS TOGETHER
2b. Explain whether you would classify Julia Ward Howe as impartial in her depiction of the opposing forces involved in the Civil War. Explain what you think Howe's priorities were in writing this song. In what way did the time in which she wrote the song affect her depiction of the Civil War?

PERSPECTIVE: LOOK AT OTHER VIEWS
3a. Explain what attitude you believe Confederate soldiers might have adopted toward this song. What might they have thought about the speaker's portrayal of the Lord's relationship with Union troops? As an alternative to this question, explore what your attitude would be toward this song if you were a pacifist. What might you refute?

EMPATHY: SEE FROM INSIDE
3b. Imagine what it would be like to be in a war where American fought American, and, as sometimes was the case, brother fought brother. What conflicting feelings might soldiers have experienced? Why might religious hymns, such as Howe's, have been used to ready soldiers for battle?

Literary Tools

HYMN. A **hymn** is a song or verse of praise, often religious. What religious images and themes does Howe use in "The Battle Hymn of the Republic"?

_____

_____

_____

_____

WordWorkshop

ARCHAIC LANGUAGE. Archaic language consists of old or obsolete phrases such as *smote* for *hit*. When you read "The Battle Hymn of the Republic," you may have noticed that Howe wrote "Mine eyes have seen the glory," when standard usage today would dictate that we say "My eyes have seen the glory." Compile a list of archaic words used in the hymn and add them to the chart below. Then write down the modern equivalents of these terms.

Archaic Word or Phrase	Modern Word or Phrase
Mine eyes	My eyes

Read-Write Connection

If you were a Union soldier, how would hearing the words of this song make you feel about your role in the war?

Beyond the Reading

FIND CIVIL WAR SONGS. Although "The Battle Hymn of the Republic" is probably the most widely known Civil War song, it is far from the only one. Work with a partner to locate another Civil War song. Together, prepare an oral interpretation of the song, writing an introduction and any needed transitions between verses. You and your classmate do not have to sing the song if you are not comfortable doing so; instead, you may take turns expressively reading alternate verses.

GO ONLINE. To find links and additional activities for this selection, visit the EMC Internet Resource Center at **emcp.com/languagearts** and click on Write-In Reader.

Unit 5 READING Review

Choose and Use Reading Strategies

Before reading an excerpt from another spiritual, review and discuss with a partner how to use reading strategies with folk literature.

1. Read with a Purpose
2. Connect to Prior Knowledge
3. Write Things Down
4. Make Predictions
5. Visualize
6. Use Text Organization
7. Tackle Difficult Vocabulary
8. Monitor Your Reading Progress

Read "Go Down, Moses," another spiritual from the African-American folk tradition. "Go Down, Moses" tells the story of Moses, a Hebrew prophet who led his people, the Israelites, out of captivity in Egypt. Use the margins and mark up the lyrics. Show how you use reading strategies to read actively. After you finish reading, summarize the spiritual's ideas in two or three sentences.

> When Israel was in Egypt's land,
> Let my people go!
> Oppressed so hard they could not stand,
> Let my people go!
>
> *Chorus*
> "Go down, Moses,
> 'Way down in Egypt's land.
> Tell old Pharaoh
> To let my people go!"
>
> "Thus spoke the Lord," bold Moses said,
> "Let my people go!
> If not, I'll smite your firstborn dead,
> Let my people go!"
>
> *(Repeat Chorus)*
>
> "No more shall they in bondage toil,
> Let my people go!
> Let them come out with Egypt's spoil,
> Let my people go!"
>
> *(Repeat Chorus)*

WordWorkshop

UNIT 5 WORDS FOR EVERYDAY USE

burnished, 210	flaring, 210	transfigure, 211
fateful, 210	jubilant, 211	wrath, 209

CREATE A VOCABULARY TEST. Create a vocabulary test with five sentence-completion questions. Include three possible answers for each question. Vary the forms of the words as necessary. When you are done, exchange tests with a classmate.

EXAMPLE
My mother's _____ feelings were apparent when she yelled at me after I made a hole in the wall with my soccer ball.
a. jubilant
b. wrathful
c. burnished
Answer: *b*

1. _____

2. _____

3. _____

4. _____

5. _____

When you and your classmate finish the sentences, together create a song that uses all of the Words for Everyday Use from this unit.

_____
_____
_____
_____
_____
_____
_____
_____
_____
_____

Literary Tools

Select the best literary element on the right to complete each sentence on the left. Write the correct letter in the blank.

_____1. "Follow the Drinking Gourd" is a(n) ____ because it is a song with a deep religious and emotional character.

_____2. "My Old Kentucky Home" is a(n) ____ because it is has stanzas, a refrain, and a simple melody.

_____3. "The Battle Hymn of the Republic" is a(n) ____ because it is a religious song of praise.

_____4. The central idea in "Swing Low, Sweet Chariot," a search for freedom and heaven, is known as the song's ____.

_____5. Because "Song of the Sky Loom" explains events in the natural world as resulting from the action of some supernatural entity it is called a(n) ____.

a. folk song, 182, 206
b. hymn, 213
c. myth, 181, 187, 189
d. spiritual, 192, 195
e. theme, 200

On Your Own

FLUENTLY SPEAKING. Form small groups to research and present spirituals and folk songs from other cultures within the United States. Work together to write and present an introduction that explains the history of each work.

PICTURE THIS. Create a songbook of additional folk songs and spirituals, and include the musical notes. Illustrate the songs with images that reflect what each is about.

PUT IT IN WRITING. Imagine that you work in the public relations department of an orchestra that will perform one of the songs in this unit. Write a press release to persuade the public to attend the concert. Include the following information in your press release: date of press release, date and time of the concert, location, name of group performing, costs of the tickets, how to purchase the tickets, and why people should attend.

Unit SIX

Reading Drama

DRAMA

A **drama,** or *play*, is a story told through characters played by actors. Early groups of people around the world enacted ritual scenes related to hunting, warfare, or religion. From these, drama arose. Western drama as we know it began in ancient Greece.

Types of Drama

Most dramas can be classified as either comedies or tragedies. A **comedy** originally was any work with a happy ending. The term is widely used today to refer to any humorous work, especially one prepared for the stage or screen. A **tragedy** initially was a drama that told the story of the fall of a person of high status. In recent years, the word *tragedy* has been used to describe any play about the downfall of a central character, or *protagonist*, who wins the audience's sympathies.

The earliest American theatrical productions were vaudeville shows and **melodramas,** plays with exaggerated characters, scenes and situations. From the 1920s through the 1950s, **Realist theater**, plays emphasizing details of ordinary life, blossomed in the work of American playwrights. In this unit, *The Glass Menagerie* by Tennessee Williams is an example of Realist theater. In recent decades **modern drama** has dealt with such contemporary American problems as rootlessness, violence, and sexism, or with the realities of the African-American urban experience.

Elements of Drama

THE PLAYWRIGHT. The author of a play is the **playwright.** A playwright has limited control in deciding how his or her work is presented.

NOTE THE FACTS

What are two types of drama?

_____
_____
_____

Producers, directors, set designers, and actors all interpret a playwright's work and present their interpretations to the audience.

Script. A **script** is the written text from which a drama is produced. It contains dialogue and stage directions and may be divided into acts and scenes.

Dialogue. The speech of the actors in a play is called **dialogue.** In a play, dialogue appears after the names of characters. A speech given by one character is called a **monologue.** A speech given by a character alone onstage is called a **soliloquy.** A statement intended to be heard by the audience but not by other characters on the stage is called an **aside.**

Acts and Scenes. An **act** is a major part of the play. One-act, three-act, and five-act plays are all common. A **scene** is a short section of a drama, and typically begins with the entrance of one or more characters. The number of scenes in each act may vary.

In this unit, you will read a scene from Act 3 of *The Crucible* and Act 1, Scenes 1–3 of *The Glass Menagerie* by Tennessee Williams.

The Parts of a Stage

Up Right	Up Center	Up Left
Right Center	Center	Left Center
Down Right	Down Center	Down Left

Stage Directions. Stage directions are notes included in a script to describe how the playwright wants something to be presented or performed onstage. Stage directions can describe lighting, costumes, music, sound effects, or other elements of a play. They can also describe entrances and exits, gestures, tone of voice, or other elements related to the acting of a play. Stage directions

---

NOTE THE FACTS

What is a speech given by one character called?

_____

_____

_____

_____

Reading Strategy Review

Visualize. Using the Parts of a Stage diagram, mark where characters would go if stage directions told them to *enter up right.*

sometimes provide background information. In stage directions, the parts of the stage are described from the actor's point of view, as shown on the diagram below. As you read the excerpt from *The Crucible*, pay attention to the way the stage directions (given in parentheses) describe how the characters move and react.

SPECTACLE. The **spectacle** includes all the elements of the drama that are presented to the audience's senses. The set, props, special effects, lighting, and costumes are all part of the spectacle.

USING READING STRATEGIES WITH DRAMA

Active Reading Strategy Checklists

When reading drama, be aware of the plot (what happens), the setting, the characters, the dialogue (what the characters say), and the stage directions (how the characters say their lines and the actions they take onstage). The following checklists offer things to consider as you read drama.

1 READ WITH A PURPOSE. Before reading drama, give yourself a purpose, or something to look for, as you read. Sometimes your teacher will give you a purpose: "As you read, try to determine the theme for the play." Other times you can set your own purpose by previewing the opening lines and instructional information. Say to yourself

- ❏ I want to look for . . .
- ❏ I need to learn what happens to . . .
- ❏ I want to experience how . . .
- ❏ I want to understand why . . .
- ❏ I want to figure out what causes . . .

2 CONNECT TO PRIOR KNOWLEDGE. Being aware of what you already know and thinking about it as you read can help you understand the characters and events. As you read, say to yourself

- ❏ The setting is a lot like . . .
- ❏ What happens here is similar to what happens in . . .
- ❏ This character is like . . .
- ❏ The ending reminds me of . . .
- ❏ I like this description because . . .

Reading **TIP**

Become an actor! Practice reading parts of the play aloud using a voice that expresses what the characters feel.

USE A CODE

Here's a way to code the text.
- \+   I like this
- –   I don't like this
- √   This is important
- Yes I agree with this
- No I disagree with this
- ?   I don't understand this
- W I wonder . . .
- !   This is like something I know
- ↝ I need to come back to this later

Create additional code marks to note other reactions you have.

Reading TIP

Sketch what the setting and the characters look like. The sketch will help you envision the action.

3 **WRITE THINGS DOWN.** As you read drama, write down important ideas that the author is sharing with readers. Possible ways to write things down include

- ❑ Underline important information in the stage directions.
- ❑ Write down things you want to remember about how the characters might say their lines.
- ❑ Highlight lines you want to read aloud.
- ❑ Create a graphic organizer to keep track of people and events.
- ❑ Use a code in the margin that shows how you respond to the action.

4 **MAKE PREDICTIONS.** As you read drama, use information in the stage directions and the dialogue to make guesses about what will happen next. Make predictions like the following.

- ❑ The title makes me predict that . . .
- ❑ The stage directions make me think that . . .
- ❑ I think the selection will end with . . .
- ❑ I think there will be a conflict between . . .
- ❑ The dialogue makes me guess that . . .

5 **VISUALIZE.** Visualizing, or allowing the words on the page to create images in your mind, helps you understand the action and how the characters may say their lines. In order to visualize the setting, the characters, and the action, make statements such as

- ❑ The setting and props look . . .
- ❑ This character speaks . . .
- ❑ This character's movements are . . .
- ❑ This character wears . . .
- ❑ Over the course of the play, this character's behavior . . .
- ❑ The words help me see, hear, feel, smell, taste . . .

6 **USE TEXT ORGANIZATION.** When you read drama, pay attention to the dialogue, the characters, and the action. Learn to stop occasionally and retell what you have read. Say to yourself

- ❑ The stage directions help me pay attention to . . .
- ❑ The exposition, or introduction, is about . . .
- ❑ The central conflict centers on . . .
- ❑ The climax, or high point of interest, occurs when . . .
- ❑ The resolution, or the outcome, of the play is that . . .
- ❑ My summary of this scene is . . .

7 TACKLE DIFFICULT VOCABULARY. Difficult words in drama can get in the way of your ability to understand the characters and events. Use context, consult a dictionary, or ask someone about words you do not understand. When you come across a difficult word in a drama, say to yourself

- ❏ The lines near this word tell me that this word means . . .
- ❏ A dictionary definition shows that the word means . . .
- ❏ My work with the word before reading helps me know that the word means . . .
- ❏ A classmate said that the word means . . .
- ❏ This word is pronounced . . .

8 MONITOR YOUR READING PROGRESS. All readers encounter difficulty when they read, especially if the reading material is not self-selected. When you have to read something, note problems you are having and fix them. The key to reading success is knowing when you are having difficulty. To fix problems, say to yourself

- ❏ Because I don't understand this part, I will . . .
- ❏ Because I'm having trouble staying connected to what I'm reading, I will . . .
- ❏ Because the words in the play are too hard, I will . . .
- ❏ Because the play is long, I will . . .
- ❏ Because I can't retell what happened here, I will . . .

Become an Active Reader

The instruction with the drama selection in this unit gives you an in-depth look at how to use one strategy to read actively. Brief margin notes guide your use of additional strategies. Using one active reading strategy will greatly increase your reading success and enjoyment. Use the white space in the margins to add your own comments and strategy ideas. Learn how to use several strategies in combination to ensure your complete understanding of what you are reading. When you have difficulty, try a fix-up idea. For further information about the active reading strategies, see Unit 1, pages 4–15.

Reading TIP

Insert synonyms for difficult words into the dialogue as you read. If you are unsure about a synonym that will work, ask a classmate about the synonym he or she would use.

Fix-Up Ideas
- Reread
- Ask a question
- Read in shorter chunks
- Read aloud
- Retell
- Work with a partner
- Unlock difficult words
- Vary your reading rate
- Choose a new reading strategy
- Create a mnemonic device

How to Use Reading Strategies with Drama

Note how a reader uses active reading strategies while reading this excerpt from Act 1 of *The Crucible* by Arthur Miller.

READ WITH A PURPOSE — I want to find out why Abigail is being accused of witchcraft.	**CONNECT TO PRIOR KNOWLEDGE** — I've heard about the Salem witch trials. I'd like to know more about them.

ABIGAIL. Uncle, the rumor of witchcraft is all about; I think you'd best go down and deny it yourself. The parlor's packed with people, sir. I'll go sit with her.

PARRIS. (*pressed, turns on her*) And what shall I say to them? That my daughter and my niece I discovered dancing like the heathen in the forest?

ABIGAIL. Uncle, we did dance; let you tell them I confessed it—and I'll be whipped if I must be. But they're speakin' of witchcraft. Betty's not witched.

PARRIS. Abigail, I cannot go before the congregation when I know you have not opened with me. What did you do with her in the forest?

ABIGAIL. We did dance, uncle, and when you leaped out of the bush so suddenly, Betty was frightened and then she fainted. And there's the whole of it.

PARRIS. Child, sit you down.

ABIGAIL. (*quavering, as she sits*). I would never hurt Betty. I love her dearly.

PARRIS. Now look you, child, your punishment will come in its time. But if you trafficked with spirits in the forest I must know it now, for surely my enemies will, and they will ruin me with it.

ABIGAIL. But we never conjured spirits.

PARRIS. Then why can she not move herself since midnight? This child is desperate! (ABIGAIL *lowers her eyes.*) It must come out—my enemies will bring it out. Let me know what you done there. Abigail, do you understand that I have many enemies?

ABIGAIL. I have heard of it, uncle.

PARRIS. There is a faction sworn to drive me from my pulpit. Do you understand that?

ABIGAIL. I think so, sir.

PARRIS. Now then, in the midst of such disruption, my own household is discovered to be the very center of some obscene practice. Abominations are done in the forest—

ABIGAIL. It were sport, uncle!

VISUALIZE — I can picture the girls dancing in the forest.

MONITOR YOUR READING PROGRESS — I'll try to summarize what I've read so far.

MAKE PREDICTIONS — I predict that Parris's enemies will cause trouble for him.

USE TEXT ORGANIZATION — The capitalized names tell me who is speaking.

TACKLE DIFFICULT VOCABULARY — The context tells me that *abominations* must mean something obscene or disgusting.

WRITE THINGS DOWN — I can highlight things Parris says that reveal what kind of person he is.

FROM The Crucible
by Arthur Miller

Active READING STRATEGY

VISUALIZE

Before Reading ▶ PREPARE TO MAKE A MIND MOVIE

❏ Preview the entire selection, including the Reader's Resource on this page, the cast of characters and introductory paragraph on pages 226–228, and the activities on pages 232–234.
❏ Write down what you think the selection will be about.
❏ Create a short mind movie of a courtroom scene, including the characters described on page 226.
❏ In the graphic organizer below, you will sketch the mind movie you create as you read the selection.

Graphic Organizer: Visualization Sketches

CONNECT

Reader's resource

In 1692, a series of trials was held in Salem, Massachusetts, of persons accused of witchcraft. A number of people in the community and in surrounding areas had developed a disease resembling epilepsy, and suspicions arose that the afflictions might be the work of witches. In all, nineteen persons were hanged as a result of the trials, and one person was pressed to death. Many others were imprisoned and tortured.

Arthur Miller became interested in the Salem witch trials during the McCarthy Era of the 1950s, a time when a similar "witch hunt" occurred in the United States, this one for suspected Communists and other radicals in public office and the entertainment industry. Miller's play, *The Crucible,* explores the psychology of mob hysteria and guilt by association.

Word watch

PREVIEW VOCABULARY
confound

Reader's journal

When have you felt social pressure to do something you knew was wrong?

UNIT 6 / READING DRAMA   **225**

During Reading

MAKE A MIND MOVIE

- In groups of eight, assign each person a role. One person should read the stage directions aloud.
- Try to picture what the courtroom and the people look like, how they speak, and how they move. Imagine you are a court artist and sketch Danforth being questioned in one of the sketch boxes in the graphic organizer.
- Read the rest of the selection silently, continuing to make a mind movie. Then rejoin your group and reread the last two pages of the selection aloud, using dramatic tones and gestures.

The people in a play are its **characters.** Names of characters are given before the words that they speak. In a play the **dialogue** is the speech of the characters and is not placed in quotation marks.

Arthur Miller

Cast of Characters in This Scene

Abigail Williams. 18-year-old niece of Reverend Parris. In love with John Proctor, she pretends to be possessed in an attempt to have Proctor's wife condemned as a witch.

John Proctor. Farmer in his mid-thirties seeking to free his wife from false charges.

Mary Warren. 17-year-old servant of John Proctor.

Mercy Lewis and Susanna Walcott. Mercy is an 18-year-old servant girl; Susanna is a little younger. Along with Abigail, they claim to have been possessed by witches.

Reverend Samuel Parris. Zealous minister who begins the witch hunt in Salem.

Deputy Governor Danforth. The deputy governor of Salem, prosecutor in this case.

Reverend John Hale. A minister who is called to Salem by Reverend Parris to help determine whether witchcraft is afoot.

In this scene from Act 3 of the play, John Proctor, whose wife, Elizabeth, has been arrested as a witch, has brought to the court Mary Warren, who has evidence that Abigail and the other afflicted girls have been pretending. As the scene opens, Abigail interrupts an interrogation of John Proctor by the prosecutor, Danforth.

Abigail, with a weird, wild, chilling cry, screams up to the ceiling.
ABIGAIL. You will not! Begone! Begone, I say!
DANFORTH. What is it, child? (*But Abigail, pointing with fear, is now raising up her frightened eyes, her awed face, toward the ceiling—the girls are doing the same—and now Hawthorne, Haler, Putnam, Cheever, Herrick, and Danforth do the same.*) What's there? (*He lowers his eyes from the ceiling, and now he is frightened; there is real tension in his voice.*) Child! (*She is transfixed—with all the girls, she is whimpering open-mouthed, agape at the ceiling.*) Girls! Why do you—?
MERCY LEWIS. (*pointing*) It's on the beam! Behind the rafter!
DANFORTH. (*looking up*) Where!
ABIGAIL. Why—? (*She gulps.*) Why do you come, yellow bird?
PROCTOR. Where's a bird? I see no bird!
ABIGAIL. (*to the ceiling*) My face? My face?
PROCTOR. Mr. Hale—
DANFORTH. Be quiet!
PROCTOR. (*to Hale*) Do you see a bird?
DANFORTH. Be quiet!!
ABIGAIL. (*to the ceiling, in a genuine conversation with the "bird," as though trying to talk it out of attacking her*) But God made my face; you cannot want to tear my face. Envy is a deadly sin, Mary.
MARY WARREN. (*on her feet with a spring, and horrified, pleading*) Abby!
ABIGAIL. (*unperturbed, continuing to the "bird"*) Oh, Mary, this is a black art[1] to change your shape. No, I cannot, I cannot stop my mouth; it's God's work I do.
MARY WARREN. Abbey, I'm *here!*

---
1. **black art.** Evil magic

NOTE THE FACTS

What question does Danforth ask Mary?

_____

_____

FIX-UP IDEA

Quickwrite
After you read to the second page of the selection, stop and do a quickwrite about the situation. Describe the situation. What would you do if you were Danforth? Proctor? Mary Warren? Continue reading. When you get to the end of the third page, stop and do another quickwrite. How has the situation changed? How would you react now? Read to the last page and do a final quickwrite.

THINK AND REFLECT

What does Mary mean when she says that the girls are "sporting"? (Interpret)

_____

_____

_____

PROCTOR. (*frantically*) They're pretending, Mr. Danforth!
ABIGAIL. (*Now she takes a backward step, as though in fear the bird will swoop down momentarily.*) Oh, please, Mary! Don't come down.
SUSANNA WALCOTT. Her claws, she's stretching her claws!
PROCTOR. Lies, lies.
ABIGAIL. (*backing further, eyes still fixed above*) Mary, please don't hurt me!
MARY WARREN. (*to Danforth*) I'm not hurting her!
DANFORTH. (*to Mary Warren*) Why does she see this vision?
MARY WARREN. She sees nothin'!
ABIGAIL. (*now staring full front as though hypnotized, and mimicking the exact tone of Mary Warren's cry*) She sees nothin'!
MARY WARREN. (*pleading*) Abby, you mustn't!
ABIGAIL AND ALL THE GIRLS. (*all transfixed*) Abby, you mustn't!
MARY WARREN. (*to all the girls*) I'm here, I'm here!
GIRLS. I'm here, I'm here!
DANFORTH. (*horrified*) Mary Warren! Draw back your spirit out of them!
MARY WARREN. Mr. Danforth!
GIRLS. (*cutting her off*) Mr. Danforth!
DANFORTH. Have you compacted with the devil? Have you?
MARY WARREN. Never, never!
GIRLS. Never, never!
DANFORTH. (*growing hysterical*) Why can they only repeat you?
PROCTOR. Give me a whip—I'll stop it!
MARY WARREN. They're sporting. They—!
GIRLS. They're sporting!
MARY WARREN. (*turning on them all hysterically and stamping her feet*) Abby, stop it!
GIRLS. (*stamping their feet*) Abby, stop it!
MARY WARREN. Stop it!
GIRLS. Stop it!
MARY WARREN. (*screaming it out at the top of her lungs, and raising her fists*) Stop it!!

GIRLS. (*raising their fists*) Stop it!!

Mary Warren, utterly confounded, and becoming overwhelmed by Abigail's—and the girls'—utter conviction, starts to whimper, hands half raised, powerless, and all the girls begin whimpering exactly as she does.

DANFORTH. A little while ago you were afflicted. Now it seems you afflict others; where did you find this power?

MARY WARREN. (*staring at Abigail*) I—have no power.

GIRLS. I have no power.

PROCTOR. They're gulling[2] you, Mister!

DANFORTH. Why did you turn about this past two weeks? You have seen the Devil, have you not?

HALE. (*indicating Abigail and the girls*) You cannot believe them!

MARY WARREN. I—

PROCTOR. (*sensing her weakening*) Mary, God damns all liars!

DANFORTH. (*pounding it into her*) You have seen the Devil, you have made compact with Lucifer,[3] have you not?

Mary utters something unintelligible, staring at Abigail, who keeps watching the "bird" above.

PROCTOR. God damns liars, Mary!

DANFORTH. I cannot hear you. What do you say? (*Mary utters again unintelligibly.*) You will confess yourself or you will hang! (*He turns her roughly to face him.*) Do you know who I am? I say you will hang if you do not open with me!

PROCTOR. Mary, remember the angel Raphael—do that which is good and—

ABIGAIL. (*pointing upward*) The wings! Her wings are spreading! Mary, please, don't, don't—!

HALE. I see nothing, Your Honor!

DANFORTH. Do you confess this power! (*He is an inch from her face.*) Speak!

---

2. **gull.** To trick; dupe
3. **Lucifer.** Name for the devil

MARK THE TEXT

Underline or highlight what Danforth accuses Mary of.

THINK AND REFLECT

What might happen to Mary if the court believes Abigail and the girls? **(Predict)**

_____
_____
_____

USE THE STRATEGY

VISUALIZE. Draw a sketch in your graphic organizer illustrating the action at this point.

words for everyday use

con • found (kən found´) *vt.*, confuse; bewilder. *The results of the experiment* confounded *the physicists at first because they appeared to contradict the laws of physics.*

Use THE STRATEGY

VISUALIZE. Rejoin your group and read the last two pages of the selection aloud, using dramatic tones and gestures to act out your mind movie.

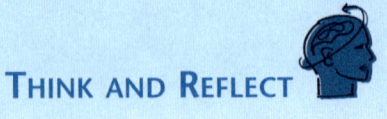

THINK AND REFLECT

Whose book does Mary accuse Proctor of asking her to sign? **(Infer)**

_____
_____
_____

Reading STRATEGY REVIEW

MAKE A PREDICTION. What do you think will happen to Mary?

_____
_____

ABIGAIL. She's going to come down! She's walking the beam!

DANFORTH. Will you speak!

MARY WARREN. (*staring in horror*) I cannot!

GIRLS. I cannot!

110 **PARRIS.** Cast the Devil out! Look him in the face! Trample him! We'll save you, Mary, only stand fast against him and—

ABIGAIL. (*looking up*) Look out! She's coming down!

She and all the girls run to one wall, shielding their eyes. And now, as though cornered, they let out a gigantic scream, and Mary, as though infected, opens her mouth and screams with them. Gradually Abigail and the girls leave off, until only Mary is left there, staring up at the "bird," screaming madly. All watch her, horrified by this evident fit. Proctor strides to her.

120 **PROCTOR.** Mary, tell the Governor what they— (*He has hardly got a word out, when seeing him coming for her, she rushes out of his reach, screaming in horror.*)

MARY WARREN. Don't touch me—don't touch me! (*At which the girls halt at the door.*)

PROCTOR. (*astonished*) Mary!

MARY WARREN. (*pointing at Proctor*) You're the Devil's man!

He is stopped in his tracks.

PARRIS. Praise God!

GIRLS. Praise God!

130 **PROCTOR.** (*numbed*) Mary, how—?

MARY WARREN. I'll not hang with you! I love God, I love God.

DANFORTH. (*to Mary*) He bid you do the Devil's work?

MARY WARREN. (*hysterically, indicating Proctor*) He come at me by night and every day to sign, to sign, to—

DANFORTH. Sign what?

PARRIS. The Devil's book? He come with a book?

MARY WARREN. (*hysterically, pointing at Proctor, fearful of him*) My name, he want my name. "I'll murder you," he
140 says, "if my wife hangs! We must go and overthrow the court," he says!

Danforth's head jerks toward Proctor, shock and horror in his face.

PROCTOR. (*turning, appealing to Hale*) Mr. Hale!

MARY WARREN. (*her sobs beginning*) He wake me every

night, his eyes were like coals and his fingers claw my neck, and I sign, I sign . . .

HALE. Excellency, this child's gone wild!

PROCTOR. (*as Danforth's wide eyes pour on him*) Mary, Mary!

MARY WARREN. (*screaming at him*) No, I love God; I go your way no more. I love God, I bless God. (*Sobbing, she rushes to Abigail.*) Abby, Abby, I'll never hurt you more! (*They all watch, as Abigail, out of her infinite charity, reaches out and draws the sobbing Mary to her, and then looks up to Danforth.*) ■

THINK AND REFLECT

How is Mary's final statement to Abigail ironic? Why do you think Mary makes this statement? **(Evaluate)**

Reflect ON YOUR READING

After Reading ➤ **DISCUSS MIND MOVIES**

- ❏ Share your Visualization Sketches with your group and explain how they illustrate your mind movie.
- ❏ Discuss the following questions: How do other people's actions and tones match the mind movie you made? Talk about your different interpretations.

Reading Skills and Test Practice

IDENTIFY AND ANALYZE LITERARY ELEMENTS

READ, THINK, AND EXPLAIN. Define *stage directions* and explain why they are a critical element of drama. Use examples from *The Crucible* to support your response.

_____
_____
_____
_____
_____
_____
_____
_____

REFLECT ON YOUR RESPONSE. Compare your response to those of your group members. What examples from the play did each of you use? How did your mind movies help you give examples?

_____
_____
_____
_____
_____
_____

THINK-ALOUD NOTES

_____
_____
_____
_____
_____
_____
_____
_____
_____
_____

Investigate, Inquire, and Imagine

RECALL: GATHER FACTS
1a. Of what does Mary accuse Proctor?

INTERPRET: FIND MEANING
1b. Why does Mary change her mind and accuse Proctor?

ANALYZE: TAKE THINGS APART
2a. In Puritan New England, debate raged over the admissibility in court of "spectral evidence," the evidence of spirits seen by some people but not by others. What example of such "spectral evidence" appears in this selection? What other "evidence" does Danforth have for believing that Proctor is "the Devil's man"?

SYNTHESIZE: BRING THINGS TOGETHER
2b. How would you describe the method of questioning that Danforth uses with Mary? Would such a method of questioning be acceptable in a court of law today? What is the weakness of this strategy? Explain.

EVALUATE: MAKE JUDGMENTS
3a. What pressures are put on Mary to denounce Proctor? Is what Mary does understandable? excusable? moral? Why, or why not?

EXTEND: CONNECT IDEAS
3b. What would you do in Mary's position?

Literary Tools

STAGE DIRECTIONS. **Stage directions** are notes that describe characters' movements and ways of speaking, the setting, or such elements of the spectacle as lighting, costumes, properties, and sound effects. Find examples in this scene of stage directions that indicate parts of the setting and stage directions that indicate how characters are to speak or move. How do the stage directions help you to visualize the action in the play?

_____
_____
_____
_____
_____
_____
_____

WordWorkshop

CONTEXT CLUES. You can often figure out the meaning of an unfamiliar word in your reading by using context clues. Three main types of context clues are restatement, apposition, and examples.

The author may use **restatement** by using different words to express the same idea in the same or another sentence.

EXAMPLE   A number of people developed a *disease* resembling epilepsy, and suspicions arose that the **afflictions** might be the work of witches.

Apposition renames something in different words. Look for a word or phrase that has been placed in the sentence to clarify the word you do not know.

EXAMPLE   Abigail interrupts the **interrogation,** or *questioning,* of John Proctor by the prosecutor.

Examples used in a sentence can help illustrate a term you do not know.

EXAMPLE   *Hanging* and *pressing* were forms of **capital punishment** during the Salem Witch Trials; now *death by injection* is more common.

On your own paper, write a sentence for each of the following words from *The Crucible* that uses restatement, apposition, or examples to convey the meaning of the word. If you wish to use restatement, you may write two sentences to help convey the meaning of the given word.

1. condemned
2. zealous
3. unperturbed
4. sporting
5. infinite

Read-Write Connection

Have you ever tried to blame someone else when you were being accused of something? What were your reasons for doing this?

Beyond the Reading

RESEARCH THE SALEM WITCH TRIALS AND THE MCCARTHY HEARINGS. Divide the class into two groups. One group will research the Salem witch trials of 1692, while the other group researches the McCarthy hearings of the early 1950s. Each group present its findings in class. Then hold a class discussion about the similarities and differences between these two historical moments.

GO ONLINE. To find links and additional activities for this selection, visit the EMC Internet Resource Center at **emcp.com/languagearts** and click on Write-In Reader.

from *The Glass Menagerie*
by Tennessee Williams

Active READING STRATEGY

WRITE THINGS DOWN

Before Reading ➤ MAKE A CHARACTERIZATION CHART

- Read the Reader's Resource on page 236. What do you learn about the character Laura from this section?
- Preview the cast of characters on page 237. Think about what the relationships might be between these four characters.
- Preview the Characterization Chart below for the two main characters in the play, Laura and Tom.
- As you read, fill in examples of Laura's and Tom's physical appearance, behavior, interaction with other characters, and internal states that reveal their personalities.

Graphic Organizer: Characterization Chart

Character	Physical Appearance	Behavior	Interaction with Others	Internal State
Laura				
Tom				

Word watch

PREVIEW VOCABULARY

aghast
cater
conglomeration
cultivate
czar
emissary
fiasco
implacable
induct
ineluctably
interfused
mastication
matriculate
menagerie
pinion
prominent
resume
sublimation
symptomatic

Reader's journal

Would you call yourself more of an extrovert or an introvert? Why?

_____
_____
_____
_____

UNIT 6 / READING DRAMA

NOTE THE FACTS

Who was the model for the central character in *The Glass Menagerie*?

_____

_____

_____

Reading TIP

As you read the stage directions for this play, try to determine what elements of the setting are unrealistic and calculated to create emotional responses in the audience.

Reader's resource

Tennessee Williams (1911–1983) was the pen name of one of America's finest dramatists. Born Thomas Lanier Williams, he grew up in Mississippi and St. Louis. Williams began writing early, publishing his first short story at the age of fourteen. The closest companion of Williams's youth, his sister Rose, provided the model for the central character in the play that was to become his first major success, **The Glass Menagerie.** This largely autobiographical play deals with a socially isolated woman, Laura, whose intense fragility is symbolized by her collection of glass figurines. Laura's nickname "Blue Roses" recalls the name of Williams's sister Rose. The character Tom in the play, a young writer, is something of a self-portrait, and critics have suggested that Williams wrote the play because of the guilt that he felt for abandoning his sister Rose, who ended up in a mental institution. Williams's sister, like Laura, collected glass figures, and this remembered detail became a central image in his work. In this excerpt from the play, you will read Act 1, Scenes 1–3.

First staged in Chicago in 1944, *The Glass Menagerie* was an immediate success, opening in New York the following year. Since then the play has been produced many times on Broadway and by theater companies throughout the world, including several film versions. Williams's plays often deal with troubled, emotionally intense social misfits and are often set in the post-Civil War South. Because of the intensity of emotion in these plays and their evocative settings, they are often referred to as *Southern Gothic.* Williams's other famous plays include *A Streetcar Named Desire* (1947), *Cat on a Hot Tin Roof* (1955), and *Suddenly Last Summer* (1958).

EXPRESSIONISM. Expressionism is the name given to a twentieth-century movement in literature and art that sought to express ideas or emotions by exaggerating the artistic medium itself. As expressionist painters did bold brush strokes and intense colors, expressionist dramatists often exaggerated the elements of spectacle and the literary techniques in their works, using lighting, sound, properties, and elements of the stage set for symbolic purposes. Tennessee Williams was one of the pioneers of American Expressionism.

from The Glass Menagerie

Tennessee Williams

ACT 1, SCENE 1
CAST OF CHARACTERS

AMANDA WINGFIELD
LAURA WINGFIELD

TOM WINGFIELD
JIM O'CONNOR

The Wingfield apartment is in the rear of the building, one of those vast hive-like conglomerations of cellular living-units that flower as warty growths in overcrowded urban centers of lower

words for everyday use

con • glom • er • a • tion (kən gläm´ər ā´shən) *n.*, collection or mixture. *During the Elizabethan period, the theater entertained a conglomeration of classes.*

During Reading

NOTE STAGE DIRECTIONS

- Listen as your teacher reads the opening stage directions. Remember that **stage directions** describe how something should be performed onstage. Try to picture what the stage looks like as you listen. When your teacher stops reading, sketch or diagram the stage. In your own words, quickly describe the pictures you created.
- Begin to read Act 1 on your own. Think about what the characters look like, their movements, and their tones of voice. Note how the stage directions provide information about how the characters act and react.
- Stop occasionally to add information about Laura and Tom in your Characterization Chart.

Reading TIP

As you read the stage directions for Act 1, Scene 1, pay attention to what Williams says about the economic and social setting in which the characters live.

middle-class population and are <u>symptomatic</u> of the impulse of this largest and fundamentally enslaved section of American society to avoid fluidity and differentiation and to exist and function as one <u>interfused</u> mass of automatism. The apartment faces an alley and is entered by a fire-escape, a structure whose name is a touch of accidental poetic truth, for all of these huge buildings are always burning with the slow and <u>implacable</u> fires of human desperation. The fire-escape is included in the set—that is, the landing of it and steps descending from it. (Note that the stage L. alley may be entirely omitted, since it is never used except for TOM's first entrance, which can take place stage R.) The scene is memory and is therefore nonrealistic. Memory takes a lot of poetic license. It omits some details, others are exaggerated, according to the emotional value of the articles it touches, for memory is seated predominantly in the heart. The interior is therefore rather dim and poetic. (CUE #1. As soon as the house lights dim, dance-hall music heard on-stage R. Old popular music of, say 1915–1920 period. This continues until TOM is at fire-escape landing, having lighted cigarette, and begins speaking.)

AT RISE: *At the rise of the house curtain, the audience is faced with the dark, grim rear wall of the Wingfield tenement. (The stage set proper is screened out by a gauze curtain, which suggests the front part, outside, of the building.) This building, which runs parallel to the footlights, is flanked on both sides by dark, narrow alleys which run into murky canyons of tangled clotheslines, garbage cans and the sinister lattice-work of neighboring fire-escapes. (The alleys are actually in darkness, and the objects just mentioned are not visible.) It is up and down these side alleys that exterior entrances and exits are made, during the play. At the end of* TOM's *opening commentary, the dark tenement wall slowly reveals (by means of a transparency) the interior of the ground-floor Wingfield apartment. (Gauze curtain, which suggests front part of building, rises on the interior set.) Downstage is the living-room, which also serves as a sleeping*

NOTE THE FACTS

What does the author say about memory?

_____
_____
_____

FIX-UP IDEA

Read Short Sections
Try reading Act 1 in smaller sections. Think about reading each scene as a separate section. When you finish reading each section, talk with a few of your classmates about the section you just read. Discuss what action, symbol, emotion, or idea you found most striking in that section.

---

words for everyday use

symp • to • mat • ic (simp´tə mat´ik) *adj.*, indicative; that constitutes a condition. *Sneezing and watery eyes are <u>symptomatic</u> of allergies.*
in • ter • fused (in tər fyüzd´) *adj.*, combined, blended. *Snorkeling among the coral reefs, we were awed by the color of the water <u>interfused</u> with light.*
im • pla • ca • ble (im plā´kə bəl) *adj.*, cannot be appeased or pacified. *The <u>implacable</u> tourist insisted someone at the hotel desk speak to her in English.*

room for LAURA, *the day-bed unfolding to make her bed. Just above this is a small stool or table on which is a telephone.*

Up-stage, C., *and divided by a wide arch or second proscenium[1] with transparent faded portieres (or second curtain, "second curtain" is actually the inner gauze curtain between the living-room and the dining-room, which is up-stage of it), is the dining-room. In an old-fashioned whatnot in the living-room are seen scores of transparent glass animals. A blown-up photograph of the father hangs on the wall of the living-room, facing the audience, to the* L. *of the archway. It is the face of a very handsome young man in a doughboy's[2] First World War cap. He is gallantly smiling,* <u>ineluctably</u> *smiling, as if to say, "I will be smiling forever." (Note that all that is essential in connection with dance-hall is that the window be shown lighting lower part of alley. It is not necessary to show any considerable part of dance-hall.) The audience hears and sees the opening scene in the dining-room through both the transparent fourth wall (this is the gauze curtain which suggests outside of building) of the building and the transparent gauze portieres of the dining-room arch. It is during this revealing scene that the fourth wall slowly ascends, out of sight. This transparent exterior wall is not brought down again until the very end of the play, during* TOM's *final speech. The narrator is an undisguised convention of the play. He takes whatever license with dramatic convention as is convenient to his purposes.*

TOM *enters, dressed as a merchant sailor, from alley, stage* L. *(i.e., stage* R. *if* L. *alley is omitted), and strolls across the front of the stage to the fire-escape. (*TOM *may lean against grillwork of this as he lights cigarette.) There he stops and lights a cigarette. He addresses the audience.*

TOM.   I have tricks in my pocket—I have things up my sleeve—but I am the opposite of the stage magician. He gives you illusion that has the appearance of truth. I give you truth in the pleasant disguise of illusion. I take you

---

1. **proscenium.** Plane, including the arch and the curtain, separating the stage proper from the audience
2. **doughboy.** World War I United States infantryman

words for everyday use   in • e • luc • ta • bly (in´ē luk´tə blē) *adv.,* in an inescapable or unavoidable manner. *In a Greek drama, fate* <u>ineluctably</u> *draws protagonists to their doom.*

Reading STRATEGY REVIEW

VISUALIZE. As you read the stage directions, try to visualize the Wingfields' apartment.

MARK THE TEXT

Underline or highlight what Tom, the narrator, says about the nature of truth and illusion in this play.

THINK AND REFLECT

What do you think is meant by a "memory play"? What is memory associated with in this play? **(Interpret)**

_____
_____
_____
_____

MARK THE TEXT

Underline what the gentleman caller is a symbol of.

NOTE THE FACTS

Where is Tom and Laura's father?

_____
_____
_____
_____

back to an alley in St. Louis. The time that quaint period when the huge middle class of America was <u>matriculating</u> from a school for the blind. Their eyes had failed them, or they had failed their eyes, and so they were having their fingers pressed forcibly down on the fiery Braille alphabet of a dissolving economy.—In Spain there was revolution.— Here there was only shouting and confusion and labor disturbances, sometimes violent, in otherwise peaceful cities such as Cleveland—Chicago—Detroit.... That is the social background of this play.... The play is memory. (MUSIC CUE #2.) Being a memory play, it is dimly lighted, it is sentimental, it is not realistic.—In memory everything seems to happen to music.—That explains the fiddle in the wings. I am the narrator of the play, and also a character in it. The other characters in the play are my mother, Amanda, my sister, Laura, and a gentleman caller who appears in the final scenes. He is the most realistic character in the play, being an <u>emissary</u> from a world that we were somehow set apart from.—But having a poet's weakness for symbols, I am using this character as a symbol—as the long-delayed but always expected something that we live for.—There is a fifth character who doesn't appear other than in a photograph hanging on the wall. When you see the picture of this grinning gentleman, please remember this is our father who left us a long time ago. He was a telephone man who fell in love with long distance—so he gave up his job with the telephone company and skipped the light fantastic out of town.... The last we heard of him was a picture postcard from the Pacific coast of Mexico, containing a message of two words—"Hello—Good-bye!" and no address.
(LIGHTS UP IN DINING-ROOM. TOM *exits* R. *He goes off downstage, takes off his sailor overcoat and skull-fitting knitted cap and remains off-stage by dining-room* R. *door for his entrance cue.* AMANDA's *voice becomes audible through the portieres—i.e., gauze curtains separating dining-room and living-room.* AMANDA *and* LAURA *are seated at a drop-leaf table.*

words for everyday use

ma • tric • u • late (mə trik′yü lāt′) *vt.*, enroll. *Durrell* <u>matriculated</u> *at the University of Wisconsin, enrolling with two of his friends.*

em • is • sar • y (em′i ser′ē) *n.*, person or agent sent on a mission. *The* <u>emissary</u> *from the king of Spain requested an audience with Queen Elizabeth I to discuss the king's marriage proposal.*

(AMANDA *is sitting in* C. *chair and* LAURA *in* L. *chair. Eating is indicated by gestures without food or utensils.* AMANDA *faces the audience. The interior of the dining-room has lit up softly and through the scrim[3]—gauze curtains—we see* AMANDA *and* LAURA *seated at the table in the upstage area.*)

AMANDA. You know, Laura, I had the funniest experience in church last Sunday. The church was crowded except for one pew way down front and in that was just one little woman. I smiled very sweetly at her and said, "Excuse me, would you mind if I shared this pew?" "I certainly would," she said, "this space is rented." Do you know that is the first time that I ever knew that the Lord rented space. (*Dining-room gauze curtains open automatically.*) These Northern Episcopalians! I can understand the Southern Episcopalians, but these Northern ones, no. (TOM *enters dining-room* R., *slips over to table and sits in chair* R.) Honey, don't push your food with your fingers. If you have to push your food with something, the thing to use is a crust of bread. You must chew your food. Animals have secretions in their stomachs which enable them to digest their food without <u>mastication</u>, but human beings must chew their food before they swallow it down, and chew, chew. Oh, eat leisurely. Eat leisurely. A well-cooked meal has many delicate flavors that have to be held in the mouth for appreciation, not just gulped down. Oh, chew, chew—chew! (*At this point the scrim curtain—if the director decides to use it—the one suggesting exterior wall, rises here and does not come down again until just before the end of the play.*) Don't you want to give your salivary glands a chance to function?

TOM. Mother, I haven't enjoyed one bite of my dinner because of your constant directions on how to eat it. It's you that makes me hurry through my meals with your hawk-like attention to every bite I take. It's disgusting—all this discussion of animal's secretion—salivary glands—

READ ALOUD

Read aloud Amanda's highlighted speech. If you were the son or daughter of Amanda Wingfield, how would you feel about your mother?

_____
_____
_____

---

3. **scrim.** Hanging of light cloth as a semitransparent curtain in a theatrical production

words for everyday use

mas • ti • ca • tion (mas´ti kā´shən) *n.*, chewing. "With good dental hygiene," the dentist said, "you can enjoy <u>mastication</u> with your own teeth for the rest of your life."

Note the Facts

Why does Amanda tell Laura to remain seated?

_____
_____

Think and Reflect

How does Laura feel about her mother's expectations? **(Interpret)**

_____
_____
_____

Note the Facts

What event in her life does Amanda enjoy remembering?

_____
_____
_____

mastication! *(Comes down to armchair in living-room* R., *lights cigarette.)*

AMANDA. Temperament like a Metropolitan star! You're not excused from this table.

TOM. I'm getting a cigarette.

AMANDA. You smoke too much.

LAURA *(Rising)*. Mother, I'll bring in the coffee.

AMANDA. No, no, no, no. You sit down. I'm going to be the servant today and you're going to be the lady.

LAURA. I'm already up.

AMANDA. <u>Resume</u> your seat. Resume your seat. You keep yourself fresh and pretty for the gentlemen callers. (LAURA *sits.*)

LAURA. I'm not expecting any gentlemen callers.

AMANDA *(Who has been gathering dishes from table and loading them on tray).* Well, the nice thing about them is they come when they're least expected. Why, I remember one Sunday afternoon in Blue Mountain when your mother was a girl . . .

(Goes out for coffee, U. R.*)*

TOM. I know what's coming now! (LAURA *rises.)*

LAURA. Yes. But let her tell it. *(Crosses to* L. *of day-bed, sits.)*

TOM. Again?

LAURA. She loves to tell it.

AMANDA *(Entering from* R. *in dining-room and coming down into living-room with tray and coffee).* I remember one Sunday afternoon in Blue Mountain when your mother was a girl she received—seventeen—gentlemen callers! (AMANDA *crosses to* TOM *at armchair* R., *gives him coffee, and crosses* C. LAURA *comes to her, takes cup, resumes her place on* L. *of day-bed.* AMANDA *puts tray on small table* R. *of day-bed, sits* R. *on day-bed. Inner curtain closes, light dims out.)* Why sometimes there weren't chairs enough to accommodate them all and we had to send the servant over to the parish house to fetch the folding chairs.

TOM. How did you entertain all those gentlemen callers? (TOM *finally sits in armchair* R.*)*

---

words for everyday use

re • sume (ri züm´) *vt.,* take, get, or occupy again. *The car alarm <u>resumed</u> its horrible noise just as we were drifting off to sleep again.*

AMANDA. I happened to understand the art of conversation!

TOM. I bet you could talk!

AMANDA. Well, I could. All the girls in my day could, I tell you.

TOM. Yes?

AMANDA. They knew how to entertain their gentlemen callers. It wasn't enough for a girl to be possessed of a pretty face and a graceful figure—although I wasn't slighted in either respect. She also needed to have a nimble wit and a tongue to meet all occasions.

TOM. What did you talk about?

AMANDA. Why, we'd talk about things of importance going on in the world! Never anything common or coarse or vulgar. My callers were gentlemen—all! Some of the most <u>prominent</u> men on the Mississippi Delta—planters and sons of planters! There was young Champ Laughlin. (MUSIC CUE #3.) He later became Vice-President of the Delta Planters' Bank. And Hadley Stevenson; he was drowned in Moon Lake.—My goodness, he certainly left his widow well provided for—a hundred and fifty thousand dollars in government bonds. And the Cutrere Brothers—Wesley and Bates. Bates was one of my own bright particular beaus! But he got in a quarrel with that wild Wainwright boy and they shot it out on the floor of Moon Lake Casino. Bates was shot through the stomach. He died in the ambulance on his way to Memphis. He certainly left his widow well provided for, too—eight or ten thousand acres, no less. He never loved that woman; she just caught him on the rebound. My picture was found on him the night he died. Oh and that boy, that boy that every girl in the Delta was setting her cap for! That beautiful (MUSIC FADES OUT.) brilliant young Fitzhugh boy from Greene County!

TOM. What did he leave his widow?

MARK THE TEXT

Underline or highlight the qualities Amanda says the girls in her day needed to entertain gentlemen callers.

THINK AND REFLECT

What qualities does Amanda think are most important in a gentleman caller? (Infer)

_____
_____
_____
_____

words for everyday use

prom • i • nent (präm´ə nənt) *adj.*, widely and favorably known. *The most <u>prominent</u> celebrities appeared on her talk show.*

THINK AND REFLECT

What does Amanda regret? (Infer)

_____
_____
_____

NOTE THE FACTS

What reason does Amanda give for the lack of gentlemen callers? What does Laura see as the reason?

_____
_____
_____

THINK AND REFLECT

How do you think her mother's joking and prodding might make Laura feel? (Empathize)

_____
_____
_____

210 **AMANDA.** He never married! What's the matter with you—you talk as though all my old admirers had turned up their toes to the daisies!
TOM. Isn't this the first you've mentioned that still survives?
AMANDA. He made an awful lot of money. He went North to Wall Street and made a fortune. He had the Midas touch—everything that boy touched just turned to gold! *(Gets up.)* And I could have been Mrs. J. Duncan Fitzhugh—mind you! *(Crosses* L. C.*)* But—what did I do?—I just went out of my way and picked your father! *(Looks at picture on* L.
220 *wall. Goes to small table* R. *of day-bed for tray.)*
LAURA *(Rises from day-bed).* Mother, let me clear the table.
AMANDA *(Crossing* L. *for* LAURA*'s cup, then crossing* R. *for* TOM*'s).* No, dear, you go in front and study your typewriter chart. Or practice your shorthand a little. Stay fresh and pretty! It's almost time for our gentlemen callers to start arriving. How many do you suppose we're going to entertain this afternoon? *(*TOM *opens curtains between dining-room and living-room for her. These close behind her, and she exits into kitchen* R. TOM *stands* U. C. *in living-room.)*
230 **LAURA** *(To* AMANDA, *off-stage).* I don't believe we're going to receive any, Mother.
AMANDA *(Off-stage).* Not any? Not one? Why, you must be joking! Not one gentleman caller? What's the matter? Has there been a flood or a tornado?
LAURA *(Crossing to typing table).* It isn't a flood. It's not a tornado, Mother. I'm just not popular like you were in Blue Mountain. Mother's afraid that I'm going to be an old maid. (MUSIC CUE #4.) *(Lights dim out.* TOM *exits* U. C. *in blackout.* LAURA *crosses to* menagerie R.*)*

words for everyday use
me • nag • er • ie (mə naj´ər ē) *n.*, collection of wild or strange animals kept in enclosures for exhibition. *The heiress owned a private* menagerie *whose various animals rivaled those in the local zoo.*

Act 1, Scene 2

Scene is the same. Lights dim up on living-room.
LAURA discovered by menagerie, polishing glass. Crosses to phonograph, plays record. She times this business so as to put needle on record as MUSIC CUE #4 *ends. Enter* AMANDA *down alley* R. *Rattles key in lock.* LAURA *crosses guiltily to typewriter and types. (Small typewriter table with typewriter on it is still on stage in living-room* L.) AMANDA *comes into room* R. *closing door. Crosses to armchair, putting hat, purse and gloves on it. Something has happened to* AMANDA. *It is written in her face: a look that is grim and hopeless and a little absurd. She has on one of those cheap or imitation velvety-looking cloth coats with imitation fur collar. Her hat is five or six years old, one of those dreadful cloche[4] hats that were worn in the late twenties and she is clasping an enormous black patent-leather pocketbook with nickel clasps and initials. This is her fulldress outfit, the one she usually wears to the D.A.R.[5] She purses her lips, opens her eyes very wide, rolls them upward and shakes her head. Seeing her mother's expression,* LAURA *touches her lips with a nervous gesture.*

LAURA. Hello, Mother, I was just . . .

AMANDA. I know. You were just practicing your typing, I suppose. *(Behind chair* R.*)*

LAURA. Yes.

AMANDA. Deception, deception, deception!

LAURA *(Shakily)*. How was the D.A.R. meeting, Mother?

AMANDA *(Crosses to* LAURA*)*. D.A.R. meeting!

LAURA. Didn't you go to the D.A.R. meeting, Mother?

AMANDA *(Faintly, almost inaudibly)*. No, I didn't go to any D.A.R. meeting. *(Then more forcibly.)* I didn't have the strength—I didn't have the courage. I just wanted to find a hole in the ground and crawl in it and stay there the rest of my entire life.

(Tears type charts, throws them on floor.)

LAURA *(Faintly)*. Why did you do that, Mother?

---

4. **cloche.** Close-fitting, bell-shaped hat
5. **D.A.R.** Daughters of the American Revolution, a civic organization

---

NOTE THE FACTS

How does Amanda say she feels?

_____
_____

THINK AND REFLECT

What effect does she hope to produce in Laura? (Analyze)

_____
_____
_____

Think and Reflect

Why does Amanda ask Laura how old she is? (Interpret)

_____
_____
_____

Note the Facts

Why is Amanda angry with her daughter?

_____
_____
_____

AMANDA *(Sits on R. end of day-bed).* Why? Why? How old are you, Laura?

LAURA. Mother, you know my age.

AMANDA. I was under the impression that you were an adult, but evidently I was very much mistaken. *(She stares at LAURA.)*

40 **LAURA.** Please don't stare at me, Mother! *(AMANDA closes her eyes and lowers her head. Pause.)*

AMANDA. What are we going to do? What is going to become of us? What is the future? *(Pause.)*

LAURA. Has something happened, Mother? Mother, has something happened?

AMANDA. I'll be all right in a minute. I'm just bewildered—by life . . .

LAURA. Mother, I wish that you would tell me what's happened!

50 **AMANDA.** I went to the D.A.R. this afternoon, as you know; I was to be <u>inducted</u> as an officer. I stopped off at Rubicam's Business College to tell them about your cold and to ask how you were progressing down there.

LAURA. Oh . . .

AMANDA. Yes, oh—oh—oh. I went straight to your typing instructor and introduced myself as your mother. She didn't even know who you were. Wingfield, she said? We don't have any such scholar enrolled in this school. I assured her she did. I said my daughter Laura's been coming to classes 60 since early January. "Well, I don't know," she said, "unless you mean that terribly shy little girl who dropped out of school after a few days' attendance?" "No," I said, "I don't mean that one. I mean my daughter, Laura, who's been coming here every single day for the past six weeks!" "Excuse me," she said. And she took down the attendance book and there was your name, unmistakable, printed, and all the dates you'd been absent. I still told her she was wrong. I still said, "No, there must have been some mistake! There must have been some mix-up in the records!" "No,"

words for everyday use   in • duct (in dukt´) *vt.,* place in official position. *Theresa was <u>inducted</u> into the club with much ceremony.*

246   THE EMC WRITE-IN READER

she said, "I remember her perfectly now. She was so shy and her hands trembled so that her fingers couldn't touch the right keys! When we gave a speed-test—she just broke down completely—was sick at the stomach and had to be carried to the washroom! After that she never came back. We telephoned the house every single day and never got any answer." *(Rises from day-bed, crosses R. C.)* That was while I was working all day long down at that department store, I suppose, demonstrating those—*(With hands indicates brassiere.)* Oh! I felt so weak I couldn't stand up! *(Sits in armchair.)* I had to sit down while they got me a glass of water! (LAURA *crosses up to phonograph.*) Fifty dollars' tuition. I don't care about the money so much, but all my hopes for any kind of future for you—gone up the spout, just gone up the spout like that. (LAURA *winds phonograph up.*) Oh, don't do that, Laura!—Don't play that victrola![6]

LAURA. Oh! *(Stops phonograph, crosses to typing table, sits.)*

AMANDA. What have you been doing every day when you've gone out of the house pretending that you were going to business college?

LAURA. I've just been going out walking.

AMANDA. That's not true!

LAURA. Yes, it is, Mother, I just went walking.

AMANDA. Walking? Walking? In winter? Deliberately courting pneumonia in that light coat? Where did you walk to, Laura?

LAURA. All sorts of places—mostly in the park.

AMANDA. Even after you'd started catching that cold?

LAURA. It was the lesser of two evils, Mother. I couldn't go back. I threw up on the floor!

AMANDA. From half-past seven till after five every day you mean to tell me you walked around in the park, because you wanted to make me think that you were still going to Rubicam's Business College?

LAURA. Oh, Mother, it wasn't as bad as it sounds. I went inside places to get warmed up.

AMANDA. Inside where?

LAURA. I went in the art museum and the bird-houses at the Zoo. I visited the penguins every day! Sometimes I did

---

6. **victrola.** Record player

NOTE THE FACTS

How has Laura been spending her time?

_____
_____
_____

Literary TOOLS

IRONY. **Irony** is a difference between appearance and reality. Why is Amanda's reference to her husband ironic in view of her plans for Laura?

_____
_____
_____

MARK THE TEXT

Underline or highlight the sort of future Amanda envisions.

---

110 without lunch and went to the movies. Lately I've been spending most of my afternoons in the Jewelbox, that big glass house where they raise the tropical flowers.

AMANDA.   You did all that to deceive me, just for deception! Why? Why? Why? Why?

LAURA.   Mother, when you're disappointed, you get that awful suffering look on your face, like the picture of Jesus' mother in the Museum! *(Rises.)*

AMANDA.   Hush!

LAURA   *(Crosses R. to menagerie).* I couldn't face it. I couldn't. (MUSIC CUE #5.)

120 AMANDA   *(Rising from day-bed).* So what are we going to do now, honey, the rest of our lives? Just sit down in this house and watch the parades go by? Amuse ourselves with the glass menagerie? Eternally play those worn-out records your father left us as a painful reminder of him? *(Slams phonograph lid.)* We can't have a business career. (END MUSIC CUE #5.) No, we can't do that—that just gives us indigestion. *(Around R. day-bed.)* What is there left for us now but dependency all our lives? I tell you, Laura, I know so well what happens to unmarried women who aren't prepared to occupy a position

130 in life. *(Crosses L., sits on day-bed.)* I've seen such pitiful cases in the South—barely tolerated spinsters living on some brother's wife or a sister's husband—tucked away in some mousetrap of a room—encouraged by one in-law to go on and visit the next in-law—little birdlike women—without any nest—eating the crust of humility all their lives! Is that the future that we've mapped out for ourselves? I swear I don't see any other alternative. And I don't think that's a very pleasant alternative. Of course—some girls *do* marry. My goodness, Laura, haven't you ever liked some boy?

140 LAURA.   Yes, Mother, I liked one once.

AMANDA.   You did?

LAURA.   I came across his picture a while ago.

AMANDA.   He gave you his picture too? *(Rises from day-bed, crosses to chair R.)*

LAURA.   No, it's in the year-book.

AMANDA   *(Sits in armchair).* Oh—a high-school boy.

LAURA.   Yes. His name was Jim. *(Kneeling on floor; gets year-book from under menagerie.)* Here he is in "The Pirates of Penzance."

150 **AMANDA** *(Absently).* The what?
LAURA. The operetta the senior class put on. He had a wonderful voice. We sat across the aisle from each other Mondays, Wednesdays and Fridays in the auditorium. Here he is with a silver cup for debating! See his grin?
AMANDA. So he had a grin, too! *(Looks at picture of father on wall behind phonograph. Hands year-book back.)*
LAURA. He used to call me—Blue Roses.
AMANDA. Blue Roses? What did he call you a silly name like that for?

160 **LAURA** *(Still kneeling).* When I had that attack of pleurosis[7]—he asked me what was the matter when I came back. I said pleurosis—he thought that I said "Blue Roses." So that's what he always called me after that. Whenever he saw me, he'd holler, "Hello, Blue Roses!" I didn't care for the girl that he went out with. Emily Meisenbach. Oh, Emily was the best-dressed girl at Soldan. But she never struck me as being sincere . . . I read in a newspaper once that they were engaged. *(Puts year-book back on a shelf of glass menagerie.)* That's a long time ago—they're probably married by now.

170 **AMANDA.** That's all right, honey, that's all right. It doesn't matter. Little girls who aren't cut out for business careers sometimes end up married to very nice young men. And I'm just going to see that you do that, too!
LAURA. But, Mother—
AMANDA. What is it now?
LAURA. I'm—crippled!
AMANDA. Don't say that word! *(Rises, crosses to* C. *Turns to* LAURA.*)* How many times have I told you never to say that word! You're not crippled, you've just got a slight defect.

180 *(*LAURA *rises.)* If you lived in the days when I was a girl and they had long graceful skirts sweeping the ground, it might have been considered an asset. When you've got a slight disadvantage like that, you've just got to <u>cultivate</u> something

---

7. **pleurosis.** Inflammation of the lungs

NOTE THE FACTS

What does Amanda set as her goal?

_____
_____
_____

Reading STRATEGY REVIEW

MAKE PREDICTIONS. Predict what Amanda might do to find a husband for Laura.

_____
_____
_____

words for everyday use

cul • ti • vate (kul′tə vāt) *vt.*, acquire and develop. *Jeremy <u>cultivated</u> his interest in jazz by buying CDs and going to jazz clubs.*

Literary TOOLS

CONFLICT. A **conflict** is a struggle between two forces in a literary work. A struggle that takes place between a character and some outside force is called an *external conflict.* A conflict that takes place within a character is called an *internal conflict.* As you read, determine what Tom's conflicts are in this scene.

NOTE THE FACTS

What does Tom say about his mother's plan? How does it change his mother and sister?

_____
_____
_____

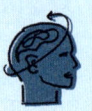

THINK AND REFLECT

Does Tom see this plan as realistic? **(Evaluate)**

_____
_____

else to take its place. You have to cultivate charm—or vivacity—or *charm!* (*Spotlight on photograph. Then dim out.*) That's the only thing your father had plenty of—charm! (AMANDA *sits on day-bed.* LAURA *crosses to armchair and sits.*) (MUSIC CUE #6.) (*Blackout.*)

ACT 1, SCENE 3

SCENE: *The same. Lights up again but only on* R. *alley and fire-escape landing, rest of the stage dark.* (*Typewriter table and typewriter have been taken offstage.*) *Enter* TOM, *again wearing merchant sailor overcoat and knittedcap, in alley* R. *As* MUSIC CUE #6 *ends,* TOM *begins to speak.*

TOM   (*Leans against grill of fire-escape, smoking*). After the <u>fiasco</u> at Rubicam's Business College, the idea of getting a gentleman caller for my sister Laura began to play a more and more important part in my mother's calculations. It became an obsession. Like some archetype[8] of the universal unconscious, the image of the gentleman caller haunted our small apartment. An evening at home rarely passed without some allusion to this image, this spectre, this hope. . . . And even when he wasn't mentioned, his presence hung in my mother's preoccupied look and in my sister's frightened, apologetic manner. It hung like a sentence passed upon the Wingfields! But my mother was a woman of action as well as words. (MUSIC CUE #7.) She began to take logical steps in the planned direction. Late that winter and in the early spring—realizing that extra money would be needed to properly feather the nest and plume the bird—she began a vigorous campaign on the telephone, roping in subscribers to one of those magazines for matrons called "The Homemaker's Companion," the type of journal that features the serialized <u>sublimations</u> of ladies of letters who think in

---
8. **archetype.** Original pattern; prototype

words for everyday use
fi • as • co (fē as′kō) *n.,* complete failure. *Jeff's ownership of a cinema cafe turned into a complete <u>fiasco</u>.*
sub • li • ma • tion (sub′lə ma′shən) *n.,* expression of socially or personally unacceptable impulses in constructive, acceptable forms. *The still life of food on Paul's dining room wall was a <u>sublimation</u> of his desire to eat while on his diet.*

terms of delicate cup-like breasts, slim, tapering waists, rich creamy thighs, eyes like wood-smoke in autumn, fingers that soothe and caress like soft, soft strains of music. Bodies as powerful as Etruscan[9] sculpture. *(He exits down R. into wings. Light in alley R. is blacked out, and a head-spot falls on AMANDA, at phone in living-room. MUSIC CUE #7 ends as TOM stops speaking.)*

AMANDA. Ida Scott? *(During this speech TOM enters dining-room U. R. unseen by audience, not wearing overcoat or hat. There is an unlighted reading lamp on table. Sits C. of dining-room table with writing materials.)* This is Amanda Wingfield. We missed you at the D.A.R. last Monday. Oh, first I want to know how's your sinus condition? You're just a Christian martyr. That's what you are. You're just a Christian martyr. Well, I was just going through my little red book, and I saw that your subscription to the "Companion" is about to expire just when that wonderful new serial by Bessie Mae Harper is starting. It's the first thing she's written since "Honeymoon for Three." Now, that was unusual, wasn't it? Why, Ida, this one is even lovelier. It's all about the horsey set on Long Island and a debutante is thrown from her horse while taking him over the jumps at the—regatta. Her spine—her spine is injured. That's what the horse did—he stepped on her. Now, there is only one surgeon in the entire world that can keep her from being completely paralyzed, and that's the man she's engaged to be married to and he's tall and he's blond and he's handsome. That's unusual, too, huh? Oh, he's not perfect. Of course he has a weakness. He has the most terrible weakness in the entire world. He just drinks too much. What? Oh, no, Honey, don't let them burn. You go take a look in the oven and I'll hold on . . . Why, that woman! Do you know what she did? She hung up on me. *(Dining-room and living-room lights dim in. Reading lamp lights up at same time.)*

LAURA. Oh, Mother, Mother, Tom's trying to write. *(Rises from armchair where she was left at curtain of previous scene, goes to curtain between dining-room and living-room, which is already open.)*

---

9. **Etruscan.** Of a culture that flourished on the Italian peninsula before the Romans

THINK AND REFLECT

What is the real purpose of Amanda's telephone call to Ida Scott? **(Interpret)**

_____

_____

_____

NOTE THE FACTS

What does Amanda say is the most terrible weakness in the world?

_____

_____

THINK AND REFLECT

What does Tom enjoy doing? In what way do this activity and his mother's personality conflict? **(Analyze)**

_____

_____

_____

AMANDA. Oh! So he is. So he is. *(Crosses from phone, goes to dining-room and up to* TOM.*)*

TOM *(At table).* Now what are you up to?

AMANDA. I'm trying to save your eyesight. *(Business with lamp.)* You've only got one pair of eyes and you've got to take care of them. Oh, I know that Milton was blind, but that's not what made him a genius.

TOM. Mother, will you please go away and let me finish my writing?

AMANDA *(Squares his shoulders).* Why can't you sit up straight? So your shoulders don't stick through like sparrows' wings?

TOM. Mother, please go busy yourself with something else. I'm trying to write.

AMANDA *(Business with* TOM*).* Now, I've seen a medical chart, and I know what that position does to your internal organs. You sit up and I'll show you. Your stomach presses against your lungs, and your lungs press against your heart, and that poor little heart gets discouraged because it hasn't got any room left to go on beating for you.

TOM. What in hell! . . . *(Inner curtains between living-room and dining-room close. Lights dim down in dining-room.* LAURA *crosses, stands C. of curtains in living-room listening to following scene between* TOM *and* AMANDA.*)*

AMANDA. Don't you talk to me like that—

TOM. —am I supposed to do?

AMANDA. What's the matter with you? Have you gone out of your senses?

TOM. Yes, I have. You've driven me out of them.

AMANDA. What is the matter with you lately, you big—big—idiot?

TOM. Look, Mother—I haven't got a thing, not a single thing left in this house that I can call my own.

AMANDA. Lower your voice!

TOM. Yesterday you confiscated my books! You had the nerve to——

AMANDA. I did. I took that horrible novel back to the library—that awful book by that insane Mr. Lawrence.[10] I

---

10. **Mr. Lawrence.** D. H. Lawrence (1858–1930) was a poet and novelist whose writings were considered outrageous by some of his contemporaries.

cannot control the output of a diseased mind or people who cater to them, but I won't allow such filth in my house. No, no, no, no, no!

TOM. House, house! Who pays the rent on the house, who makes a slave of himself to—!

AMANDA. Don't you dare talk to me like that! (LAURA *crosses* D. L. *to back of armchair.*)

110 **TOM.** No, *I* mustn't say anything! I've just got to keep quiet and let you do all the talking.

AMANDA. Let me tell you something!

TOM. I don't want to hear any more.

AMANDA. You will hear more—(LAURA *crosses to phonograph.*)

TOM (*Crossing through curtains between dining-room and living-room. Goes up stage of door* R. *where, in a dark spot, there is supposedly a closet*). Well, I'm not going to listen. I'm going out. (*Gets out coat.*)

AMANDA (*Coming through curtains into living-room, stands*
120 C.). You are going to listen to me, Tom Wingfield. I'm tired of your impudence.—And another thing—I'm right at the end of my patience!

TOM (*Putting overcoat on back of armchair and crossing back to* AMANDA). What do you think I'm at the end of, Mother? Aren't I supposed to have any patience to reach the end of? I know, I know. It seems unimportant to you, what I'm *doing*—what I'm trying to do—having a difference between them! You don't think that.

AMANDA. I think you're doing things that you're ashamed
130 of, and that's why you act like this. (TOM *crosses to day-bed and sits.*) I don't believe that you go every night to the movies. Nobody goes to the movies night after night. Nobody in their right minds goes to the movies as often as you pretend to. People don't go to the movies at nearly midnight and movies don't let out at two A.M. Come in stumbling, muttering to yourself like a maniac. You get three hours' sleep and then go to work. Oh, I can picture the way you're doing down there. Moping, doping, because you're in no condition.

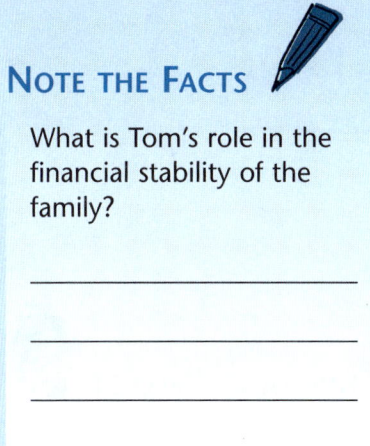

NOTE THE FACTS

What is Tom's role in the financial stability of the family?

_____
_____
_____

MARK THE TEXT

Underline or highlight why Amanda thinks Tom is acting this way.

words for everyday use

ca • ter (kāt´ər) *vi.*, take special pains in seeking to gratify another's needs or desires. *In deciding on a trip to Florida, we did not cater to Raymond's wishes to spend a week in the mountains.*

THINK AND REFLECT

How does Tom feel about his job? Why does he continue doing it? What has he had to give up? (Interpret)

_____

_____

_____

Use THE STRATEGY

WRITE THINGS DOWN. What does Tom's anger tell you about his personality? Make a note in your Characterization Chart.

TOM. That's true—that's very, very true. I'm in no
140   condition!

AMANDA. How dare you jeopardize your job? Jeopardize our security? How do you think we'd manage—? (*Sits armchair* R.)

TOM. Look, Mother, do you think I'm *crazy* about the *warehouse?* You think I'm in love with the Continental Shoemakers? You think I want to spend fifty-five years of my life down there in that—*celotex interior!* with *fluorescent tubes?!* Honest to God, I'd rather somebody picked up a crow-bar and battered out my brains—than go back mornings! But I
150   *go!* Sure, every time you come in yelling that bloody *Rise and Shine!* Rise and shine!! I think how lucky dead people are. But I get up. (*Rises from day-bed.*) I *go!* For sixty-five dollars a month I give up all that I dream of doing and being *ever!* And you say that is all I think of. Oh, God! Why, Mother, if self is all I ever thought of, Mother, *I'd* be where *he* is—GONE! (*Crosses to get overcoat on back of armchair.*) As far as the system of transportation reaches! (AMANDA *rises, crosses to him and grabs his arm.*) Please don't grab at me, Mother!

AMANDA (*Following him*). I'm not grabbing at you. I want
160   to know where you're going now.

TOM (*Taking overcoat and starts crossing to door* R.) I'm going to the movies!

AMANDA (*Crosses* C.). I don't believe that lie!

TOM (*Crosses back to* AMANDA). No? Well, you're right. For once in your life you're right. I'm not going to the movies. I'm going to opium dens! Yes, Mother, opium dens, dens of vice and criminals' hang-outs, Mother. I've joined the Hogan gang. I'm a hired assassin, I carry a tommy-gun in a violin case! I run a string of cathouses in the valley!
170   They call me Killer, Killer Wingfield, I'm really leading a double life. By day I'm a simple, honest warehouse worker, but at night I'm a dynamic <u>czar</u> of the underworld. Why, I go to gambling casinos and spin away a fortune on the roulette table! I wear a patch over one eye and a false

words for everyday use

czar (zar) *n.*, emperor. *The Russian <u>czar</u> was an absolute monarch.*

254   THE EMC WRITE-IN READER

moustache, sometimes I wear green whiskers. On those occasions they call me—El Diablo![11] Oh, I could tell you things to make you sleepless! My enemies plan to dynamite this place some night! Some night they're going to blow us all sky-high. And will I be glad! Will I be happy! And so will you be. You'll go up—up—over Blue Mountain on a broomstick! With seventeen gentlemen callers. You ugly babbling old witch! *(He goes through a series of violent, clumsy movements, seizing his overcoat, lunging to R. door, pulling it fiercely open. The women watch him, aghast. His arm catches in the sleeve of the coat as he struggles to pull it on. For a moment he is pinioned by the bulky garment. With an outraged groan he tears the coat off again, splitting the shoulder of it, and hurls it across the room. It strikes against the shelf of LAURA's glass collection, there is a tinkle of shattering glass. LAURA cries out as if wounded.)*

LAURA. My glass!—menagerie . . . *(She covers her face and turns away.* MUSIC CUE #8 *through to end of scene.)*

AMANDA *(In an awful voice).* I'll never speak to you again as long as you live unless you apologize to me! *(AMANDA exits through living-room curtains. TOM is left with LAURA. He stares at her stupidly for a moment. Then he crosses to shelf holding glass menagerie. Drops awkwardly on his knees to collect fallen glass, glancing at LAURA as if he would speak, but couldn't. Blackout. TOM, AMANDA, and LAURA exit in blackout.)* ■

---

11. **El Diablo.** Spanish for "the devil"

NOTE THE FACTS

What happens to the glass menagerie?

_____
_____
_____

THINK AND REFLECT

What feelings for his sister are revealed by Tom's actions? **(Analyze)**

_____
_____
_____

Literary TOOLS

SYMBOL. A **symbol** is a thing that stands for or represents both itself and something else. Of what is the glass menagerie a symbol? What similarities do the menagerie and Laura have?

_____
_____
_____

words for everyday use

a • ghast (ə gast´) *adj.,* feeling great horror or dismay. *When Sheila dropped my homework down the stairwell, I looked at her, aghast!*

pin • ion (pin´yən) *vt.,* disable or impede. *They pinioned the prize parrot's wings so that it could not fly away.*

Reflect ON YOUR READING

After Reading → ANALYZE THE MAIN CHARACTERS

❑ Review the information you have added to your Characterization Chart for Laura and Tom. Which methods of characterization revealed the most about each character?

❑ With your group, discuss the following questions: What do Laura's pastimes at home reveal about her character? How do Tom's dreams contrast with his mother's?

Reading Skills and Test Practice

ANALYZE LITERARY TECHNIQUES

With a partner, discuss how to answer these questions about the selection. Use the Think-Aloud Notes to write down your reasons for eliminating the incorrect answers.

____1. Why is the glass menagerie a good symbol for Laura?
  a. Laura loves animals and collects glass figurines.
  b. Laura is beautiful but fragile like the glass animals.
  c. The glass menagerie is a once favored item that has been passed over.
  d. The rigidity of the glass represents Laura's unyielding nature.

____2. Why is Tom interested in the magician's trick of escaping from a coffin without removing a nail?
  a. Tom would like to be a magician.
  b. Tom understands the other tricks the magician does, but he can't figure out this one.
  c. Tom is the opposite of the stage magician.
  d. Tom is looking for a way to escape from an impossible situation.

How did using the reading strategy help you to answer the questions?

_____
_____
_____
_____

THINK-ALOUD NOTES

Investigate, Inquire, and Imagine

RECALL: GATHER FACTS
1a. After expressing her worries about Laura's future, what does Amanda ask her daughter? How does Laura respond? Why did the boy call Laura "Blue Roses"?

INTERPRET: FIND MEANING
1b. What does the nickname "Blue Roses" signify? What does it underline about Laura's personality?

ANALYZE: TAKE THINGS APART
2a. In what ways does Amanda Wingfield live in a world of illusion? How accurate is her memory and her assessment of the present?

SYNTHESIZE: BRING THINGS TOGETHER
2b. What is the significance of the shattered glass animals?

EVALUATE: MAKE JUDGMENTS
3a. Which character possesses the most determination—Amanda, Tom, or Laura? Why?

EXTEND: CONNECT IDEAS
3b. What could Tom and Laura do to equal their mother's determination?

Literary Tools

CONFLICT. A **conflict** is a struggle between two forces in a literary work. A struggle that takes place between a character and some outside force is called an *external conflict*. A conflict that takes place within a character is called an *internal conflict*. In the chart below, write examples of Tom's conflicts in Scene 3. On the right, identify whether each example demonstrates an external or an internal conflict (see example).

Conflict	Type of Conflict
Tom is trying to write but is interrupted by his mother	External

WordWorkshop

Prefixes. Learning prefixes, roots, and suffixes can help you build your vocabulary by helping you figure out the meaning of new words that you do not know. Review the Prefix Chart in Unit 9 on pages 400–401. Several words in Act 1 of *The Glass Menagerie* use the Latin prefix *in–*. Other forms of this prefix include *il–*, *im–*, and *ir–*. The prefix *in–* means "not" or "against" and "in," "into," "on," or "put or go into."

Try to determine the meaning of each of the following words. Then use a dictionary to check your answer.

1. irrational _____
2. insubordinate _____
3. inspiring _____
4. ingratiate _____
5. impassioned _____

Use each of the following words from the selection in a sentence.

6. implacable _____
7. induct _____
8. ineluctably _____
9. interfused _____
10. interior _____

Read-Write Connection

What strategies have you seen people use to escape a situation they are not happy with?

Beyond the Reading

Stage a Scene from a Play. With other students in your class, select a cutting from a modern drama selection such as *Our Town, Spoon River Anthology, Long Day's Journey into Night,* or *The Crucible.* Write an introduction for your cutting; decide what gestures, facial expressions, and body language to use; and rehearse. Then present your drama to the rest of the class.

Go Online. To find links and additional activities for this selection, visit the EMC Internet Resource Center at **emcp.com/languagearts** and click on Write-In Reader.

Unit 6 Reading Review

Choose and Use Reading Strategies

Before reading an excerpt from the play *Our Town* by Thornton Wilder, review with a partner how to use reading strategies with drama.

1. Read with a Purpose
2. Connect to Prior Knowledge
3. Write Things Down
4. Make Predictions
5. Visualize
6. Use Text Organization
7. Tackle Difficult Vocabulary
8. Monitor Your Reading Progress

Next, apply at least two of these reading strategies as you read the excerpt below. Use the margins and mark up the text to show how you are using the reading strategies to read actively. You may find it helpful to choose a graphic organizer from Appendix B to gather information as you read the excerpt, or use the Summary Chart on page B-12 to create a graphic organizer that summarizes the excerpt.

> **STAGE MANAGER.** Mr. Webb is Publisher and Editor of the Grover's Corners *Sentinel*. That's our local paper, y'know.
>
> MR. WEBB *enters from his house, pulling on his coat. His finger is bound in a handkerchief.*
>
> **MR. WEBB.** Well . . . I don't have to tell you we're run here by a Board of Selectmen.—All males vote at the age of twenty-one. Women vote indirect. We're lower middle class: sprinkling of professional men . . . ten per cent illiterate laborers. Politically, we're eighty-six percent Republicans; six per cent Democrats; four per cent Socialists; rest, indifferent.
>
> Religiously, we're eighty-five per cent Protestants; twelve per cent Catholics; rest, indifferent.
>
> **STAGE MANAGER.** Have you any comments, Mr. Webb?
>
> **MR. WEBB.** Very ordinary town, if you ask me. Little better behaved than most. Probably a lot duller.

But our young people here seem to like it well enough. Ninety per cent of 'em graduating from high school settle down right here to live—even when they've been away to college.

STAGE MANAGER. Now, is there anyone in the audience who would like to ask Editor Webb anything about the town?

WOMAN IN THE BALCONY. Is there much drinking in Grover's Corners?

MR. WEBB. Well, ma'am, I wouldn't know what you'd call *much*. Satiddy nights the farmhands meet down in Ellery Greenough's stable and holler some. We've got one or two town drunks, but they're always having remorses every time an evangelist comes to town. No, ma'am, I'd say likker ain't a regular thing in the home here, except in the medicine chest. Right good for snake bite, y'know—always was.

BELLIGERENT MAN AT BACK OF AUDITORIUM. Is there no one in town aware of—

STAGE MANAGER. Come forward, will, you, where we can all hear you—What were you saying?

BELLIGERENT MAN. Is there no one in town aware of social injustice and industrial inequality?

MR. WEBB. Oh, yes, everybody is—somethin' terrible. Seems like they spend most of their time talking about who's rich and who's poor.

BELLIGERENT MAN. Then why don't they do something about it?

He withdraws without waiting for an answer.

MR. WEBB. Well, I dunno. . . . I guess we're all hunting like everybody else for a way the diligent and sensible can rise to the top and the lazy and quarrelsome can sink to the bottom. But it ain't easy to find. Meanwhile, we do all we can to help those that can't help themselves and those that can we leave alone.—Are there any other questions?

WordWorkshop

UNIT 6 WORDS FOR EVERYDAY USE

aghast, 255
cater, 253
confound, 233
conglomeration, 237
cultivate, 249
czar, 254
emissary, 240
fiasco, 250
implacable, 238
induct, 246
ineluctably, 239
interfused, 238
mastication, 241
matriculate, 240
menagerie, 244
pinion, 255
prominent, 243
resume, 242
sublimation, 250
symptomatic, 238

CREATE A CROSSWORD PUZZLE. In a small group, put together a list of words to include in a crossword puzzle. Your list should contain ten of the Unit 6 Words for Everyday Use from the above list and ten words that everybody knows. Use as many of the words as you can from your list (you may not be able to use all of them). Use your own paper for the CLUES ACROSS and CLUES DOWN. Refer to the Crossword Puzzle activity in Appendix A on page A-3 for examples. After you fill in your puzzle and finish your clues, make another blank numbered puzzle. Exchange blank puzzles and clues with another group. See which group can solve their puzzle first.

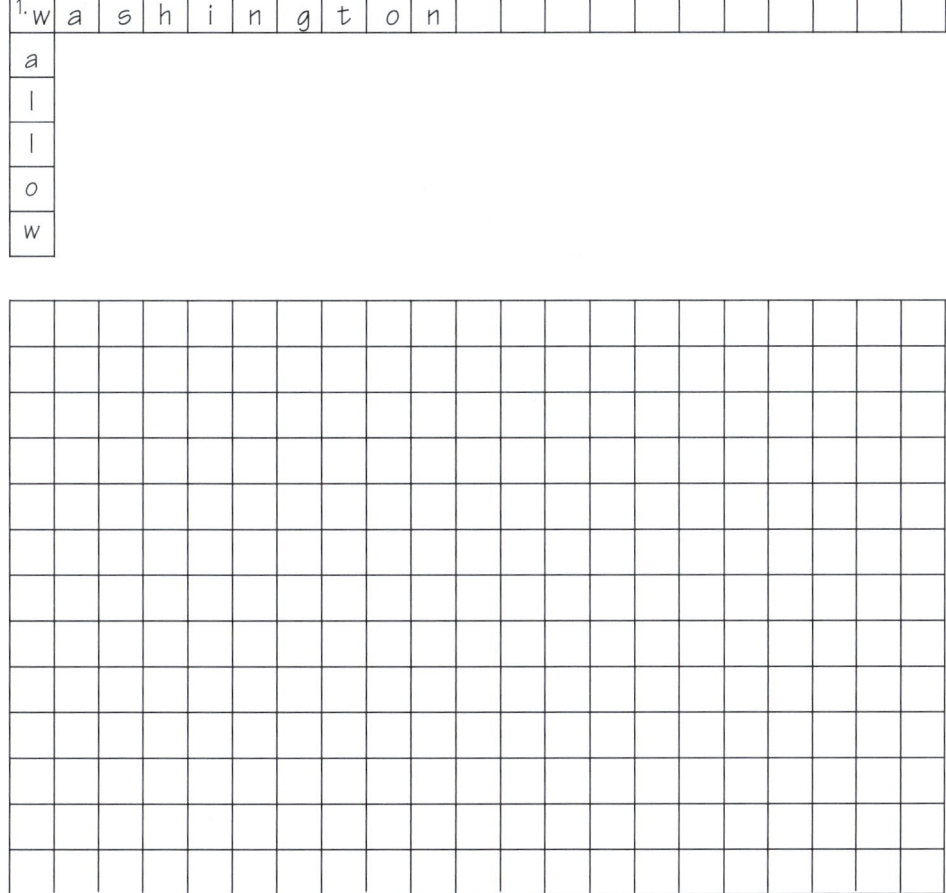

Literary Tools

Select the best literary element on the right to complete each sentence on the left. Write the correct letter in the blank.

____ 1. ___ are notes included in a play to describe how something should look, sound, or be performed.

____ 2. In *The Glass Menagerie,* Tom's frustration over needing to support his family and wanting to pursue his dreams is an example of internal ___.

____ 3. In a play, the ___ between characters does not appear in quotation marks.

____ 4. The glass menagerie is a(n) ___ of Laura's beauty, fragility, and world of illusion.

____ 5. ___ is a difference between appearance and reality.

____ 6. Tennessee Williams was one of the pioneers of American ___.

a. conflict, 250, 257

b. dialogue, 220, 226

c. Expressionism, 236

d. irony, 248

e. stage directions, 220, 227, 233, 237

f. symbol, 255

On Your Own

Find a scene from a play that you like by looking through drama anthologies, screenplays, and scripts in the library. Then choose one of the following activities.

FLUENTLY SPEAKING. Work with a small group or partner to do a dramatic reading of one scene. Introduce the scene with background information that will help your audience understand what the scene is about. Practice your lines until you and the other actors can present the dramatic reading smoothly and with appropriate feeling.

PICTURE THIS. Adapt the scene you have chosen into a comic strip or short comic book. As you sketch the characters, use their gestures, body language, and facial expressions to show how they are feeling about the events and the other characters. Use word bubbles to show what they are saying or thinking.

PUT IT IN WRITING. Pick one of the characters from the scene you have chosen. Write a dramatic monologue in which the character shares his or her thoughts and feelings about what happened in the scene.

Unit SEVEN

Reading Nonfiction

NONFICTION

Nonfiction is writing about real people, places, things, and events. It can also explore thoughts and ideas. Categories of nonfiction writing follow.

Forms of Nonfiction

ARTICLE. An **article** is a brief work of nonfiction on a specific topic. You can find articles in encyclopedias, newspapers, and magazines.

AUTOBIOGRAPHY. An **autobiography** is the story of a person's life told by that person. Consequently, autobiographies are told from the first-person point of view.

BIOGRAPHY. A **biography** is the story of a person's life told by another person. Although biographies are told from a third-person point of view, autobiographical excerpts such as **letters**, **diaries**, and **journals** may be included.

DOCUMENTARY WRITING. **Documentary writing** is writing that records an event or subject in accurate detail. A profile of the Jazz Age or a report on human rights abuses in China would be examples of documentary writing.

ESSAY. An **essay**, originally meaning "a trial or attempt," is a short nonfiction work that explores a single subject and is typically a more lasting work than an article. Among the many types of essays are personal and expository essays. A **personal**, or **expressive**, **essay** deals with the life or interests of the writer. Personal essays are often, but not always, written in the first person. The excerpt from *Walden* is a personal essay. An **expository essay** features the developed ideas of the writer on a certain topic. The excerpt from "Self-Reliance" is an example of an expository essay.

THINK AND REFLECT

Give examples of nonfiction you have read. Why do you read nonfiction? **(Analyze and Synthesize)**

_____
_____
_____

NOTE THE FACTS

What is the difference between a biography and an autobiography?

_____
_____
_____

Reading TIP

Nonfiction can use techniques of fiction, such as characterization and dialogue, to make events come alive. In this unit, John Hersey combines journalism and literature to create a compelling history of six people who survived the atomic bombing of Hiroshima.

NOTE THE FACTS

Memoir is similar to what other forms of nonfiction?

_____
_____
_____

Reading TIP

A nonfiction work can have more than one purpose. For example, an essay writer could entertain with an anecdote and then reflect on the experience. In a speech, a speaker could tell a story to illustrate a point and then persuade the listener to take action.

HISTORY. A **history** is an account of past events. To write their histories, writers may use **speeches, sermons, contracts, deeds, constitutions, laws, political tracts**, and other types of public records. Patrick Henry's Speech in the Virginia Convention and Abraham Lincoln's Gettysburg Address are two speeches that are read as history.

HOW-TO WRITING. **How-to writing** is writing that explains a procedure or strategy. A manual that explains how to operate a DVD player is an example of how-to writing.

MEMOIR. A **memoir** is a nonfiction narration that tells a story autobiographically or biographically. Memoirs are based on a person's experiences and reactions to events.

SPEECH. A **speech** is a public address that was originally delivered orally. In this unit, Chief Joseph's "I will fight no more forever" is an example of a speech.

Purposes and Methods of Writing in Nonfiction

PURPOSE. A writer's **purpose**, or aim, is a writer's reason for writing. The following chart classifies modes, or categories, of prose writing by purpose.

Modes and Purposes of Writing

Mode	Purpose	Writing Forms
personal/ expressive writing	to reflect	diary entry, memoir, personal letter, autobiography, personal essay
imaginative/ descriptive writing	to entertain, to describe, to enrich, and to enlighten	poem, character sketch, play, short story
narrative writing	to tell a story, to narrate a series of events	short story, biography, legend, myth, history
informative/ expository writing	to inform, to explain	news article, research report, expository essay, book review
persuasive/ argumentative writing	to persuade	editorial, petition, political speech, persuasive essay

Types of Nonfiction Writing

In order to write effectively, a writer can choose to organize a piece of writing in different ways. The following chart describes types of writing that are commonly used in nonfiction, and tells how they are organized.

Type of Writing	Description
narration	Narrative writing tells a story or describes events. It may use chronological, or time, order.
dialogue	Dialogue reveals people's actual speech, which is set off with quotation marks.
description	Descriptive writing tells how things look, sound, smell, taste, or feel, often using spatial order.
exposition	Expository writing presents facts or opinions and is sometimes organized in one of these ways: ■ **Analysis** breaks something into its parts and shows how the parts are related. ■ **Classification** places subjects into categories according to what they have in common. ■ **Comparison-and-contrast order** presents similarities as it compares two things and differences as it contrasts them. ■ **How-to writing** presents the steps in a process or directions on how to do something.

THINK AND REFLECT

Which type of organization would a writer most likely use for a history? **(Infer)**

_____
_____
_____

USING READING STRATEGIES WITH NONFICTION

Active Reading Strategy Checklists

When reading nonfiction, it is important to know that the author is telling you about true events. The following checklists offer things to consider when reading nonfiction selections.

1 READ WITH A PURPOSE. Before reading nonfiction, give yourself a purpose, or something to look for, as you read. Sometimes a purpose will be a directive from a teacher: "Find out why the speaker will not fight anymore." Other times you can set your own purpose by previewing the title, the opening lines, and instructional information. Say to yourself

- ❑ This selection will be about . . .
- ❑ I will keep track of . . .
- ❑ The author wants readers to know . . .
- ❑ The author wrote this to . . .

2 CONNECT TO PRIOR KNOWLEDGE. Being aware of what you already know and calling it to mind as you read can help you understand a writer's views. As you read, say to yourself

- ❑ I already know this about the author's ideas . . .
- ❑ These things in the selection are similar to something I have experienced . . .
- ❑ Something similar I've read is . . .
- ❑ I agree with this because . . .

3 WRITE THINGS DOWN. As you read nonfiction, write down or mark important points that the author makes. Possible ways to keep a written record include

- ❑ Underline the author's key ideas.
- ❑ Write down your thoughts about the author's ideas.
- ❑ Highlight the author's main points and supporting details.
- ❑ Create a graphic organizer to keep track of ideas.
- ❑ Use a code to respond to the author's ideas.

4 MAKE PREDICTIONS. Before you read a nonfiction selection, use information about the author, the subject matter, and the title to guess what the selection will be about. As you read, confirm or deny your predictions, and make new ones based on what you learn. Make predictions like the following:

Reading TIP

One purpose for reading nonfiction is to gain knowledge about real people, places, things, or events.

Reading TIP

To **connect to your prior knowledge,** compare what you are reading to
- things you have read
- things you have experienced
- things you know about the topic

Reading TIP

A simple code can help you remember your reactions to what you are reading. You can use
- ! for "This is like something I have experienced"
- ? for "I don't understand this"
- ✓ for "This seems important"

- ❏ What will come next is . . .
- ❏ The author will support ideas by . . .
- ❏ I think the selection will end with . . .
- ❏ The title tells me that the selection will be about . . .

5 VISUALIZE. Visualizing, or allowing the words on the page to create images in your mind, helps you understand the author's message. In order to visualize what a selection is about, imagine that you are the narrator. Read the words in your head with the type of expression that the author means to put behind them. Make statements such as

- ❏ This parts helps me envision how . . .
- ❏ My sketch of this part would include . . .
- ❏ This part helps me see how . . .
- ❏ This part changes my views on . . .
- ❏ The author connects ideas by . . .

6 USE TEXT ORGANIZATION. When you read nonfiction, pay attention to the main idea and supporting details. Learn to stop occasionally and retell what you have read. Say to yourself

- ❏ The writer's main point is . . .
- ❏ The writer supports the main point by . . .
- ❏ In this section, the writer is saying that . . .
- ❏ I can summarize this section by . . .
- ❏ I can follow the events because . . .

7 TACKLE DIFFICULT VOCABULARY. Difficult words can hinder your ability to understand a writer's message. Use context, consult a dictionary, or ask someone about words you do not understand. When you come across a difficult word in nonfiction, say to yourself

- ❏ The lines near this word tell me that this word means . . .
- ❏ A dictionary definition shows that the word means . . .
- ❏ My work with the word before reading helps me know that the word means . . .
- ❏ A classmate said that the word means . . .

8 MONITOR YOUR READING PROGRESS. All readers encounter difficulty when they read, especially if the reading material is not self-selected. When you have to read something, take note of problems you are having and fix them. The key to reading success is knowing when you are having difficulty. To fix problems, say to yourself

---

Reading **TIP**

Read nonfiction carefully the first time through. Take notes as you read. After you finish reading, reread your notes. Mark them up and make additions or corrections. Rereading your notes and clarifying them helps you remember what you've read.

Reading **TIP**

Think about the type of nonfiction you are reading. Consider what kind of organization is likely. Look for transition words, headings, and other organizational markers to guide you through the text.

Reading **TIP**

Skim a text before you read it. Make a list of words that might slow you down, and write synonyms for each in the margins. As you read, use the synonyms in place of the words.

FIX-UP IDEAS

- Reread
- Ask a question
- Read in shorter chunks
- Read aloud
- Retell
- Work with a partner
- Unlock difficult words
- Vary your reading rate
- Choose a new reading strategy
- Create a mnemonic device

❑ Because I don't understand this part, I will . . .
❑ Because I'm having trouble staying connected to the ideas in the selection, I will . . .
❑ Because the words in the selection are too hard, I will . . .
❑ Because the selection is long, I will . . .
❑ Because I can't retell what the selection was about, I will . . .

Become an Active Reader

The instruction with the nonfiction selections in this unit gives you an in-depth look at how to use one strategy. Brief margin notes guide your use of additional strategies. Using one active reading strategy will greatly increase your reading success and enjoyment. Learn how to use several strategies in combination to ensure your complete understanding of what you are reading. When you have difficulty, use fix-up ideas to solve a problem. For further information about the active reading strategies, see Unit 1, pages 4–15.

How to Use Reading Strategies with Nonfiction

Use the following passages to discover how you might use reading strategies as you read nonfiction.

Excerpt 1. Note how a reader uses active reading strategies while reading this excerpt from *Of Plymouth Plantation* by William Bradford.

CONNECT TO PRIOR KNOWLEDGE
I know that the Pilgrims landed in Plymouth and that their first year was very difficult.

VISUALIZE
I can visualize a Thanksgiving feast. The foods mentioned aren't the ones I'd associate with Thanksgiving, though.

FIRST THANKSGIVING

They began now to gather in the small harvest they had, and to fit up their houses and dwellings against winter, being all well recovered in health and strength and had all things in good plenty. For as some were thus employed in affairs abroad, others were exercising fishing, about cod and bass and other fish, of which they took good store, of which every family had their portion. All the summer there was no want; and now began to come in store of fowl, as winter approached, of which this place did abound when they came first (but afterward decreased by degrees). And besides water fowl there was great store of wild turkeys, of which they took many, besides venison, etc. Besides they had about a peck a meal a week to a person, or now since harvest, Indian corn to that proportion. Which made many afterwards write so largely of their plenty here to their friends in England, which were not feigned but true reports.

USE TEXT ORGANIZATION
From the subheading, I know that this excerpt is about the first Thanksgiving.

TACKLE DIFFICULT VOCABULARY
I don't know the word *feigned,* but I can tell by the context that it contrasts with *true.* Maybe it means "false."

Excerpt 2. Note how a reader uses active reading strategies while reading this excerpt from *Incidents in the Life of a Slave Girl, Seven Years Concealed* by Harriet Jacobs (Linda Brent).

READ WITH A PURPOSE
I'll read to find out what slavery was like.

MONITOR YOUR READING PROGRESS
I'll reread the first section to remind myself what the narrator's mistress was like.

When I was nearly twelve years old, my kind mistress sickened and died. As I saw the cheek grow paler, and the eye more glassy, how earnestly I prayed in my heart that she might live! I loved her; for she had been almost like a mother to me. My prayers were not answered. She died, and they buried her in the little churchyard, where, day after day, my tears fell upon her grave.

I was sent to spend a week with my grandmother. I was now old enough to begin to think of the future; and again and again I asked myself what they would do with me. I felt sure I should never find another mistress so kind as the one who was gone. . . .

WRITE THINGS DOWN
I'll make a time line of events in the narrator's life.

MAKE PREDICTIONS
I predict that the narrator's new mistress will not be as kind as the previous one was.

CONNECT

Reader's resource

Jonathan Edwards was a minister whose views began the Great Awakening, a religious revival that swept across the colonies in the 1730s. Edwards's goal as a minister was to heighten his followers' commitment to religion and to enrich their religious experience. Known for his vivid and fiery sermons, Edwards sought to make religion so moving and real that it was almost a physical experience. The following excerpt is from **"Sinners in the Hands of an Angry God,"** a sermon Edwards delivered in Enfield, Connecticut, on Sunday, July 8, 1741. Another minister reported that Edwards spoke with calm dignity, yet the effect was highly emotional.

Word watch

PREVIEW VOCABULARY

abhor	incense
ascribe	induce
avail	loathsome
constitution	provoke
contrivance	sovereign
gulf	subserve

Reader's journal

What does the word *grace* mean to you? In what ways can people extend grace to those around them?

_____
_____

from "Sinners in the Hands of an Angry God"
by Jonathan Edwards

Active READING STRATEGY

READ WITH A PURPOSE

Before Reading → **IDENTIFY THE AUTHOR'S PURPOSE**

- ❏ Discuss the following question with a small group of your classmates: What would you do if you were trying to convince somebody of something you felt was important?
- ❏ Read the Reader's Resource carefully. With your group, determine Jonathan Edwards's purpose. Keep this purpose in mind as you read.
- ❏ Preview the Main Idea Chart below. As you read you will keep track of the author's techniques and main ideas in this graphic organizer.

Graphic Organizer: Main Idea Chart

Technique	Main Idea

270   THE EMC WRITE-IN READER

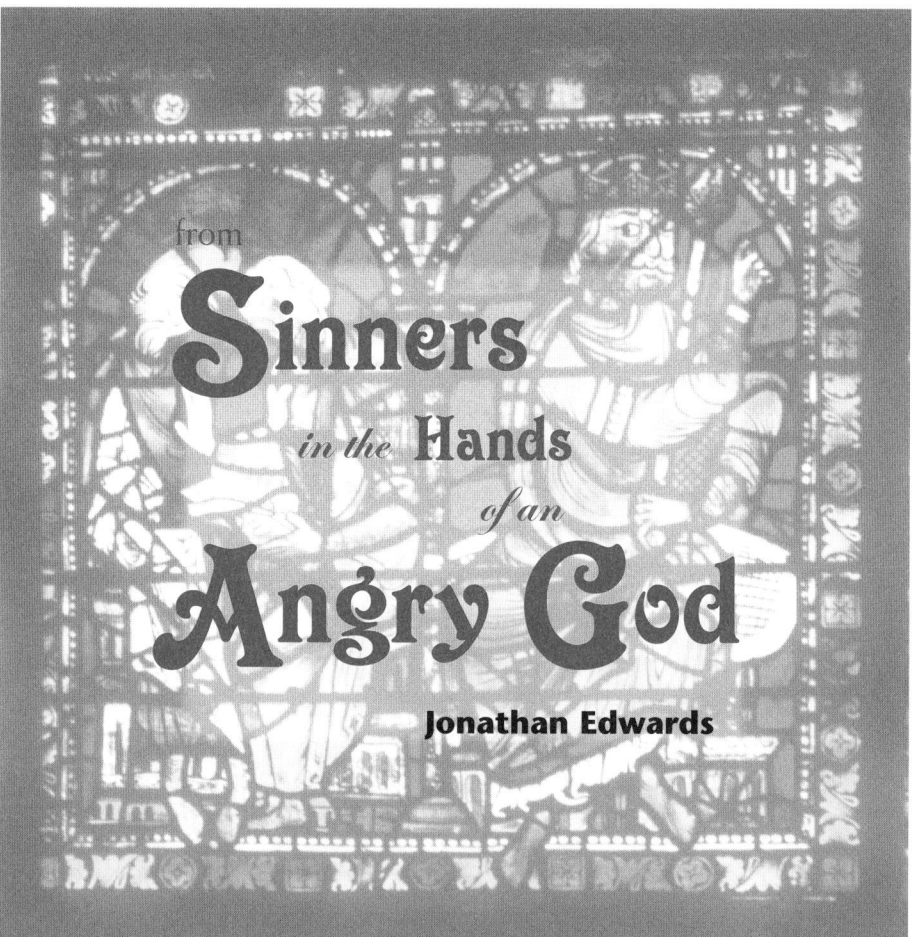

from

Sinners in the Hands of an Angry God

Jonathan Edwards

During Reading

READ WITH THE AUTHOR'S PURPOSE IN MIND

❑ Read along silently as your teacher reads the first two paragraphs aloud. What main points does Edwards make in this section? What techniques such as analogies, anecdotes, or repetition does Edwards use to make these points clear? Note the ideas and the techniques in the Main Idea Chart.

❑ Continue to read with your group, taking turns reading aloud. Keep Edwards's purpose in mind. List main ideas related to Edwards's purpose and the techniques he uses to make these points.

MARK THE TEXT

Highlight or underline what most people think keeps them alive. Highlight in a second color or circle what Edwards thinks preserves people.

NOTE THE FACTS

What makes people heavy as lead? What effect does this weight have?

_____

_____

_____

You probably are not sensible[1] of this; you find you are kept out of hell, but do not see the hand of God in it; but look at other things, as the good state of your bodily <u>constitution</u>, your care of your own life, and the means you use for your own preservation. But indeed these things are nothing; if God should withdraw His hand, they would <u>avail</u> no more to keep you from falling, than the thin air to hold up a person that is suspended in it.

Your wickedness makes you as it were heavy as lead, and to tend downwards with great weight and pressure towards hell; and if God should let you go, you would immediately sink

10

---
1. **sensible.** Aware

words for everyday use con • sti • tu • tion (kän´stə tü´shən) *n.,* physical makeup of a person. *Fran's <u>constitution</u> suffered from sitting at a desk for hours with no time to exercise.*
a • vail (ə vāl´) *vi.,* be of use or advantage. *Maurice's attempts to get concert tickets <u>availed</u> nothing, for they were sold out.*

UNIT 7 / READING NONFICTION   271

Literary TOOLS

ANALOGY. An **analogy** is a comparison of two things that are alike in some respects. Often an analogy explains or describes something unfamiliar by comparing it to something more familiar. A *simile* is an expressed analogy. A *metaphor* is an implied analogy. In this sermon, Edwards uses analogies to give his listeners a clear, concrete picture of the abstract ideas he presents. As you read, note analogies in the Main Idea Chart and identify the idea Edwards is trying to convey through each analogy.

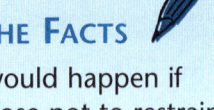

NOTE THE FACTS

What would happen if God chose not to restrain His rough wind?

_____
_____
_____

---

and swiftly descend and plunge into the bottomless <u>gulf</u>, and your healthy constitution, and your own care and prudence, and best <u>contrivance</u>, and all your righteousness, would have no more influence to uphold you and keep you out of hell, than a spider's web would have to stop a fallen rock. Were it not for the <u>sovereign</u> pleasure of God, the earth would not bear you one moment; for you are a burden to it; the creation groans with you; the creature is made subject to the bondage of your corruption, not willingly; the sun does not willingly shine upon you to give you light to serve sin and Satan; the earth does not willingly yield her increase[2] to satisfy your lusts; nor is it willingly a stage for your wickedness to be acted upon; the air does not willingly serve you for breath to maintain the flame of life in your vitals,[3] while you spend your life in the service of God's enemies. God's creatures are good, and were made for men to serve God with, and do not willingly <u>subserve</u> to any other purpose, and groan when they are abused to purposes so directly contrary to their nature and end. And the world would spew[4] you out, were it not for the sovereign hand of Him who hath subjected it in hope. There are black clouds of God's wrath now hanging directly over your heads, full of the dreadful storm, and big with thunder; and were it not for the restraining hand of God, it would immediately burst forth upon you. The sovereign pleasure of God, for the present, stays His rough wind; otherwise it would come with fury, and your destruction would come like a whirlwind, and you would be like the chaff of the summer threshing floor. . . .[5]

---

2. **increase.** Harvest
3. **vitals.** Necessary organs
4. **spew.** Throw up; eject
5. **chaff . . . threshing floor.** *Chaff*—husks of wheat that are left behind; *threshing floor*—place where grain is separated from its husks

---

words for everyday use

gulf (gulf) *n.*, wide, deep gap or separation. *People cross <u>gulfs</u> upon fallen trees in the movies, but I dared not cross the cavernous drop myself.*
con • triv • ance (kən trī′vəns) *n.*, invention; ingenious plan. *I feared we'd be trapped in the pit for days, but Mara's clever <u>contrivance</u> freed us in no time.*
sov • er • eign (sä′və rən) *adj.*, above or superior to all others. *With <u>sovereign</u> power, the superintendent decided the truant student's fate.*
sub • serve (səb sʉrv′) *vt.*, be useful or helpful; serve. *The pious nun <u>subserved</u> her God.*

40   The bow of God's wrath is bent, and the arrow made ready on the string, and justice bends the arrow at your heart, and strains the bow, and it is nothing but the mere pleasure of God, and that of an angry God, without any promise or obligation at all, that keeps the arrow one moment from being made drunk with your blood. Thus all you that never passed under a great change of heart, by the mighty power of the Spirit of God upon your souls, all you that were never born again, and made new creatures, and raised from being dead in sin, to a state of new, and before
50   altogether unexperienced light and life, are in the hands of an angry God. However you may have reformed your life in many things, and may have had religious affections,[6] and may keep up a form of religion in your families and closets,[7] and in the house of God, it is nothing but His mere pleasure that keeps you from being this moment swallowed up in everlasting destruction. However unconvinced you may now be of the truth of what you hear, by and by you will be fully convinced of it. Those that are gone from being in the like circumstances with you see that
60   it was so with them; for destruction came suddenly upon most of them; when they expected nothing of it and while they were saying, peace and safety: now they see that those things on which they depended for peace and safety, were nothing but thin air and empty shadows.

   The God that holds you over the pit of hell, much as one holds a spider or some <u>loathsome</u> insect over the fire, <u>abhors</u> you, and is dreadfully <u>provoked</u>: His wrath towards you burns like fire; He looks upon you as worthy of nothing else but to be cast into the fire; He is of purer eyes
70   than to bear to have you in His sight; you are ten thousand times more abominable in His eyes than the most hateful

---

6. **affections.** Feelings
7. **closets.** Studies; meditations

words for everyday use
 loath • some (lōth´səm) *adj.,* disgusting. *The <u>loathsome</u> beast left a trail of slime in the wake of its destruction.*
 ab • hor (ab hôr´) *vt.,* shrink from in disgust. *"I <u>abhor</u> snakes," said my aunt, looking at my reptilian pet with disgust.*
 pro • voke (prō vōk´) *vt.,* anger, irritate, annoy. *"Don't poke the dog with that stick. You'll only <u>provoke</u> him," Derek said.*

FIX-UP IDEA

Use Margin Questions
If you are having trouble identifying Edwards's main points, go back and answer the margin questions. These questions will help you focus on the points Edwards is making.

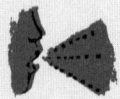

READ ALOUD

Practice reading the highlighted passage aloud. Make sure you understand the meaning of the passage. Then try to read the words the way Edwards might have said them. What, according to Edwards, will convince those who doubt his words?

_____
_____

Reading STRATEGY REVIEW

TACKLE DIFFICULT VOCABULARY. Use Words for Everyday Use and footnotes to help you understand the language in this selection. If you find other unfamiliar words, use context clues to help you find the meanings of the words. When using context clues, look for restatement of an idea, synonyms or antonyms of the word, or examples of the word.

Mark the Text

Highlight or underline the only reason listeners were not plunged into hell while they slept or since they awoke.

Note the Facts

According to Edwards, how much control do people who are sinful in the eyes of God have over their destinies?

_____
_____
_____

venomous serpent is in ours. You have offended Him infinitely more than ever a stubborn rebel did his prince; and yet it is nothing but His hand that holds you from falling into the fire every moment. It is to be <u>ascribed</u> to nothing else, that you did not go to hell the last night; that you was suffered to awake again in this world, after you closed your eyes to sleep. And there is no other reason to be given, why you have not dropped into hell since you arose in the morning, but that God's hand has held you up. There is no other reason to be given why you have not gone to hell, since you have sat here in the house of God, provoking His pure eyes by your sinful wicked manner of attending His solemn worship. Yea, there is nothing else that is to be given as a reason why you do not this very moment drop down into hell.

O sinner! Consider the fearful danger you are in: it is a great furnace of wrath, a wide and bottomless pit, full of the fire of wrath, that you are held over in the hand of that God, whose wrath is provoked and <u>incensed</u> as much against you, as against many of the damned in hell. You hang by a slender thread, with the flames of divine wrath flashing about it, and ready every moment to singe it, and burn it asunder; and you have no interest in any Mediator, and nothing to lay hold of to save yourself, nothing to keep off the flames of wrath, nothing of your own, nothing that you have done, nothing that you can do, to <u>induce</u> God to spare you one moment. ■

words for everyday use

as • cribe (ə skrīb´) *vt.*, assign; attribute. *Glenda <u>ascribed</u> her success at basketball to her mother's coaching.*
in • cense (in sens´) *vt.*, make very angry. *Muriel was <u>incensed</u> when she found Myron had stolen her idea.*
in • duce (in dūs´) *vt.*, persuade; prevail on. *Despite the rising flood waters, no one could <u>induce</u> Otto to leave his home.*

Reflect ON YOUR READING

After Reading → **SHARE HOW THE PURPOSE AFFECTED YOUR READING**

- ❑ Share your list with your group from the Before Reading activity. Do all of the points you listed relate to Edwards's purpose?
- ❑ Discuss this question with your group: Did Edwards achieve his purpose?

Reading Skills and Test Practice

IDENTIFY AUTHOR'S PURPOSE

READ, THINK, AND EXPLAIN. Write a short review of "Sinners in the Hands of an Angry God." In your review, identify what Edwards was trying to achieve and explain how he did or did not meet this goal. Use the Think-Aloud Notes to jot down your ideas.

_____
_____
_____
_____
_____
_____
_____

How did using the reading strategy help you to identify the author's purpose?

_____
_____
_____
_____

THINK-ALOUD NOTES

Investigate, Inquire, and Imagine

RECALL: GATHER FACTS
1a. What does Edwards claim is required to take a person out of the sinner classification?

INTERPRET: FIND MEANING
1b. What abstract idea is personified, or described as a person, in paragraph 3? What is this personified ideal doing? Why is this comparison frightening?

ANALYZE: TAKE THINGS APART
2a. In paragraph 4, what progression does Edwards trace in speaking of the threat to the sinner's existence?

SYNTHESIZE: BRING THINGS TOGETHER
2b. Why might this progression be particularly effective in arousing fear?

EVALUATE: MAKE JUDGMENTS
3a. Do you think that this sermon could inspire people to throw themselves on the mercy of an angry God? What short-term and long-term effects would you expect?

EXTEND: CONNECT IDEAS
3b. What is your idea of a "sinner" and of a holy or "pure" person? Write a journal entry about things you would like to do to make yourself a better person. You do not need to share this journal entry with anyone.

Literary Tools

ANALOGY. An **analogy** is a comparison of two things that are alike in some respects. Often an analogy explains or describes something unfamiliar by comparing it to something more familiar. On your own paper, complete a chart like the one below by listing analogies in the speech.

Thing being described	What it is likened to
Physical means of keeping you alive cannot prevent you from dying and going to hell if God withdraws support.	Thin air cannot hold up a person suspended in it.

Do you think the analogies Edwards uses are effective? Why, or why not?

_____

_____

_____

_____

WordWorkshop

Look Up Words with Multiple Meanings. Sometimes you will encounter a word that has multiple meanings. For example, you probably know that the word *constitution* means a written document outlining the basic principles and laws of a group, but in the following example that meaning doesn't make sense.

" . . . but look at other things, as the good state of your bodily constitution"

In this case, *constitution* means the physical makeup of a person.

If you look up a word in a dictionary and find multiple definitions, apply each definition to the sentence. Determine the meaning that makes the most sense in context.

For each of the underlined words, identify the meaning of the word as it is used in the sentence. Then identify a second meaning of each word, and write a contextual sentence for the second meaning. Use a dictionary if necessary.

1. [T]he earth does not willingly yield her <u>increase</u>.
2. The <u>bow</u> of God's wrath is bent, and the arrow made ready on the string . . .
3. You provoke and <u>incense</u> the wrath of God.
4. [Y]ou have no <u>interest</u> in any Mediator, and nothing to lay hold of to save yourself . . .
5. . . . to <u>induce</u> God to spare you one moment.

Read-Write Connection

Some of the members of Edwards's congregation wept upon hearing this sermon. Can you empathize with these listeners? Why, or why not?

_____

_____

_____

Beyond the Reading

Compare Sermons. Compare Edwards's sermon with the sermon of a contemporary preacher. You can use the sermon of a preacher you have heard in person or a sermon you find through research. How do the sermons differ? How are they similar? Are the goals and motivations of the speakers the same? Do the sermons reflect the different audiences being addressed?

Go Online. To find links and additional activities for this selection, visit the EMC Internet Resource Center at **emcp.com/languagearts** and click on Write-In Reader.

CONNECT

Reader's resource

Patrick Henry was a distinguished diplomat and orator during the American Revolution. The **Speech in the Virginia Convention** is probably Henry's best-known oration. The speech was given at a time when Britain had sent additional troops and naval forces to the colonies to maintain order in reaction to protests against taxes. The question at hand was whether to attempt reconciliation with Britain. Less than a month after Henry's speech, his prediction of open battle in the North was fulfilled in the opening skirmishes of the American Revolution.

Word watch

PREVIEW VOCABULARY

avert	prostrate
comport	remonstrate
effectual	solace
formidable	subjugation
inestimable	submission
insidious	supinely
inviolate	temporal
martial	

Reader's journal

When have a friend or relative's words motivated you to take action?

_____
_____
_____

Speech in the Virginia Convention
by Patrick Henry

Active READING STRATEGY

READ WITH A PURPOSE

Before Reading → **IDENTIFY PURPOSE**

❏ Read the Reader's Resource to focus on when and why the speech was given. What do you expect this speech to be about? What purpose do you think Henry had for giving the speech?

❏ A **rhetorical question** is one asked for effect rather than to get an answer. Usually, the answer is clear from context. As you read, pay attention to rhetorical questions and consider how they relate to Henry's purpose.

Graphic Organizer: Rhetorical Question Chart

Rhetorical Question	Assumed Answer
"Is this the part of wise men, engaged in a great and arduous struggle for liberty?"	Wise men seeking freedom open their eyes and see the truth.

Speech in the Virginia Convention

Patrick Henry

> **During Reading**
>
> **READ WITH PURPOSE IN MIND**
> - Listen as your teacher reads the first two paragraphs of the selection aloud. Identify rhetorical questions that Henry asks and write them in your chart. Also write the assumed answer to each question. What main points does Henry make?
> - Continue reading on your own. As you read, keep Henry's purpose in mind and continue to add rhetorical questions and assumed answers in the chart. Think about how these ideas support Henry's purpose.
>
>
>
> **READ ALOUD**
> Because this is a speech, you may get a better understanding from hearing it. After you have read through the speech once, practice reading it aloud with a partner. Take turns reading aloud and listening.
>
>
>
> **NOTE THE FACTS**
> What does Henry say is the only way to arrive at the truth?
> _____
> _____
> _____

Mr. President:[1] No man thinks more highly than I do of the patriotism, as well as abilities, of the very worthy gentlemen who have just addressed the house. But different men often see the same subject in different lights: and, therefore, I hope it will not be thought disrespectful to those gentlemen, if, entertaining, as I do, opinions of a character very opposite to theirs, I shall speak forth my sentiments freely and without reserve. This is no time for ceremony. The question before the house is one of awful moment to this country. For my own part, I consider it as nothing less than a question of freedom or slavery. And in proportion to the magnitude of the subject ought to be the freedom of the debate. It is only in this way that we can hope to arrive at truth, and fulfill the great responsibility which we hold to God and our country. Should I keep back my opinions at such a time, through fear of giving offense, I should consider myself as guilty of treason toward my country, and of an act of disloyalty toward the Majesty of Heaven, which I revere above all earthly kings.

---

1. **Mr. President.** President of the Virginia Convention

NOTE THE FACTS

What guides the speaker according to lines 30–31?

_____

_____

_____

Reading TIP

An **allusion** is a rhetorical technique in which reference is made to a person, event, object, or work from history or literature. When Henry says, "Suffer not yourselves to be betrayed with a kiss," he is alluding to the kiss that Judas gave to Christ when betraying the latter to Roman soldiers. The allusion reveals Henry's feelings that the English king cannot be trusted.

FIX-UP IDEA

Unlock Difficult Words
Review the Words for Everyday Use. Carefully read each word, its definition, and the sentence using it. Then go back and read the part of the selection that uses this word. If you encounter other words you do not know, first try to determine their meanings using context clues. If that doesn't work, consult a dictionary.

20   Mr. President, it is natural to man to indulge in the illusions of hope. We are apt to shut our eyes against a painful truth, and listen to the song of that siren till she transforms us into beasts. Is this the part of wise men, engaged in a great and arduous struggle for liberty? Are we disposed to be of the number of those who having eyes see not, and having ears hear not, the things which so nearly concern their <u>temporal</u> salvation? For my part, whatever anguish of spirit it may cost, I am willing to know the whole truth; to know the worst and to provide for it.

30   I have but one lamp by which my feet are guided, and that is the lamp of experience. I know of no way of judging of the future but by the past. And judging by the past, I wish to know what there has been in the conduct of the British ministry for the last ten years to justify those hopes with which gentlemen have been pleased to <u>solace</u> themselves and the house? Is it that <u>insidious</u> smile with which our petition[2] has been lately received? Trust it not, sir: it will prove a snare to your feet. Suffer not yourselves to be betrayed with a kiss. Ask yourselves how this gracious reception of our petition

40   <u>comports</u> with those warlike preparations which cover our waters and darken our land. Are fleets and armies necessary to a work of love and reconciliation? Have we shown ourselves so unwilling to be reconciled that force must be called in to win back our love? Let us not deceive ourselves, sir. These are the implements of war and <u>subjugation</u>—the last arguments to which kings resort.

I ask gentlemen, sir, what means this <u>martial</u> array,[3] if its purpose be not to force us to <u>submission</u>? Can gentlemen

---

2. **petition.** "Olive Branch Petition," in which the king was asked to intercede between Parliament and the colonies
3. **array.** Display; assembly

words for everyday use

tem • po • ral (tem´pə rəl) *adj.*, lasting only for a time; temporary. *Marty's anger was <u>temporal</u>, and soon his good-natured grin returned.*
so • lace (säl´əs) *vt.*, comfort, relieve. *The father gave <u>solace</u> to his young child with a hug.*
in • sid • i • ous (in sid´ē əs) *adj.*, sly; crafty. *The dishwasher refused to go along with the cook's <u>insidious</u> plan to steal from the restaurant manager.*
com • port (kəm pôrt´) *vi.*, agree; go along. *The politician's actions do not <u>comport</u> with his stated ideals.*
sub • ju • ga • tion (sub´jə gā´shən) *n.*, takeover; enslavement. *The <u>subjugation</u> of Earth by fifty-foot ants was the subject of the movie.*
mar • tial (mär´shəl) *adj.*, warlike; of the military. *"The Battle Hymn of the Republic" is a <u>martial</u> song.*
sub • mis • sion (sub mish´ən) *n.*, act of yielding; surrendering. *The dog showed his <u>submission</u> by dropping the stick and lying down.*

assign any other possible motive for it? Has Great Britain any enemy in this quarter of the world, to call for all this accumulation of navies and armies? No, sir, she has none. They are meant for us: they can be meant for no other. They are sent over to bind and rivet upon us those chains which the British ministry have been so long forging.

And what have we to oppose to them? Shall we try argument? Sir, we have been trying that for the last ten years. Have we anything new to offer upon the subject? Nothing. We have held the subject up in every light of which it is capable; but it has been all in vain. Shall we resort to entreaty and humble supplication? What terms shall we find which have not been already exhausted? Let us not, I beseech[4] you, sir, deceive ourselves longer.

Sir, we have done everything that could be done to avert the storm which is now coming on. We have petitioned; we have remonstrated; we have supplicated; we have prostrated ourselves before the throne, and have implored its interposition[5] to arrest the tyrannical hands of the ministry and Parliament. Our petitions have been slighted; our remonstrances have produced additional violence and insult; our supplications have been disregarded; and we have been spurned with contempt from the foot of the throne! In vain, after these things, may we indulge the fond[6] hope of peace and reconciliation. There is no longer any room for hope. If we wish to be free, if we mean to preserve inviolate those inestimable privileges for which we have been so long contending, if we mean not basely to abandon the noble struggle in which we have been so long engaged, and which we have pledged ourselves never to abandon until the glorious object of our contest shall be obtained—we must

---

4. **beseech.** Beg; plead
5. **interposition.** Intervention
6. **fond.** Foolish

words for everyday use

a • vert (ə vurt´) vt., prevent. *Snow and ice did not avert the delivery of the mail.*
re • mon • strate (ri män´strāt´) vt., demonstrate. *Dianne remonstrated her objection with a lengthy argument.*
pros • trate (präs´trāt´) vt., bow down. *The courtiers prostrated themselves before the king.*
in • vi • o • late (in vī´ə lit) adj., sacred. *Chris's Sunday morning with the comics and a doughnut is inviolate.*
in • es • ti • ma • ble (in es´tə mə bəl) adj., too great to be measured. *You have my inestimable gratitude for solving the problem.*

Reading TIP
A **metaphor** is a figure of speech in which one thing is written or spoken about as if it were another. Henry's speech is full of metaphors. For example, he compares the attempts of the British to subjugate the colonies to the forging of chains.

MARK THE TEXT
Highlight or underline the steps the colonists have taken to avert the wrath of Britain.

Reading STRATEGY REVIEW
MAKE PREDICTIONS. Henry's speech is rising to a key point. Stop and predict what action Henry will suggest.

_____
_____
_____

NOTE THE FACTS

Who is favored in battle?

_____
_____
_____

80 fight! I repeat it, sir, we must fight! An appeal to arms and to the God of Hosts is all that is left us!

They tell us, sir, that we are weak—unable to cope with so formidable an adversary. But when shall we be stronger? Will it be the next week, or the next year? Will it be when we are totally disarmed, and when a British guard shall be stationed in every house? Shall we gather strength by irresolution and inaction? Shall we acquire the means of effectual resistance by lying supinely on our backs and hugging the delusive phantom of hope until our enemies shall have bound us hand and foot?

90 Sir, we are not weak, if we make a proper use of those means which the God of nature hath placed in our power. Three millions of people, armed in the holy cause of liberty, and in such a country as that which we possess, are invincible by any force which our enemy can send against us. Besides, sir, we shall not fight our battles alone. There is a just God who presides over the destinies of nations and who will raise up friends to fight our battles for us. The battle, sir, is not to the strong alone; it is to the vigilant, the active, the brave. Besides, sir, we have no election.[7] If we were base enough to desire it,

100 it is now too late to retire from the contest. There is no retreat but in submission and slavery! Our chains are forged! Their clanging may be heard on the plains of Boston! The war is inevitable—and let it come! I repeat it, sir, let it come![8]

It is in vain, sir, to extenuate the matter. Gentlemen may cry, "Peace, peace"—but there is no peace. The war is actually begun! The next gale that sweeps from the north will bring to our ears the clash of resounding arms! Our brethren are already in the field! Why stand we here idle? What is it that gentlemen wish? What would they have? Is

110 life so dear, or peace so sweet, as to be purchased at the price of chains and slavery? Forbid it, Almighty God! I know not what course others may take; but as for me, give me liberty or give me death! ■

THINK AND REFLECT

What effect do you think Henry's closing line had on listeners? (Evaluate)

_____
_____
_____

---

7. **election.** Choice
8. **The war . . . come!** Boston had recently been occupied by British troops under the leadership of General Howe.

words for everyday use

for • mi • da • ble (fôr′mə de bəl) *adj.*, overwhelming. *Cleaning my room was a formidable task.*
ef • fec • tu • al (e fek′chü əl) *adj.*, effective. *A simple "Quiet" was effectual in silencing the class.*
su • pine • ly (sü′pīn′ lə) *adv.*, passively. *I refuse to sit supinely while you shirk your responsibilities.*

Reflect ON YOUR READING

After Reading → **SHARE YOUR IDEAS**

❑ With a small group of classmates, share the rhetorical questions you identified in your graphic organizer and the assumed answer to each question.
❑ Talk about how these ideas relate to Henry's purpose.

Reading Skills and Test Practice

IDENTIFY AUTHOR'S PURPOSE

Discuss with a partner how to answer questions that require you to identify purpose. Use the Think-Aloud Notes to write down your reasons for eliminating the incorrect answers.

_____ 1. What was the purpose of this speech?
   a. to convince the Virginia Convention to seek peace with Great Britain
   b. to identify the problems with the Stamp Act
   c. to persuade the Virginia Convention that war was necessary
   d. to entertain the convention with brilliant rhetoric

_____ 2. What position did the previous speakers take?
   a. They argued for a study on the feasibility of winning war.
   b. They expressed concern about going to war.
   c. They urged their audience to fight for liberty.
   d. They pressed for moderation and a peaceful attitude toward Britain.

How did using the reading strategy help you to answer the questions?

_____
_____
_____
_____

THINK-ALOUD NOTES

UNIT 7 / READING NONFICTION 283

Investigate, Inquire, and Imagine

RECALL: GATHER FACTS
1a. What is Henry's response to the possibility that war may break out soon?

INTERPRET: FIND MEANING
1b. What does Henry see as an unthinkable alternative to war?

ANALYZE: TAKE THINGS APART
2a. Compare the colonists' and the British authorities' attempts to resolve the conflict in the colonies.

SYNTHESIZE: BRING THINGS TOGETHER
2b. What British actions would probably have appeased Henry so that he would not have called for war?

EVALUATE: MAKE JUDGMENTS
3a. Is Henry's speech diplomatic? Explain your response.

EXTEND: CONNECT IDEAS
3b. What groups of people in the news today seem to agree with Henry's declaration that death is preferable to a life without liberty?

Literary Tools

RHETORICAL QUESTION. A **rhetorical question** is one asked for effect but not meant to be answered because the answer is clear from context. Speakers use rhetorical questions to reinforce a point that they have already made or that should, from the speaker's point of view, be obvious to the audience. Review the rhetorical questions you noted in your graphic organizer. What points did Henry emphasize through the use of rhetorical questions?

WordWorkshop

TEST YOUR WORD KNOWLEDGE. Review the Words for Everyday Use from the Speech in the Virginia Convention by looking at the definitions and how the words are used in context. Then answer the following questions.

1. Why would an inestimable debt be formidable?

2. Would you react supinely to an attack on rights you hold inviolate? Explain.

3. Name a situation when you would solace a friend.

4. Does prostrating yourself suggest a proud or a submissive attitude? Explain.

5. Explain whether you would trust someone with an <u>insidious</u> smile.

   _____

6. Identify a relationship between <u>subjugation</u> and <u>submission</u>.

   _____

7. Write a sentence that contrasts <u>temporal</u> with an antonym.

   _____

8. Does lying <u>comport</u> with your expectations of Honest Abe? Why?

   _____

9. Would you <u>remonstrate</u> if you agreed or disagreed with somebody's opinion?

   _____

10. Name two kinds of situations you would want to <u>avert</u>.

    _____

Read-Write Connection

If you had heard Henry's speech in 1775, what stand would you have decided to take toward the British? Would you have been in favor of war or of a peaceful resolution of the conflict?

_____

_____

_____

_____

Beyond the Reading

GIVE A SPEECH. An **extemporaneous speech** is thoroughly researched and prepared ahead of time and is sometimes given from notes. Prepare an extemporaneous speech about a cause you believe in. Deliver your speech to your class. Try to persuade your listeners to support the cause that you believe in.

GO ONLINE. To find links and additional activities for this selection, visit the EMC Internet Resource Center at **emcp.com/languagearts** and click on Write-In Reader.

CONNECT

Reader's resource

Ralph Waldo Emerson was considered the greatest American thinker of his day. Emerson was a leader of the Transcendentalist Movement. The Transcendentalists believed in a deep spiritual connection between people and nature, and the soul of each individual was thought to be a microcosm of the world itself. The essay **"Self-Reliance"** expresses his beliefs on individualism. It is a combination of different ideas from his journal in which Emerson recorded his thoughts for years. Emerson used his journal as a source of ideas for his frequent lectures. He tested and perfected his style and wording before audiences, noting their reactions. He then condensed his ideas into essay form.

Word watch

PREVIEW VOCABULARY

arduous   predominate
aversion   squalid

Reader's journal

Have you ever been in a situation where you had to choose between what you thought was right and the course that others thought you should take? What was your final decision?

"Self-Reliance"
by Ralph Waldo Emerson

Active READING STRATEGY

WRITE THINGS DOWN

Before Reading ➤ **PREVIEW LITERARY ELEMENTS**

❏ An **aphorism** is a short saying or pointed statement. An aphorism that gains currency and is passed from generation to generation is called a *proverb* or *adage*. An example of an aphorism is "Life is short, art is long." With a few of your classmates, identify some aphorisms you know.

❏ Talk about the kind of advice or ideas Emerson might put forth in an essay titled "Self-Reliance."

❏ Look for aphorisms as you read the selection and think about the themes the aphorisms suggest. Keep track of the aphorisms and their meanings in the graphic organizer below.

Graphic Organizer: Aphorism Chart

Aphorism	Meaning

286   THE EMC WRITE-IN READER

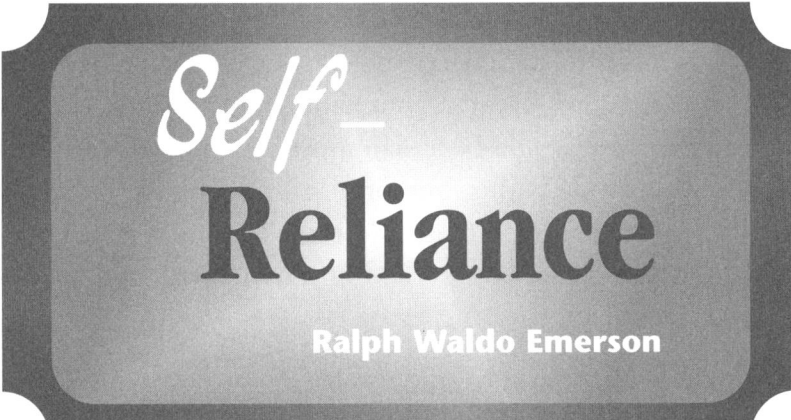

Self-Reliance
Ralph Waldo Emerson

There is a time in every man's education when he arrives at the conviction that envy is ignorance; that imitation is suicide; that he must take himself for better, for worse, as his portion; that though the wide universe is full of good, no kernel of nourishing corn can come to him but through his toil bestowed on that plot of ground which is given to him to till.

♦ ♦ ♦

Trust thyself: every heart vibrates to that iron string. Accept the place the divine Providence has found for you; the society of your contemporaries, the connexion of events. Great men have always done so and confided themselves childlike to the genius of their age, betraying their perception that the Eternal was stirring at their heart, working through their hands, <u>predominating</u> in all their being.

♦ ♦ ♦

Society everywhere is in conspiracy against the manhood of every one of its members. Society is a joint-stock company[1] in which the members agree for the better securing of his bread to each shareholder, to surrender the

---

1. **joint-stock company.** Company in which joint owners hold the capital

words for everyday use

pre • dom • i • nate (prē däm´ə nāt´) vi., have authority or influence over others. Her opinions <u>predominate</u> and everyone does what she says.

During Reading

RECORD LITERARY ELEMENTS

❑ Listen as your teacher reads the first two sections of "Self-Reliance" aloud. Write down any aphorisms in your chart. Restate the aphorism in your own words in the right-hand column of your chart and comment on how it might apply to your life.

❑ Continue reading on your own. Stop at the end of each segment and add aphorisms and comments to your chart.

Note the Facts

Whom should you trust? What should you accept?

_____

_____

_____

Literary TOOLS

ESSAY AND THEME. An **essay** is a brief work of prose nonfiction. A good essay develops a single idea. A **theme** is a central idea in a literary work. What do you expect the theme to be, based on the title of this essay? As you read, look for details that support this theme.

Fix-Up Idea

Think Aloud
Work with a partner to read the essay aloud. Read one section aloud. Then pause and do a think aloud about what you have read. Share images or advice you feel is most striking, discuss what makes them striking, what questions you have, and what Emerson's ideas might mean in your own life. Have your partner read the next segment. Again stop and think aloud. Do this until you have read the whole essay.

Note the Facts

By what opinion is it easy to live? Whose opinion should you follow?

_____
_____
_____

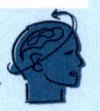

Think and Reflect

What evidence does the speaker offer to suggest that being misunderstood is not bad? Who else might be included in the list of those who have been misunderstood? **(Extend)**

_____
_____
_____

liberty and culture of the eater. The virtue in most request is conformity. Self-reliance is its <u>aversion</u>. It loves not realities and creators, but names and customs.

Whoso would be a man must be a nonconformist. He who would gather immortal palms must not be hindered by the name of goodness, but must explore if it be goodness. Nothing is at last sacred but the integrity of our own mind.

♦ ♦ ♦

What I must do, is all that concerns me, not what the people think. This rule, equally <u>arduous</u> in actual and in intellectual life, may serve for the whole distinction between greatness and meanness. It is the harder, because you will always find those who think they know what is your duty better than you know it. It is easy in the world to live after the world's opinion; it is easy in solitude to live after our own; but the great man is he who in the midst of the crowd keeps with perfect sweetness the independence of solitude.

♦ ♦ ♦

A foolish consistency is the hobgoblin of little minds, adored by little statesmen and philosophers and divines. With consistency a great soul has simply nothing to do. He may as well concern himself with his shadow on the wall. Out upon your guarded lips! Sew them up with packthread, do. Else, if you would be a man, speak what you think today in words as hard as cannon balls, and tomorrow speak what tomorrow thinks in hard words again, though it contradict every thing you said today. Ah, then, exclaim the aged ladies, you shall be sure to be misunderstood. Misunderstood! It is a right fool's word. Is it so bad then to be misunderstood? Pythagoras was misunderstood, and Socrates, and Jesus, and Luther, and Copernicus, and Galileo, and Newton, and every pure and wise spirit that ever took flesh. To be great is to be misunderstood.

words for everyday use

a•ver•sion (ə vʉr´zhən) *n.*, definite dislike. *Since she was allergic to nuts, she developed an <u>aversion</u> to them.*

ar•du•ous (är´jü əs) *adj.*, difficult. *The farmer endured a life of <u>arduous</u> toil.*

♦ ♦ ♦

I hope in these days we have heard the last of conformity and consistency. Let the words be gazetted and ridiculous henceforward.² **Instead of the gong for dinner, let us hear a whistle from the Spartan fife.**³ Let us bow and apologize never more. A great man is coming to eat at my house. I do not wish to please him: I wish that he should wish to please me. I will stand here for humanity, and though I would make it kind, I would made it true. Let us affront and reprimand the smooth mediocrity and <u>squalid</u> contentment of the times, and hurl in the face of custom, and trade, and office, the fact which is the upshot of all history, that there is a great responsible Thinker and Actor moving wherever moves a man; that a true man belongs to no other time or place, but is the center of things. Where he is, there is nature. . . . Every true man is a cause, a country, and an age; requires infinite spaces and numbers and time fully to accomplish his thought;—and posterity seem to follow his steps as a procession. A man Cæsar is born, and for ages after, we have a Roman Empire. Christ is born, and millions of minds so grow and cleave⁴ to his genius, that he is confounded with virtue and the possible of man. An institution is the lengthened shadow of one man; as, the Reformation, of Luther; Quakerism, of Fox; Methodism, of Wesley; Abolition, of Clarkson.⁵ Scipio,⁶ Milton called, "the height of Rome;" and all history resolves itself very easily into the biography of a few stout and earnest persons. ■

THINK AND REFLECT

Read the highlighted line. Restate Emerson's meaning in your own words. **(Paraphrase)**

_____
_____
_____

NOTE THE FACTS

How does Emerson describe history?

_____
_____
_____

---

2. **gazetted and ridiculous henceforward.** Labeled and not used from now on
3. **gong . . . fife.** The gong stands for ease and leisure, and the fife represents disciplined, alert life.
4. **cleave.** Cling; adhere
5. **Reformation . . . Clarkson.** Martin Luther (1483–1546), founder of the Reformation; George Fox (1624–1691), founder of Quakerism; John Wesley (1703–1791), founder of Methodism; and Thomas Clarkson (1760–1846), abolitionist
6. **Scipio.** (237–183 BC) Roman conqueror of Carthage, a city-state of ancient Africa

words for everyday use

squal • id (skwäl´id) *adj.*, wretched; miserable. *The destitute family lived in a squalid shack.*

Reflect ON YOUR READING

After Reading ➤ IDENTIFY THEME

- ❑ Share your Aphorism Charts with your group from the Before Reading activity.
- ❑ Discuss other ways you can apply the aphorisms you identified.
- ❑ As a group, identify a theme of the selection.

Reading Skills and Test Practice

SYNTHESIZE INFORMATION

READ, THINK, AND EXPLAIN. Identify a major theme in "Self-Reliance," and use examples from the essay to support this theme.

_____
_____
_____
_____
_____
_____
_____
_____
_____

How did using the reading strategy help you to identify the theme?

_____
_____
_____
_____

THINK-ALOUD NOTES

Investigate, Inquire, and Imagine

RECALL: GATHER FACTS
1a. What type of behavior does Emerson say is easy? What type of behavior does Emerson say is difficult but essential for greatness?

INTERPRET: FIND MEANING
1b. What does Emerson mean by the phrase "the independence of solitude" (line 33)? Why is it something for which to strive?

ANALYZE: TAKE THINGS APART
2a. Consider some of the people Emerson says were misunderstood in their time. What qualities distinguish them from other people?

SYNTHESIZE: BRING THINGS TOGETHER
2b. Why might great people sometimes be inconsistent? Summarize Emerson's view of the importance of consistency.

EVALUATE: MAKE JUDGMENTS
3a. Do you agree with Emerson that it is better to rely on yourself rather than upon others for your values and your principles? What are some of the benefits of being self-reliant?

EXTEND: CONNECT IDEAS
3b. In your opinion, if society values conformity over individualism, why do nonconformists seem to have the greatest impact on society? What contemporary nonconformists can you think of that have had a great impact on our culture?

WordWorkshop

USE VOCABULARY IN APHORISMS. Review the aphorisms you found in Emerson's "Self-Reliance." First, define each of the following vocabulary words from the essay. Then use each word in an original aphorism.

1. aversion _____

   Aphorism _____
   _____

2. arduous _____

   Aphorism _____
   _____

3. predominate _____

   Aphorism _____
   _____

4. squalid _____

   Aphorism _____
   _____

Literary Tools

ESSAY AND THEME. An **essay** is a brief work of prose nonfiction. A good essay develops a single idea. A **theme** is a central idea in a literary work. Identify at least one theme that runs through this essay. Explain how Emerson develops this idea.

_____
_____
_____
_____
_____

Read-Write Connection

With which quote from "Self-Reliance" do you agree most strongly, and why?

_____
_____
_____
_____
_____
_____
_____
_____

Beyond the Reading

WRITE A BIOGRAPHY. A **biography** is the story of a person's life told by someone other than that person. Read about the life of one of the nonconformists Emerson mentions in "Self-Reliance." Write a brief biography of that person. Include the most memorable events from that person's life and illustrate why the person was great.

GO ONLINE. To find links and additional activities for this selection, visit the EMC Internet Resource Center at **emcp.com/languagearts** and click on Write-In Reader.

from *Walden*

by Henry David Thoreau

Active READING STRATEGY

USE TEXT ORGANIZATION

Before Reading ▶ **PREVIEW ORGANIZATION**

❑ Read the Reader's Resource to understand what kind of selection this is. Then skim through the selection looking at photographs and headings. Note that the selection is divided into shorter segments separated by bullets. Each segment covers a new topic.

❑ Write down expectations you have about this essay based on your preview. What kinds of subjects do you think it will talk about? Why?

_____

_____

Graphic Organizer: Cluster Chart

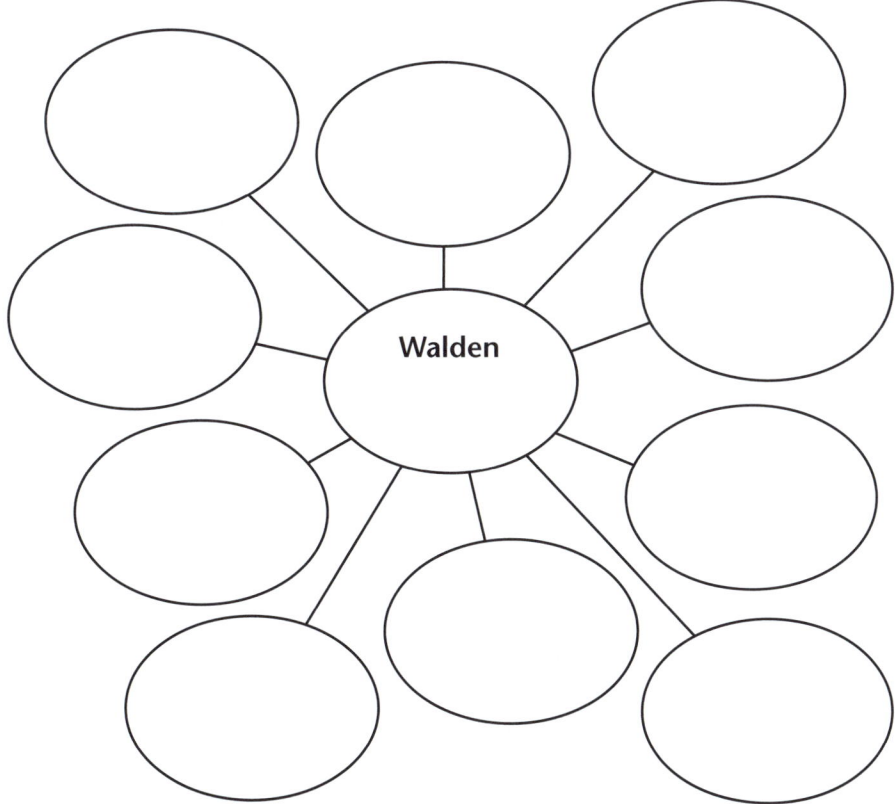

CONNECT

Reader's resource

Henry David Thoreau was a writer, philosopher, and naturalist. Thoreau lived for two years in a cabin he built on Ralph Waldo Emerson's property at Walden Pond. *Walden* is drawn from the journals Thoreau kept before, during, and after his stay at Walden Pond. The book firmly established Thoreau's reputation as a writer as well as an outspoken individualist. Thoreau's work demonstrates how the abstract ideals of individualism and libertarianism can be effectively instilled in a person's life.

Word watch

PREVIEW VOCABULARY

aspiration   perennial
cessation   posterity
earnest   resignation
encumbrance   saturated
endeavor   superfluous
ethereal   undulation
fluctuate   unwieldy
laxly   volatile
paltry

Reader's journal

What do you need in order to be happy?

_____

_____

_____

UNIT 7 / READING NONFICTION   293

During Reading

USE ORGANIZATION AS YOU READ

❑ Read the subheading of the first section. What can you guess about the section based on the subheading?

❑ Read the first sentence. Do you agree with this statement? Continue reading to see how Thoreau explains this statement. Read to the bullets on page 295. Stop and note in the Cluster Chart important ideas you find in the passage. Discuss the first passage with your classmates.

❑ Continue reading. Pause at section breaks to add your thoughts to the Cluster Chart. What important ideas did you find? Which quotations stay in your head? What do these quotations mean to you?

NOTE THE FACTS

What kind of lives do most people lead? What does Thoreau call resignation?

_____

_____

_____

Walden
Henry David Thoreau

from "Economy"

The mass of men lead lives of quiet desperation. What is called <u>resignation</u> is confirmed desperation. From the desperate city you go into the desperate country, and have to console yourself with the bravery of minks and muskrats. A stereotyped but unconscious despair is concealed even under what are called the games and amusements of mankind. There is no play in them, for this comes after work. But it is a characteristic of wisdom not to do desperate things.

10   When we consider what, to use the words of the catechism, is the chief end of man,[1] and what are the true necessaries and means of life, it appears as if men had deliberately chosen the common mode of living because they preferred it to any other. Yet they honestly think there is no choice left. But alert and healthy natures remember

---

1. **When . . . man.** Refers to a line from the shorter Catechism in the *New England Primer,* "What is the chief end of man? Man's chief end is to glorify God and enjoy him forever."

words for everyday use

res • ig • na • tion (rez ig nā´shən) *n.,* submission; patient acceptance. *Micah had to accept his grade with <u>resignation</u> since he could not change it.*

that the sun rose clear. It is never too late to give up our prejudices. No way of thinking or doing, however ancient, can be trusted without proof. What every body echoes or in silence passes by as true today may turn out to be falsehood tomorrow, mere smoke of opinion, which some had trusted for a cloud that would sprinkle fertilizing rain on their fields. What old people say you cannot do you try and find that you can. Old deeds for old people, and new deeds for new. Old people did not know enough once, perchance, to fetch fresh fuel to keep the fire a-going; new people put a little dry wood under a pot, and are whirled round the globe with the speed of birds, in a way to kill old people, as the phrase is. Age is no better, hardly so well, qualified for an instructor as youth, for it has not profited so much as it has lost. One may almost doubt if the wisest man has learned any thing of absolute value by living. Practically, the old have no very important advice to give the young, their own experience has been so partial, and their lives have been such miserable failures, for private reasons, as they must believe; and it may be that they have some faith left which belies that experience, and they are only less young than they were. I have lived some thirty years on this planet and I have yet to hear the first syllable of valuable or even <u>earnest</u> advice from my seniors. They have told me nothing, and probably cannot tell me any thing, to the purpose. Here is life, an experiment to a great extent untried by me; but it does not avail me that they have tried it. If I have any experience which I think valuable, I am sure to reflect that this my Mentors[2] said nothing about.

◆ ◆ ◆

Near the end of March, 1845, I borrowed an axe and went down to the woods by Walden Pond, nearest to where I

---

2. **Mentors.** Wise advisors; from Mentor, the friend of Odysseus in Homer's *Odyssey* who educated Odysseus's son

words for everyday use

ear • nest (ur´nist) *adj.*, serious; sincere. *If you are <u>earnest</u> about getting on the team, you must condition for it in every way possible.*

NOTE THE FACTS

What happens to things we believe to be true?

_____
_____
_____

THINK AND REFLECT

Does Thoreau believe in the wisdom of old age? Why, or why not? **(Infer)**

_____
_____
_____

MARK THE TEXT

Highlight or underline how Thoreau describes life.

Reading Strategy Review

VISUALIZE. When you visualize, you form a picture or an image in your mind of the action and descriptions in a text. Read the highlighted text. Picture the scene Thoreau describes. When you come to other passages of description, stop and visualize the scene.

Note the Facts

To what does Thoreau compare the condition of humans?

_____
_____
_____

---

intended to build my house, and began to cut down some tall arrowy white pines, still in their youth, for timber. It is difficult to begin without borrowing, but perhaps it is the most generous course thus to permit your fellow-men to have an interest in your enterprise. The owner of the axe, as he released his hold on it, said that it was the apple of his eye; but I returned it sharper than I received it. It was a pleasant hillside where I worked, covered with pine woods, through which I looked out on the pond, and a small open field in the woods where pines and hickories were springing up. The ice in the pond was not yet dissolved, though there were some open spaces, and it was all dark colored and saturated with water. There were some slight flurries of snow during the days that I worked there, but for the most part when I came out on to the railroad, on my way home, its yellow sand heap stretched away gleaming in the hazy atmosphere, and the rails shone in the spring sun, and I heard the lark and pewee and other birds already come to commence another year with us. They were pleasant spring days, in which the winter of man's discontent was thawing as well as the earth, and the life that had lain torpid began to stretch itself. One day, when my axe had come off and I had cut a green hickory for a wedge, driving it with a stone and had placed the whole to soak in a pond hole in order to swell the wood, I saw a striped snake run into the water, and he lay on the bottom, apparently without inconvenience, as long as I staid there, or more than a quarter of an hour; perhaps because he had not yet fairly come out of the torpid state. It appeared to me that for a like reason men remain in their present low and primitive condition; but if they should feel the influence of the spring of springs arousing them, they would of necessity rise to a higher and more ethereal life. I had previously seen the snakes in frosty mornings in my path with portions of their bodies still numb and inflexible, waiting for the sun to thaw them. On

---

words for everyday use

sat • u • rat • ed (sach´ə rāt´ əd) *adj.*, thoroughly soaked. *When the sponge is saturated, it weighs twice as much as it does when it is dry.*

e • the • re • al (ē thir´ē əl) *adj.*, heavenly. *Many listeners think a harp sounds ethereal and call it a heavenly instrument.*

the 1st of April it rained and melted the ice, and in the early part of the day, which was very foggy, I heard a stray goose groping about over the pond and cackling as if lost, or like the spirit of the fog.

So I went on for some days cutting and hewing timber, and also studs and rafters, all with my narrow axe, not having many communicable or scholarlike thoughts, singing to myself,—

> Men say they know many things;
> But lo! they have taken wings,—
> The arts and sciences
> And a thousand appliances
> The wind that blows
> Is all that any body knows.

I hewed the main timbers six inches square, most of the studs on two sides only, and the rafters and floor timbers on one side, leaving the rest of the bark on, so that they were just as straight and much stronger than sawed ones. Each stick was carefully mortised or tenoned[3] by its stump, for I had borrowed other tools by this time. My days in the woods were not very long ones, yet I usually carried my dinner of bread and butter, and read the newspaper in which it was wrapped, at noon, sitting amid the green pine boughs which I had cut off, and to my bread was imparted some of their fragrance, for my hands were covered with a thick coat of pitch. Before I had done I was more the friend than the foe of the pine tree, though I had cut down some of them, having become better acquainted with it. Sometimes a rambler in the wood was attracted by the sound of my axe, and we chatted pleasantly over the chips which I had made.

By the middle of April, for I made no haste in my work, but rather made the most of it, my house was framed and ready for the raising. I had already bought the shanty of James Collins, an Irishman who worked on the Fitchburg Railroad, for boards. James Collins' shanty was considered an uncommonly fine one. When I called to see it he was not at home. I walked about the outside, at first unobserved from

---

3. **mortised or tenoned.** Joined or fastened

FIX-UP IDEA

Read Shorter Sections
If you have trouble staying focused in this long essay, try reading smaller sections at a time. Use natural breaks marked by bullets and subheads as stopping points. Stop more frequently if you need to. Answer any margin questions included in the section you just read. Then note important ideas in your Cluster Chart and move on to the next section.

THINK AND REFLECT

Describe in your own words what Thoreau's days in the woods were like. (Synthesize)

_____
_____
_____

DRAW A PICTURE

Visualize the shanty Thoreau describes. Then draw a picture of it.

NOTE THE FACTS

What agreement did Thoreau make with James Collins?

_____
_____
_____

within, the window was so deep and high. It was of small dimensions, with a peaked cottage roof, and not much else to be seen, the dirt being raised five feet all around as if it were a compost heap. The roof was the soundest part, though a good deal warped and made brittle by the sun. Door-sill there was none, but a <u>perennial</u> passage for the hens under the door board. Mrs. C. came to the door and asked me to view it from the inside. The hens were driven in by my approach. It was dark, and had a dirt floor for the most part, dank, clammy, and aguish, only here a board and there a board which would not bear removal. She lighted a lamp to show me the inside of the roof and the walls, and also that the board floor extended under the bed, warning me not to step into the cellar, a sort of dust hole two feet deep. In her own words, they were "good boards overhead, good boards all around, and a good window,"—of two whole squares originally, only the cat had passed out that way lately. There was a stove, a bed, and a place to sit, an infant in the house where it was born, a silk parasol, gilt-framed looking-glass, and a patent new coffee mill nailed to an oak sapling, all told. The bargain was soon concluded, for James had in the mean while returned. I to pay four dollars and twenty-five cents tonight, he to vacate at five tomorrow morning, selling to nobody else meanwhile: I to take possession at six. It were well, he said, to be there early, and anticipate certain indistinct but wholly unjust claims on the score of ground rent and fuel. This he assured me was the only <u>encumbrance</u>. At six I passed him and his family on the road. One large bundle held their all,—bed, coffee-mill, looking-glass, hens, all but the cat, she took to the woods and became a wild cat, and, as I learned afterward, trod in a trap set for woodchucks, and so became a dead cat at last.

 I took down this dwelling the same morning, drawing the nails, and removed it to the pond side by small cartloads, spreading the boards on the grass there to bleach and warp

words for everyday use

per • en • ni • al (pər en´ē əl) *adj.*, throughout the year; perpetual. *My father gave me a magazine subscription, saying his <u>perennial</u> present could be enjoyed all year.*
en • cum • brance (en kum´brəns) *n.*, hindrance. *My dachshund is beginning to find her extra weight an <u>encumbrance</u> to moving quickly.*

160 back again in the sun. One early thrush gave me a note or two as I drove along the woodland path. I was informed treacherously by a young Patrick that neighbor Seeley, an Irishman, in the intervals of the carting, transferred the still tolerable, straight, and drivable nails, staples, and spikes to his pocket, and then stood when I came back to pass the time of day, and look freshly up, unconcerned, with spring thoughts, at the devastation; there being a dearth[4] of work, as he said. He was there to represent spectatordom, and help make this seemingly insignificant event one with the
170 removal of the gods of Troy.[5]

I dug my cellar in the side of a hill sloping to the south, where a woodchuck had formerly dug his burrow, down through sumach and blackberry roots, and the lowest stain of vegetation, six feet square by seven deep, to a fine sand where potatoes would not freeze in any winter. The sides were left shelving, and not stoned; but the sun having never shone on them, the sand still keeps its place. It was but two hours' work. I took particular pleasure in this breaking of ground, for in almost all latitudes men dig into the earth for
180 an equable temperature. Under the most splendid house in the city is still to be found the cellar where they store their roots as of old, and long after the superstructure has disappeared posterity remark its dent in the earth. The house is still but a sort of porch at the entrance of a burrow.

At length, in the beginning of May, with the help of some of my acquaintances, rather to improve so good an occasion for neighborliness than from any necessity, I set up the frame of my house. No man was ever more honored in the character of his raisers than I. They are destined, I trust, to
190 assist at the raising of loftier structures one day. I began to occupy my house on the 4th of July, as soon as it was boarded and roofed, for the boards were carefully

---

4. **dearth.** Scarcity
5. **gods of Troy.** Reference to Virgil's *Aeneid* in which Aeneas escapes with his household gods

THINK AND REFLECT

What effect does a spectator have on Thoreau's work? **(Infer)**

_____
_____
_____

NOTE THE FACTS

Why is the cellar of a house so important?

_____
_____
_____

words for everyday use

pos • ter • i • ty (päs ter´ə tē) *n.,* succeeding generations. *Often an author honored during his or her lifetime is judged insignificant by posterity.*

feather-edged and lapped, so that it was perfectly impervious to rain;[6] but before boarding I laid the foundation of a chimney at one end, bringing two cartloads of stones up the hill from the pond in my arms. I built the chimney after my hoeing in the fall, before a fire became necessary for warmth, doing my cooking in the mean while out of doors on the ground, early in the morning: which mode I still think is in some respects more convenient and agreeable than the usual one. When it stormed before my bread was baked, I fixed a few boards over the fire, and sat under them to watch my loaf, and passed some pleasant hours in that way. In those days, when my hands were much employed, I read but little, but the least scraps of paper which lay on the ground, my holder, or table-cloth, afforded me as much entertainment, in fact answered the same purpose as the Iliad.[7]

◆ ◆ ◆

from "Where I Lived and What I Lived For"

Every morning was a cheerful invitation to make my life of equal simplicity, and I may say innocence, with Nature herself. I have been as sincere a worshipper of Aurora[8] as the Greeks. I got up early and bathed in the pond; that was a religious exercise, and one of the best things which I did. They say that characters were engraven on the bathing tub of king Tching-thang to this effect: "Renew thyself completely each day; do it again, and again, and forever again."[9] I can understand that. Morning brings back the heroic ages. I was as much affected by the faint hum of a mosquito making its invisible and unimaginable tour through my apartment at earliest dawn, when I was sitting with door and windows open, as I could be by any trumpet that ever sang of fame. It was Homer's requiem; itself an Iliad and Odyssey in the air, singing its own wrath and wanderings. There was something

---

6. **feather-edged . . . rain.** The boards' thin edges overlapped, making the roof watertight.
7. **Iliad.** Greek epic by Homer
8. **Aurora.** Goddess of dawn
9. **"Renew . . . again."** From Confucius, Chinese philosopher

cosmical about it, a standing advertisement, till forbidden,[10] of the everlasting vigor and fertility of the world. The morning, which is the most memorable season of the day, is the awakening hour. Then there is least somnolence in us; and for an hour, at least, some part of us awakes which slumbers all the rest of the day and night. Little is to be expected of that day, if it can be called a day, to which we are not awakened by our Genius, but by the mechanical nudgings of some servitor, are not awakened by our own newly-acquired force and <u>aspirations</u> from within, accompanied by the <u>undulations</u> of celestial music, instead of factory bells and a fragrance filling the air—to a higher life than we fell asleep from; and thus the darkness bear its fruit, and prove itself to be good, no less than the light. That man who does not believe that each day contains an earlier, more sacred, and auroral hour than he has yet profaned, has despaired of life, and is pursuing a descending and darkening way. After a partial <u>cessation</u> of his sensuous life, the soul of man, or its organs rather, are reinvigorated each day, and his Genius tries again what noble life it can make. All memorable events, I should say, transpire in morning time and in a morning atmosphere. The Vedas[11] say, "All intelligences awake with the morning." Poetry and art, and the fairest and most memorable of the actions of men, date from such an hour. All poets and heroes, like Memnon,[12] are the children of Aurora, and emit their music at sunrise. To him whose elastic and vigorous thought keeps pace with the sun, the day is a perpetual morning. It matters not what the clocks say or the attitudes and labors of men. Morning is when I am awake and there is a dawn in me. Moral reform is the effort to throw off sleep. Why is it that men give so poor an account of their day if they have not been slumbering? They are not such

NOTE THE FACTS
How does Thoreau think we should awaken?
_____
_____
_____

NOTE THE FACTS
Why is morning important?
_____
_____
_____

---

10. **standing . . . forbidden.** Advertisement that was to be run "till forbidden" or stopped by the advertiser
11. **Vedas.** Hindu scriptures
12. **Memnon.** King killed by Achilles in the Trojan War

words for everyday use
as • pi • ra • tion (as pə rā´shən) n., strong ambition. *Many musicians practice long hours if they have <u>aspirations</u> of becoming famous.*
un • du • la • tion (un dyü lā´shən) n., act of moving in waves. *The athlete was overcome by <u>undulations</u> of pain sweeping over him.*
ces • sa • tion (se sā´shən) n., stopping. *Until the <u>cessation</u> of the drill, no one could hear anything.*

MARK THE TEXT

Highlight or underline what Thoreau believes the word *awake* means.

Use THE STRATEGY

USE TEXT ORGANIZATION. Look at the picture on this page. How does it compare to the description Thoreau gave? How does it relate to his purpose?

_____
_____
_____

NOTE THE FACTS

Why did Thoreau go to the woods?

_____
_____
_____

260 poor calculators. If they had not been overcome with drowsiness they would have performed something. The millions are awake enough for physical labor; but only one in a million is awake enough for effective intellectual exertion, only one in a hundred millions to a poetic or divine life. To be awake is to be alive. I have never yet met a man who was quite awake. How could I have looked him in the face?

We must learn to reawaken and keep ourselves awake, not by mechanical aids, but by an infinite expectation of the dawn, which does not forsake us in our soundest sleep. I know of no more encouraging fact than the unquestionable ability of man to elevate his life by a conscious <u>endeavor</u>. It 270 is something to be able to paint a particular picture, or to carve a statue, and so to make a few objects beautiful; but it is far more glorious to carve and paint the very atmosphere and medium through which we look, which morally we can do. To affect the quality of the day, that is the highest of arts. Every man is tasked to make his life, even in its details, worthy of the contemplation of his most elevated and critical hour. If 280 we refused, or rather used up, such <u>paltry</u> information as we get, the oracles[13] would distinctly inform us how this might be done.

I went to the woods because I wished to live deliberately, to front only the essential facts of life, and see if I could not learn what it had to teach, and not, when I came to die, discover that I had not lived. I did not wish to live what was 290 not life, living is so dear; nor did I wish to practice

---

13. **oracles.** People in communication with the gods

words for everyday use

en • deav • or (en dev´ər) *n.*, effort; attempt. *Serious work has been done in the <u>endeavor</u> to promote world peace.*

pal • try (pȯl´trē) *adj.*, insignificant. *The help he offered was so <u>paltry</u> that I ended up doing most of the work myself.*

resignation, unless it was quite necessary. I wanted to live deep and suck out all the marrow of life, to live so sturdily and Spartan-like[14] as to put to rout all that was not life, to cut a broad swath and shave close, to drive life into a corner, and reduce it to its lowest terms, and, if it proved to be mean, why then to get the whole and genuine meanness of it, and publish its meanness to the world; or if it were sublime, to know it by experience, and be able to give a true account of it in my next excursion. For most men, it appears to me, are in a strange uncertainty about it, whether it is of the devil or of God, and have somewhat hastily concluded that it is the chief end of man here to "glorify God and enjoy him forever."[15]

Still we live meanly, like ants; though the fable tells us that we were long ago changed into men;[16] like pygmies we fight with cranes; it is error upon error, and clout upon clout, and our best virtue has for its occasion a <u>superfluous</u> and evitable wretchedness. Our life is frittered away by detail. An honest man has hardly need to count more than his ten fingers, or in extreme cases he may add his ten toes, and lump the rest. Simplicity, simplicity, simplicity! I say, let your affairs be as two or three, and not a hundred or a thousand; instead of a million count half a dozen, and keep your accounts on your thumb nail. In the midst of this chopping sea of civilized life, such are the clouds and storms and quicksands and thousand-and-one items to be allowed for, that a man has to live, if he would not founder and go to the bottom and not make his port at all, by dead reckoning, and he must be a great calculator indeed who succeeds. Simplify, simplify. Instead of three meals a day, if it be necessary eat but one, instead of a hundred dishes, five; and reduce other things in proportion. Our life is like a German Confederacy, made up of petty states, with its boundary forever <u>fluctuating</u>, so that even a German cannot tell you how it is bounded at any moment.

---

14. **Spartan-like.** Without excess comforts
15. **"glorify . . . forever."** Reference to the *New England Primer*
16. **fable . . . men.** Refers to a Greek fable in which Zeus turns ants into men

words for everyday use

su • per • flu • ous (sə pur´ flü əs) *adj.*, excessive. *After she had thanked me a dozen times, her gratitude began to seem <u>superfluous</u>.*

fluc • tu • ate (fluk´ chü āt´) *vi.*, change or vary continuously. *The unpredictable stock market <u>fluctuates</u> from minute to minute.*

MARK THE TEXT

Highlight or underline what happens to our lives.

READ ALOUD

Read the highlighted passage aloud. Repeat the passage until you can read it smoothly and with expression. What advice does Thoreau give?

_____
_____
_____

THINK AND REFLECT

What does Thoreau think of progress? **(Infer)**

_____
_____
_____

THINK AND REFLECT

How do you think Thoreau would react to the world today? **(Extend)**

_____
_____
_____

330

340

350

The nation itself, with all its so called internal improvements, which, by the way, are all external and superficial, is just such an <u>unwieldy</u> and overgrown establishment, cluttered with furniture and tripped up by its own traps, ruined by luxury and heedless expense, by want of calculation and a worthy aim, as the million households in the land; and the only cure for it as for them is in a rigid economy, a stern and more than Spartan simplicity of life and elevation of purpose. It lives too fast. Men think that it is essential that the Nation have commerce, and export ice, and talk through a telegraph, and ride thirty miles an hour, without a doubt, whether they do or not; but whether we should live like baboons or like men, is a little uncertain. If we do not get out sleepers,[17] and forge rails, and devote days and nights to the work, but go to tinkering upon our lives to improve them, who will build railroads? And if railroads are not built, how shall we get to heaven in season? But if we stay at home and mind our business, who will want railroads? We do not ride on the railroad; it rides upon us. Did you ever think what those sleepers are that underlie the railroad? Each one is a man, an Irish-man, or a Yankee man. The rails are laid on them, and they are covered with sand, and the cars run smoothly over them. They are sound sleepers, I assure you. And every few years a new lot is laid down and run over; so that, if some have the pleasure of riding on a rail, others have the misfortune to be ridden upon. And when they run over a man that is walking in his sleep, a supernumerary[18] sleeper in the wrong position, and wake him up, they suddenly stop the cars, and make a hue and cry about it, as if this were an exception. I am glad to know that it takes a gang of men for every five miles to keep the sleepers down and level in their beds as it is, for this is a sign that they may sometime get up again.

Why should we live with such hurry and waste of life? We are determined to be starved before we are hungry. Men say that a stitch in time saves nine, and so they take a thousand

---

17. **sleepers.** Railroad ties
18. **supernumerary.** Extra

words for everyday use

un • wield • y (un wēl´dē) *adj.*, hard to manage. *That large box is light but too <u>unwieldy</u> to move up the stairs alone.*

stitches today to save nine tomorrow. As for work, we haven't any of any consequence. We have the Saint Vitus' dance[19] and cannot possibly keep our heads still. If I should only give a few pulls at the parish bell-rope, as for a fire, that is, without setting the bell, there is hardly a man on his farm in the outskirts of Concord, notwithstanding that press of engagements which was his excuse so many times this morning, nor a boy, nor a woman, I might almost say, but would forsake all and follow that sound, not mainly to save property from the flames, but, if we will confess the truth, much more to see it burn, since burn it must, and we, be it known, did not set it on fire,—or to see it put out, and have a hand in it, if that is done as handsomely; yes, even if it were the parish church itself. Hardly a man takes a half hour's nap after dinner, but when he wakes he holds up his head and asks "What's the news?" as if the rest of mankind had stood his sentinels. Some give directions to be waked every half hour, doubtless for no other purpose; and then, to pay for it, they tell what they have dreamed. After a night's sleep the news is as indispensable as the breakfast. "Pray tell me any thing new that has happened to a man any where on this globe",—and he reads it over his coffee and rolls, that a man had had his eyes gouged out this morning on the Wachito River; never dreaming the while that he lives in the dark unfathomed mammoth cave of this world, and has but the rudiment of an eye himself.[20]

♦ ♦ ♦

from "Conclusion"

I left the woods for as good a reason as I went there. Perhaps it seemed to me that I had several more lives to live, and could not spare any more time for that one. It is remarkable how easily and insensibly we fall into a particular route, and make a beaten track for ourselves. I had not lived there a week before my feet wore a path from my door to the pond-side; and though it is five or six years since I trod it, it is still quite distinct. It is true, I fear that others may have

NOTE THE FACTS

To what does Thoreau compare a person who wakes up with a demand for the news?

_____
_____
_____

NOTE THE FACTS

Why did Thoreau leave the woods?

_____
_____
_____

---

19. **Saint Vitus' dance.** Refers to a nervous disorder with symptoms of jerky motions
20. dark . . . himself. Reference to sightless fish found in Mammoth Cave

fallen into it, and so helped to keep it open. The surface of the earth is soft and impressible by the feet of men; and so with the paths which the mind travels. How worn and dusty, then, must be the highways of the world, how deep the ruts of tradition and conformity! I did not wish to take a cabin passage, but rather to go before the mast and on the deck of the world, for there I could best see the moonlight amid the mountains. I do not wish to go below now.

I learned this, at least, by my experiment; that if one advances confidently in the direction of his dreams, and endeavors to live the life which he has imagined, he will meet with a success unexpected in common hours. He will put some things behind, will pass an invisible boundary; new, universal, and more liberal laws will begin to establish themselves around and within him; or old laws be expanded, and interpreted in his favor in a more liberal sense, and he will live with the license of a higher order of beings. In proportion as he simplifies his life, the laws of the universe will appear less complex, and solitude will not be solitude, nor poverty poverty, nor weakness weakness. If you have built castles in the air, your work need not be lost; that is where they should be. Now put the foundations under them.

It is a ridiculous demand which England and America make, that you shall speak so that they can understand you. Neither men nor toadstools grow so. As if that were important, and there were not enough to understand you without them. As if Nature could support but one order of understandings, could not sustain birds as well as quadrupeds, flying as well as creeping things, and *hush* and *who*, which Bright[21] can understand, were the best English. As if there were safety in stupidity alone. I fear chiefly lest my expression may not be *extra-vagant* enough, may not wander far enough beyond the narrow limits of my daily experience, so as to be adequate to the truth of which I have been convinced. *Extra vagance!* it depends on how you are yarded. The migrating buffalo, which seeks new pastures in another latitude, is not extravagant like the cow which kicks over the pail, leaps the cow-yard fence, and runs after her calf, in milking time. I

NOTE THE FACTS

What did Thoreau learn from living in the woods?

_____
_____
_____

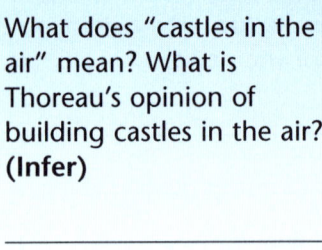

THINK AND REFLECT

What does "castles in the air" mean? What is Thoreau's opinion of building castles in the air? (Infer)

_____
_____
_____

---

21. **Bright.** Name for an ox

desire to speak somewhere *without* bounds; like a man in a waking moment, to men in their waking moments; for I am convinced that I cannot exaggerate enough even to lay the foundation of a true expression. Who that has heard a strain of music feared then lest he should speak extravagantly any more forever? In view of the future or possible, we should live quite laxly and undefined in front, our outlines dim and misty on that side; as our shadows reveal an insensible perspiration toward the sun. The volatile truth of our words should continually betray the inadequacy of the residual statement. Their truth is instantly *translated*; its literal monument alone remains. The words which express our faith and piety are not definite; yet they are significant and fragrant like frankincense[22] to superior natures.

Why level downward to our dullest perception always, and praise that as common sense? The commonest sense is the sense of men asleep, which they express by snoring. Sometimes we are inclined to class those who are once-and-a-half witted with the half-witted, because we appreciate only a third part of their wit. Some would find fault with the morning-red, if they ever got up early enough. "They pretend," as I hear, "that the verses of Kabir have four different senses; illusion, spirit, intellect, and the exoteric doctrine of the Vedas"; but in this part of the world it is considered a ground for complaint if a man's writings admit of more than one interpretation. While England endeavors to cure the potato-rot, will not any endeavor to cure the brain-rot, which prevails so much more widely and fatally?

I do not suppose that I have attained to obscurity, but I should be proud if no more fatal fault were found with my pages on this score than was found with the Walden ice. Southern customers objected to its blue color, which is the evidence of its purity, as if it were muddy, and preferred the Cambridge ice, which is white, but tastes of weeds. The

---

22. **frankincense.** Type of incense

> **words for everyday use**
> lax • ly (laks´lē) *adv.,* loosely; not strictly. *Jenna's parents enforce her curfew so laxly that she sometimes stays out all night.*
> vol • a • tile (väl´ə təl) *adj.,* unstable; fleeting. *"Stand back," said the science teacher, "because this chemical mixture is quite volatile."*

NOTE THE FACTS

What complaint is common about writing? What would Thoreau like to cure?

_____
_____
_____

THINK AND REFLECT

What idea does Thoreau express using the ice analogy? (Infer)

_____
_____
_____

purity men love is like the mists which envelop the earth, and not like the azure ether beyond.

    Some are dinning in our ears that we Americans, and moderns generally, are intellectual dwarfs compared with the ancients, or even the Elizabethan[23] men. But what is that to the purpose? A living dog is better than a dead lion.[24] Shall a man go and hang himself because he belongs to the race of pygmies, and not be the biggest pygmy that he can? Let every one mind his own business, and endeavor to be what he was made.

    Why should we be in such desperate haste to succeed, and in such desperate enterprises? If a man does not keep pace with his companions, perhaps it is because he hears a different drummer. Let him step to the music which he hears, however measured or far away. It is not important that he should mature as soon as an apple-tree or an oak. Shall he turn his spring into summer? If the condition of things which we were made for is not yet, what were any reality which we can substitute? We will not be shipwrecked on a vain reality. Shall we with pains erect a heaven of blue glass over ourselves, though when it is done we shall be sure to gaze still at the true ethereal heaven far above, as if the former were not? ■

---

23. **Elizabethan.** From the time of Queen Elizabeth I (1533–1603)
24. **A living . . . lion.** From Ecclesiastes 9:4: "But anyone who is alive in the world of the living has some hope; a live dog is better off than a dead lion."

Literary TOOLS

APHORISM. An **aphorism** is a short saying or pointed statement. What aphorism does Thoreau use at the end of this section?

Reflect ON YOUR READING

After Reading → **SHARE YOUR CONNECTIONS**

❏ Share your written comments and Cluster Chart with a partner.
❏ Discuss memorable parts of the selection. Was the selection what you expected it to be based on your previewing activities? Why, or why not?

Reading Skills and Test Practice

IDENTIFY AUTHOR'S PURPOSE

Discuss with a partner how to answer questions about the author's purpose. Use the Think-Aloud Notes to write down your reasons for eliminating the incorrect answers.

____1. How is Thoreau's tone related to his purpose in this selection?
   a. The tone is challenging; Thoreau wants readers to consider the idea of a worthwhile life.
   b. The tone is satiric; Thoreau is poking fun at conventions to make the reader recognize the problems with living in cities.
   c. The tone is mildly persuasive; Thoreau wants to influence his audience, but he thinks he can do it best by offering his ideas in a nonconfrontational way.
   d. The tone is angry; Thoreau is disgusted by the way people live and demands that they change their ways.

____2. How do the aphorisms with which Thoreau opens and closes the selection address his ideas about individuality?
   a. The first aphorism shows the way people should live and the second shows how they do live.
   b. Both challenge the reader to engage in life more thoroughly.
   c. One points out the flaws of being an individual and the other points out the flaws of thinking for yourself.
   d. The first suggests a problem with the way we live; the second encourages us to be individuals.

How did using the reading strategy help you to answer the questions?

_____
_____
_____
_____

THINK-ALOUD NOTES

Investigate, Inquire, and Imagine

RECALL: GATHER FACTS
1a. Why did Thoreau decide to live in the woods? Why did he leave?

INTERPRET: FIND MEANING
1b. What does Thoreau mean when he urges the reader to "Simplify, simplify"?

ANALYZE: TAKE THINGS APART
2a. In what ways do you think Thoreau heard "a different drummer"?

SYNTHESIZE: BRING THINGS TOGETHER
2b. What did Thoreau learn from his experiments with life in the woods?

EVALUATE: MAKE JUDGMENTS
3a. What is Thoreau's attitude toward progress? Do you agree with his philosophy? Why, or why not?

EXTEND: CONNECT IDEAS
3b. If every person lived by Thoreau's philosophy that each person should be concerned only with his or her own business, how would the development of society be affected?

Literary Tools

APHORISM. An **aphorism** is a short saying or pointed statement. "The mass of men lead lives of quiet desperation" and "If a man does not keep pace with his companions, perhaps it is because he hears a different drummer" are two aphorisms from this selection. Compare these aphorisms from *Walden* with aphorisms from Emerson's "Self-Reliance" on page 287.

WordWorkshop

TEST YOUR WORD KNOWLEDGE. Review the vocabulary words from the selection from *Walden*. Make sure you know the definition and understand how the word is used in context. Then answer the following questions.

1. What are your <u>aspirations</u> for the future?

   _____

2. How would you feel if your parents responded <u>laxly</u> to your breaking a rule? Why?

   _____

3. Why would an <u>unwieldy</u> package be an <u>encumbrance</u>?

   _____

4. Give an antonym for <u>ethereal</u>.

   _____

5. What kind of weather would leave a garden <u>saturated</u>?

   _____

6. What other words might you use to describe an <u>earnest</u> person?

   _____

7. In what way are <u>undulations</u> similar to <u>fluctuations</u>? How do they differ?

   _____

8. How would you feel if you got a <u>paltry</u> raise? Explain.

   _____

9. Describe supplies that would be <u>superfluous</u> for a day-long hike.

   _____

10. Would a <u>cessation</u> of your allowance make you happy? Why, or why not?

    _____

Read-Write Connection

Imagine you have lived like Thoreau in communion with nature in a location of your choice. What lessons do you think you might learn?

_____

_____

_____

Beyond the Reading

KEEP A JOURNAL. Both Emerson and Thoreau kept journals from which they took ideas for many of their writings. Keep a journal for one week. Take some time each day to note observations about the world around you; collect ideas, inspirations, and wonderings; or reflect on something that happened, that you read, or that you heard. Then share part of your journal with a partner. Talk about how you might follow up on something in your journal.

GO ONLINE. To find links and additional activities for this selection, visit the EMC Internet Resource Center at **emcp.com/languagearts** and click on Write-In Reader.

CONNECT

Reader's resource

Gettysburg was the site of one of the bloodiest battles of the Civil War; in July 1863, Union and Confederate troops fought for a grueling three days. Many historians feel that this battle signified the turning point of the Civil War. On November 19, 1863, President Abraham Lincoln delivered his famous address at the dedication of the national cemetery at Gettysburg. In light of the bitterness of the conflict, one of the most remarkable aspects of **The Gettysburg Address** is its avoidance of angry or inflammatory rhetoric. Instead the speech focuses on the sacrifices of the soldiers and the need for rededication to the principles of the nation's founders.

Word watch

PREVIEW VOCABULARY

consecrate   score

Reader's journal

If you were the leader of a group that needed encouragement, what would you say to inspire your followers to continue their struggle?

_____
_____
_____

The Gettysburg Address
by Abraham Lincoln

Active READING STRATEGY

USE TEXT ORGANIZATION

Before Reading ➤ **PREVIEW ORGANIZATIONAL FEATURES**

❑ Parallelism and antithesis are rhetorical techniques. Through **parallelism,** a writer emphasizes the equal value or weight of two or more ideas by expressing them in the same grammatical form. Through **antithesis,** a writer strongly contrasts words, phrases, or ideas, usually by repeating grammatical structures.

❑ Lincoln uses both of these rhetorical techniques to organize and give coherence to his speech. Keep these techniques in mind as you read the selection.

Graphic Organizer: Parallelism Chart

Example of Parallelism	Paraphrase
that from these honored dead we take increased devotion to that cause for which they gave the last full measure of devotion	that the dead may inspire us to continue the struggle for which they gave their lives

312 THE EMC WRITE-IN READER

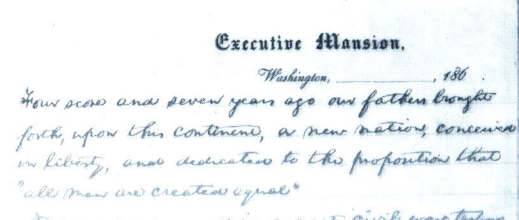

The Gettysburg Address

Abraham Lincoln

Four score and seven years ago our fathers brought forth on this continent, a new nation, conceived in Liberty, and dedicated to the proposition that all men are created equal.

Now we are engaged in a great civil war, testing whether that nation, or any nation so conceived and so dedicated, can long endure. We are met on a great battlefield of that war. We have come to dedicate a portion of that field, as a final resting place for those who here gave their lives that that nation might live. It is altogether fitting and proper that we should do this.

But, in a larger sense, we can not dedicate—we can not consecrate—we can not hallow—this ground. The brave men, living and dead, who struggled here, have consecrated it, far above our poor power to add or detract. The world will little note, nor long remember what we say here, but it can never forget what they did here. It is for us the living, rather, to be dedicated here to the unfinished work which they who fought here have thus far so nobly advanced. It is rather for us to be here dedicated to the great task remaining before us—that from these honored dead we take increased devotion to that cause for which they gave the last full measure of devotion—that we here highly resolve that these dead shall not have died in vain—that this nation, under God, shall have a new birth of freedom—and that government of the people, by the people, for the people, shall not perish from the earth. ■

words for everyday use

score (skôr) *n.*, set of twenty. "We don't need one hundred eggs!" Corky exclaimed when she heard Lou order five *score*.
con • se • crate (kän´si krāt´) *vt.*, make or declare sacred. The bishop *consecrated* the church before the minister held the first service.

During Reading

USE ORGANIZATIONAL FEATURES AS YOU READ

- Listen to the speech as it is read once. As you listen, try to recognize parallelism. Write down in the graphic organizer any examples that stand out to you as you listen.
- Read the speech carefully. Look for further examples of parallelism and add them to your chart. Underline or highlight examples of antithesis.

NOTE THE FACTS

What event is taking place at the time this speech is given? What is this event testing?

_____
_____

Fix-Up Idea

Vary Reading Rate
If you are having trouble following Lincoln's speech, try slowing down. A comma or dash indicates a pause. Take some extra time whenever you come to a comma or dash to think about what you have just read. Then continue until you come to the next comma or dash. Continue this way until you have finished the speech.

Reflect ON YOUR READING

After Reading → **DISCUSS THE EFFECT OF ORGANIZATIONAL FEATURES**

❑ Compare your Parallelism Chart with a partner. Complete your chart by paraphrasing the examples of parallelism you found.
❑ Identify the main ideas that are emphasized by the use of parallelism and antithesis.

_____
_____
_____
_____

Reading Skills and Test Practice

IDENTIFY CAUSE AND EFFECT

Discuss with a partner how to answer questions that require you to identify cause and effect. Use the Think-Aloud Notes to write down your reasons for eliminating the incorrect answers.

____1. According to Lincoln, why is it "fitting and proper" to dedicate the cemetery on the Gettysburg battlefield?
　　a. to make the world remember what the soldiers did
　　b. because the soldiers died to save the nation
　　c. because Gettysburg was where the last battle of the war was fought
　　d. to show that all men are created equal

____2. What main effect does Lincoln hope that his speech will have?
　　a. It will honor the men who died.
　　b. It will consecrate, or make holy, the ground where so many men died.
　　c. People will rededicate themselves to the Union cause.
　　d. People will feel better about their lost loved ones.

How did using the reading strategy help you to answer the questions?

_____
_____
_____
_____

THINK-ALOUD NOTES

Investigate, Inquire, and Imagine

RECALL: GATHER FACTS
1a. Who has consecrated the cemetery better than Lincoln or his audience could?

INTERPRET: FIND MEANING
1b. Under what circumstances would the dead have died in vain?

ANALYZE: TAKE THINGS APART
2a. Lincoln uses the word *dedicate* six times in the course of this brief speech. Look up the word and decide which of the meanings Lincoln intended.

SYNTHESIZE: BRING THINGS TOGETHER
2b. Summarize the most important message that Lincoln is trying to make.

EVALUATE: MAKE JUDGMENTS
3a. Lincoln said, "The world will little note, nor long remember what we say here." However, this speech has been repeated for over one hundred years. Why do you think this speech has touched Americans so deeply since 1863?

EXTEND: CONNECT IDEAS
3b. Have you heard any speeches by the president or others in government that you think are likely to be remembered for many years to come?

Literary Tools

PARALLELISM AND ANTITHESIS. Parallelism is a rhetorical technique in which a writer emphasizes the equal value or weight of two or more ideas by expressing them in the same grammatical form. **Antithesis** is a rhetorical technique in which words, phrases, or ideas are sharply contrasted, usually by repeating grammatical structures. Review the examples of parallelism you noted in your Parallelism Chart. Then complete the chart below by writing examples of antithesis and paraphrasing each example.

Example of Antithesis	Paraphrase

What purpose do these techniques serve in this speech?

_____

_____

WordWorkshop

WORDS WITH MULTIPLE MEANINGS. Many words in English have more than one meaning. For example, if you thought the word *score* meant the points earned in a game or on a test, you might have been confused by the opening of the Gettysburg Address: "Four score and seven years ago. . . ." In this context, score means "twenty."

The word *score* has several other meanings. Try to determine the meaning of the word in each sentence below. Then use a dictionary to verify your definitions and write your own sentence for each meaning.

1. Use a knife to <u>score</u> the top of the cake before you cut it into pieces.
   Meaning in sentence: _____
   Verified definition: _____
   Sentence: _____
2. George was determined to settle the <u>score</u> with his long-time enemy.
   Meaning in sentence: _____
   Verified definition: _____
   Sentence: _____
3. Which composer do you think will win the award for the best <u>score</u>?
   Meaning in sentence: _____
   Verified definition: _____
   Sentence: _____
4. Sela <u>scored</u> an autographed copy of the book at an auction.
   Meaning in sentence: _____
   Verified definition: _____
   Sentence: _____
5. The Titans need to <u>score</u> a touchdown to win the game.
   Meaning in sentence: _____
   Verified definition: _____
   Sentence: _____

Read-Write Connection

If you had been in the audience when Lincoln gave the Gettysburg Address, how would you have reacted to such a short speech about such a long war?

Beyond the Reading

UNDERSTAND THE WIT AND WISDOM OF ABRAHAM LINCOLN. "You can fool all the people some of the time, and some of the people all of the time, but you cannot fool all of the people all of the time" is a famous quote by Abraham Lincoln. Do an Internet search or use a book of quotations to find other sayings by Abraham Lincoln. Explain what you think Lincoln meant, or apply his words to a situation in your own life.

GO ONLINE. To find links and additional activities for this selection, visit the EMC Internet Resource Center at **emcp.com/languagearts** and click on Write-In Reader.

"I will fight no more forever"
by In-mut-too-yag-lat-lat, Chief Joseph of the Nez Percé

Active READING STRATEGY

CONNECT TO PRIOR KNOWLEDGE

Before Reading ➤ **THINK ABOUT WHAT YOU KNOW**

❑ Read the Reader's Resource carefully. With a few of your classmates, discuss this information and other things you know about Native American history, especially the relationship between Native Americans and the United States government.
❑ Read the Reader's Journal question and discuss this question with your group.
❑ Note things you know about Native American history, about the Nez Percé, and about Chief Joseph in the "What I *Know*" column of the graphic organizer below. Write questions you hope to answer in the "What I *Want* to Learn" column.

Graphic Organizer: K-W-L Chart

What I *Know*	What I *Want* to Learn	What I Have *Learned*

CONNECT

Reader's resource

In-mut-too-yag-lat-lat, or Thunder Traveling over the Mountains, is known in English as Chief Joseph. He was a valiant leader who tried to preserve the way of life of his people, the Nez Percé. In 1877, Chief Joseph was preparing to move with his people to a reservation in Idaho when he learned of an attack by three Native Americans on settlers. Fearing reprisal, he fled with his people to Canada. After a long journey marked by fighting, when they were only forty miles from the Canadian border, Chief Joseph and his weakened band surrendered. **"I will fight no more forever"** is his surrender speech.

Reader's journal

How would you feel if you were forced to give up your home?

_____
_____
_____
_____
_____

UNIT 7 / READING NONFICTION

During Reading

USE WHAT YOU KNOW

- Think about Chief Joseph's situation at the time he delivered this speech. How would you feel if you were in this situation? Note your ideas in the "What I *Know*" column. Then begin the selection. What details do you learn in the first three lines? How do these details affect your mood? Note these ideas in the "What I Have *Learned*" column.
- Continue reading, taking notes about ideas and the effects these ideas have on your mood.

Fix-Up Idea

Read Aloud

Hearing the selection may help you connect to Chief Joseph's mood and meaning. With a partner, take turns reading aloud. After you have both had a chance to listen to the selection, talk about which images or ideas had the biggest effect on you.

NOTE THE FACTS

What does Chief Joseph want time to do? What does he expect to find?

_____
_____
_____

I will fight no more forever

Chief Joseph

Tell General Howard[1] I know his heart. What he told me before, I have in my heart. I am tired of fighting. Our chiefs are killed. Looking Glass is dead. Toohoolhoolzote[2] is dead. The old men are all dead. It is the young men who say yes and no. He who led on the young men is dead. It is cold and we have no blankets. The little children are freezing to death. My people, some of them, have run away to the hills and have no blankets, no food; no one knows where they are—perhaps freezing to death. I want to have time to look for my children and see how many I can find. Maybe I shall find them among the dead. Hear me, my chiefs. I am tired; my heart is sick and sad. From where the sun now stands I will fight no more forever. ■

10

---

1. **General Howard.** Oliver Howard (1830–1909), who conducted the operation against Chief Joseph and the Nez Percé (1877)
2. **Looking Glass . . . Toohoolhoolzote.** Two Nez Percé leaders

Reflect ON YOUR READING

After Reading ▶ **DISCUSS WHAT YOU LEARNED**

- ❑ Review your K-W-L Chart. What have you learned from reading the selection? What do you still want to know?
- ❑ With your group from the Before Reading activity, discuss your reaction to Chief Joseph's speech. How does this speech compare to other things you know about Native American history?
- ❑ With your group, prepare a brief summary of the speech's mood and content.

Reading Skills and Test Practice

IDENTIFY AUTHOR'S PURPOSE

Discuss with a partner how to answer questions that require you to identify an author's purpose. Use the Think-Aloud Notes to write down your reasons for eliminating the incorrect answers.

_____1. Why does Chief Joseph list people who are dead and dying?
   a. to show the ranks he will soon join because he is tired and sick
   b. to persuade General Howard to provide burial rights for these people
   c. to inform the general why he will continue to fight
   d. to express why he has lost his will to continue fighting

_____2. Why does Chief Joseph mention the sun?
   a. The sun is shining in his eyes while he speaks.
   b. He says the sun is going down on his people, meaning their way of life is ending.
   c. He calls on the sun as a witness to his surrender.
   d. The sun offers hope for the future of the Nez Percé.

How did using the reading strategy help you to answer the questions?

_____
_____
_____
_____

THINK-ALOUD NOTES

Investigate, Inquire, and Imagine

RECALL: GATHER FACTS
1a. What has happened to all the Nez Percé's leaders, the chiefs, and the old men?

INTERPRET: FIND MEANING
1b. What is dangerous about having the young men in charge?

ANALYZE: TAKE THINGS APART
2a. Distinguish a way in which Chief Joseph would feel his situation eased.

SYNTHESIZE: BRING THINGS TOGETHER
2b. Why does Chief Joseph mention the sun?

EVALUATE: MAKE JUDGMENTS
3a. What makes Chief Joseph's speech touching and memorable?

EXTEND: CONNECT IDEAS
3b. Two years after he made this speech, Chief Joseph said that "all people should have equal rights upon [the earth]." Read the opening paragraphs of the Declaration of Independence on page 368. What similarities and differences exist between Chief Joseph's beliefs and those expressed by Thomas Jefferson?

Literary Tools

ORAL TRADITION. An **oral tradition** is a work, a motif, an idea, or a custom that is passed by word of mouth from generation to generation. Fill in the left-hand column of the chart that follows with memorable lines from the speech. In the right-hand column, explain why the lines are memorable and could be repeated by future generations.

Memorable Lines	Explanation
"Looking Glass is dead. Toohoolhoolzote is dead."	These lines are memorable because they make the listener recall the glorious deeds of these dead warriors and leaders. They also have parallel structure, making them easy to remember.

WordWorkshop

SYNONYMS. **Synonyms** are words that have the same or similar meanings. With a few of your classmates, brainstorm synonyms for the words *fight, forever, tired,* and *sad.* Record your ideas in the chart below. Then write a paragraph using a variety of the synonyms you listed.

Word	Synonyms
fight	
forever	
tired	
sad	

Read-Write Connection

If you were Chief Joseph, how would you feel about the broken promises made by white politicians? Explain your answer.

_____
_____
_____
_____
_____
_____

Beyond the Reading

RESEARCH TREATIES. Research a Native American treaty. Relate its original terms and whether or not the treaty was broken. Tell whether the tribe still lives on the same territory as stipulated by the treaty or if it has moved. If it has moved, report why. Report also on any current litigation—for example, a dispute over hunting and fishing rights that dates back to the treaty.

GO ONLINE. To find links and additional activities for this selection, visit the EMC Internet Resource Center at **emcp.com/languagearts** and click on Write-In Reader.

CONNECT

Reader's resource

On August 6, 1945, the United States dropped an atomic bomb on the city of Hiroshima, Japan, in order to bring an end to World War II. The city was largely destroyed, and more than 70,000 people are believed to have been killed. Thousands more who survived the initial blast died of radiation sickness. In his book *Hiroshima*, John Hersey tells the story of six individuals who survived the atomic bombing of the city. "A Noiseless Flash" is the first chapter in the book. Hersey, a novelist, short story and nonfiction writer, and journalist, combines literary techniques and the factual air of reporting to describe a real event. Some critics say *Hiroshima* began the literary genre of the nonfiction novel.

Word watch

PREVIEW VOCABULARY

abstinence	intermittent
buffet	philanthropy
convivial	pommel
finicky	rendezvous
hedonistic	repugnant
hullabaloo	theological
incendiary	volition
incessant	xenophobic

Reader's journal

When has something good or bad happened to you just because you varied your routine?

"A Noiseless Flash"
from *Hiroshima* by John Hersey

Active READING STRATEGY

WRITE THINGS DOWN

Before Reading → **PREPARE TO TRACK CHARACTERS**

❑ The selection deals with the experiences of six individuals who survived the atomic bombing of Hiroshima: Miss Toshiko Sasaki, Dr. Masakazu Fujii, Mrs. Hatsuyo Nakamura, Father Wilhelm Kleinsorge, Dr. Terufumi Sasaki, and Reverend Mr. Kiyoshi Tanimoto.

❑ As you read you will track information about and events experienced by each character in the Character Chart below.

Graphic Organizer: Character Chart

Character	Experiences
Miss Toshiko Sasaki	
Dr. Masakazu Fujii	
Mrs. Hatsuyo Nakamura	
Father Wilhelm Kleinsorge	
Dr. Terufumi Sasaki	
Reverend Mr. Kiyoshi Tanimoto	

A Noiseless Flash

John Hersey

At exactly fifteen minutes past eight in the morning, on August 6, 1945, Japanese time, at the moment when the atomic bomb flashed above Hiroshima, Miss Toshiko Sasaki, a clerk in the personnel department of the East Asia Tin Works, had just sat down at her place in the plant office and was turning her head to speak to the girl at the next desk. At that same moment, Dr. Masakazu Fujii was settling down cross-legged to read the Osaka *Asahi* on the porch of his private hospital, overhanging one of the seven deltaic[1] rivers which divide Hiroshima; Mrs. Hatsuyo Nakamura, a tailor's widow, stood by the window of her kitchen, watching a neighbor tearing down his house because it lay in the path of an air-raid-defense fire lane; Father Wilhelm Kleinsorge, a German priest of the Society of Jesus, reclined in his underwear on a cot on the top floor of his order's three-story mission house, reading a Jesuit magazine, *Stimmen der Zeit*;[2] Dr. Terufumi Sasaki, a young member of the surgical staff of the city's large, modern Red Cross Hospital, walked along one of the hospital corridors with a blood

---

1. **deltaic.** Related to the triangular deposits at the mouth of a river
2. ***Stimmen der Zeit.*** German for "Voices of the Time"

During Reading

ADD DETAILS AND REACT TO CHARACTERS

- ❏ Listen as your teacher reads the first paragraph aloud. The paragraph introduces each character. Write down what you learn about each character in your chart.
- ❏ Continue reading on your own. As you read, fill in details that you think are important about each character and details about each character's experiences. Also add your reactions to the characters and their experiences.

THINK AND REFLECT

What do the activities of the six people have in common? **(Compare)**

_____
_____
_____

NOTE THE FACTS

What were the residents of Hiroshima expecting?

_____
_____
_____

MARK THE TEXT

Underline or highlight what each of the six people credits with his or her survival.

THINK AND REFLECT

What mood does Hersey create in the first paragraph? (Infer)

_____
_____
_____

specimen for a Wassermann test[3] in his hand; and the Reverend Mr. Kiyoshi Tanimoto, pastor of the Hiroshima Methodist Church, paused at the door of a rich man's house in Koi, the city's western suburb, and prepared to unload a handcart full of things he had evacuated from town in fear of the massive B-29 raid which everyone expected Hiroshima to suffer. A hundred thousand people were killed by the atomic bomb, and these six were among the survivors. They still wonder why they lived when so many others died. Each of them counts many small items of chance or <u>volition</u>—a step taken in time, a decision to go indoors, catching one streetcar instead of the next—that spared him. And now each knows that in the act of survival he lived a dozen lives and saw more death than he ever thought he would see. At the time, none of them knew anything.

The Reverend Mr. Tanimoto got up at five o'clock that morning. He was alone in the parsonage,[4] because for some time his wife had been commuting with their year-old baby to spend nights with a friend in Ushida, a suburb to the north. Of all the important cities of Japan, only two, Kyoto and Hiroshima, had been visited in strength by *B-san*, or Mr. B, as the Japanese, with a mixture of respect and unhappy familiarity, called the B-29; and Mr. Tanimoto, like all his neighbors and friends, was almost sick with anxiety. He had heard uncomfortably detailed accounts of mass raids on Kure, Iwakuni, Tokuyama, and other nearby towns; he was sure Hiroshima's turn would come soon. He had slept badly the night before, because there had been several air raid warnings. Hiroshima had been getting such warnings almost every night for weeks, for at that time the B-29s were using Lake Biwa, northeast of Hiroshima, as a <u>rendezvous</u> point, and no matter what city the Americans planned to hit, the Superfortresses streamed in over the coast near Hiroshima.

---

3. **Wassermann test.** Blood test used to diagnose syphilis
4. **parsonage.** Home that a church provides for its pastor

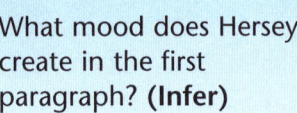

vo • li • tion (vō li' shən) *n.*, choice or decision made. *Margot had to drag Omar to the conference, but he stayed of his own <u>volition</u>.*
ren • dez • vous (rän' di vü) *adj.*, planned meeting. *At the amusement park, we decided to set a <u>rendezvous</u> point in case we were separated in the crowd.*

The frequency of the warnings and the continued <u>abstinence</u> of Mr. B with respect to Hiroshima had made its citizens jittery; a rumor was going around that the Americans were saving something special for the city.

Mr. Tanimoto is a small man, quick to talk, laugh, and cry. He wears his black hair parted in the middle and rather long; the prominence of the frontal bones just above his eyebrows and the smallness of his mustache, mouth, and chin give him a strange, old-young look, boyish and yet wise, weak and yet fiery. He moves nervously and fast, but with a restraint which suggests that he is a cautious, thoughtful man. He showed, indeed, just those qualities in the uneasy days before the bomb fell. Besides having his wife spend the nights in Ushida, Mr. Tanimoto had been carrying all the portable things from his church, in the close-packed residential district called Nagaragawa, to a house that belonged to a rayon manufacturer in Koi, two miles from the center of town. The rayon man, a Mr. Matsui, had opened his then unoccupied estate to a large number of his friends and acquaintances, so that they might evacuate whatever they wished to a safe distance from the probable target area. Mr. Tanimoto had had no difficulty in moving chairs, hymnals, Bibles, altar gear, and church records by pushcart himself, but the organ console and an upright piano required some aid. A friend of his named Matsuo had, the day before, helped him get the piano out to Koi; in return, he had promised this day to assist Mr. Matsuo in hauling out a daughter's belongings. That is why he had risen so early.

Mr. Tanimoto cooked his own breakfast. He felt awfully tired. The effort of moving the piano the day before, a sleepless night, weeks of worry and unbalanced diet, the cares of his parish—all combined to make him feel hardly adequate to the new day's work. There was another thing, too: Mr. Tanimoto had studied theology at Emory College, in Atlanta, Georgia; he had graduated in 1940; he spoke

NOTE THE FACTS

What actions show Mr. Tanimoto's "cautious, thoughtful nature"?

_____
_____
_____

NOTE THE FACTS

Why had Mr. Tanimoto risen early on the day of the bombing?

_____
_____
_____

words for everyday use

ab • sti • nence (ab′ stə nən[t]s) *n.*, habitual going without. Dora's <u>abstinence</u> from dairy products helped her lose ten pounds.

excellent English; he dressed in American clothes; he had corresponded with many American friends right up to the time the war began; and among a people obsessed with a fear of being spied upon—perhaps almost obsessed himself—he found himself growing increasingly uneasy. The police had questioned him several times, and just a few days before, he had heard that an influential acquaintance, a Mr. Tanaka, a retired officer of the Toyo Kisen Kaisha steamship line, an anti-Christian, a man famous in Hiroshima for his showy philanthropies and notorious for his personal tyrannies, had been telling people that Tanimoto should not be trusted. In compensation, to show himself publicly a good Japanese, Mr. Tanimoto had taken on the chairmanship of his local *tonarigumi*, or Neighborhood Association, and to his other duties and concerns this position had added the business of organizing air raid defense for about twenty families.

Before six o'clock that morning, Mr. Tanimoto started for Mr. Matsuo's house. There he found that their burden was to be a *tansu*, a large Japanese cabinet, full of clothing and household goods. The two men set out. The morning was perfectly clear and so warm that the day promised to be uncomfortable. A few minutes after they started, the air raid siren went off—a minute-long blast that warned of approaching planes but indicated to the people of Hiroshima only a slight degree of danger, since it sounded every morning at this time, when an American weather plane came over. The two men pulled and pushed the handcart through the city streets. Hiroshima was a fanshaped city, lying mostly on the six islands formed by the seven estuarial rivers[5] that branch out from the Ota River; its main commercial and residential districts, covering about four square miles in the center of the city, contained three-quarters of its population, which had been reduced by

---

5. **estuarial rivers.** Rivers that meet the sea

words for everyday use

phi • lan • thro • py (fə lan[t]' thrə pē) *n.*, act or gift of dispensing aid or funds set aside for humanitarian purposes. *One of Carnegie's principal philanthropies was establishing public libraries.*

NOTE THE FACTS

What rumors had arisen about Mr. Tanimoto? What did he do to try to disprove the rumors?

_____

_____

_____

NOTE THE FACTS

Why didn't the people of Hiroshima worry much about the air raid siren?

_____

_____

_____

several evacuation programs from a wartime peak of 380,000 to about 245,000. Factories and other residential districts, or suburbs, lay compactly around the edges of the city. To the south were the docks, an airport, and the island-studded Inland Sea. A rim of mountains runs around the other three sides of the delta. Mr. Tanimoto and Mr. Matsuo took their way through the shopping center, already full of people, and across two of the rivers to the sloping streets of Koi, and up them to the outskirts and foothills. As they started up a valley away from the tight-ranked houses, the all-clear sounded. (The Japanese radar operators, detecting only three planes, supposed that they comprised a reconnaissance.)[6] Pushing the handcart up to the rayon man's house was tiring, and the men, after they had maneuvered their load into the driveway and to the front steps, paused to rest awhile. They stood with a wing of the house between them and the city. Like most homes in this part of Japan, the house consisted of a wooden frame and wooden walls supporting a heavy tile roof. Its front hall, packed with rolls of bedding and clothing, looked like a cool cave full of fat cushions. Opposite the house, to the right of the front door, there was a large, <u>finicky</u> rock garden. There was no sound of planes. The morning was still; the place was cool and pleasant.

   Then a tremendous flash of light cut across the sky. Mr. Tanimoto has a distinct recollection that it traveled from east to west, from the city toward the hills. It seemed a sheet of sun. Both he and Mr. Matsuo reacted in terror—and both had time to react (for they were 3,500 yards, or two miles, from the center of the explosion). Mr. Matsuo dashed up the front steps into the house and dived among the bedrolls and buried himself there. Mr. Tanimoto took four or five steps and threw himself between two big rocks in the garden. He bellied up very hard against one of them. As his face was

Literary TOOLS

IRONY. **Irony** is a difference between appearance and reality. Why is it ironic that the all-clear signal sounded? Look for other examples of irony as you read.

_____
_____
_____

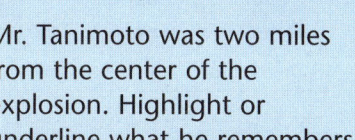

MARK THE TEXT

Mr. Tanimoto was two miles from the center of the explosion. Highlight or underline what he remembers about the flash.

---

6. **reconnaissance.** Exploratory military survey of enemy territory

words for everyday use

fin • ick • y (fi′ ni kē) *adj.*, excessively nice or exacting in taste or standards. *Mrs. Bucket's <u>finicky</u> preparations resulted in an exquisite candlelight supper.*

NOTE THE FACTS

What did most residents hear when the bomb dropped? What did a fisherman who was nearly twenty miles from Hiroshima hear?

_____

_____

_____

Reading STRATEGY REVIEW

MAKE PREDICTIONS. Think about Mr. Tanimoto's experience. Predict what the other people might witness. As you learn more about each person's experience, you may want to adjust some of these predictions.

_____

_____

_____

Literary TOOLS

VERBAL IRONY. Verbal irony is a statement that implies its opposite. Why does Hersey put "safe areas" in quotation marks?

_____

_____

_____

against the stone, he did not see what happened. He felt a sudden pressure, and then splinters and pieces of board and fragments of tile fell on him. He heard no roar. (Almost no one in Hiroshima recalls hearing any noise of the bomb. But a fisherman in his sampan[7] on the Inland Sea near Tsuzu, the man with whom Mr. Tanimoto's mother-in-law and sister-in-law were living, saw the flash and heard a tremendous explosion; he was nearly twenty miles from Hiroshima, but the thunder was greater than when the B-29s hit Iwakuni, only five miles away.)

When he dared, Mr. Tanimoto raised his head and saw that the rayon man's house had collapsed. He thought a bomb had fallen directly on it. Such clouds of dust had risen that there was a sort of twilight around. In panic, not thinking for the moment of Mr. Matsuo under the ruins, he dashed out into the street. He noticed as he ran that the concrete wall of the estate had fallen over—toward the house rather than away from it. In the street, the first thing he saw was a squad of soldiers who had been burrowing into the hillside opposite, making one of the thousands of dugouts in which the Japanese apparently intended to resist invasion, hill by hill, life for life; the soldiers were coming out of the hole, where they should have been safe, and blood was running from their heads, chests, and backs. They were silent and dazed.

Under what seemed to be a local dust cloud, the day grew darker and darker.

At nearly midnight, the night before the bomb was dropped, an announcer on the city's radio station said that about two hundred B-29s were approaching southern Honshu[8] and advised the population of Hiroshima to evacuate to their designated "safe areas." Mrs. Hatsuyo Nakamura, the tailor's widow, who lived in the section called Noboricho and who had long had a habit of doing as she was told, got her three children—a ten-year-old boy, Toshio, an eight-year-old girl, Yaeko, and a five-year-old girl, Myeko—out of bed and dressed them and walked with

---

7. **sampan.** Small, flat-bottomed, Asian boat
8. **Honshu.** Largest island of Japan

them to the military area known as the East Parade Ground, on the northeast edge of the city. There she unrolled some mats and the children lay down on them. They slept until about two, when they were awakened by the roar of the planes going over Hiroshima.

As soon as the planes had passed, Mrs. Nakamura started back with her children. They reached home a little after two-thirty and she immediately turned on the radio, which, to her distress, was just then broadcasting a fresh warning. When she looked at the children and saw how tired they were, and when she thought of the number of trips they had made in past weeks, all to no purpose, to the East Parade Ground, she decided that in spite of the instructions on the radio, she simply could not face starting out all over again. She put the children in their bedrolls on the floor, lay down herself at three o'clock, and fell asleep at once, so soundly that when the planes passed over later, she did not waken to their sound.

The siren jarred her awake at about seven. She arose, dressed quickly, and hurried to the house of Mr. Nakamoto, the head of her Neighborhood Association, and asked him what she should do. He said that she should remain at home unless an urgent warning—a series of <u>intermittent</u> blasts of the siren—was sounded. She returned home, lit the stove in the kitchen, set some rice to cook, and sat down to read that morning's Hiroshima *Chugoku*. To her relief, the all-clear sounded at eight o'clock. She heard the children stirring, so she went and gave each of them a handful of peanuts and told them to stay on their bedrolls, because they were tired from the night's walk. She had hoped that they would go back to sleep, but the man in the house directly to the south began to make a terrible <u>hullabaloo</u> of hammering, wedging, ripping, and splitting. The prefectural[9] government, convinced, as everyone in Hiroshima was, that the city

---

9. **prefectural.** Relating to a district governed by a chief officer

words for everyday use

in • ter • mit • tent (in tər mi′ tənt) *adj.*, coming and going at intervals, not continuous. *We could occasionally hear the announcer between the <u>intermittent</u> blasts of static.*

hul • la • ba • loo (hə lə bə lü′) *n.*, confused noise. *Mr. Auriemma shouted to be heard over the <u>hullabaloo</u> in the gym.*

Use THE STRATEGY

WRITE THINGS DOWN. Hersey has introduced the second character: Mrs. Nakamura. Remember to jot down notes about her experience and your reaction to her.

NOTE THE FACTS

Why didn't Mrs. Nakamura return to the East Parade Ground despite the warning she heard on the radio?

_____
_____
_____

Literary TOOLS

DRAMATIC IRONY. Dramatic irony occurs when the reader or audience knows something that the characters do not know. Why is Mrs. Nakamoto's relief at hearing the all-clear ironic?

_____
_____
_____

NOTE THE FACTS

Why was Mrs. Nakamura's neighbor tearing down his house?

_____
_____
_____

THINK AND REFLECT

What different kinds of pity did Mrs. Nakamura feel? Which do you think was strongest? **(Analyze and Evaluate)**

_____
_____
_____

NOTE THE FACTS

What did Mrs. Nakamura do when the flash came? What happened to her?

_____
_____
_____

240 would be attacked soon, had begun to press with threats and warnings for the completion of wide fire lanes, which, it was hoped, might act in conjunction with the rivers to localize any fires started by an <u>incendiary</u> raid; and the neighbor was reluctantly sacrificing his home to the city's safety. Just the day before, the prefecture had ordered all able-bodied girls from the secondary schools to spend a few days helping to clear these lanes, and they started work soon after the all-clear sounded.

Mrs. Nakamura went back to the kitchen, looked at the rice, and began watching the man next door. At first, she was annoyed with him for making so much noise, but then she was moved almost to tears by pity. Her emotion was specifically directed toward her neighbor, tearing down his home, board by board, at a time when there was so much unavoidable destruction, but undoubtedly she also felt a generalized, community pity, to say nothing of self-pity. She
250 had not had an easy time. Her husband, Isawa, had gone into the Army just after Myeko was born, and she had heard nothing from or of him for a long time, until, on March 5, 1942, she received a seven-word telegram: "Isawa died an honorable death at Singapore." She learned later that he had died on February 15th, the day Singapore fell, and that he had been a corporal. Isawa had been a not particularly prosperous tailor, and his only capital was a Sankoku sewing machine. After his death, when his allotments[10] stopped coming, Mrs. Nakamura got out the machine and began to
260 take in piecework herself, and since then had supported the children, but poorly, by sewing.

As Mrs. Nakamura stood watching her neighbor, everything flashed whiter than any white she had ever seen. She did not notice what happened to the man next door; the reflex of a mother set her in motion toward her children. She had taken a single step (the house was 1,350 yards, or three-quarters of a mile, from the center of the explosion) when something

---

10. **allotments.** Monetary payments provided by the government

words for everyday use

in • cen • di • ar • y (in sen′ dē er ē) *adj.,* relating to or involving deliberate burning of property. *During the riots in the inner city, residents were most afraid of <u>incendiary</u> crime.*

picked her up and she seemed to fly into the next room over the raised sleeping platform, pursued by parts of her house.

Timbers fell around her as she landed, and a shower of tiles pommelled her; everything became dark, for she was buried. The debris did not cover her deeply. She rose up and freed herself. She heard a child cry, "Mother, help me!," and saw her youngest—Myeko, the five-year-old—buried up to her breast and unable to move. As Mrs. Nakamura started frantically to claw her way toward the baby, she could see or hear nothing of her other children.

In the days right before the bombing, Dr. Masakazu Fujii, being prosperous, hedonistic, and at the time not too busy, had been allowing himself the luxury of sleeping until nine or nine-thirty, but fortunately he had to get up early the morning the bomb was dropped to see a house guest off on a train. He rose at six, and half an hour later walked with his friend to the station, not far away, across two of the rivers. He was back home by seven, just as the siren sounded its sustained warning. He ate breakfast and then, because the morning was already hot, undressed down to his underwear and went out on the porch to read the paper. This porch—in fact, the whole building—was curiously constructed. Dr. Fujii was the proprietor of a peculiarly Japanese institution: a private, single-doctor hospital. This building, perched beside and over the water of the Kyo River, and next to the bridge of the same name, contained thirty rooms for thirty patients and their kinfolk—for, according to Japanese custom, when a person falls sick and goes to a hospital, one or more members of his family go and live there with him, to cook for him, bathe, massage, and read to him, and to offer incessant familial sympathy, without which a Japanese patient would be miserable indeed. Dr. Fujii had no beds— only straw mats—for his patients. He did, however, have all

FIX-UP IDEA

Unlock Difficult Words
If you are struggling with the vocabulary in the selection, read through the selection once to gather important ideas without worrying about the meaning of every word. Then go back and reread. Use context clues to help you figure out meanings. If that doesn't work, try to use word parts such as prefixes and word roots to help you figure out meanings. Use a dictionary if you are still unsure of what the words mean. Write the words and definitions in your word study notebook.

MARK THE TEXT

Highlight or underline why Dr. Masakazu Fujii had to get up early the morning the bomb was dropped.

Use THE STRATEGY

WRITE THINGS DOWN. What do you know about Dr. Masakazu Fujii? What opinions do you have about him? Note your answers in your chart.

---

words for everyday use

pom • mel (pə′məl) *vt.*, pound or beat. *After the punk pommelled him and took his wallet, Steve went to the police station to file a report.*

he • do • nis • tic (hē dən is′tik) *adj.*, relating to or characterized by pleasure. *Kleo planned to devote himself to a hedonistic lifestyle during vacation.*

in • ces • sant (in se′sənt) *adj.*, continuing or following without interruption. *The incessant noise of the drum beating gave Tanja a headache.*

sorts of modern equipment: an x-ray machine, diathermy apparatus,[11] and a fine tiled laboratory. The structure rested two-thirds on the land, one-third on piles over the tidal waters of the Kyo. This overhang, the part of the building where Dr. Fujii lived, was queer-looking, but it was cool in summer and from the porch, which faced away from the center of the city, the prospect of the river, with pleasure boats drifting up and down it, was always refreshing. Dr. Fujii had occasionally had anxious moments when the Ota and its mouth branches rose to flood, but the piling was apparently firm enough and the house had always held.

Dr. Fujii had been relatively idle for about a month because in July, as the number of untouched cities in Japan dwindled and as Hiroshima seemed more and more inevitably a target, he began turning patients away, on the ground that in case of a fire raid he would not be able to evacuate them. Now he had only two patients left—a woman from Yano, injured in the shoulder, and a young man of twenty-five recovering from burns he had suffered when the steel factory near Hiroshima in which he worked had been hit. Dr. Fujii had six nurses to tend his patients. His wife and children were safe; his wife and one son were living outside Osaka, and another son and two daughters were in the country on Kyushu.[12] A niece was living with him, and a maid and a manservant. He had little to do and did not mind, for he had saved some money. At fifty, he was healthy, convivial, and calm, and he was pleased to pass the evenings drinking whiskey with friends, always sensibly and for the sake of conversation. Before the war, he had *affected* brands imported from Scotland and America; now he was perfectly satisfied with the best Japanese brand, Suntory.

Dr. Fujii sat down cross-legged in his underwear on the spotless matting of the porch, put on his glasses, and started reading the Osaka *Asahi*. He liked to read the Osaka news

---

11. **diathermy apparatus.** Equipment for heat treatments
12. **Kyushu.** Southernmost of the main islands of Japan

words for everyday use

con • viv • i • al (kən viv′ yəl) *adj.*, relating to feasting, drinking, and good company. "Eat, drink, and be merry" describes Leslie's convivial attitude toward life.

NOTE THE FACTS

Why had Dr. Fujii been turning away patients? How many patients did he have at the time of the bombing?

THINK AND REFLECT

How did Dr. Fujii seem to feel about the war? (Infer)

because his wife was there. He saw the flash. To him—faced away from the center and looking at his paper—it seemed a brilliant yellow. Startled, he began to rise to his feet. In that moment (he was 1,550 yards from the center), the hospital leaned behind his rising and, with a terrible ripping noise, toppled into the river. The Doctor, still in the act of getting to his feet, was thrown forward and around and over; he was <u>buffeted</u> and gripped; he lost track of everything, because things were so speeded up; he felt the water.

350   Dr. Fujii hardly had time to think that he was dying before he realized that he was alive, squeezed tightly by two long timbers in a V across his chest, like a morsel suspended between two huge chopsticks—held upright, so that he could not move, with his head miraculously above water and his torso and legs in it. The remains of his hospital were all around him in a mad assortment of splintered lumber and materials for the relief of pain. His left shoulder hurt terribly. His glasses were gone.

360   Father Wilhelm Kleinsorge, of the Society of Jesus, was, on the morning of the explosion, in rather frail condition. The Japanese wartime diet had not sustained him, and he felt the strain of being a foreigner in an increasingly <u>xenophobic</u> Japan; even a German, since the defeat of the Fatherland,[13] was unpopular. Father Kleinsorge had, at thirty-eight, the look of a boy growing too fast—thin in the face, with a prominent Adam's apple, a hollow chest, dangling hands, big feet. He walked clumsily, leaning forward a little. He was tired all the time. To make matters worse, he had suffered for two days,
370 along with Father Cieslik, a fellow-priest, from a rather painful and urgent diarrhea, which they blamed on the beans and black ration bread they were obliged to eat. Two other priests then living in the mission compound, which

READ ALOUD

Read the highlighted passage aloud. What did Dr. Fujii notice when the bomb struck? What happened to him?

_____
_____
_____

NOTE THE FACTS

What were three reasons for Father Kleinsorge's frail condition?

_____
_____
_____

---

13. **defeat of the Fatherland.** Germany surrendered in May 1945.

words for everyday use

buf • fet (bə′ fət) *vt.*, batter or drive by force. *During the storm, the ship was <u>buffeted</u> by heavy winds and sank.*

xe • no • pho • bic (zē nə fō′ bik) *adj.*, fearful of or showing hatred toward foreigners. *My <u>xenophobic</u> neighbor did not welcome the immigrants who moved in next door.*

Use THE STRATEGY

WRITE THINGS DOWN. Make notes in your chart about Father Kleinsorge. How is he different from the other people introduced so far? What does he have in common with Mr. Tanimoto?

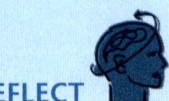

THINK AND REFLECT

How does Father Kleinsorge react to the alarm and the all-clear? Compare his reactions to those of the other characters. **(Compare)**

_____
_____
_____

was in the Noboricho section—Father Superior LaSalle and Father Schiffer—had happily escaped this affliction.

Father Kleinsorge woke up about six the morning the bomb was dropped, and half an hour later—he was a bit tardy because of his sickness—he began to read Mass in the mission chapel, a small Japanese-style wooden building which was without pews, since its worshipers knelt on the usual Japanese matted floor, facing an altar graced with splendid silks, brass, silver, and heavy embroideries. This morning, a Monday, the only worshipers were Mr. Takemoto, a <u>theological</u> student living in the mission house; Mr. Fukai, the secretary of the diocese;[14] Mrs. Murata, the mission's devoutly Christian housekeeper; and his fellow-priests. After Mass, while Father Kleinsorge was reading the Prayers of Thanksgiving, the siren sounded. He stopped the service and the missionaries retired across the compound to the bigger building. There, in his room on the ground floor, to the right of the front door, Father Kleinsorge changed into a military uniform which he had acquired when he was teaching at the Rokko Middle School in Kobe and which he wore during air raid alerts.

After an alarm, Father Kleinsorge always went out and scanned the sky, and in this instance, when he stepped outside, he was glad to see only the single weather plane that flew over Hiroshima each day about this time. Satisfied that nothing would happen, he went in and breakfasted with the other Fathers on substitute coffee and ration bread, which, under the circumstances, was especially <u>repugnant</u> to him. The Fathers sat and talked a while, until, at eight, they heard the all-clear. They went then to various parts of the building. Father Schiffer retired to his room to do some writing. Father Cieslik sat in his room in a straight chair with a pillow over his stomach to ease his pain, and read. Father Superior LaSalle stood at the window of his room,

---

14. **diocese.** Territorial jurisdiction of a bishop

words for everyday use
theo • log • i • cal (thē ə lä′ ji kəl) *adj.*, of or relating to theology, or the study of religious faith, practice, and experience. *The <u>theological</u> magazine was published by a Catholic press.*
re • pug • nant (ri pug′ nənt) *adj.*, exciting distaste or aversion. *The idea of conceding defeat was <u>repugnant</u> to our team.*

thinking. Father Kleinsorge went up to a room on the third floor, took off all his clothes except his underwear, and stretched out on his right side on a cot and began reading his *Stimmen der Zeit*.

After the terrible flash—which, Father Kleinsorge later realized, reminded him of something he had read as a boy about a large meteor colliding with the earth—he had time (since he was 1,400 yards from the center) for one thought: A bomb has fallen directly on us. Then, for a few seconds or minutes, he went out of his mind.

Father Kleinsorge never knew how he got out of the house. The next things he was conscious of were that he was wandering around in the mission's vegetable garden in his underwear, bleeding slightly from small cuts along his left flank; that all the buildings round about had fallen down except the Jesuits' mission house, which had long before been braced and double-braced by a priest named Groppe, who was terrified of earthquakes; that the day had turned dark; and that Murata-*san*, the housekeeper, was nearby, crying over and over, "*Shu Jesusu, awaremi tamia!* Our Lord Jesus, have pity on us!"

On the train on the way into Hiroshima from the country, where he lived with his mother, Dr. Terufumi Sasaki, the Red Cross Hospital surgeon, thought over an unpleasant nightmare he had had the night before. His mother's home was in Mukaihara, thirty miles from the city, and it took him two hours by train and tram[15] to reach the hospital. He had slept uneasily all night and had wakened an hour earlier than usual, and, feeling sluggish and slightly feverish, had debated whether to go to the hospital at all; his sense of duty finally forced him to go, and he had started out on an earlier train than he took most mornings. The dream had particularly frightened him because it was so closely associated, on the surface at least, with a disturbing actuality. He was only twenty-five years old and had just completed his training at the Eastern Medical University, in Tsingtao,[16] China. He was

---

15. **tram.** Streetcar
16. **Tsingtao.** Large Chinese city on the Yellow River, which was occupied by Japan during World War II

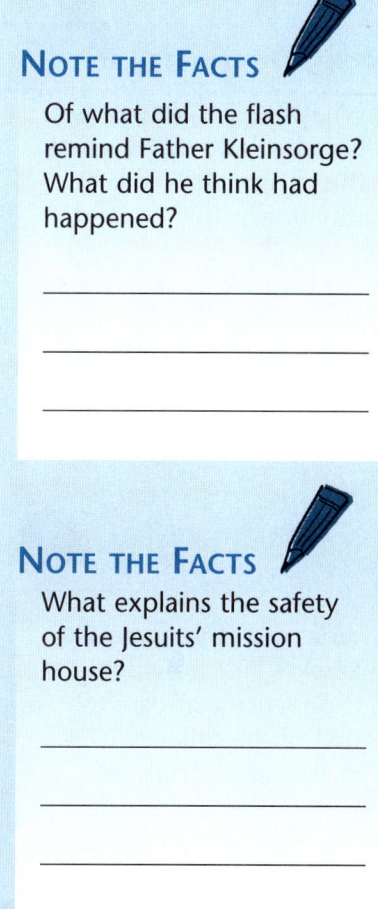

NOTE THE FACTS

Of what did the flash remind Father Kleinsorge? What did he think had happened?

_____
_____
_____

NOTE THE FACTS

What explains the safety of the Jesuits' mission house?

_____
_____
_____

MARK THE TEXT

Highlight or underline how this day began differently for Dr. Terufumi Sasaki.

NOTE THE FACTS

What had Dr. Sasaki dreamed about? How was this dream related to his situation?

_____
_____
_____

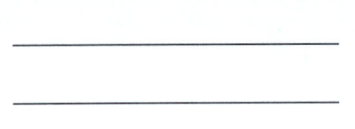

THINK AND REFLECT

What probably saved Dr. Sasaki's life? How does his experience compare to that of the other characters? (**Analyze**)

_____
_____
_____

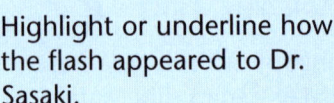

MARK THE TEXT

Highlight or underline how the flash appeared to Dr. Sasaki.

---

something of an idealist and was much distressed by the inadequacy of medical facilities in the country town where his mother lived. Quite on his own, and without a permit, he had begun visiting a few sick people out there in the evenings, after his eight hours at the hospital and four hours' commuting. He had recently learned that the penalty for practicing without a permit was severe; a fellow-doctor whom he had asked about it had given him a serious scolding. Nevertheless, he had continued to practice. In his dream, he had been at the bedside of a country patient when the police and the doctor he had consulted burst into the room, seized him, dragged him outside, and beat him up cruelly. On the train, he just about decided to give up the work in Mukaihara, since he felt it would be impossible to get a permit, because the authorities would hold that it would conflict with his duties at the Red Cross Hospital.

At the terminus,[17] he caught a streetcar at once. (He later calculated that if he had taken his customary train that morning, and if he had had to wait a few minutes for the streetcar, as often happened, he would have been close to the center at the time of the explosion and would surely have perished.) He arrived at the hospital at seven-forty and reported to the chief surgeon. A few minutes later, he went to a room on the first floor and drew blood from the arm of a man in order to perform a Wassermann test. The laboratory containing the incubators for the test was on the third floor. With the blood specimen in his left hand, walking in a kind if distraction he had felt all morning, probably because of the dream and his restless night, he started along the main corridor on his way toward the stairs. He was one step beyond an open window when the light of the bomb was reflected, like a gigantic photograph flash, in the corridor. He ducked down on one knee and said to himself, as only a Japanese would, "Sasaki, *gambare!* Be brave!" Just then (the building was 1,650 yards from the center), the blast ripped through the hospital. The glasses he was wearing flew off his face; the bottle of blood crashed against one wall, his

---

17. **terminus.** Station at the end of a transportation line

Japanese slippers zipped out from under his feet—but otherwise, thanks to where he stood, he was untouched.

Dr. Sasaki shouted the name of the chief surgeon and rushed around to the man's office and found him terribly cut by glass. The hospital was in horrible confusion: heavy partitions and ceilings had fallen on patients, beds had overturned, windows had blown in and cut people, blood was spattered on the walls and floors, instruments were everywhere, many of the patients were running about screaming, many more lay dead. (A colleague working in the laboratory to which Dr. Sasaki had been walking was dead; Dr. Sasaki's patient, whom he had just left and who a few moments before had been dreadfully afraid of syphilis, was also dead.) Dr. Sasaki found himself the only doctor in the hospital who was unhurt.

Dr. Sasaki, who believed that the enemy had hit only the building he was in, got bandages and began to bind the wounds of those inside the hospital; while outside, all over Hiroshima, maimed and dying citizens turned their unsteady steps toward the Red Cross Hospital to begin an invasion that was to make Dr. Sasaki forget his private nightmare for a long, long time.

Miss Toshiko Sasaki, the East Asia Tin Works clerk, who is not related to Dr. Sasaki, got up at three o'clock in the morning on the day the bomb fell. There was extra housework to do. Her eleven-month-old brother, Akio, had come down the day before with a serious stomach upset; her mother had taken him to the Tamura Pediatric Hospital and was staying there with him. Miss Sasaki, who was about twenty, had to cook breakfast for her father, a brother, a sister, and herself, and—since the hospital, because of the war, was unable to provide food—to prepare a whole day's meals for her mother and the baby, in time for her father, who worked in a factory making rubber earplugs for artillery crews, to take the food by on his way to the plant. When she had finished and had cleaned and put away the cooking things, it was nearly seven. The family lived in Koi, and she had a forty-five-minute trip to the tin works, in the section of town called

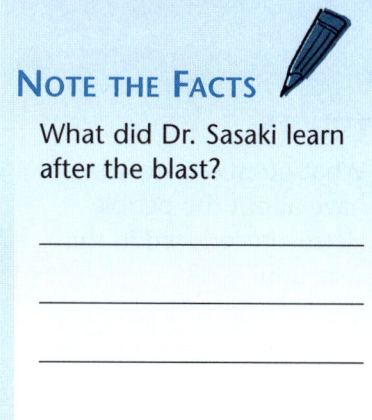

NOTE THE FACTS

What did Dr. Sasaki learn after the blast?

_____
_____
_____

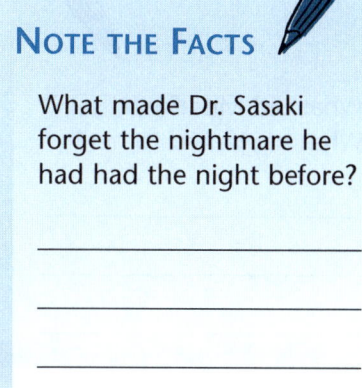

NOTE THE FACTS

What made Dr. Sasaki forget the nightmare he had had the night before?

_____
_____
_____

Use THE STRATEGY

WRITE THINGS DOWN. What do you learn about Miss Toshiko Sasaki in this paragraph? Add notes about her to your Character Chart.

What Do You Wonder?

What questions do you have about the people Hersey introduced in this selection?

_____
_____
_____

Note the Facts

What did Miss Sasaki see? What happened to her?

_____
_____
_____

Think and Reflect

A writer's **aim** is his or her purpose or goal. Hersey's aim is to inform the reader of the horrors of nuclear war and how it devastates the lives of ordinary, innocent people. How effectively do you think Hersey met his purpose? **(Evaluate)**

_____
_____

Kannonmachi. She was in charge of the personnel records in the factory. She left Koi at seven, and as soon as she reached the plant, she went with some of the other girls from the personnel department to the factory auditorium. A prominent local Navy man, a former employee, had committed suicide the day before by throwing himself under a train—a death considered honorable enough to warrant a memorial service, which was to be held at the tin works at ten o'clock that morning. In the large hall, Miss Sasaki and the others made suitable preparations for the meeting. This work took about twenty minutes.

Miss Sasaki went back to her office and sat down at her desk. She was quite far from the windows, which were off to her left, and behind her were a couple of tall bookcases containing all the books of the factory library, which the personnel department had organized. She settled herself at her desk, put some things in a drawer, and shifted papers. She thought that before she began to make entries in her lists of new employees, discharges, and departures for the Army, she would chat for a moment with the girl at her right. Just as she turned her head away from the windows, the room was filled with a blinding light. She was paralyzed by fear, fixed still in her chair for a long moment (the plant was 1,600 yards from the center).

Everything fell, and Miss Sasaki lost consciousness. The ceiling dropped suddenly and the wooden floor above collapsed in splinters and the people up there came down and the roof above them gave way; but principally and first of all, the bookcases right behind her swooped forward and the contents threw her down, with her left leg horribly twisted and breaking underneath her. There, in the tin factory, in the first moment of the atomic age, a human being was crushed by books. ■

Reflect ON YOUR READING

After Reading ▶ **SHARE YOUR IDEAS**

❑ With a few of your classmates, compare your Character Charts.
❑ Discuss why you think Hersey chose to focus on six individuals rather than writing a more objective history of the bombing. What effect does this decision have on your view of the Hiroshima bombing?

_____
_____
_____
_____

Reading Skills and Test Practice

IDENTIFY AUTHOR'S PURPOSE

Discuss with a partner how to answer questions about the author's purpose. Use the Think-Aloud Notes to write down your reasons for eliminating the incorrect answers.

____1. Why does the author describe what these people were doing at the very moment the bomb exploded?
   a. to introduce the characters and let the reader know what job each person held
   b. to contrast the normalcy of the day with the horrors that followed the dropping of the bomb
   c. to create conflict between the characters
   d. to develop sympathy for the characters

____2. What idea did the author emphasize?
   a. Each person deserved to survive the bombing.
   b. These people were all closely connected through various organizations and affiliations.
   c. Small changes in schedule and chance account for the survival of these people.
   d. It is unbelievable that any of these people survived.

How did using the reading strategy help you to answer the questions?

_____
_____
_____
_____

THINK-ALOUD NOTES

Investigate, Inquire, and Imagine

RECALL: GATHER FACTS
1a. Whom does Hersey identify in the opening paragraph? What was each person doing?

INTERPRET: FIND MEANING
1b. Why does Hersey focus on six individuals? Why does he give the distance away from the center of the explosion of each of the survivors?

ANALYZE: TAKE THINGS APART
2a. Identify the images Hersey uses to describe the explosion of the atomic bomb, as seen by each of the survivors.

SYNTHESIZE: BRING THINGS TOGETHER
2b. Hersey combines literary techniques with factual reporting to describe the impact of the nuclear blast on the six survivors' lives. Why do you think he uses literary techniques?

EVALUATE: MAKE JUDGMENTS
3a. Hersey observed that journalism "allows the reader to witness history; fiction gives its readers an opportunity to live it." Assess this statement in relation to the selection you have just read.

EXTEND: CONNECT IDEAS
3b. Compare Hersey's account to journalistic or literary accounts of bombings you have read.

Literary Tools

IRONY. **Irony** is a difference between appearance and reality. *Verbal irony* is a statement that implies its opposite. *Dramatic irony* occurs when the reader or audience knows something that the characters do not know. *Irony of situation* occurs when an event violates the expectations of the characters, the reader, or the audience. Complete the following chart with examples of irony from the selection. Which example of irony is most powerful? Why?

Example of Irony	Type of Irony
Miss Sasaki is seriously injured when books, which are symbols of civilization, fall on her.	irony of situation

WordWorkshop

ROOTS AND AFFIXES. Look at the following words from "A Noiseless Flash."

    philanthropy   theological   xenophobic

Even if you didn't know what these words meant, you could figure out something about them from their affixes and roots.

- *Phil* means loving. It can appear at the beginning of a word as *phil* or *philo* or at the end of a word as *phil* or *phile*. In *philanthropy*, it is combined with *anthropy* meaning humans.
- *The* or *theo* refers to God or a god. In this case *logy* means study or doctrine. *Theology* is the study or doctrine of God (or a god). *Logy* can also refer to written or oral expression
- *Phobe* or *phobia* means fear. *Phobic* means afraid of. *Xen* or *xeno* means foreign or foreigner. Combined as *xenophobic*, they mean "afraid of foreigners."

Use the information above and what you know about other affixes and roots to try to determine the meaning of each of the following words. Use a dictionary to check your guess. Then use each word in a sentence.

1. xenophile
2. theocracy
3. bibliophile
4. hydrophobic
5. monotheistic

Read-Write Connection

Hersey says, "And now each [of the survivors] knows that in the act of survival he lived a dozen lives and saw more death than he ever thought he would see." Describe the positive and negative aspects of being a survivor of an atomic bomb.

Beyond the Reading

CREATE A FRONT PAGE. With a group of your classmates, create a front page for a newspaper dated August 7, 1945, the day after the nuclear bomb exploded in Hiroshima. Write headlines and stories. Think about what kinds of pictures you would include. Do any research necessary to provide accurate facts for your articles.

GO ONLINE. To find links and additional activities for this selection, visit the EMC Internet Resource Center at **emcp.com/languagearts** and click on Write-In Reader.

Unit 7 READING Review

Choose and Use Reading Strategies

Before reading the excerpt below, review with a partner how to use each of these reading strategies with nonfiction.

1. Read with a Purpose
2. Connect to Prior Knowledge
3. Write Things Down
4. Make Predictions
5. Visualize
6. Use Text Organization
7. Tackle Difficult Vocabulary
8. Monitor Your Reading Progress

Now apply at least two of these reading strategies as you read the excerpt from Joan Didion's "On the Mall." Use the margins and mark up the text to show how you are using the reading strategies to read actively. After reading, summarize the excerpt in your own words.

> A few aspects of shopping-center theory do in fact remain impenetrable to me. I have no idea why the Community Builders' Council ranks "Restaurant" as deserving a Number One (or "Hot Spot") location but exiles "Chinese Restaurant" to a Number Three, out there with "Power and Light Office" and "Christian Science Reading Room." Nor do I know why the Council approves of enlivening a mall with "small animals" but specifically, vehemently, and with no further explanation, excludes "monkeys." If I had a center I would have monkeys, and Chinese restaurants, and Mylar kites and bands of small girls playing tambourine.

WordWorkshop

UNIT 7 WORDS FOR EVERYDAY USE

abhor, 273	consecrate, 313	formidable, 282
abstinence, 325	constitution, 271	gulf, 272
arduous, 288	contrivance, 272	hedonistic, 331
ascribe, 274	convivial, 332	hullabaloo, 329
aspiration, 301	earnest, 295	incendiary, 330
avail, 271	effectual, 282	incense, 274
aversion, 288	encumbrance, 298	incessant, 331
avert, 281	endeavor, 302	induce, 274
buffet, 333	ethereal, 296	inestimable, 281
cessation, 301	finicky, 327	insidious, 280
comport, 280	fluctuate, 303	intermittent, 329

inviolate, 281	provoke, 273	submission, 280
laxly, 307	remonstrate, 281	subserve, 272
loathsome, 273	rendezvous, 324	superfluous, 303
martial, 280	repugnant, 334	supinely, 282
paltry, 302	resignation, 294	temporal, 280
perennial, 298	saturated, 296	theological, 334
philanthropy, 326	score, 313	undulation, 301
pommel, 331	solace, 280	unwieldy, 304
posterity, 299	sovereign, 272	volatile, 307
predominate, 287	squalid, 289	volition, 324
prostrate, 281	subjugation, 280	xenophobic, 333

WORD GAME. Create a word game such as a crossword puzzle or word search using Words for Everyday Use from Unit 7. Give definitions, synonyms, or incomplete sentences to identify each word needed for the puzzle. Switch puzzles with a partner. See if you can complete your partner's puzzle.

Literary Tools

Select the best literary element on the right to complete each sentence on the left. Write the correct letter in the blank.

_____ 1. "Self-Reliance" is a(n) ____.
_____ 2. A(n) ____ is passed by word of mouth from generation to generation.
_____ 3. Jonathan Edwards uses a(n) ____ of a spider over a fire to show his listeners how precarious their place on earth is.
_____ 4. The ___ in "as a final resting place for those who here gave their lives that the nation might live" contrasts life and death.
_____ 5. The term "safe areas" in Hiroshima is an example of ___.
_____ 6. "Is this the part of wise men, engaged in a great and arduous struggle for liberty?" is an example of a(n) ____.
_____ 7. Emphasizing the equal weight of two or more ideas by expressing them in the same grammatical form is ____.
_____ 8. "A foolish consistency is the hobgoblin of little minds" is an example of a(n) ____.
_____ 9. Soldiers in Hiroshima digging trenches in preparation for an invasion is an example of ____.
_____10. Simplifying and being an individual are ____ in *Walden*.

a. analogy, 272, 276
b. antithesis, 312, 315
c. aphorism, 286, 308, 310
d. dramatic irony, 329, 340
e. essay, 287, 291
f. irony of situation, 340
g. irony, 327, 340
h. oral tradition, 320
i. parallelism, 312, 315
j. rhetorical question, 278, 284
k. themes, 287, 291
l. verbal irony, 328, 340

On Your Own

FLUENTLY SPEAKING. Several of the selections in this unit address war. Look at Henry's speech, Lincoln's address, and Hersey's book chapter. Give a brief speech expressing your feelings about war. You may want to talk about war in general or about a specific war.

PICTURE THIS. Choose an aphorism from this unit. Make an illustrated poster with this aphorism as a caption.

PUT IT IN WRITING. Write an essay about individualism and conformity. Do you agree with Emerson that to be great is to be misunderstood? Do you think Thoreau was right when he said that some people hear a different drummer? What analogy or examples can you give to support being an individual?

Unit EIGHT

Reading Informational and Visual Media

INFORMATIONAL AND VISUAL MEDIA

Learning how to read online and print reference works, graphic aids, and other visuals will help you access, process, and think about the vast amount of information available to you.

Informational Media

Media are channels or systems of communication, information, or entertainment. *Mass media*, designed to reach the mass of the people, refers specifically to means of communication, such as newspapers, radio, or television. *Journalism* is the gathering, evaluating, and disseminating, through various media, of news and facts of current interest. Journalism has expanded from printed matter (newspapers and periodicals) to include radio, television, documentary films, the Internet, and computer news services.

Newspapers, issued on a daily or weekly basis, report the news, provide commentary on the news, advocate various public policies, and furnish special information and advice to readers.

Periodicals, released at regular intervals, are publications that include journals, magazines, or newsletters. They feature material of special interest to particular audiences.

Technical writing refers to scientific or process-oriented instructional writing that is of a technical or mechanical nature, such as **instruction manuals**, **how-to instructional guides**, and **procedural memos**.

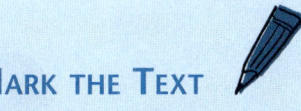

MARK THE TEXT

Underline or highlight three kinds of periodicals.

Reading **TIP**

When reading directions or procedures, read through all the steps before you begin. Make sure you have on hand any necessary materials or tools, and note any safety issues or time requirements.

Use diagrams, pictures, and icons. They may help you identify parts, understand difficult instructions, or recognize safety issues, optional steps, or other special features.

Reading TIP

When reading editorials and commentaries, look for facts to support opinions. Also consider whether your experience or knowledge of the subject supports the opinions.

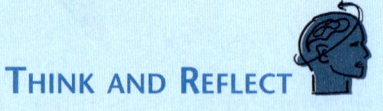

THINK AND REFLECT

How might a movie or book review be helpful? (Evaluate)

_____
_____
_____

Elements of Informational Media

NEWS ARTICLES. News articles are informational pieces of writing about a particular topic, issue, event, or series of events. They can be found in newspapers, periodicals, and on Internet sites such as newsgroups or information services.

EDITORIALS AND COMMENTARIES. An **editorial** is an article in a newspaper or periodical that gives the opinions of the editors or publishers. A **commentary** is a report of an event that expresses the opinion of a participant or observer.

ESSAYS. An **essay** is a brief work of prose nonfiction that need not be a complete or exhaustive treatment of a subject.

INTERVIEWS. An **interview** is a question and answer exchange between a reporter who wants precise information from a reliable source and the person who has that information.

REVIEWS. A **review**, or *critique*, is a critical evaluation of a work, such as a book, play, movie, musical performance, or recording.

Electronic Media

Electronic media includes online magazines and journals, known as **webzines** or **e-zines; computer news services;** and many **web-based newspapers** that are available on the **Internet**. In addition to handling web documents, the Internet also allows people to send e-mail, access archives of files, and participate in discussion groups.

Multimedia is the presentation of information using a combination of text, sound, pictures, animation, and video. Common multimedia computer applications include **game**s, **learning software, presentation software, reference materials,** and **web pages**. Using multimedia can provide a varied and informative interactive experience.

Elements of Electronic Media

ELECTRONIC MAIL. Electronic mail, or **e-mail**, is used to send written messages between individuals or groups on the Internet. E-mail messages tend to be more informal and conversational in style than letters.

WEB PAGES. A **web page** is an electronic "page" on the World Wide Web or Internet that may contain text, pictures, and sometimes animations related to a particular topic. A *website* is a collection of pages grouped together to organize the information offered by the person, company, or group that owns it.

NEWSGROUPS. Another use of e-mail is listservers, in which discussions on a particular subject are grouped together into **newsgroups** on a wide range of subjects. Messages to a newsgroup are accessible in the form of a list on a local news server that has a worldwide reach. Users can choose which messages they want to read and reply by posting messages to the newsgroup.

INFORMATION SERVICES. **Information services**, or *news services*, are providers of electronic news, information, and e-mail services.

BULLETIN BOARD SYSTEMS. A **bulletin board system**, or BBS, is an online service that allows users to post and read messages on a particular topic, converse in a *chat room*, play games with another person, and copy, or download, programs to their personal computers.

WEBZINES OR E-ZINES. **Webzines** or **e-zines** are periodicals that are available online. They may be available only online, or they may also be available in a magazine distributed by traditional methods.

ONLINE NEWSPAPERS. Major newspapers are now available online. Past editions of the paper are usually accessible through an online archive.

Visual Media

Many books and news media rely on **visual arts**, such as **fine art**, **illustrations**, and **photographs**, to convey ideas. Critically viewing a painting or photograph can add meaning to your understanding of a text.

Elements of Visual Media

GRAPHIC AIDS. **Graphic aids** are visual materials with information such as **drawings**, **illustrations**, **diagrams**, **charts**, **graphs**, **maps**, and **spreadsheets**.

PHOTOGRAPHS. Photographs can accompany news stories or historical documents, serve as scientific evidence or works of art, and record everyday life. New photographic technology allows for digital formats to be stored on disk and downloaded to computers.

THINK AND REFLECT

Identify a website that you like. What topic does it cover? **(Apply)**

THINK AND REFLECT

Give a situation in which a graphic aid would be helpful. **(Apply)**

NOTE THE FACTS

What is the difference between regular photography and digital photography?

_____
_____
_____
_____

Reading TIP

Scan the first and last paragraphs, or any headings, pictures, and graphs, before you read. This will give you a quick picture of what the writer wants you to understand.

DIGITAL PHOTOGRAPHY. With **digital photography**, images are converted into a code of ones and zeroes that a computer can read. Digital photographs can be manipulated into new images.

PHOTOJOURNALISM. **Photojournalism** is documentary photography that tells a particular story in visual terms. Photojournalists, who usually work for newspapers and periodicals, cover cultural and news events in areas such as politics, war, business, sports, and the arts.

VISUAL ARTS. The **visual arts** include painting, sculpture, drawing, printmaking, collage, photography, video, and computer-assisted art. With art, the artist tries to communicate with viewers, who may have different ideas about how to interpret the work. Learning about the location and time period of an artwork can contribute to a better understanding of it.

USING READING STRATEGIES WITH INFORMATIONAL AND VISUAL MEDIA

Active Reading Strategy Checklists

When reading informational and visual media, you will need to identify how the text is structured. Scan the material first. Headings, pictures, and directions will reveal what the selection wants to communicate. Use the following checklists when you read informational and visual media.

1 READ WITH A PURPOSE. Before reading informational and visual media, give yourself a purpose, or something to look for, as you read. Know why you are reading and what information you seek. Sometimes your teacher will set a purpose for reading: "Look for propaganda in this advertisement." Other times you can set your own purpose by previewing the title, the opening and closing paragraphs, and instructional information. Say to yourself

- ❏ I need to look for . . .
- ❏ I must keep track of . . .
- ❏ I need to understand the writer's views on . . .
- ❏ It is essential that I figure out how . . .
- ❏ I want to learn what happened when . . .

2 CONNECT TO PRIOR KNOWLEDGE. Connect to information you already know about the writer's topic. As you read, build on what you know. Say to yourself

- ❏ I know this about the topic already . . .
- ❏ Other information I've read about this topic said . . .
- ❏ I've used similar visual aids by . . .
- ❏ I did something similar when . . .
- ❏ This information is like . . .

3 WRITE THINGS DOWN. As you read informational and visual media, write down or mark ideas that help you understand the writer's views. Possible ways to keep a written record include

- ❏ Underline information that answers a specific question.
- ❏ Write down steps in a process.
- ❏ Highlight conclusions the writer draws.
- ❏ Create a graphic organizer that shows how to do something.
- ❏ Use a code to respond to the writer's ideas.

4 MAKE PREDICTIONS. Before you read informational and visual media, use the title and subject matter to guess what the selection will be about. As you read, confirm or deny your predictions, and make new ones based on what you learn. Make predictions like the following:

- ❏ The title tells me that the selection will be about . . .
- ❏ Graphic aids show me that . . .
- ❏ I predict that the writer will want me to . . .
- ❏ This selection will help me to . . .
- ❏ This writer will conclude by . . .

5 VISUALIZE. Visualizing, or allowing the words on the page to create images in your mind, helps you understand what informational and visual media is trying to communicate. In order to visualize what an informational and visual media selection is telling you, you need to picture the people, events, or procedure that a writer describes. Make statements such as

- ❏ I imagine these people will . . .
- ❏ A drawing of this part would include . . .
- ❏ I picture that this is happening in this section . . .
- ❏ I envision the situation as . . .

Reading TIP

Instead of writing down a short response, use a symbol or a short word to indicate your response.
- + I like this
- − I don't like this
- √ This is important
- Yes I agree with this
- No I disagree with this
- ? I don't understand this
- ! This is like something I know
- ↩ I need to come back to this later

Reading TIP

Make a diagram of a process. It will help you remember the steps and see how parts fit together.

6 **USE TEXT ORGANIZATION.** When you read informational and visual media, pay attention to the text's structure. Learn to stop occasionally and retell what you have read. Say to yourself

- ❏ The title, headings, and pictures tell me this selection will be about . . .
- ❏ The writer's directions tell me . . .
- ❏ There is a pattern to how the writer presents . . .
- ❏ The writer presents the information by . . .
- ❏ The writer includes helpful sections that . . .

7 **TACKLE DIFFICULT VOCABULARY.** Difficult words can hinder your ability to understand informational and visual media. Use context, consult a dictionary, or ask someone about words you do not understand. When you come across a difficult word in the selection, say to yourself

- ❏ The writer defines this word by . . .
- ❏ A dictionary definition shows that the word means . . .
- ❏ My work with the word before reading helps me know that the word means . . .
- ❏ A classmate said that the word means . . .

8 **MONITOR YOUR READING PROGRESS.** All readers encounter difficulty when they read, especially if they haven't chosen the reading material. When you have to read something, note problems you are having and fix them. The key to reading success is knowing when you are having difficulty. To fix problems, say to yourself

- ❏ Because I don't understand this part, I will . . .
- ❏ Because I'm having trouble staying connected to the ideas in the selection, I will . . .
- ❏ Because the words in the selection are too hard, I will . . .
- ❏ Because the selection is long, I will . . .
- ❏ Because I can't retell what the selection was about, I will . . .

Become an Active Reader

Active reading strategy instruction in this unit gives you an in-depth look at how to use one active reading strategy with each selection. Learning how to use several strategies in combination increases your chances of success even more. For more information about the active reading strategies, see Unit 1, pages 4–15.

Reading TIP

Every word may be critical in informational and visual media. If words are not defined in the text, use a glossary or dictionary to find the meanings.

Fix-Up Ideas

- Reread
- Ask a question
- Read in shorter chunks
- Read aloud
- Retell
- Work with a partner
- Unlock difficult words
- Vary your reading rate.
- Choose a new reading strategy
- Create a mnemonic device

How to Use Reading Strategies with Informational and Visual Media

To see how readers use active reading strategies, look over the responses one reader has while reading excerpts from informational and visual media. As you look over the reader's responses, underline or highlight responses that demonstrate that the reader is reading actively.

Excerpt 1. Note how a reader uses active reading strategies while reading this excerpt from "*Seabiscuit*: A Good Bet."

READ WITH A PURPOSE
I want to decide whether to see *Seabiscuit*.

Seabiscuit is the story of the little horse that could. Before you stop reading, saying, "I don't like horses," or "I don't care about racing . . . or even sports for that matter," take a closer look. *Seabiscuit* is a lot more than a horse or racing movie.

Seabiscuit is also the story of a nation in need of a winner for the underdog. The United States was deep in the Depression, when Seabiscuit rose to fame. People were looking for an escape from dismal lives and struggles—and for hope that they might climb out of the struggle. The little horse with the funny name who beat the big guys became their icon.

Seabiscuit is a story not only for horse lovers and history buffs but also for anyone who likes a human interest story or who wants to see the little guy triumph over adversity.

VISUALIZE
I can see and hear the crowds going wild for this horse after he beat the horse expected to win.

TACKLE DIFFICULT VOCABULARY
I'm not sure what *adversity* means, but from the context I think it means something hard you overcome.

WRITE THINGS DOWN
I'll make a pro and con chart to write down things that should be interesting or not interesting to me.

Excerpt 2. Note how a reader uses active reading strategies while reading this text from a website on Amy Tan.

USE TEXT ORGANIZATION
The underlined text shows me the main categories I could click on for more information.

MAKE PREDICTIONS
This would be a good source for my report on Amy Tan.

CONNECT TO PRIOR KNOWLEDGE
I know Amy Tan is Chinese American. The quote here talks about that.

MONITOR YOUR READING PROGRESS
I'm not sure why the site says "Blessing from America." I'll explore to find out.

UNIT 8 / READING INFORMATIONAL AND VISUAL MEDIA

CONNECT

Reader's resource

The Very Brief Relation of the Devastation of the Indies exposes the savage behavior of Spanish explorers in the New World toward the native people. Bartolomé de las Casas, once a slave owner, became a priest and an ardent spokesperson for the rights of the indigenous peoples of the new World. He argued against the Spaniards' brutal treatment and enslavement of the native population. This excerpt focuses on Spanish actions at Hispaniola, the island home of the Arawak people and one of Christopher Columbus's first landing sites. In this selection, the Spanish are called Christians.

Word watch

PREVIEW VOCABULARY

buffet
burnish
depopulate
flourish
infest
inhuman
oppression
ruffian
subjection
suffice
vestige

Reader's journal

What makes one person stand up against injustice when others are afraid to voice their opinions?

_____
_____

---

from The *Very Brief Relation* of the DEVASTATION OF THE INDIES
from *Hispaniola*
by Bartolomé de las Casas

Active READING STRATEGY

TACKLE DIFFICULT VOCABULARY

Before Reading ➤ **PREVIEW NEW WORDS**

❑ With a partner, preview the Words for Everyday Use at the bottom of the selection pages. Read each word, its meaning, and the sentence in which it is used.
❑ Choose a word, and have your partner use it in a sentence of his or her own. Then have your partner choose a word, and you use it in a sentence of your own. Continue taking turns until you have covered all of the words.
❑ Preview the graphic organizer below. During reading write down unfamiliar words in the Vocabulary Chart.

Graphic Organizer: Vocabulary Chart

Word	Meaning	Sentence

352 THE EMC WRITE-IN READER

from The *Very Brief Relation* of the DEVASTATION OF THE INDIES

from *Hispaniola*

Bartolomé de las Casas

This was the first land in the New World to be destroyed and <u>depopulated</u> by the Christians, and here they began their <u>subjection</u> of the women and children, taking them away from the Indians to use them and ill use them, eating the food they provided with their sweat and toil. The Spaniards did not content themselves with what the Indians gave them of their own free will, according to their ability, which was always too little to satisfy enormous appetites, for a Christian eats and consumes in one day an amount of food that would <u>suffice</u> to feed three houses inhabited by ten Indians for one month. And they committed other acts of force and violence and <u>oppression</u> which made the Indians realize that these men had not come from Heaven.[1] And some of the Indians concealed their foods while others concealed their wives and

---

1. **realize . . . Heaven.** Columbus and other early European voyagers reported that the natives took them to be gods who had come from the heavens.

words for everyday use

de • pop • u • late (dē päp´yə lāt´) *vt.*, reduce the population of, especially by violence or disease. *Plagues and famines <u>depopulated</u> medieval Europe.*

sub • jec • tion (sub jek´shən) *n.*, bringing under control or dominion. *The <u>subjection</u> of the American colonies by the British sparked the American Revolution.*

suf • fice (sə fīs´) *vi.*, be enough. *One small salad per day will not <u>suffice</u> to nourish a growing adolescent.*

op • pres • sion (ə presh´ən) *n.*, keeping down by cruel or unjust use of authority. *The people protested the <u>oppression</u> committed by the controlling government.*

During Reading

USE CONTEXT CLUES

- ❏ Follow along in your text as your teacher reads the first three paragraphs aloud. If you encounter words with which you are unfamiliar, write them in your Vocabulary Chart. When your teacher has finished reading, review the words you listed and try to determine their meanings by using context clues.
- ❏ Continue reading the selection on your own. Jot down unfamiliar words, and try to define them by using context clues. If the context clues do not provide the meaning, try analyzing the word parts—prefixes, roots, and suffixes—to determine meaning. If that strategy fails, consult a dictionary.
- ❏ Record the definitions in your chart.

READ ALOUD

Practice saying the Words for Everyday Use aloud. Use the pronunciation guide to help you. Then read the highlighted passage aloud.

NOTE THE FACTS

According to the author, how much did the Christians eat?

_____

_____

NOTE THE FACTS

What did the native people begin to seek?

_____
_____
_____

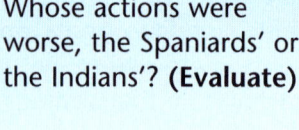

THINK AND REFLECT

Whose actions were worse, the Spaniards' or the Indians'? **(Evaluate)**

_____
_____
_____

children and still others fled to the mountains to avoid the terrible transactions of the Christians.

And the Christians attacked them with <u>buffets</u> and beatings, until finally they laid hands on the nobles of the villages. . . . From that time onward the Indians began to seek ways to throw the Christians out of their lands. They took up arms, but their weapons were very weak and of little service in offense and still less in defense. (Because of this, the wars of the Indians against each other are little more than games played by children.) And the Christians, with their horses and swords and pikes began to carry out massacres and strange cruelties against them. . . .

And because all the people who could do so fled to the mountains to escape these <u>inhuman</u>, ruthless, and ferocious acts, the Spanish captains, enemies of the human race, pursued them with the fierce dogs they kept which attacked the Indians, tearing them to pieces and devouring them. And because on few and far between occasions, the Indians justifiably killed some Christians, the Spaniards made a rule among themselves that for every Christian slain by the Indians, they would slay a hundred Indians.

From *The Coast of Pearls, Paria, and the Island of Trinidad*

[The Spaniards] have brought to the island of Hispaniola and the island of San Juan[2] more than two million souls taken captive, and have sent them to do hard labor in the mines, labors that caused many of them to die. And it is a great sorrow and heartbreak to see this coastal land which was so <u>flourishing</u>, now a depopulated desert.

This is truth that can be verified, for no more do they bring ships loaded with Indians that have been thus attacked and captured as I have related. No more do they cast overboard into the sea the third part of the numerous Indians they stow

---
2. **San Juan.** Puerto Rico

words for everyday use

buf • fet (buf´it) *n.*, blow with the hand or fist. *Unable to avoid the <u>buffets</u> of his opponent, the boxer was knocked out.*
in • hu • man (in hyü´mən) *adj.*, unfeeling; cruel; barbarous. *The brutal actions of the Spanish conquistadors were <u>inhuman</u>.*
flour • ish (flʉr´ish) *vi.*, grow vigorously; thrive; prosper. *Because of the rainfall, the vegetable garden <u>flourished</u>.*

on their vessels, these dead being added to those they have killed in their native lands, the captives crowded into the holds of their ships, without food or water, or with very little, so as not to deprive the Spanish tyrants who call themselves ship owners and who carry enough food for themselves on their voyages of attack. And for the pitiful Indians who died of hunger and thirst, there is no remedy but to cast them into the sea. And verily, as a Spaniard told me, their ships in these regions could voyage without compass or chart, merely by following for the distance between the Lucayos Islands[3] and Hispaniola, which is sixty or seventy leagues,[4] the trace of those Indian corpses floating in the sea, corpses that had been cast overboard by earlier ships.

Afterward, when they disembark on the island of Hispaniola, it is heartbreaking to see those naked Indians, heartbreaking for anyone with a vestige of piety, the famished state they are in, fainting and falling down, weak from hunger, men, women, old people, and children.

Then, like sheep, they are sorted out into flocks of ten or twenty persons, separating fathers from sons, wives from husbands, and the Spaniards draw lots, the ship owners carrying off their share, the best flock, to compensate them for the moneys they have invested in their fleet of two or three ships, the ruffian tyrants getting their share of captives who will be house slaves, and when in this "*repartimiento*"[5] a tyrant gets an old person or an invalid, he says, "Why do you give me this one? To bury him? And this sick one, do you give him to me to make him well?" See by such remarks in what esteem the Spaniards hold the Indians and judge if they are accomplishing the divine concepts of love for our fellow man, as laid down by the prophets.

---

3. **Lucayos Islands.** The Bahamas
4. **leagues.** Linear unit of measure that varies in different periods of time; usually equal to about three miles
5. ***repartimiento***. Distribution (Spanish). A royal decree in 1503 ordered masters of native persons to try to convert them to Christianity and hold their property. In reality it was a system of slavery.

---

words for everyday use

ves • tige (ves´tij) *n.*, trace; bit. *The Roanoke colony disappeared and not a vestige remained of its settlers.*

ruf • fi • an (ruf´ē an) *adj.*, brutal; violent; lawless. *The principal warned the bully to cease his ruffian ways.*

FIX-UP IDEA

Reread
If you find it difficult to unlock word meanings on the first time through a passage, reread the passage focusing on finding the meaning of the entire passage.

NOTE THE FACTS

What condition were the native people in when they arrived at Hispaniola?

_____
_____

MARK THE TEXT

Highlight or underline what happened to a pearl diver if he wanted to rest.

Literary TOOLS

POINT OF VIEW. Point of view is the vantage point from which a story is told. The story may be told from a *first-person point of view* by one of the participants, who uses *I* to refer to himself or herself. It may also be told from a *third-person point of view* by an outsider who avoids the use of *I*. As you read, look for clues about the point of view.

The tyranny exercised by the Spaniards against the Indians in the work of pearl fishing is one of the most cruel that can be imagined. There is no life as infernal and desperate in this century that can be compared with it, although the mining of gold is a dangerous and burdensome way of life. The pearl fishers dive into the sea at a depth of five fathoms, and do this from sunrise to sunset, and remain for many minutes without breathing, tearing the oysters out of their rocky beds where the pearls are formed. They come to the surface with a netted bag of these oysters where a Spanish torturer is waiting in a canoe or skiff, and if the pearl diver shows signs of wanting to rest, he is showered with blows, his hair is pulled, and he is thrown back into the water, obliged to continue the hard work of tearing out the oysters and bringing them again to the surface.

The food given the pearl divers is codfish, not very nourishing, and the bread made of maize, the bread of the Indies. At night the pearl divers are chained so they cannot escape.

Often a pearl diver does not return to the surface, for these waters are <u>infested</u> with maneating sharks of two kinds, both vicious marine animals that can kill, eat, and swallow a whole man.

In this harvesting of pearls let us again consider whether the Spaniards preserve the divine concepts of love for their fellow men, when they place the bodies of the Indians in such mortal danger, and their souls, too, for these pearl divers perish without the holy sacraments.[6] And it is solely because of the Spaniards' greed for gold that they force the Indians to lead such a life, often a brief life, for it is impossible to continue for long diving into the cold water and holding the breath for minutes at a time, repeating this hour after hour, day after day; the continual cold penetrates

---

6. **sacraments.** Christian rites, such as baptism or the Eucharist, believed to have been ordained by Christ and that are held to be means of divine grace or to be signs or symbols of a spiritual reality

words for everyday use

in • fest (in fest´) *vt.*, overrun or inhabit in large numbers. *The old house was <u>infested</u> with termites that gnawed upon the wood.*

them, constricts the chest, and they die spitting blood, or weakened by diarrhea.

The hair of these pearl divers, naturally black, is as if <u>burnished</u> by the saltpeter in the water, and hangs down their backs making them look like sea dogs or monsters of another species. And in this extraordinary labor, or, better put, in this infernal labor, the Lucayan Indians are finally consumed, as are captive Indians from other provinces. And all of them were publicly sold for one hundred and fifty castellanos,[7] these Indians who had lived happily on their islands until the Spaniards came, although such a thing was against the law. But the unjust judges did nothing to stop it. For all the Indians of these islands are known to be great swimmers.[8] ∎

---

7. **castellanos.** Spanish gold coin bearing the arms of Castile
8. **But the unjust . . . great swimmers.** Spanish judges ignored the mistreatment of the native peoples because their abilities at pearl diving were impressive.

THINK AND REFLECT

What effect did pearl diving under force from the Spaniards have on the Lucayan Indians? **(Infer)**

_____

_____

words for everyday use

bur • nish (bur´nish) *vt.,* make shiny by rubbing. *I <u>burnished</u> the candlesticks to make them gleam.*

Reflect ON YOUR READING

After Reading → PRACTICE USING NEW WORDS

❑ Share the list of words in your Vocabulary Chart with a partner.
❑ Work together to write two sentences for each of the listed words. Make sure your sentences show that you understand the definition of each word. Write your sentences in your chart.

Reading Skills and Test Practice

USE CONTEXT CLUES

Discuss with a group how best to answer questions that require you to use context clues. Use the Think-Aloud Notes to write down your reasons for eliminating the incorrect answers.

Read the following passage. Then answer the questions that follow the passage.

> And because all the people who could do so fled to the mountains to escape these inhuman, ruthless, and ferocious acts, the Spanish captains, enemies of the human race, pursued them with the fierce dogs they kept.... And because on few and far between occasions, the Indians justifiably killed some Christians, the Spaniards made a rule among themselves that for every Christian slain by the Indians, they would slay a hundred Indians.

_____1. What is the best definition of *ruthless* based on the context clues in the passage above?
   a. scary
   b. kindly
   c. cruel
   d. helpless

_____2. Which of the following is a synonym of *slain*?
   a. harmed
   b. killed
   c. captured
   d. devoured

How did using the reading strategy help you to answer the questions?

_____
_____
_____
_____

THINK-ALOUD NOTES

Investigate, Inquire, and Imagine

RECALL: GATHER FACTS
1a. How did the Spaniards, or Christians, react to native efforts at self-defense?

INTERPRET: FIND MEANING
1b. Why did they punish the natives so severely?

ANALYZE: TAKE THINGS APART
2a. List actions that show that the Spaniards disregard the divine concept of love for their fellow humans.

SYNTHESIZE: BRING THINGS TOGETHER
2b. What motivated the Spaniards in their relations with the natives? What do you think motivated de las Casas in his relations with the natives after his conversion in 1515?

PERSPECTIVE: LOOK AT OTHER VIEWS
3a. Why do you think Bartolomé de las Casas risked everything, even being charged with treason against Spain, to write the *Relation*?

EMPATHY: SEE FROM INSIDE
3b. What would you do if you were a native of Hispaniola and suffered such mistreatment at the hands of the Spaniards? Would you resist or submit? Explain.

Literary Tools

POINT OF VIEW. Point of view is the vantage point from which a story is told. The story may be told from a *first-person point of view* by one of the participants, who uses *I* to refer to himself or herself. It may also be told from a *third-person point of view* by an outsider who avoids the use of *I*. From what point of view is this story told? Why do you think de las Casas uses this point of view?

_____

_____

_____

WordWorkshop

CONTEXT CLUES. If you come across an unfamiliar word, you can often figure out its meaning by using context clues. For more information on context clues, see Unit 9, pages 398–399.

Use context clues to determine the meaning of the following words from *The Very Brief Relation of the Devastation of the Indies*. Identify the word or words that help you understand the meaning of each given word. Identify each context clue as a comparison or contrast clue. Then write a definition in your own words and use the word in a sentence.

1. buffets _____

2. ruthless _____

3. flourishing _____

4. famished _____

5. invalid _____

Read-Write Connection

How do you think Bartolomé de las Casas felt when he witnessed his own people behaving so terribly? How would you feel if you saw a friend act cruelly? What would you do?

_____

Beyond the Reading

RESEARCH EUROPEAN EXPLORERS. Research Christopher Columbus or another explorer who landed in the New World. Chart the routes of the explorer. Identify the purpose of the voyage, the explorer's point of origin, and lands claimed. Discuss interactions between the explorer and the natives of the lands he reached.

GO ONLINE. To find links and additional activities for this selection, visit the EMC Internet Resource Center at **emcp.com/languagearts** and click on Write-In Reader.

from

THE NEW ENGLAND Primer

by Anonymous

Active READING STRATEGY

CONNECT TO PRIOR KNOWLEDGE

Before Reading ➡ **THINK ABOUT WHAT YOU KNOW**

- ❏ Share your response to the Reader's Journal activity with a partner.
- ❏ Talk about lessons you were taught when you were young.
- ❏ What kinds of things do you expect to see in the illustrated alphabet from *The New England Primer*?
- ❏ Preview the graphic organizer below. As you read, you will **paraphrase**, or restate in your own words, each couplet from the primer.

Graphic Organizer: Paraphrase Chart

A		N	
B		O	
C		P	
D		Q	
E		R	
F		S	
G		T	
H		U	
I		V	
J		W	
K		X	
L		Y	
M		Z	

CONNECT

Reader's resource

The New England Primer was the first textbook produced in America to teach reading. The New England colonies were founded for religious reasons, and religious matters play a large role in the book. *The New England Primer* included the Lord's Prayer, the Apostles' Creed, a series of moral and instructive sentences from the Bible, and an illustrated alphabet. The selection you are about to read is the illustrated alphabet.

Reader's journal

What do you remember learning from illustrated alphabet books with rhymes or pictures when you were younger?

_____
_____
_____
_____

During Reading

USE WHAT YOU KNOW

- Read along as your teacher reads the first three couplets. How are these couplets similar to or different from ABC rhymes you are familiar with? What religious allusions can you find in the first three couplets?
- Paraphrase each couplet in your Paraphrase Chart.
- Read and paraphrase the rest of the couplets on your own.

Reading TIP

There are many religious or biblical references in this selection. For example, in the *A* line, the reference to Adam is a biblical reference to the story of Adam and Eve. The book in the *B* line is the Bible.

Fix-Up Idea

Tackle Archaic Language
You may see many words you do not recognize in this selection. That's because language has changed since the selection was written. For example, *doth* is an old way of saying "does." The footnote points out another difference. Use footnotes and context clues to help you figure out archaic language.

FROM

THE NEW ENGLAND Primer

Anonymous

A	In *Adam's* Fall We finned[1] all.
B	Thy Life to mend This *Book* attend.
C	The *Cat* doth play And after flay.
D	A *Dog* will bite A Thief at Night.
E	An *Eagles* Flight Is out of Sight.
F	An idle *Fool* Is whipt at School.
G	As runs the *Glafs* Man's life doth pafs.
H	My *Book* and *Heart* Shall never part.
J	*Job* feels the Rod Yet bleffes GOD.

---

1. **finned.** Sinned. The letter *s* often appears as an *f* in the early print style of the *Primer*.

K — Our *KING* the good
No man of blood.

L — The *Lion* bold
The *Lamb* doth hold.

M — The *Moon* gives light
In time of night.

N — *Nightingales* fing
In Time of Spring.

O — The *Royal Oak* it was the Tree
That fav'd His Royal Majeftie.

P — *Peter* denies
His Lord and cries

Q — Queen *Efther* comes in Royal State
To Save the Jews from difmal Fate

R — *Rachol* doth mourn
For her firft born.

S — *Samuel* anoints
Whom God appoints:

T — *Time* cuts down all
Both great and fmall.

U — *Uriah's* beauteous Wife
Made *David* feek his Life.

W — *Whales* in the Sea
God's Voice obey.

X — *Xerxes* the great did die,
And fo muft you & I

Y — *Youth* forward flips
Death fooneft nips

Z — *Zacheus* he Did climb the Tree
His Lord to Fee. ∎

THINK AND REFLECT

What might the description "No man of blood" mean in the description for letter *K*? **(Infer)**

_____
_____
_____

Literary TOOLS

COUPLET. A **couplet** is a pair of rhyming lines that express a complete thought. This selection is made up of couplets.

THINK AND REFLECT

What attitude toward death is expressed in the entries for *X* and *Y*? **(Interpret)**

_____
_____
_____

Reflect ON YOUR READING

After Reading → **SHARE YOUR CONNECTIONS**

- ❏ Share your paraphrases with your partner from the Before Reading activity. If you have different ideas for some letters, talk about how you came up with your answer.
- ❏ If some letters confused you, try to figure them out together. Use all of the information available to you, including the Reader's Resource and the illustrations.
- ❏ Make a note of any couplets that you still don't understand. Discuss your responses with the rest of the class.

Reading Skills and Test Practice

IDENTIFY AUTHOR'S PURPOSE

Discuss with a partner how to answer questions that require you to identify purpose. Use the Think-Aloud Notes to write down your reasons for eliminating the incorrect answers.

_____1. Aside from the alphabet, what does this selection mainly teach?
  a. how to write rhyming poetry
  b. history of the Puritans in New England
  c. moral lessons
  d. the importance of education

_____2. What lesson do the couplets for G, T, and X share?
  a. We are all sinners who must strive to mend our lives.
  b. The Bible will help us improve our lives.
  c. Even the great must obey God.
  d. Life is short and death inevitable.

How did using the reading strategy help you to answer the questions?

_____
_____
_____
_____

THINK-ALOUD NOTES

Investigate, Inquire, and Imagine

RECALL: GATHER FACTS
1a. What animals appear in the rhyme for the letter *L*?

INTERPRET: FIND MEANING
1b. What qualities might the animals referenced in the *L* line represent?

ANALYZE: TAKE THINGS APART
2a. During an era of political chaos and revolution in seventeenth-century England, the king saved himself from enemies by hiding in a tree. Which letter has a rhyme that refers to this incident? Which other rhymes refer to political leadership of the day?

SYNTHESIZE: BRING THINGS TOGETHER
2b. Based on this selection, how did the Puritans feel about their leadership?

EVALUATE: MAKE JUDGMENTS
3a. At least three rhymes warn of age and death. Identify the letters with these rhymes. Do you think that these are appropriate rhymes for children? Why, or why not?

EXTEND: CONNECT IDEAS
3b. Make up new rhymes to replace ones that you don't think are appropriate for children today. Try to include topics that are important in schools today.

Literary Tools

COUPLET. A **couplet** is a pair of rhyming lines that express a complete thought. This selection is made up of couplets. Classify each couplet based on the subject by writing the letter in the appropriate column below.

Animals and Nature	Biblical References	Aging and Death	Moral Lessons	Politics

UNIT 8 / READING INFORMATIONAL AND VISUAL MEDIA   365

WordWorkshop

VISUAL CONTEXT CLUES. Visual clues can help you understand the meaning of text. For example, the picture that accompanies *B* in the alphabet verse from *The New England Primer* helps you recognize that the book the verse refers to is the Bible. The picture for verse G helps you to understand that the "glass" is an hourglass. Pictures or visual images can also help you remember the meaning of a new word. For example, for the word *beauteous*, you might imagine a person admiring himself or herself in a mirror to remind you that the word means "beautiful."

Choose five words from the selection that you want to remember and create a vocabulary card for each. Use the same format as the sample below.

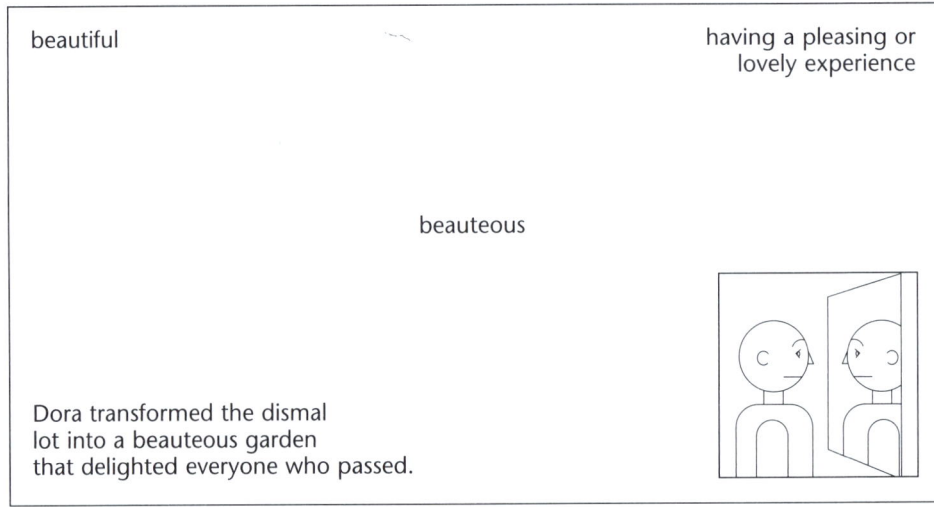

Read-Write Connection

If you were a young, colonial child reading the *Primer*, what would you learn about religion and attitudes toward life?

_____

_____

Beyond the Reading

WRITE ANNOTATIONS. An **annotation** for a literary work is an explanatory note for some part of that work. For example, annotations often appear as footnotes that explain difficult vocabulary or obscure references. If you are unfamiliar with references in the *Primer,* research the references. Then write two annotations for the alphabet.

GO ONLINE. To find links and additional activities for this selection, visit the EMC Internet Resource Center at **emcp.com/languagearts** and click on Write-In Reader.

DECLARATION of INDEPENDENCE
by Thomas Jefferson

Active READING STRATEGY

READ WITH A PURPOSE

Before Reading ➤ ESTABLISH A PURPOSE

- Read the Reader's Resource carefully and think about the name of this document.
- With a partner, discuss why the Declaration of Independence was written and what you know about it.

Graphic Organizer: Cluster Chart

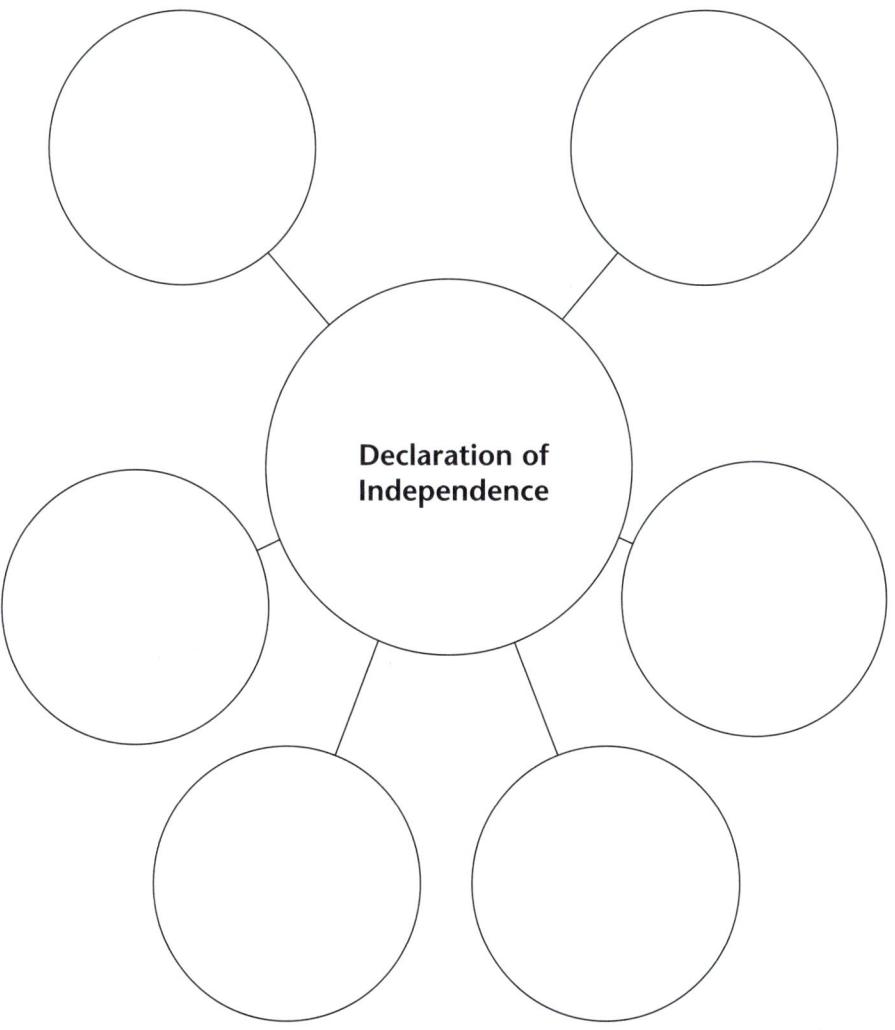

CONNECT

Reader's resource

The **Declaration of Independence** is a key document in American history. In 1776, the Continental Congress decided to separate from Great Britain and form a new government. The Declaration of Independence stated these two purposes and the reasons for creating a new government. Thomas Jefferson, with Benjamin Franklin, John Adams, and others, drafted the Declaration of Independence. It was adopted on July 4, 1776.

Word watch

PREVIEW VOCABULARY

abdicate	naturalization
acquiesce	rectitude
assent	redress
compliance	sufferance
convulsion	tenure
evince	transient
inestimable	unalienable
insurrection	usurpation
magnanimity	

Reader's journal

What rights do you have at home, school, and work?

_____

_____

_____

UNIT 8 / READING INFORMATIONAL AND VISUAL MEDIA   367

During Reading

KEEP THE PURPOSE IN MIND

- ❑ Listen as your teacher reads the first two paragraphs aloud. Then with your partner, list in your Cluster Chart important ideas found in these paragraphs. How do these ideas relate to the purpose of the document?

- ❑ Continue reading on your own, keeping track of the main ideas. The middle section of the document contains many short paragraphs. Don't try to note the idea of each, but see how the ideas relate to one another.

NOTE THE FACTS

What reason for drafting the Declaration of Independence is stated in the opening paragraph?

_____
_____
_____

MARK THE TEXT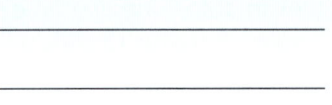

Highlight or underline the unalienable rights noted in the Declaration.

DECLARATION *of* INDEPENDENCE

Thomas Jefferson

The Drafting of the Declaration of Independence, c.1900. Jean Leon Jerome Ferris. Private Collection.

IN CONGRESS, JULY 4, 1776

When in the course of human events, it becomes necessary for one people to dissolve the political bands which have connected them with another, and to assume, among the powers of the earth, the separate and equal station to which the laws of nature and of nature's God entitle them, a decent respect to the opinions of mankind requires that they should declare the causes which impel them to the separation.

We hold these truths to be self-evident:—that all men are created equal; that they are endowed by their Creator with certain <u>unalienable</u> rights; that among these are life, liberty, and the pursuit of happiness. That, to secure these rights, governments are instituted among men, deriving their just powers from the consent of the governed; that, whenever any form of government becomes destructive of these ends, it is the right of the people to alter or to abolish it, and to institute a new government, laying its foundation on such principles, and organizing its powers in such form, as to them shall seem most likely to effect their safety and happiness. Prudence, indeed, will dictate that governments long established should not be changed for light and

words for everyday use

un • al • ien • a • ble (un āl´yən ə bəl) *adj.,* that which may not be taken away.
Melody argued with her parents that staying up late was an <u>unalienable</u> right.

368   THE EMC WRITE-IN READER

transient causes; and, accordingly, all experience hath shown that mankind are more disposed to suffer, while evils are sufferable, than to right themselves by abolishing the forms to which they are accustomed. But, when a long train of abuses and usurpations, pursuing invariably the same object, evinces a design to reduce them under absolute despotism,[1] it is their right, it is their duty, to throw off such government, and to provide new guards for their future security. Such has been the patient sufferance of these colonies; and such is now the necessity that constrains them to alter their former systems of government. The history of the present King of Great Britain[2] is a history of repeated injuries and usurpations, all having, in direct object, the establishment of an absolute tyranny over these States. To prove this, let facts be submitted to a candid world.

He has refused his assent to laws the most wholesome and necessary for the public good.

He has forbidden his Governors to pass laws of immediate and pressing importance, unless suspended in their operation till his assent should be obtained; and when so suspended, he has utterly neglected to attend to them.

He has refused to pass other laws for the accommodation of large districts of people, unless these people would relinquish the right of representation in the legislature—a right inestimable to them, and formidable to tyrants only.

He has called together legislative bodies at places unusual, uncomfortable, and distant from the depository of their public records, for the sole purpose of fatiguing them into compliance with his measure.

---

1. **despotism.** Government by a tyrant
2. **present King of Great Britain.** King George III (1760–1820)

words for everyday use

tran • si • ent (tran′sē ənt) *adj.,* not permanent; temporary. *Colds are transient; they go away after a week or so.*
u • sur • pa • tion (yü zər pā′shən) *n.,* unlawful or violent taking of power. *The prime minister was accused of usurpation of rights belonging to the king.*
e • vince (ē vin[t]s′) *vt.,* show plainly. *By scowling, the server evinced his displeasure at the small size of the tip.*
suf • fer • ance (suf′ər əns) *n.,* power to tolerate pain. *The workers' long sufferance of poor working conditions ended when they decided to go on strike.*
as • sent (ə sent′) *n.,* agreement. *Marie nodded in assent.*
in • es • ti • ma • ble (in es′tə mə bəl) *adj.,* too great to be measured. *Leonardo da Vinci's paintings are of inestimable value.*
com • pli • ance (kəm plī′ən[t]s) *n.,* act of giving in to wishes or demands. *Compliance with the tax laws is required.*

Reading STRATEGY REVIEW

TACKLE DIFFICULT VOCABULARY. Remember to use footnotes and Words for Everyday Use to help you understand difficult words in this selection. What is another strategy you can use to find the meaning of an unfamiliar word?

_____

_____

THINK AND REFLECT

Why is the right of representation in the legislature very important to the people? Why is it threatening to tyrants? **(Infer)**

_____

_____

_____

NOTE THE FACTS

What effect has dissolving the representative houses had?

_____
_____
_____

Literary TOOLS

PARALLELISM. Parallelism is a rhetorical technique in which a writer emphasizes the equal value or weight of two or more ideas by expressing them in the same grammatical form. The highlighted text shows an example of parallelism. The grievances against the king begin with "He has." Look for other examples of parallelism as you read.

THINK AND REFLECT

How does this long list of grievances against the king support the purpose stated in the opening of the Declaration? **(Infer)**

_____
_____
_____

He has dissolved representative houses repeatedly, for opposing, with manly firmness, his invasions on the rights of the people.

He has refused, for a long time after such dissolutions, to cause others to be elected; whereby the legislative powers, incapable of annihilation, have returned to the people at large for their exercise; the State remaining, in the meantime, exposed to all dangers of invasion from without, and <u>convulsions</u> within.

60   He has endeavored to prevent the population of these States; for that purpose obstructing the laws for the <u>naturalization</u> of foreigners; refusing to pass others to encourage their migration hither, and raising the conditions of new appropriations of lands.

He has obstructed the administration of justice, by refusing his assent to laws for establishing judiciary powers.

He has made judges dependent on his will alone for the <u>tenure</u> of their offices, and the amount and payment of their salaries.

70   He has erected a multitude of new offices, and sent hither swarms of officers to harass our people and eat out their substance.

He has kept among us in times of peace, standing armies, without the consent of our legislatures.

He has affected to render the military independent of, and superior to, the civil power.

He has combined with others to subject us to a jurisdiction foreign to our constitutions, and unacknowledged by our laws; giving his assent to their acts

80   of pretended legislation:

For quartering large bodies of armed troops among us;

For protecting them, by a mock trial, from punishment for any murders which they should commit on the inhabitants of these States;

For cutting off our trade with all parts of the world;

For imposing taxes on us without our consent;

---

words for everyday use

con • vul • sion (kən vul´shən) *n.,* sudden, violent disturbance. *The feverish patient was shaken by <u>convulsions</u>.*
nat • u • ral • i • za • tion (nach´ər əl iz ā´shən) *n.,* bestowal of the rights of citizenship. *Before his <u>naturalization</u>, Juan needed a green card to work in the United States.*
ten • ure (ten´yər) *n.,* right to hold a position permanently. *The governor's <u>tenure</u> in office is four years.*

> **FIX-UP IDEA**
>
> **Use Margin Questions**
> If you are having trouble recognizing important ideas and their connections to the purpose, go back and answer the questions in the margins. These questions will help you identify key ideas in the selection. Use these ideas to help you understand other sections of the document.

For depriving us, in many cases, of the benefits of trial by jury;

For transporting us beyond the seas, to be tried for pretended offences;

For abolishing the free system of English laws in a neighboring province, establishing there an arbitrary government, and enlarging its boundaries, so as to render it at once an example and fit instrument for introducing the same absolute rule into these colonies;

For taking away our charters, abolishing our most valuable laws, and altering, fundamentally, the forms of our governments;

For suspending our own legislatures, and declaring themselves invested with power to legislate for us in all cases whatsoever.

He has <u>abdicated</u> government here, by declaring us out of his protection, and waging war against us.

THINK AND REFLECT

Choose two of the grievances listed on this page. Restate the grievances in your own words. (**Paraphrase**)

_____
_____
_____

NOTE THE FACTS

How has the king abdicated government in the colonies?

_____
_____
_____

words for everyday use
ab • di • cate (ab´ di kāt´) vt., give up a right or a responsibility. *The powerful barons forced the king to <u>abdicate</u> his throne.*

MARK THE TEXT

Highlight or underline three groups of people the king has sent to fight against the colonists.

NOTE THE FACTS

What steps had the colonists taken prior to writing the Declaration of Independence?

_____
_____
_____

He has plundered our seas, ravaged our coasts, burnt our towns, and destroyed the lives of our people.

He is at this time transporting large armies of foreign mercenaries[3] to complete the works of death, desolation, and tyranny, already begun with circumstances of cruelty and perfidy[4] scarcely paralleled in the most barbarous ages, and totally unworthy the head of a civilized nation.

He has constrained our fellow-citizens, taken captive on the high seas, to bear arms against their country, to become the executioners of their friends and brethren, or to fall themselves by their hands.

He has excited domestic <u>insurrection</u> amongst us, and has endeavored to bring on the inhabitants of our frontiers the merciless Indian savages, whose known rule of warfare is an undistinguished destruction of all ages, sexes, and conditions.

In every state of these oppressions we have petitioned for <u>redress</u>, in the most humble terms; our repeated petitions have been answered only by repeated injury. A prince whose character is thus marked by every act which may define a tyrant is unfit to be the ruler of a free people.

Nor have we been wanting in our attentions to our British brethren. We have warned them, from time to time, of attempts by their legislature to extend an unwarrantable jurisdiction over us. We have reminded them of the circumstances of our emigration and settlement here. We have appealed to their native justice and <u>magnanimity</u>; and we have conjured them, by the ties of our common kindred, to disavow these usurpations, which would inevitably interrupt our connections and correspondence. They, too, have been deaf to the voice of justice and of consanguinity.[5] We must, therefore, <u>acquiesce</u> in the necessity which

---

3. **mercenaries.** Hired soldiers
4. **perfidy.** Betrayal of trust
5. **consanguinity.** Close connection; relatedness

words for everyday use

in • sur • rec • tion (in′sə rek′shən) *n.*, uprising. *In 1913, Irish patriots took over the Dublin Post Office, but British troops put down the <u>insurrection</u>.*
re • dress (rē′dres′) *n.*, compensation. *Mrs. Blount demanded <u>redress</u> from the driver who dented her car.*
mag • na • nim • i • ty (mag′nə nim′ə tē) *n.*, state of being above pettiness. *A good leader treats the people with <u>magnanimity</u>.*
ac • qui • esce (ak′wē es′) *vi.*, agree without protest. *We asked the people next door to turn down their music, but they would not <u>acquiesce</u> to our request.*

denounces our separation; and hold them, as we hold the rest of mankind, enemies in war, in peace friends.

We, Therefore, the Representatives of the United States of America, in General Congress assembled, appealing to the Supreme Judge of the world for the rectitude of our intentions, do, in the name and by the authority of the good people of these colonies, solemnly publish and declare, That these United Colonies are, and of right ought to be, Free and Independent States; that they are absolved from all allegiance to the British crown, and that all political connection between them and the state of Great Britain is, and ought to be, totally dissolved; and that, as free and independent states, they have full power to levy war, conclude peace, contract alliances, establish commerce, and to do all other acts and things which independent states may of right do. And, for the support of this declaration, with a firm reliance on the protection of Divine Providence, we mutually pledge to each other our lives, our fortunes, and our sacred honor. ∎

Read Aloud

Read the highlighted lines aloud. Summarize the point of this statement.

Note the Facts

What are the signers willing to give up in support of this declaration?

_____
_____
_____

words for everyday use

rec • ti • tude (rek´ tə tüd´) *n.*, correctness. *The judge will determine the rectitude of your case.*

Reflect ON YOUR READING

After Reading → SHARE YOUR CONNECTIONS

❑ Share the main ideas you identified with your partner, and discuss how these points are related to the purpose.
❑ Write a summary of the Declaration of Independence.

_____
_____
_____
_____
_____

Reading Skills and Test Practice

IDENTIFY AUTHOR'S PURPOSE

Discuss with your partner how to answer questions about the authors' purpose. Use the Think-Aloud Notes to write down your reasons for eliminating the incorrect answers.

____1. What is the purpose of the Declaration of Independence?
    a. to identify the rights of all people
    b. to complain about wrongs done to the colonies
    c. to dissolve the bonds between the colonies and Great Britain
    d. to persuade the king to free the colonies

____2. How does the first paragraph relate to the purpose of the document?
    a. It contains the most direct declaration of independence in the piece.
    b. It identifies the purpose and some of the reasons for dissolving bonds with Great Britain.
    c. It tries to persuade the king that he has wronged the colonies.
    d. It explains the arguments that led up to the decision to declare independence.

How did using the reading strategy help you to answer the questions?

_____
_____
_____
_____

THINK-ALOUD NOTES

Investigate, Inquire, and Imagine

RECALL: GATHER FACTS
1a. What is an "unalienable" right? What rights does Jefferson consider unalienable?

INTERPRET: FIND MEANING
1b. How does the Declaration help protect unalienable rights?

ANALYZE: TAKE THINGS APART
2a. Into how many sections is the Declaration of Independence divided? What is the purpose of each section?

SYNTHESIZE: BRING THINGS TOGETHER
2b. How does this document reflect John Locke's idea that people are born with "natural rights" that cannot be taken away from them, and Jean-Jacques Rousseau's belief that government is a social contract entered into by the people for their protection and well-being?

EVALUATE: MAKE JUDGMENTS
3a. Draw your own conclusions about how the Declaration of Independence was received by King George.

EXTEND: CONNECT IDEAS
3b. How good a job is the government doing today at protecting Americans' "unalienable rights"? What debates have you heard recently about these rights?

Literary Tools

PARALLELISM. **Parallelism** is a rhetorical technique in which a writer emphasizes the equal value or weight of two or more ideas by expressing them in the same grammatical form. Map the way Jefferson uses parallelism in his presentation of the grievances against King George. Fill in the chart with examples of unlawful jurisdiction of the British, working from the section in which Jefferson uses parallel structure by starting each clause with the word *for*. Add circles as necessary.

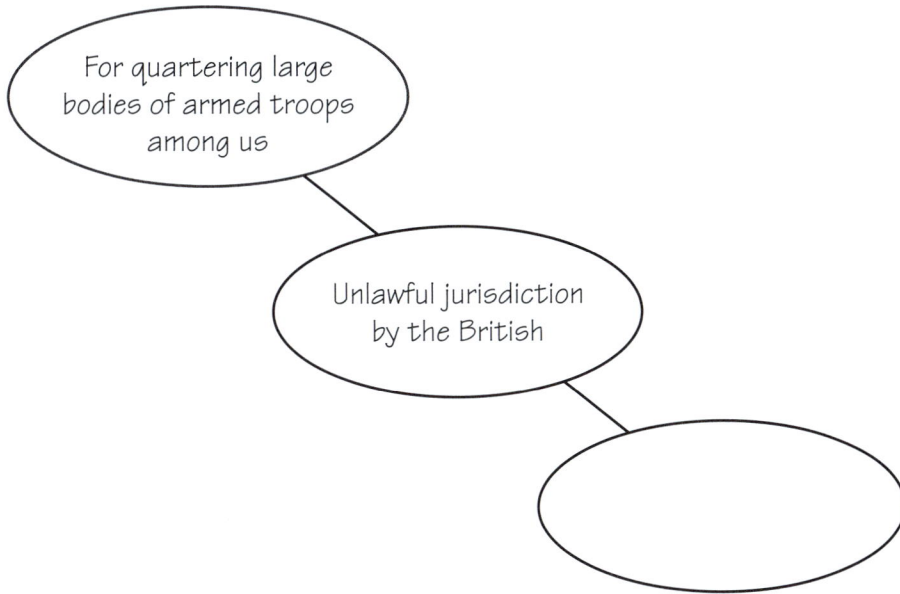

WordWorkshop

SEMANTIC FEATURE ANALYSIS. **Semantic feature analysis** can help you explore how related words differ from one another. Use the Semantic Feature Chart below to examine the differences between the following terms of agreement. Use a dictionary if necessary to understand the connotations of any words you are unsure of. Consider whether each feature applies to each term. Put a plus sign for "yes" and a minus sign for "no."

Terms of agreement	Agree under pressure	Accept with enthusiasm	Related to opinions or propositions	Related to will or feelings
Agreement				
Accede				
Acquiesce				
Assent				
Compliance				
Consent				
Subscribe				

When you are done, explain the similarities and differences among the terms.

Read-Write Connection

Write a personal declaration of independence. State why you are declaring independence and what you are willing to give up to attain your freedom.

Beyond the Reading

RESEARCH THE BILL OF RIGHTS. The Bill of Rights, the first ten amendments to the Constitution, outline the rights of individual citizens. Find and read the Bill of Rights. Then choose one that is especially important to you. Write an essay or speech explaining why this amendment is important. Draw upon personal experience or current events to illustrate your point.

GO ONLINE. To find links and additional activities for this selection, visit the EMC Internet Resource Center at **emcp.com/languagearts** and click on Write-In Reader.

"The Susan B. Anthony Dollar"

Active READING STRATEGY

WRITE THINGS DOWN

Before Reading ➤ MAKE A PLAN

- ❑ Read the Reader's Resource. Look at the picture of the Susan B. Anthony coin on page 378. Jot down your preliminary thoughts about the selection in the Main Ideas Chart.
- ❑ Decide how you will write down information as you read. You may want to highlight or underline key information or use the graphic organizer that follows.

Graphic Organizer: Main Ideas Chart

Part of Selection	Main Idea
Prereading	
Paragraph 1	
Paragraph 2	
Paragraph 3	
Paragraph 4	
Paragraph 5	
Paragraph 6	

CONNECT

Reader's resource

Susan B. Anthony fought for women's suffrage. She cast an illegal vote in the presidential election of 1872. The nineteenth amendment to the Constitution, sometimes called the Susan B. Anthony amendment, gave women the right to vote in 1920, fourteen years after Anthony's death. Anthony was commemorated on a dollar coin minted from 1979 to 1981. The article "**The Susan B. Anthony Dollar**" discusses the history of the coin.

Reader's journal

If a new coin were created, what American do you think should be pictured on it? Why?

_____
_____
_____
_____
_____
_____

UNIT 8 / READING INFORMATIONAL AND VISUAL MEDIA   377

During Reading

WRITE THINGS DOWN AS YOU READ

❑ Listen as your teacher reads the first paragraph aloud. What is the main idea of this paragraph? Underline or highlight key words and phrases. Write the main idea of the paragraph in the Main Ideas Chart.

❑ Continue reading on your own. Keep marking key words and phrases and writing main ideas in your chart.

NOTE THE FACTS

To what cause did Susan B. Anthony dedicate her life?

_____
_____

FIX-UP IDEA

Refocus
If you are having trouble identifying main ideas, try refocusing. First, write down what you know about the Susan B. Anthony dollar. Then write down two or three questions that you have about the coin. As you read, try to find answers to your questions.

The Susan B. Anthony Dollar

On October 10, 1978, President Jimmy Carter signed into law the Susan B. Anthony Dollar Act, authorizing the United States Mint to manufacture small-sized dollars, dated 1979 to 1981. The historical significance of Susan B. Anthony's portrait on the silver dollar lies in her contributions to the women's movement. The coin symbolizes the long and difficult struggle of American women to obtain equal rights, a struggle to which Susan B. Anthony dedicated her life.

The United States Mint and the Treasury Department originally intended the new dollar coin to carry a "Flowing Hair Liberty" instead of Anthony's portrait. A political controversy erupted when Representative Mary Rose Oakar introduced a bill providing for the portrait of Susan B. Anthony. For more than 115 years, the only female images to appear on coins had been allegorical female figures known simply as "Miss Liberty." The only male figures to appear on currency had all been United States presidents. Despite opposition, both houses of Congress approved the use of Anthony's portrait.

The Anthony dollar quickly earned the nickname the "mini-dollar," since it was 30 percent smaller than its predecessor, the Eisenhower dollar. The creation of a smaller coin was primarily an economic consideration. The Treasury Department estimated that replacing the Eisenhower dollar with mini-dollars would result in savings of 4.5 million dollars. Even greater savings were projected by replacing circulating

378   THE EMC WRITE-IN READER

paper dollar notes with the mini-dollar coin, since the dollar coin would have a 15-year estimated service life, while a $1 note had only an 18-month life span. It was also intended to broaden the scope of the vending machine industry and increase efficiency of automated coin returns for cashiers. Its eleven-sided inner border was designed to provide physical recognition for the visually challenged.

The American Banker's Association opposed the production of the coin, however, fearing that the Treasury did not have an adequate plan to promote the circulation of the coin. While representatives of the vending-machine industry endorsed the concept of a smaller dollar coin, they failed to convert equipment to accommodate the new coin.

Hindsight proved the bankers' concerns to be justified when the coin failed to catch on with the public. Many people rejected the Anthony dollar because they confused it with the quarter, and the majority of vending machines did not accept the new coin. Production of Susan B. Anthony dollars ceased in 1981.

By the late 1990s, the reserves of the Susan B. Anthony dollar were running low and the U.S. Mint determined that a new dollar coin was needed. In December 1997, Congress passed a law entitled "The United States Dollar Coin Act of 1997," to create a new dollar coin. To learn about the process of selecting and designing the new Sacagawea dollar coin, visit http://www.usmint.gov/, the Internet site of the United States Mint. ■

Literary TOOLS

ARTICLE. An **article** is a brief work of nonfiction on a specific topic. The term *article* typically refers to encyclopedia entries and short nonfiction works that appear in newspapers and magazines. What is the topic of this article?

_____

_____

MARK THE TEXT

Highlight or underline two reasons why the Susan B. Anthony dollar didn't catch on.

THINK AND REFLECT

What steps could be taken to make the Sacagawea dollar more popular than the Susan B. Anthony dollar? **(Apply)**

_____

_____

_____

Reflect ON YOUR READING

After Reading ➤ SUMMARIZE WHAT YOU WROTE

❑ Discuss with a partner the main ideas you wrote in your Main Ideas Chart. Talk about the overall main idea of the article.
❑ Write a one-paragraph summary of the article.

_____
_____
_____
_____

Reading Skills and Test Practice

IDENTIFY MAIN IDEAS

Discuss with a partner how to answer questions that require you to identify main ideas. Use the Think-Aloud Notes to write down your reasons for eliminating the incorrect answers.

____1. Why wasn't the Susan B. Anthony dollar a success?
  a. The coin was worth less than a dollar bill.
  b. Not enough of them were made.
  c. The treasury did not promote circulation.
  d. People were upset that Susan B. Anthony was pictured on the coin.

____2. What do Susan B. Anthony and Sacagawea have in common?
  a. Both of them fought for women's rights.
  b. Both are pictured on dollar coins.
  c. Both are considered allegories of liberty.
  d. They are the most recognizable women in American history.

How did using the reading strategy help you to answer the questions?

_____
_____
_____

THINK-ALOUD NOTES

_____
_____
_____
_____
_____
_____
_____
_____
_____

Investigate, Inquire, and Imagine

RECALL: GATHER FACTS
1a. Who was originally supposed to be pictured on the small-sized dollar coin authorized in 1978?

INTERPRET: FIND MEANING
1b. Why was the decision to put Susan B. Anthony on a coin controversial?

ANALYZE: TAKE THINGS APART
2a. List reasons for the creation of the small-sized dollar coin. List reasons the coin did not catch on.

SYNTHESIZE: BRING THINGS TOGETHER
2b. What could have been done differently to make the coin a success?

EVALUATE: MAKE JUDGMENTS
3a. Judge how successful the Sacagawea dollar coin is.

EXTEND: CONNECT IDEAS
3b. Do you think the Sacagawea dollar coin will catch on better than previous dollar coins? Why?

Literary Tools

ARTICLE. An **article** is a brief work of nonfiction on a specific topic. The term *article* typically refers to encyclopedia entries and short nonfiction works that appear in newspapers and popular magazines. What do you think would be an appropriate place to publish for this article? Why?

_____
_____
_____
_____
_____

WordWorkshop

PREFIXES. Using word parts can help you find the meaning of unfamiliar words. **Prefixes** are word parts that come at the beginning of words. Look at the chart below to find the meaning of some common prefixes.

Prefix or Suffix	Meaning
auto–	self
pre–	before

Then give the meaning of each of the following words from the selection and write a sentence using each word.

1. **predecessor** _____

   _____

2. **automated** _____

   _____

Identify two other words with each prefix.

1. **auto–** _____

   _____

2. **pre–** _____

   _____

Read-Write Connection

Do you think Sacagawea deserved to be depicted on a coin? Why, or why not?

_____

_____

Beyond the Reading

TAKE AN ONLINE TOUR. The house where Susan B. Anthony lived from 1866 until her death in 1906 is now a museum in Rochester, New York, called the **Susan B. Anthony House**. Visit the website of the museum, **http://www.susanbanthonyhouse.org/**, and take the online tour. Make a list of important facts about Susan B. Anthony.

GO ONLINE. To find links and additional activities for this selection, visit the EMC Internet Resource Center at **emcp.com/languagearts** and click on Write-In Reader.

FROM *THE BIG MONEY*, "Newsreel LXVIII"
THE THIRD VOLUME IN THE TRILOGY *U.S.A.*

by John Dos Passos

Active READING STRATEGY

USE TEXT ORGANIZATION

Before Reading ➤ PREVIEW ORGANIZATION

- ❑ Read about collage in the Reader's Resource. The selection you are about to read is pieced together from a variety of media.
- ❑ Scan the selection. You will see different kinds of type—all capitals or italics. The changing type will help you recognize when a different type of material is being introduced. For example, the italicized bits are parts of a song, while the capitalized bits are headlines. Other bits are mostly excerpts from newspaper articles. Keep this in mind as you read.
- ❑ Preview the graphic organizer below. As you read, you will use the Connections Chart to identify types of media, interpret meaning, and make connections among the ideas in "Newsreel LXVIII."

Graphic Organizer: Connections Chart

Type of Media	Meaning	Connection

CONNECT

Reader's resource

"Newsreel LXVIII" is a literary **collage**. It uses allusions, quotations, bits of song, headlines, and other materials. John Dos Passos created the form of the literary newsreel based on newsreels that used to be shown before movies. "Newsreel LXVIII" focuses on issues related to the Great Depression of the 1930s. During this time, millions of Americans were without work and facing severe economic hardship. At the time, strong and sometimes violent conflicts arose between those who felt that government should help and those who felt that it should not.

Word watch

PREVIEW VOCABULARY

disbar
hem
ideology
indefinite
meddling
placard
pontoon
propagandist
rickety
solidarity
tallowy

Reader's journal

What headlines, song lyrics, phrases, and slogans have you been exposed to today? Why do they tell you about contemporary American culture?

UNIT 8 / READING INFORMATIONAL AND VISUAL MEDIA 383

FROM *THE BIG MONEY*

Newsreel LXVIII

John Dos Passos

WALL STREET STUNNED

*This is not Thirtyeight, but it's old Ninetyseven
You must put her in Center on time*[1]

MARKET SURE TO RECOVER FROM SLUMP

DECLINE IN CONTRACTS

POLICE TURN MACHINE GUNS ON
COLORADO MINE STRIKERS KILL 5 WOUND 40

sympathizers appeared on the scene just as thousands of office workers were pouring out of the buildings at the lunch hour. As they raised their placard high and started an indefinite march from one side to the other, they were jeered and hooted not only by the office workers but also by workmen on a building under construction

---

1. **This is not . . . on time.** This is a line from the railroad ballad "The Wreck of the Old Ninety-Seven," which immortalized the wreck of train number 97 on the Southern Railway in Danville, Virginia, in 1909. One recording of such a railroad ballad sold over a million copies in the 1920s, making it one of the earliest pop singles.

words for everyday use
plac • ard (pla′ kärd; pla′ kərd) *n.*, notice for display in a public place; sign. *The placard directed us to the festival entrance.*
in • def • i • nite (in def′ ə nit) *adj.*, having no exact limits. *George prepared food for an indefinite number of guests, since he wasn't sure how many people would show up for his party.*

NEW METHODS OF SELLING SEEN

RESCUE CREWS TRY TO UPEND ILL-FATED CRAFT
WHILE WAITING FOR PONTOONS

> *He looked 'round an' said to his black greasy fireman*
>   *Jus' shovel in a little more coal*
> *And when we cross that White Oak Mountain*
> 20   *You can watch your Ninety-seven roll*

I find your column interesting and need advice. I have saved four thousand dollars which I want to invest for a better income. Do you think I might buy stocks?

POLICE KILLER FLICKS CIGARETTE AS HE GOES
TREMBLING TO DOOM

PLAY AGENCIES IN RING OF SLAVE GIRL MARTS

MAKER OF LOVE DISBARRED AS LAWYER

> *Oh the right wing clothesmakers*
> *And the Socialist fakers*
> 30   *They make by the workers . . .*
> *Double cross*
>
> *They preach Social-ism*
> *But practice Fasc-ism*
> *To keep capitalism*
> *By the boss*[2]

MOSCOW CONGRESS OUSTS OPPOSITION

> *It's a mighty rough road from Lynchburg to Danville*
>   *An' a line on a three mile grade*
> *It was on that grade he lost his average*
> 40   *An' you see what a jump he made*

---

2. **Oh the . . . By the boss.** Socialist labor-union protest song that is interspersed throughout the work

words for everyday use
pon • toon (pän tün´) *n.*, flat-bottomed boat; floating object used for support. *The airplane was able to land on water by floating on its pontoons.*
dis • bar (dis bär´) *vt.*, deprive (a lawyer) of the right to practice law. *The lawyer was disbarred for embezzling funds from his client.*

Reading TIP

The highlighted text on this page continues the song about the "old Ninety-seven" that began on page 384.

Literary TOOLS

COLLAGE. In literature, a **collage** is a work that incorporates or brings together an odd assortment of materials, such as allusions, quotations, bits of song, dialogue, foreign words, mythical or folkloric elements, headlines, and pictures or other graphic devices. What kinds of materials do you find on this page of the collage?

_____

_____

_____

THINK AND REFLECT

Why do you think Dos Passos weaves the song about the "old Ninety-seven" throughout this work? What themes does it suggest? **(Infer)**

_____

_____

_____

THINK AND REFLECT

What might the "rescue of men" have referred to in the newspaper headline? What other meaning might it have in this work? **(Interpret)**

_____
_____
_____

NOTE THE FACTS

What happened to the driver of the "old Ninety-seven"?

_____
_____
_____

THINK AND REFLECT

What does Dos Passos suggest about the president's view by juxtaposing it with these song lyrics? **(Infer)**

_____
_____
_____

MILL THUGS IN MURDER RAID

here is the most dangerous example of how at the decisive moment the bourgeois <u>ideology</u> liquidates class <u>solidarity</u> and turns a friend of the workingclass of yesterday into a most miserable <u>propagandist</u> for imperialism[3] today

RED[4] PICKETS FINED FOR PROTEST HERE

We leave our home in the morning
    We kiss our children goodbye

OFFICIALS STILL HOPE FOR RESCUE OF MEN

50 *He was goin' downgrade makin' ninety miles an hour*
    When his whistle broke into a scream
    He was found in the wreck with his hand on the throttle
    An' was scalded to death with the steam

RADICALS FIGHT WITH CHAIRS AT UNITY MEETING

PATROLMEN PROTECT REDS
U.S. CHAMBER OF COMMERCE
URGES CONFIDENCE
REAL VALUES UNHARMED

While we slave for the bosses
60   *Our children scream an' cry*
    But when we draw our money
    Our grocery bills to pay

PRESIDENT SEES PROSPERITY NEAR

Not a cent to spend for clothing
    Not a cent to lay away

---

3. **imperialism.** Policy or practice of seeking to dominate the economic or political affairs of underdeveloped areas or weaker countries
4. **red.** Political radical or reactionary, especially a communist

words for everyday use

i • de • ol • o • gy (ī´dē äl´ə gē) *n.*, doctrine, opinion, or way of thinking. Communism and capitalism are economic <u>ideologies</u> that propose very different ways of distributing wealth.
sol • i • dar • i • ty (säl´ə dar´ə tē) *n.*, combination or agreement of all elements or individuals. Due to their <u>solidarity</u>, the striking pilots were able to force management to meet their demands.
prop • a • gan • dist (präp´ə gan´dist) *n.*, one who spreads ideas for a particular cause. The <u>propagandist</u> issued statements encouraging Americans to buy the expensive running shoes.

STEAMROLLER IN ACTION AGAINST MILITANTS

MINERS BATTLE SCABS[5]

But we cannot buy for our children
   Our wages are too low
Now listen to me you workers
   Both you women and men
Let us win for them the victory
   I'm sure it ain't no sin

CARILLON PEALS IN SINGING TOWER[6]

the President declared it was impossible to view the increased advantages for the many without smiling at those who a short time ago expressed so much fear lest our country might come under the control of a few individuals of great wealth.

HAPPY CROWDS THRONG CEREMONY

on a tiny island nestling like a green jewel in the lake that mirrors the singing tower, the President today participated in the dedication of a bird sanctuary and its pealing carillon, fulfilling the dream of an immigrant boy

The Camera Eye (51)

at the head of the valley in the dark of the hills on the broken floor of a lurchedover[7] cabin a man halfsits halflies propped up by an old woman two wrinkled girls that might be young   chunks of coal flare in the hearth flicker in his face white and sagging as dough   blacken the cavedin mouth the taut throat the belly swelled enormous with the wound he got working on the minetipple[8]

the barefoot girl brings him a tincup of water   the woman wipes sweat off his streaming face with a dirty

---

5. **scabs.** Derogatory term for workers who refuse to join a union, or who work for lower wages or under different conditions than those accepted by the union; workers who refuse to strike or who take the place of a striking worker

6. **carillon . . . singing tower.** *Carillon*—set of stationary bells, each producing one tone of the chromatic scale; *singing tower*—the Spring Tower erected in Florida; President Calvin Coolidge spoke at the dedication of the tower in 1929.

7. **lurchedover.** Dos Passos has run together the words *lurched* and *over*. The selection contains several more run-together words.

8. **minetipple.** Equipment that tips cars in a coal mine to unload the coal

denim sleeve   the firelight flares in his eyes stretched big with fever in the women's scared eyes and in the blanched faces of the foreigners

without help in the valley <u>hemmed</u> by dark strike-silent hills the man will die (my father died we know what it is like to see a man die) the women will lay him out on the <u>rickety</u> cot the miners will bury him

100   in the jail it's light too hot the steamheat hisses we talk through the greenpainted iron bars to a tall white mustachioed old man some smiling miners in shirtsleeves a boy   faces white from mining have already the <u>tallowy</u> look of jailfaces

foreigners what can we say to the dead?   foreigners what can we say to the jailed?   the representative of the political party talks fast through the bars join up with us and no other union we'll send you tobacco candy solidarity our lawyers will write briefs speakers will shout your names at
110   meetings they'll carry your names on cardboard on picketlines   the men in jail shrug their shoulders smile thinly our eyes look in their eyes through the bars

what can I say?   (in another continent I have seen the faces looking out through the barred basement windows behind the ragged sentry's boots I have seen before day the straggling footsore prisoners herded through the streets limping between bayonets   heard the volley

I have seen the dead lying out in those distant deeper valleys)   what can we say to the jailed?

120   in the law's office we stand against the wall the law is a big man with eyes angry in a big pumpkinface   who sits and stares at us <u>meddling</u> foreigners through the door the deputies crane with their guns   they stand guard at the mines

words for everyday use

hem (hem) *adj.,* encircle; surround. *The mansion was <u>hemmed</u> in by a wall that kept out intruders.*
rick • e • ty (rik´it ē) *adj.,* shaky. *The <u>rickety</u> fire escape was replaced.*
tal • low • y (tal´ō ē) *adj.,* fatty and pale. *<u>Tallowy</u> clumps of congealed lard floated on the dishwater.*
med • dling (med´liŋ) *adj.,* interfering; concerning oneself with other people's affairs without being asked. *Christopher's <u>meddling</u> personality would not allow him to stay out of other people's problems.*

they blockade the miners' soupkitchens they've cut off the road up the valley   the hiredmen with guns stand ready to shoot (they have made us foreigners in the land where we were born they are the conquering army that has filtered into the country unnoticed they have taken the hilltops by stealth they levy toll they stand at the minehead   they stand at the polls   they stand by when the bailiffs carry the furniture of the family evicted from the city tenement out on the sidewalk they are there when the bankers foreclose[9] on a farm they are ambushed and ready to shoot down the strikers marching behind the flag up the switchback road to the mine   those that the guns spare they jail)

the law stares across the desk out of angry eyes his face reddens in splotches like a gobbler's neck with the strut of the power of submachine guns sawedoffshotguns teargas and vomitinggas the power that can feed you or leave you to starve

sits easy at his desk his back is covered he feels strong behind him he feels the prosecutingattorney the judge an owner himself the political boss the minesuperintendent the board of directors   the president of the utility the manipulator of the holdingcompany

he lifts his hand towards the telephone

the deputies crowd in the door

we have only words against ■

---

9. **foreclose.** Legally force someone to sell their farm because they are unable to pay their debts

NOTE THE FACTS

What powers does the law have? Who supports the law?

_____

_____

_____

Reflect ON YOUR READING

After Reading → SUMMARIZE AND SHARE CONNECTIONS

- ❏ Share your Connections Chart with a few of your classmates.
- ❏ If you had trouble making connections among some elements of the collage, talk with your group about how to figure out the meaning of these sections.
- ❏ Use the Investigate, Inquire, and Imagine questions on page 391 to help you focus on issues in the selection.

Reading Skills and Test Practice

IDENTIFY A THEME

Discuss with a partner how to answer questions that require you to identify theme. Use the Think-Aloud Notes to write down your reasons for eliminating the incorrect answers.

____1. Which of the following is *not* a major theme in "Newsreel LXVIII"?
   a. the effects of the Great Depression on working-class people
   b. solidarity of the powerful oppressing the poor
   c. the importance of preserving natural resources
   d. prejudice against foreigners.

____2. What best summarizes the overall theme of the selection?
   a. The law has too much power.
   b. The working class often has to do dangerous jobs and many people die as a result.
   c. The country was facing social and economic disaster but was starting to see some change for the positive.
   d. A few people control the wealth and power, which has major effects on the lives of individuals.

How did using the reading strategy help you to answer the questions?

_____
_____
_____
_____

THINK-ALOUD NOTES

Investigate, Inquire, and Imagine

RECALL: GATHER FACTS
1a. What did the workers say they wanted for their families?

INTERPRET: FIND MEANING
1b. Why couldn't workers buy what their families needed?

ANALYZE: TAKE THINGS APART
2a. Identify the principal themes that are raised throughout "Newsreel LXVIII."

SYNTHESIZE: BRING THINGS TOGETHER
2b. What overall point do the materials selected by Dos Passos make?

EVALUATE: MAKE JUDGMENTS
3a. How effective is the newsreel structure in presenting a portrait of life at a particular time?

EXTEND: CONNECT IDEAS
3b. What themes would you cover in a collage about contemporary American society?

WordWorkshop

VOCABULARY COLLAGE. In the space below, create a vocabulary collage of the Words for Everyday Use from the selection. You may use words, parts of words, prefixes or suffixes, pronunciations, parts of speech, definitions, contextual sentences, and images to represent the words. You may handwrite the words or cut out letters from newspapers or magazines. You may draw images or cut them out from other sources.

Literary Tools

COLLAGE. In literature, a **collage** is a work that incorporates or brings together an odd assortment of materials, such as allusions, quotations, bits of song, dialogue, foreign words, mythical or folkloric elements, headlines, and pictures or other graphic devices. Review your Connections Chart. Which material used by Dos Passos in "Newsreel LXVIII" has the most impact in expressing the selection's theme?

_____
_____
_____
_____

Read-Write Connection

If you were a mineworker in the 1930s, do you think Dos Passos would be sympathetic to your poor working conditions? Why, or why not?

_____
_____
_____
_____
_____
_____
_____

Beyond the Reading

MAKE A COLLAGE. Use the collage structure to create an impression of the current year. Use headlines, editorials, newspaper columns, letters to the editor, song lyrics, advertisements, and images of people in various situations. Try to follow the approach used in "Newsreel LXVIII," juxtaposing elements in a thoughtful and thought-provoking way.

GO ONLINE. To find links and additional activities for this selection, visit the EMC Internet Resource Center at **emcp.com/languagearts** and click on Write-In Reader.

Unit 8

Choose and Use Reading Strategies

Before reading the excerpt below, review with a partner how to use each of these reading strategies with informational and visual media.

1. Read with a Purpose
2. Connect to Prior Knowledge
3. Write Things Down
4. Make Predictions
5. Visualize
6. Use Text Organization
7. Tackle Difficult Vocabulary
8. Monitor Your Reading Progress

Now apply at least two of these reading strategies as you read the excerpt from "The New England Renaissance (1800–1860)." Use the margins and mark up the text to show how you are using the reading strategies to read actively. After you finish reading the excerpt, fill in the time line on page 394 with the dates and events mentioned.

> **Social Expansion and Democratization**
>
> After the **Louisiana Purchase** of 1803, which doubled the size of the country, the United States expanded rapidly across the continent. By 1836, the original thirteen colonies had grown into twenty-five states, stretching as far west as Arkansas. Two important technological developments helped to make that expansion seem less daunting. The invention of the telegraph by **Samuel Morse** in 1838 made it possible to communicate across distances instantly. The introduction of the steam locomotive by **John Stevens** in 1825 made possible the development of a railway system to connect towns and cities across the vast country. By the 1850s, the East Coast was connected to Chicago by rail and beyond that to the western side of the Mississippi. Still, while industrial transformation was well under way in various parts of the East, the rest of the country remained predominantly agricultural, with many new farms springing up in the new territories.

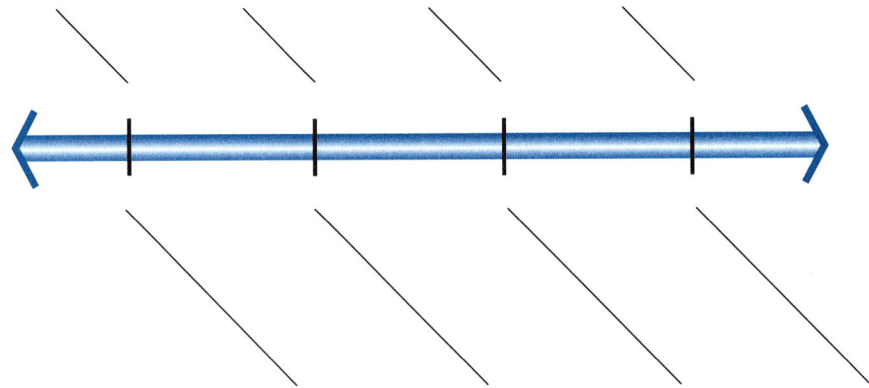

Literary Tools

Select the best literary element on the right to complete each sentence on the left. Write the correct letter in the blank.

_____ 1. "Thy love is such I can no way repay / The heavens reward thee manifold, I pray" is a(n) _____.

_____ 2. A(n) _____ is a brief work of nonfiction; "The Susan B. Anthony Dollar" is an example.

_____ 3. A(n) _____ combines a variety of materials, including headlines, bits of dialogue, song lyrics, and allusions.

_____ 4. De las Casas uses third-person _____ to separate himself from the Spaniards he discusses.

_____ 5. Thomas Jefferson used _____ in the Declaration of Independence to stress the equal value of the grievances of the king against the colonies.

a. article, 379, 381

b. collage, 383, 392

c. couplet, 363, 365

d. parallelism, 370, 375

e. point of view, 356, 359

WordWorkshop

UNIT 8 WORDS FOR EVERYDAY USE

abdicate, 371
acquiesce, 372
assent, 369
buffet, 354
burnish, 357
compliance, 369
convulsion, 370
depopulate, 353
disbar, 385
evince, 369
flourish, 354
hem, 388
ideology, 386
indefinite, 384
inestimable, 369
infest, 356
inhuman, 354
insurrection, 372
magnanimity, 372
meddling, 388
naturalization, 370
oppression, 353
placard, 384
pontoon, 385
propagandist, 386
rectitude, 373
redress, 372
rickety, 388
ruffian, 355
solidarity, 386
subjection, 353
sufferance, 369
suffice, 353
tallowy, 388
tenure, 370
transient, 369
unalienable, 368
usurpation, 369
vestige, 355

MNEMONIC DEVICES. A **mnemonic device** is a catchy phrase or striking image that helps you remember information. For example, you may have heard the phrase "the principal is your pal" to help you remember to use *principal* instead of *principle* for the leader of a school. Vocabulary mnemonics can be sayings, drawings, or jingles.

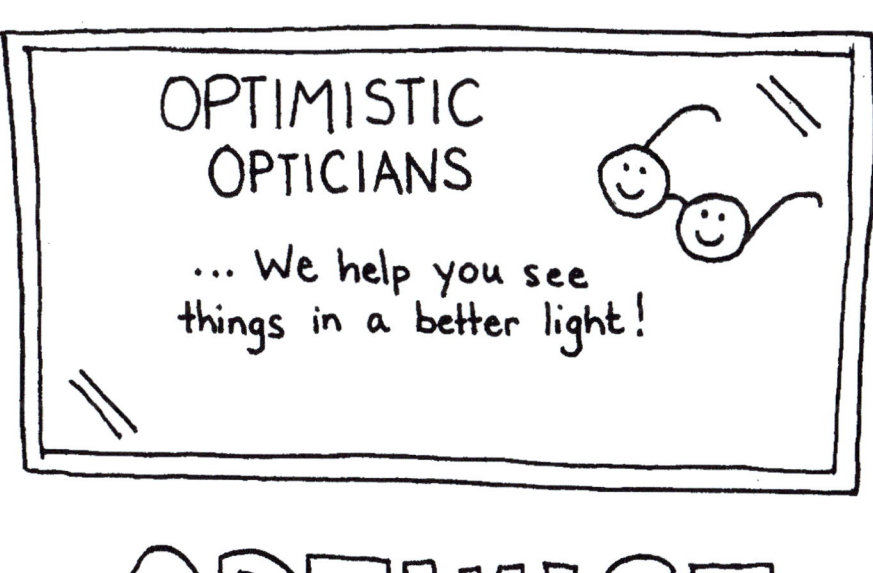

Work with a partner or small group to create mnemonic devices for ten of the Words for Everyday Use listed above.

On Your Own

FLUENTLY SPEAKING. Deliver an extemporaneous speech about human rights, injustices in the world, or equality. Think about the inalienable rights identified in the Declaration of Independence, the inhumane treatment of the natives in de las Casas's *Relation,* and Susan B. Anthony's struggle for the right to vote. Consider the struggle for rights and justice today. Choose one example for the focus of your speech, or use several examples to make your point.

PICTURE THIS. Make a visual collage about the world today. In your collage, you may want to include photographs of people, places, or events; drawings or sketches; splashes of color that create a mood; headlines, bits of news stories, or song lyrics; small objects; or other materials. Share your collage with your class. Talk about why you included certain items.

PUT IT IN WRITING. Choose a topic of interest to you. Write an article for a magazine or newspaper about your topic. You may need to do some research to help you write the article. Add photographs, charts, diagrams, or other graphics to add interest to your article or to help explain things.

Unit NINE

Developing Vocabulary Skills

TACKLING DIFFICULT VOCABULARY AS YOU READ

To understand what you read, you need a set of tools for dealing with words you don't know. Glossaries and footnotes, context clues, prior knowledge of word parts and word families, and dictionaries are tools that can help you unlock the meaning of unfamiliar words.

Using Definitions, Footnotes, Endnotes, and Glossaries

Some textbooks, like this one, provide **definitions** of selected words on the page on which the word is used. **Footnotes**, like definitions, also appear on the same page as the words to which they refer. Specifically, footnotes appear at the foot, or bottom, of a page and are numbered to correspond to the words or phrases they explain. Sometimes footnotes cite a source of information. Other times they define uncommon words and phrases. If you see a superscripted number next to a word in the text you are reading (*martinet*[6]), but can't find the footnote at the foot of the page, check the end of the article, chapter, or book. A footnote that comes at the end of a document is called an **endnote**. A **glossary** is an alphabetized list of important words and their definitions. Glossaries usually appear at the end of an article, a chapter, or a book.

To use definitions, footnotes, endnotes, and glossaries, follow these steps:

1. Read the paragraph or short section containing the unfamiliar word to get a sense of the meaning.
2. Check the definition, footnote, endnote, or glossary entry for the word.
3. Reread the paragraph or section, this time keeping in mind the definition of the new word.

MARK THE TEXT

Underline or highlight four text features that might provide definitions of unfamiliar words.

Using Context Clues

You can often figure out the meaning of an unfamiliar word by using context clues. **Context clues**, or hints you gather from the words and sentences around the unfamiliar word, prevent you from having to look up every unknown word in the dictionary. The chart below defines the types of context clues and gives you an example of each. It also lists words that signal each type of clue.

THINK AND REFLECT

If a text reads, "Yesterday the lake was rough and dangerous, but today it is completely *placid*," what do you think *placid* means? **(Apply)**

_____

_____

_____

Context Clues

comparison clue	shows a comparison, or how the unfamiliar word is like something that might be familiar to you
signal words	*and, like, as, just as, as if, as though*

EXAMPLE
As she *ruminates* over which college she should attend, Candice reminds me of a statue by Auguste Rodin called *The Thinker*. (If Candice looks like something called *The Thinker*, she must be deep in thought, so *ruminates* must mean "thinks or contemplates deeply.")

contrast clue	shows that something contrasts, or differs in meaning, from something else
signal words	*but, nevertheless, on the other hand, however, although, though, in spite of*

EXAMPLE
Devon reacts with *magnanimity* even when everyone around him is resorting to pettiness and judgment. (The words *even when* suggest that Devon's reaction contrasts with what would be expected of him. In other words, he resists the pettiness and judgment around him. *Magnanimity* must mean something like "being above pettiness.")

restatement clue	uses different words to express the same idea
signal words	*that is, in other words, or*

EXAMPLE
Can you *distill* the chemistry lecture for me? I just want to know the most important points. (The second sentence indicates that *distill* means "reduce to the most essential parts.")

examples clue	gives examples of other items to illustrate the meaning of something
signal words	*including, such as, for example, for instance, especially, particularly*

EXAMPLE
Greg is interested in all sorts of *celestial* beings, including angels, seraphs, and cherubims. (If you know what angels, seraphs, and cherubims are, you can tell that *celestial* means "relating to heaven or divinity.")

CONTINUED

cause-and-effect clue	tells you that something happened as a result of something else
signal words	*if/then, when/then, thus, therefore, because, so, as a result of, consequently*

EXAMPLE

In Minnesota, warm, pleasant weather is so *ephemeral* that everyone wants to be outside while it lasts. (If one has to rush to take advantage of warm weather "while it lasts," *ephemeral* must mean "short-lived.")

Using Your Prior Knowledge

You can often use your knowledge of word parts and other words to help you figure out the meaning of a new word.

BREAKING WORDS INTO BASE WORDS, WORD ROOTS, PREFIXES, AND SUFFIXES

Many words are formed by adding prefixes and suffixes to main word parts called **base words** (if they can stand alone) or **word roots** (if they can't). A **prefix** is a letter or group of letters added to the beginning of a word to change its meaning. A **suffix** is a letter or group of letters added to the end of a word to change its meaning.

Word Part	Definition	Example
base word	main word part that can stand alone	port
word root	main word part that can't stand alone	annu
prefix	letter or group of letters added to the beginning of the word	counter–
suffix	letter or group of letters added to the end of the word	–ic

When you encounter an unfamiliar word, check to see if you recognize the meaning of the prefix, suffix, base word, or word root. In combination with context clues, these meanings can help you unlock the meaning of the entire word. On the following pages are charts listing the meanings of the most common prefixes, suffixes, and word roots.

Reading STRATEGY REVIEW

READ WITH A PURPOSE. Rather than read the charts on the following pages all the way through from beginning to end, set a purpose for reading, and then let that purpose guide how you read the charts. For example, if you just want to become familiar with what prefixes, suffixes, and word roots are, read only a few lines from each chart, but read them carefully, studying how each word part contributes to the meaning of the words in the "Example" column. Your teacher might set a purpose for you, too. If so, approach the charts as your teacher directs.

Common Prefixes

Prefix	Meaning	Examples
ambi–/amphi–	both	ambidextrous, amphibian
anti–/ant–	against; opposite	antibody, antacid
bi–	two	bicycle, biped
circum–	around; about	circumnavigate, circumstance
co–/col–/com–/con–/cor–	together	cooperate, collaborate, commingle, concentrate, correlate
counter–	contrary; complementary	counteract, counterpart
de–	opposite; remove; reduce	decipher, defrost, devalue
dia–	through; apart	dialogue, diaphanous
dis–	not; opposite of	dislike, disguise
dys–	abnormal; difficult; bad	dysfunctional, dystopia
em–/en–	into or onto; cover with; cause to be; provide with	embark, empower, enslave, enfeeble
ex–	out of; from	explode, export, extend
extra–/extro–	outward; outside; beyond	extraordinary, extrovert
hyper–	too much, too many, or extreme	hyperbole, hyperactive
hypo–	under	hypodermic
il–, im–, in–, ir–	not	illogical, impossible, inoperable, irrational
	in; within; toward; on	illuminate, imperil, infiltrate, irrigate
inter–	among or between	international, intersect
intra–/intro–	into; within; inward	introvert, intramural
meta–	after; changed	metamorphosis, metaphor
mis–	wrongly	mistake, misfire
non–	not	nonsense, nonsmoker
out–	in a manner that goes beyond	outrun, outmuscle
over–	excessive	overdone, overkill
per–	through, throughout	permeate, permanent
peri–	all around	perimeter, periscope
post–	after; later	postgame, postpone
pre–	before	prefix, premature

CONTINUED

Common Prefixes (continued)

Prefix	Meaning	Examples
pro–	before; forward	proceed, prologue
re–	again; back	redo, recall
retro–	back	retrospect, retroactive
semi–	half; partly	semicircle, semidry
sub–/sup–	under	substandard, subfloor, support
super–	above; over; exceeding	superstar, superfluous
sym–/syn–	with; together	sympathy, synonym, synergy
trans–	across; beyond	transatlantic, transfer, transcend
ultra–	too much, too many, extreme	ultraviolet, ultrasound
un–	not	unethical, unhappy
under–	below or short of a quantity or limit	underestimate, understaffed
uni–	one	unicorn, universe

Common Suffixes

Noun Suffix	Meaning	Examples
–ance/–ancy/–ence/–ency	quality or state	defiance, independence, emergency
–age	action or process	marriage, voyage
–ant/–ent	one who	defendant, assistant, resident
–ar/–er/–or	one who	lawyer, survivor, liar
–dom	state or quality of	freedom, boredom
–es/–s	plural form of noun	siblings, trees
–ion/–tion	action or process	revolution, occasion
–ism	act; state; or system of belief	plagiarism, barbarism, Buddhism
–ist	one who does or believes something	ventriloquist, idealist
–itude, –tude	quality of, state of	multitude, magnitude
–ity/–ty	state of	longevity, infinity
–ment	action or process; state or quality; product or thing	development, government, amusement, amazement, ointment, fragment
–ness	state of	kindness, happiness

CONTINUED

Common Suffixes (continued)		
Adjective Suffix	**Meaning**	**Examples**
–able/–ible	capable of	attainable, possible
–al	having characteristics of	personal, governmental
–er	more	higher, calmer, shorter
–est	most	lowest, craziest, tallest
–ful	full of	helpful, gleeful, woeful
–ic	having characteristics of	scientific, chronic
–ish	like	childish, reddish
–ive	performs or tends toward	creative, pensive
–less	without	hapless, careless
–ous	possessing the qualities of	generous, joyous
–y	indicates description	happy, dirty, flowery
Adverb Suffix	**Meaning**	**Examples**
–ly	in such a way	quickly, studiously, invisibly
–ward, –ways, –wise	in such a direction	toward, sideways, crosswise
Verb Suffix	**Meaning**	**Examples**
–ate	make or cause to be	fixate, activate
–ed	past tense of verb	walked, acted, fixed
–ify/–fy	make or cause to be	vilify, magnify, glorify
–ing	indicates action in progress (present participle); can also be a noun (gerund)	running, thinking, being
–ize	bring about; cause to be	colonize, legalize

Common Word Roots		
Word Root	**Meaning**	**Examples**
acr	highest point	acrobat
act	do	actor, reaction
ann/annu/enni	year	annual, bicentennial
aqu	water	aquarium, aquatic
aster, astr	star	asteroid, disastrous
aud	hear	audition, auditorium

CONTINUED

Common Word Roots (continued)

Word Root	Meaning	Examples
bene	good	beneficial, benefactor
bibl, bibli	book	Bible
chron	time	chronic
cosm	universe; order	cosmic, cosmos
cred	believe; trust	credit, credible
cycl	circle	bicycle, cyclone
dem/demo	people	democracy
derm	skin	dermatologist
dic/dict	say	dictate, dictionary
duc/duct	lead; pull	conduct, reproduction
dyn	force, power	dynamic, dynamite
equ/equi/iqui	equal	equidistant, equitable, iniquity
fer	carry	transfer, refer
fin	end	finish, infinite
firm	firm, strong	confirm, reaffirm
flect/flex	bend	deflect, reflex, flexible
fort	strong	fortify, comfort
ge	earth	geode, geography
gress	go	progress, regress
hydr	water	hydrate
ign	fire	ignite, ignition, igneous
ject	throw	projector, eject
judic	judgment	prejudice, judicial
lect/leg	read; choose	lecture, election, collect
liber	free	liberate, liberal
loc	place	location, relocate
locut/loqu	speak	elocution, loquacious, colloquial
log/logue	word, speech, discourse	logic, dialogue
luc/lumin	shine; light	translucent, illuminate
mal	bad	malevolent
man/manu	hand	manufacture, manual

CONTINUED

Common Word Roots (continued)		
Word Root	**Meaning**	**Examples**
metr	measure	metric
morph	form	morpheme, metamorphosis
mot	move	motor, emotion
mut	change	mutation, transmutable
nov	new	novelty, renovate
onym	name	synonym, antonym
path	feel; suffer; disease	sympathy, pathology
ped	foot, child	pedal, pediatrics
phon/phony	sound; voice; speech	symphony
phot	light	photography
physi	nature	physical, physics
pop	people	popular, populate
port	carry	transport, portable
psych	mind; soul	psychology, psychic
reg	rule	register, regulate
rupt	break	disrupt, interruption, rupture
scrib/script	write	describe, prescription
son	sound	sonic
spec/spect/spic	look	speculate, inspect, despicable
spir	breathe	spirit, inspiration
ter/terr	earth	inter, extraterrestrial, terrain
therm	heat	thermal
top	place	topography, topical
tract	draw; drag	retract, tractor, contract
typ	stamp; model	typical, type
ver	truth	veracity, verifiable
vert	turn	divert, introvert, extrovert
vid/vis	see	video, visual
viv	alive	vivacious, vivid
vol/volv	turn	evolution, revolve

The more meanings of prefixes, suffixes, and word roots you know, the better equipped you are to tackle difficult vocabulary words.

Even if you don't know the meaning of a word part, however, you can often figure out the meaning of a word using word parts. To do this, think of as many familiar words as you can that contain each part of the word.

For example, if you were tackling the word *quadruped*, you might first think of words beginning with the prefix *quad–*: *quadrangle*, *quadrant*, and *quadruplet*. You know from your geometry class that a quadrangle is something having four angles and four sides. You're pretty sure that the other two words also have something to do with the number four. (If you wanted to be really thorough, you could check out this hunch with a friend or a dictionary.) Then you might think of words that contain *ped*: *pedal*, *pedestrian*, and *pedestal*. A pedal and a pedestal are both things you step on with your foot. A pedestrian is someone who walks. From this information, you might guess (correctly) that *ped* means "foot." A quadruped is something, usually an animal, with four feet.

This process is even easier when you work with a partner. Think aloud with your partner about how to break apart a word. Then discuss the meanings of each part and a possible meaning for the entire word.

RECOGNIZING COMBINING FORMS

Some word roots have become very common in English and are used all the time in combination with each other and with base words to create new scientific, medical, and technical terms. These combining forms can look like prefixes and suffixes, but contain more core meaning. The chart on the next page defines and gives examples of some common combining forms that will help you tackle new words.

NOTE THE FACTS

How can you use word parts to figure out the meaning of a new word?

_____
_____
_____
_____
_____

THINK AND REFLECT

Think aloud about how you would use word parts to figure out the meaning of the word *retroactive*. Record notes from your think aloud here. **(Apply)**

_____
_____
_____
_____
_____

Combining Forms

Word Part	Meaning	Examples
acro–	heights	acrophobia
anthropo–	human being	anthropologist
archaeo–/arche–	old	archeology
astr–/astro–	star	astronaut, astrology
audio–	hear	audiovisual
auto–	self	autobiography, automatic
bi–/bio–	life	biography, biosphere
bibli–/biblio–	book	bibliography
–centric	having such a center	egocentric
chron–/chrono–	time	chronology
–cracy	form of government; social or political class	aristocracy, democracy
ethno–	race; people; cultural group	ethnography
ge–/geo–	earth; soil	geography, geology
–graph/–graphy	something written, drawn, or represented by graphics	telegraph, photography
hydr–/hydro–	water	hydroelectric, hydrometer
–logy/–ology	study of	geology, biology
mal–	bad	malfunction, malnutrition
–mania	madness	kleptomania, megalomania
–metry	having to do with measure	geometry, symmetry
micro–	small; minute	microscope, microcosm
omni–	all	omnipresent, omnibus
–onym	name	synonym, antonym
–phile	one who loves	bibliophile
–phobe	one who has an irrational fear	arachnophobe, acrophobe
–phobia	exaggerated fear of	claustrophobia, photophobia
phon–/–phone/phono–	sound; voice; speech	telephone, phonograph
phot–/–photo–	light	photograph, telephoto
physi–/physio–	nature; physical	physiological
pseud–/pseudo–	false	pseudonym, pseudointellectual
psych–/psycho–	mind	psychiatrist, psychology
–scope/–scopy	view	telescope, microscopy
–ster	one who does or is	mobster, spinster
therm–/thermo–	heat	thermometer, thermodynamics
tel–/tele–	distant	telegram, telephone

Exploring Word Origins and Word Families

The English language expands constantly and gathers new words from many different sources. Understanding the source of a word can help you unlock its meaning.

One source of new words is the names of people and places associated with the thing being named. Words named for people and places are called **eponyms**.

> **EXAMPLES**
> **boycott** A group of people in Ireland decided to cease doing business and associating with Captain Charles Cunningham Boycott because of the high rents he was charging people to live on his land.
> **aphrodisiac** This word for a love potion or other substance that causes love is named after Aphrodite, the Greek goddess of love and beauty.

Another source for new words is **acronyms**. Acronyms are words formed from the first letter or letters of the major parts of terms.

> **EXAMPLES**
> **ASAP**, from *as soon as possible*
> **RSVP**, from *répondez s'il vous plaît* (French for "please reply")

Some words in the English language are borrowed from other languages.

> **EXAMPLES**
> **aficionado** (Spanish), **ukulele** (Hawaiian), **typhoon** (Chinese)

Many words are formed by shortening longer words.

> **EXAMPLES**
> **prom**, from *promenade*
> **limo**, from *limousine*
> **typo**, from *typographical error*

Brand names are often taken into the English language. People begin to use these words as common nouns, even though most of them are still brand names.

> **EXAMPLES**
> Kool-Aid   Wite Out   Band-Aid

THINK AND REFLECT

Name three other words that have been created by shortening other words. (Apply)

_____
_____
_____
_____
_____
_____

Using a Dictionary

When you can't figure out a word using the strategies already described, or when the word is important to the meaning of the text and you want to make sure you have it right, use a dictionary.

There are many parts to a dictionary entry. Study the following sample. Then read the explanations of each part of an entry below.

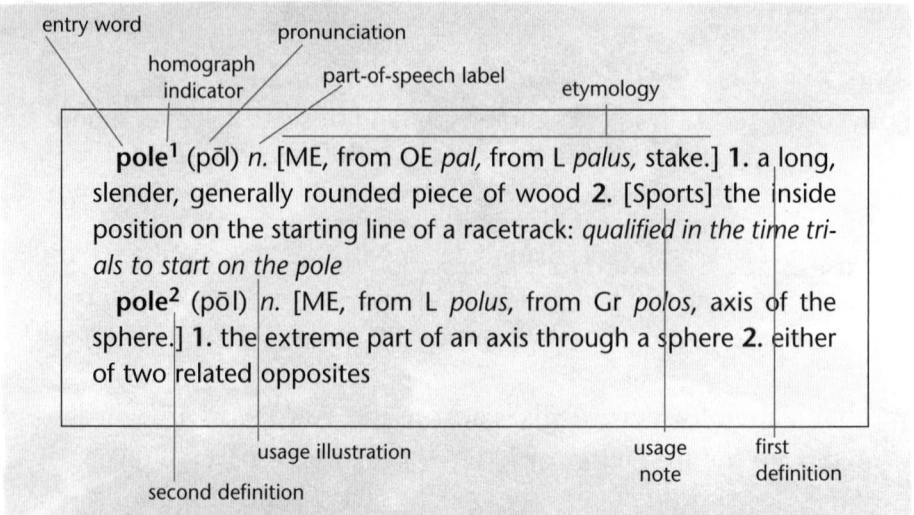

The **pronunciation** is given immediately after the entry word. The dictionary's table of contents will tell you where you can find a complete key to pronunciation symbols. In some dictionaries, a simplified pronunciation key is provided at the bottom of each page.

An abbreviation of the **part of speech** usually follows the pronunciation. This label tells how the word can be used. If a word can be used as more than one part of speech, a separate entry is provided for each part of speech.

An **etymology** is the history of the word. In the first entry, the word *pole* can be traced back through Middle English (ME) and Old English (OE) to the Latin (L) word *palus*, which means "stake." In the second entry, the word *pole* can be traced back through Middle English to the Latin word *polus*, which comes from the Greek (Gr) word *polos*, meaning "axis of the sphere."

Sometimes the entry will include a list of **synonyms**, or words that have the same or very similar meanings. The entry may also include a **usage illustration,** which is an example of how the word is used in context.

Understanding Multiple Meanings

Each definition in the entry gives a different meaning of the word. When a word has more than one meaning, the different definitions are numbered. The first definition in an entry is the most common meaning of the word, but you will have to choose the meaning that fits the context in which you have found the word. Try substituting each definition for the word until you find the one that makes the most sense.

If you come across a word that doesn't seem to make sense in context, consider whether that word might have another, lesser known meaning. Can the word be used as more than one part of speech, for example, as either a noun or a verb? Does it have a broader meaning than the one that comes to your mind? For example, in the short story "An Occurrence at Owl Creek Bridge," you will find this sentence: "It is now dry and would burn like tow." The most common meaning of *tow* is "to pull," but that doesn't make sense here. Consulting the footnote at the bottom of the page, you would discover that the word *tow* can also mean "flammable fibers of hemp or flax."

Keep in mind that some words not only have multiple meanings but also different pronunciations. Words that are spelled the same but are pronounced differently are called **homographs**.

Understanding Denotation and Connotation

The **denotation** of a word is its dictionary definition. Sometimes, in order to understand a passage fully, it is helpful to know the connotations of the words as well. A **connotation** of a word is an emotional association the word has in addition to its literal meaning. For example, the words *freakish* and *unique* both denote "different from what is typical," but *freakish* has a negative connotation similar to *ugly* or *scary*, whereas *unique* has a positive connotation involving being special or one-of-a-kind. The best way to learn the connotation of a word is to pay attention to the context in which the word appears or to ask someone more familiar with the word.

IMPROVING YOUR ACTIVE VOCABULARY

Keeping a Word Study Notebook

Keeping a **word study notebook** is a convenient way to log new words, their meanings, and their spellings, as well as prefixes, suffixes, word roots, and other concepts. In addition, you can use your word study notebook to write down words that you have trouble remembering how to spell. You may even want to set aside a section of your notebook for

THINK AND REFLECT

How would it be different if one character called another character's dress *freakish* rather than *unique*? What would that tell you about the characters? **(Apply)**

_____
_____
_____
_____
_____

Reading TIP

In your word study notebook, record for each word:
- definition
- pronunciation
- etymology
- sample sentence or illustration

word play. You can use this area to create jokes, silly rhymes, jingles, skits, acrostics, and games using the words you have logged.

When you record a new word in your notebook, include its definition, pronunciation, and origins, along with an example sentence or drawing to help you remember it.

Here is a sample page from a word study notebook.

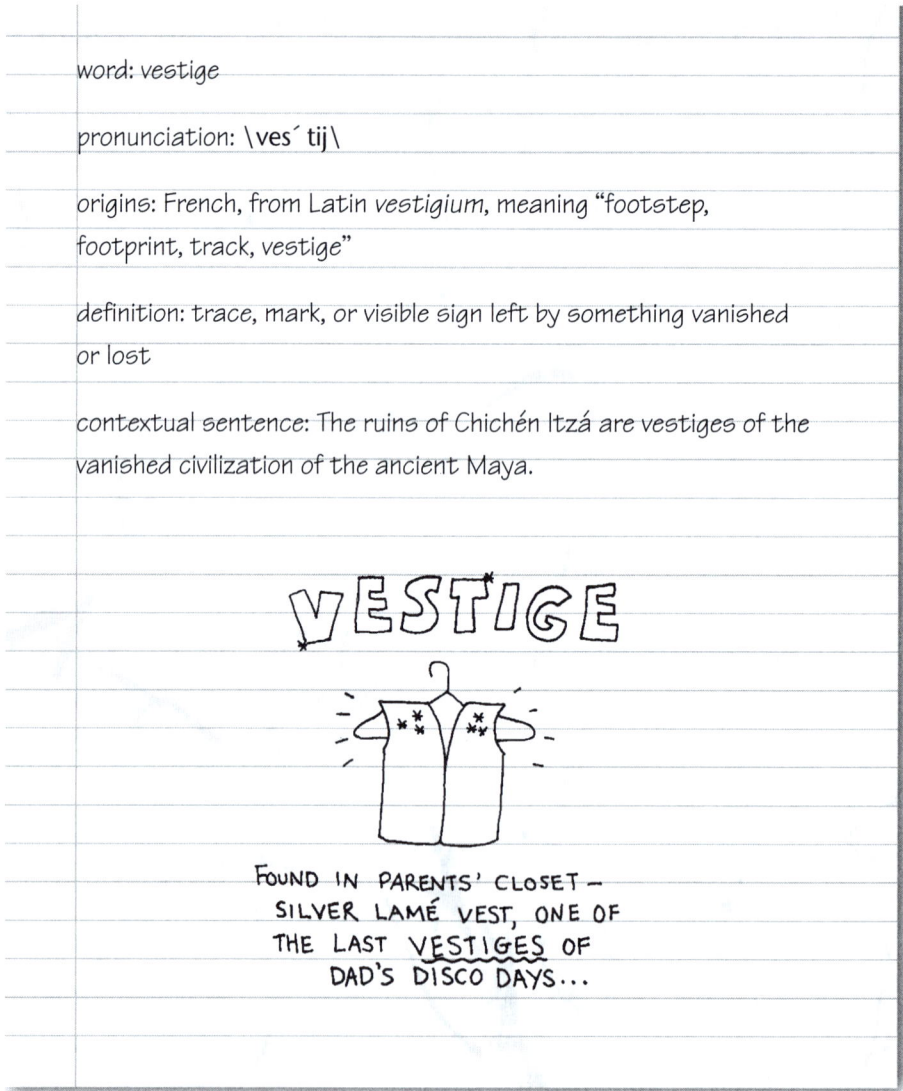

Review the words in your word study notebook and practice using the words in your speech and writing. Also, look for the words from your notebook as you read and listen. The more associations you develop and the more encounters you have with a word, the more likely you are to remember it.

Using Mnemonic Devices

A **mnemonic** (ni mä′ nik) **device** is a catchy phrase or striking image that helps you remember information. For example, you might have heard the phrase "the princiPAL is your PAL" as a trick for remembering the difference between *principal*, the person, and *principle*, the idea. The rhyme "*I* before *E* except after *C*" is a mnemonic for a spelling pattern.

Mnemonic devices are effective in learning new vocabulary words because you learn new information by linking it to words, images, and concepts that are already familiar to you. Vocabulary mnemonics can be sayings, drawings, jingles, or whatever works for you. To remember the definition of *neophyte*, you could say, "A neophyte fighter is new to fighting." To remember how to spell *museum*, you could associate the word with others like it: we are a<u>muse</u>d at the <u>muse</u>um. A mental picture can also help you remember meaning and spelling.

NOTE THE FACTS

What is a mnemonic device?

_____
_____
_____

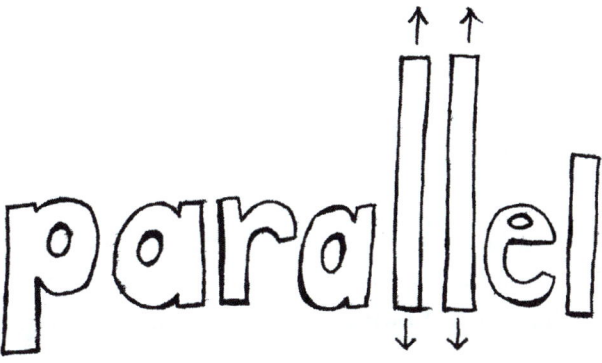

THINK AND REFLECT

Why is the graphic to the left an effective mnemonic for remembering the meaning of *parallel*? (Interpret)

_____
_____
_____

Categorizing and Classifying Words

Another technique for learning vocabulary words is categorizing and classifying the words. To categorize or classify a list of vocabulary words, sort them into groups that share a theme, topic, or characteristic. Then label each group. Like mnemonic devices, this technique works because it helps you create associations with and among new words.

For example, imagine that you need to learn the meanings of the following vocabulary words from the sermon "Sinners in the Hands of an Angry God" (Unit 7, page 270).

abhor	constitution	induce
abominable	contrivance	loathsome
ascribe	corruption	obligation
asunder	gulf	provoke
avail	incense	prudence

CONTINUED

righteousness	spew	wrath
sensible	subserve	
sovereign	venomous	

THINK AND REFLECT

In what other ways can these words be classified? (Apply)

_____
_____
_____
_____
_____
_____
_____
_____
_____
_____
_____
_____

Here is how one student classified these words.

"Sinners in the Hands of an Angry God" Vocabulary	
anger and hatred words	abhor, abominable, incense, loathsome, provoke, spew, venomous, wrath
words about power relationships	induce, obligation, righteousness, sovereign, subserve
words about virtue and sense	corruption, prudence, sensibility
words about who does what	ascribe, avail, contrivance
words about empty spaces and matter	asunder, constitution, gulf

Learning Synonyms, Antonyms, and Homonyms

A good way to expand your vocabulary is to learn synonyms, antonyms, and homonyms. As with using mnemonic devices and classifying or categorizing words, working with synonyms, antonyms, and homonyms will help you build associations for new words.

synonym	same (or nearly the same) meaning	stubborn, willful
antonym	opposite meaning	impolite, gallant
homonym	same pronunciation but different meaning	wave, waive

One way of using synonyms and antonyms to make many connections to a new word is to create a **concept map**. In a concept map, you list synonyms, antonyms, examples, nonexamples, and a contextual sentence for the word you are studying. The best way to use a concept map is to fill it out with a small group or as a whole class. That way, you get to hear everyone else's associations with the word, too. Look at the concept map for *rambunctious* on the next page.

Real-Life Contexts

The <u>rambunctious</u> class terrified the substitute teacher with their ornery behavior.

Horses are always more <u>rambunctious</u> when the weather turns cooler, giving them more energy.

Synonyms
- rowdy
- unruly
- lively
- energetic
- raucous
- boisterous
- loud
- overexcited

Antonyms
- calm
- restrained
- orderly
- obedient
- passive
- reserved
- apathetic
- lethargic

rambunctious

Examples
- puppies at play
- soccer players after a big win
- kids that have been trapped inside all day

Nonexamples
- sleeping cats
- couch potatoes
- students in a boring lecture

THINK AND REFLECT

Add one more synonym, antonym, example, and nonexample to the boxes in the chart. **(Apply)**

_____
_____
_____
_____

Unit 9 Vocabulary Review

Choose and Use Vocabulary Strategies

Before completing the vocabulary activities below, review with a partner how to use each of these vocabulary strategies.

TACKLING DIFFICULT VOCABULARY

- ❏ Use definitions, footnotes, endnotes, and glossaries
- ❏ Use context clues
- ❏ Use prior knowledge of word parts, word origins, and word families
- ❏ Use a dictionary
- ❏ Understand multiple meanings
- ❏ Understand connotation and denotation

IMPROVING YOUR ACTIVE VOCABULARY

- ❏ Keep a word study notebook
- ❏ Use mnemonic devices
- ❏ Categorize and classify words
- ❏ Learn synonyms, antonyms, and homonyms

Now read the passage below using the strategies from this unit to tackle difficult vocabulary in this excerpt from *Crisis, No. 1* by Thomas Paine. After you finish the passage, answer the vocabulary questions that follow.

> These are the times that try men's souls. The summer soldier and the sunshine patriot will, in this crisis, shrink from the service of their country, but he that stands it now, deserves the love and thanks of man and woman. Tyranny, like hell, is not easily conquered; yet we have this consolation with us, that the harder the conflict, the more glorious the triumph. What we obtain too cheap, we esteem too lightly: it is dearness only that gives everything its value. Heaven knows how to put a proper price on its goods; and it would be strange indeed if so celestial an article as freedom should not be highly rated. Britain, with an army to enforce her tyranny, has declared that she has a right (not only to tax) but "to bind us in all cases whatsoever," and if being bound in that manner is not slavery, then is there not such a thing as slavery upon earth. Even the expression is impious; for so unlimited a power can belong only to God.
>
> Whether the independence of the continent was declared too soon, or delayed too long, I will not now enter into as an

argument; my own simple opinion is, that had it been eight months earlier, it would have been much better. We did not make a proper use of last winter, neither could we, while we were in a dependent state. However, the fault, if it were one, was all our own; we have none to blame but ourselves. But no great deal is lost yet. All that Howe has been doing for this month past is rather a ravage than a conquest, which the spirit of the Jerseys, a year ago, would have quickly repulsed, and which time and a little resolution will soon recover.

1. In the first sentence of this passage, what is the meaning of the word *try*?
   a. attempt
   b. inspire
   c. pry open
   d. test

2. A "summer soldier" is most likely
   a. a young person, unlike "winter soldiers," who are more experienced.
   b. a soldier who joins the army in the summer.
   c. someone who supports a cause as long as it is going well.
   d. any soldier during the summer.

3. The best synonym for *tyranny* as it is used in this selection is
   a. oppression.
   b. dictatorship.
   c. success.
   d. urgency.

4. Which of the following words is the most helpful context clue in determining the meaning of *esteem*?
   a. conflict
   b. cheap
   c. value
   d. article

5. Use a dictionary and your knowledge of word parts to determine the meaning of each of these words. Then, on your own paper, do the following activities.

apparition	exploit	relinquish
calamity	hypocrisy	repulse
celestial	impious	resolution
conquest	infidel	try
consolation	pretense	tyranny
esteem	ravage	

   a. Create a word study notebook entry for one of the words.
   b. Create a mnemonic device for one of the words.
   c. Categorize the words.

On Your Own

FLUENTLY SPEAKING. Learn the pronunciations of each of the vocabulary words from the previous activity. Then practice reading the words aloud until you can read the entire list without stumbling. Use the Word Recognition Skills: Word Race form in Appendix A, page A-4. Record your personal best time.

PICTURE THIS. Choose a story, article, or poem that contains at least three words that are new to you. For each word, create a drawing that will help you remember its meaning. Then create a drawing that illustrates some aspect of the story, poem, or article and shows that you understand it.

PUT IT IN WRITING. Find and read a book, story, article, or poem that interests you. Create a list of vocabulary words from the text you have chosen. If the text doesn't have many difficult words in it, pick easy words and use a thesaurus to learn more difficult synonyms for those words. Then use these words to create a crossword puzzle, an acrostic, or some other word game. Look at the Word Workshop activities in the Unit Reading Reviews in this book for ideas. Write instructions for your puzzle or game. Then have a partner study the list of vocabulary words and complete your activity.

Unit TEN

Test-Taking Strategies

PREPARING FOR TESTS IN YOUR CLASSES

Tests are a common part of school life. You take tests in your classes to show what you have learned in each class. In addition, you might have to take one or more standardized tests each year. Standardized tests measure your skills against local, state, or national standards and may determine whether you graduate, what kind of job you can get, or which college you can attend. Learning test-taking strategies will help you succeed on the tests you are required to take.

These guidelines will help you to prepare for and take tests on the material you have covered in class.

Preparing for a Test

- ❑ **Know what will be covered on the test.** If you have questions about what will be covered, ask your teacher.
- ❑ **Make a study plan** to allow yourself time to go over the material. Avoid last-minute cramming.
- ❑ **Review the subject matter.** Use the graphic organizers and notes you made as you read as well as notes you took in class. Review any study questions given by your teacher.
- ❑ **Make lists** of important names, dates, definitions, or events. Ask a friend or family member to quiz you on them.
- ❑ **Try to predict questions** that may be on the test. Make sure you can answer them.
- ❑ **Get plenty of sleep** the night before the test. Eat a nutritious breakfast on the morning of the test.

Reading STRATEGY REVIEW

CONNECT TO PRIOR KNOWLEDGE. Which of these test strategies do you already use? Which might help you on your next test?

_____
_____
_____
_____
_____
_____
_____
_____
_____
_____

Taking a Test

❑ **Survey the test** to see how long it is and what types of questions are included.

❑ **Read all directions and questions carefully.** Make sure you know exactly what to do.

❑ **Plan your time.** Answer easy questions first. Allow extra time for complicated questions. If a question seems too difficult, skip it and go back to it later. Work quickly, but do not rush.

❑ **Save time for review.** Once you have finished, look back over the test. Double-check your answers, but do not change answers too readily. Your first ideas are often correct.

Answering Objective Questions

An **objective question** has a single correct answer. This chart describes the kinds of questions you may see on objective tests. It also gives you strategies for tackling each kind of question.

MARK THE TEXT

Underline or highlight the guidelines in the chart that you want to try next time you take a test.

Questions Found on Objective Tests

Description	Guidelines
True/False. You are given a statement and asked to tell whether the statement is true or false.	■ If any part of a statement is false, then the statement is false. ■ Words like *all, always, never,* and *every* often appear in false statements. ■ Words like *some, usually, often,* and *most* often appear in true statements. ■ If you do not know the answer, guess. You have a 50/50 chance of being right.
Matching. You are asked to match items in one column with items in another column.	■ Check the directions. See if each item is used only once. Also check to see if some are not used at all. ■ Read all items before starting. ■ Match those items you know first. ■ Cross out items as you match them.
Multiple Choice. You are asked to choose the best answer from a group of answers given.	■ Read *all* choices first. ■ Rule out incorrect answers. ■ Choose the answer that is most complete or accurate. ■ Pay particular attention to choices such as *none of the above* or *all of the above*.

Short Answer. You are asked to answer the question with a word, phrase, or sentence.

- Read the directions to find out if you are required to answer in complete sentences.
- Use correct spelling, grammar, punctuation, and capitalization.
- If you cannot think of the answer, move on. Something in another question might remind you of the answer.

Answering Essay Questions

An essay question asks you to write an answer that shows what you know about a particular subject. Read the following essay question on "The Story of an Hour" (Unit 3, page 69).

> Discuss the various emotions Mrs. Mallard experiences and identify the cause of each emotion.

A simplified writing process will help you tackle questions like this. Follow these steps:

❶ ANALYZE THE QUESTION. Essay questions contain clues about what is expected of you. Sometimes you will find key words that will help you determine exactly what is being asked. See the list below for some typical key words and their meanings.

Key Words for Essay Questions

analyze; identify	break into parts, and describe the parts and how they are related
compare	tell how two or more subjects are similar; in some cases, also mention how they are different
contrast	tell how two or more subjects are different from each other
describe	give enough facts about or qualities of a subject to make it clear to someone who is unfamiliar with it
discuss	provide an overview and analysis; use details for support
evaluate; argue	judge an idea or concept, telling whether you think it is good or bad, or whether you agree or disagree with it
explain	make a subject clearer, providing supporting details and examples
interpret	tell the meaning and importance of an event or concept
justify	explain or give reasons for decisions; be persuasive
prove	provide factual evidence or reasons for a statement
summarize	state only the main points of an event, concept, or debate

THINK AND REFLECT

Using the information in the chart, explain in your own words what the prompt above about "The Story of an Hour" is asking you to do. **(Apply)**

_____
_____
_____

2 PLAN YOUR ANSWER. As soon as the essay prompt is clear to you, collect and organize your thoughts about it. First, gather ideas using whatever method is most comfortable for you. If you don't immediately have ideas, try freewriting for five minutes. When you **freewrite**, you write whatever comes into your head without letting your hand stop moving. You might also gather ideas in a **cluster chart**. (See Appendix B, page B-7, for an example of this kind of chart.) Then, organize the ideas you came up with. A simple outline or chart can help. For example, the following graphic organizer might help you organize your response to the essay question on "The Story of an Hour" on the previous page.

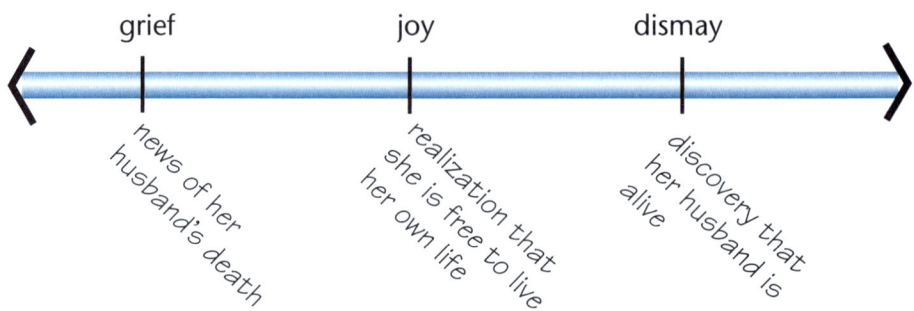

Get to know other graphic organizers that might help you by reviewing those on the before-reading pages and in Appendix B of this book.

3 WRITE YOUR ANSWER. Start with a clear thesis statement in your opening paragraph. Your **thesis statement** is a single sentence that sums up your answer to the essay question. Then follow your organizational plan to provide support for your thesis. Devote one paragraph to each major point of support for your thesis. Use plenty of details as evidence for each point. Write quickly and keep moving. Don't spend too much time on any single paragraph, but try to make your answer as complete as possible. End your essay with a concluding sentence that sums up your major points.

4 REVISE YOUR ANSWER. Make sure you have answered all parts of the question and included everything you were asked to include. Check to see that you have supplied enough details to support your thesis. Check for errors in grammar, spelling, punctuation, and paragraph breaks. Make corrections to your answer.

MARK THE TEXT

Underline or highlight what a thesis should do. Also mark where the thesis should go.

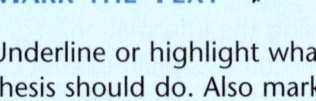

Steps for answering essay questions:
1. Analyze the question
2. Plan your answer
3. Draft your answer
4. Revise your answer

TAKING STANDARDIZED TESTS

Standardized tests are given to large groups of students in a school district, a state, or a country. Statewide tests measure how well students are meeting the learning standards the state has set. Other tests, such as the Scholastic Aptitude Test, or SAT, are used to help determine admission to colleges and universities. Others must be taken to enter certain careers. These tests are designed to measure overall ability or skills acquired so far. Learning how to take standardized tests will help you to achieve your goals.

You can get better at answering standardized test questions by practicing the types of questions that will be on the test. Use the Reading Skills and Test Practice questions in this book and other sample questions your teacher gives you to practice. Think aloud with a partner or small group about how you would answer each question. Notice how other students tackle the questions and learn from what they do.

In addition, remember these points:

- **Rule out some choices** when you are not sure of the answer. Then guess from the remaining possibilities.
- **Skip questions that seem too difficult** and go back to them later. Be aware, however, that most tests allow you to go back only within a section.
- **Follow instructions exactly.** The test monitor will read instructions to you, and instructions may also be printed in your test booklet. Make sure you know what to do.

Answering Multiple-Choice Questions

On many standardized tests, questions are multiple choice and have a single correct answer. The guidelines below will help you answer these kinds of questions effectively.

- **Read each question carefully.** Pay special attention to any words that are bolded, italicized, written in all capital letters, or otherwise emphasized.
- **Read all choices** before selecting an answer.
- **Eliminate** any answers that do not make sense, that disagree with what you remember from reading a passage, or that seem too extreme. Also, if two answers have exactly the same meaning, you can eliminate both.

MARK THE TEXT

Underline or highlight the suggestions in this list that are new to you.

- ❏ **Beware of distractors.** These are incorrect answers that look attractive because they are partially correct. They might contain a common misunderstanding, or they might apply the right information in the wrong way. Distractors are based on common mistakes students make.
- ❏ **Fill in circles completely** on your answer sheet when you have selected your answer.

Answering Reading Comprehension Questions

Reading comprehension questions ask you to read a passage and answer questions about it. These questions measure how well you perform the essential reading skills covered in Unit 2 of this book.

The Reading Skills and Test Practice questions that follow each literature selection in this book are reading comprehension questions. Use them to help you learn how to answer these types of questions correctly. Work through each question with a partner using a **think aloud**. Say out loud how you are figuring out the answer. Talk about how you can eliminate incorrect answers and determine the correct choice. You may want to make notes as you eliminate answers. By practicing this thinking process with a partner, you will be more prepared to use it silently when you have to take a standardized test.

The following steps will help you answer the reading comprehension questions on standardized tests.

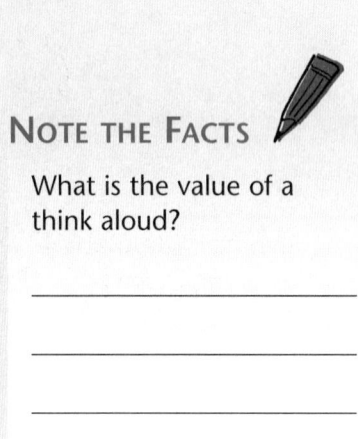

NOTE THE FACTS

What is the value of a think aloud?

_____
_____
_____

- ❏ **Preview the passage and questions** and predict what the text will be about.
- ❏ **Use the reading strategies** you have learned to read the passage. Mark the text and make notes in the margins.
- ❏ **Reread the first question carefully.** Make sure you know exactly what it is asking.
- ❏ **Read the answers.** If you are sure of the answer, select it and move on. If not, go on to the next step.
- ❏ **Scan the passage** to look for key words related to the question. When you find a key word, slow down and read carefully.
- ❏ **Answer the question** and go on to the next one. Answer each question in this way.

Answering Analogy Questions

Analogy questions ask you to find the relationship between two words and then to recognize a similar relationship in another pair of words. Look at the example below.

> SLEEP : REJUVENATION ::
> a. REST : CELEBRATION
> b. CONFLAGRATION : BURN
> c. BACON : PIG
> d. FAMINE : DROUGHT

In an analogy question, the symbols : and :: mean "is to" and "as." The example above would be read aloud as "*Sleep* is to *rejuvenation* as. . . ." Follow these guidelines for answering analogy questions:

> ❑ Think of a sentence that relates the two words. For the example above, you might think "Sleep results in rejuvenation."
> ❑ Try substituting the words from each answer pair in the sentence.
>   "Rest results in celebration."
>   "A conflagration results in a burn."
>   "Bacon results in a pig."
>   "Famine results in drought."
> ❑ Decide which sentence makes the most sense.
> ❑ If none of the options makes sense, try to think of a different sentence that relates the words, and work through the same process with the new sentence.

THINK AND REFLECT

Using the process described here, how would you answer the analogy question above? **(Apply)**

_____
_____
_____

The following chart lists some common relationships used in analogy questions.

Common Analogy Relationships	
Relationship	**Example**
synonyms	hateful : odious
antonyms	acclivity : decline
cause and effect	death : mourn
effect and cause	stillness : cessation
general and specific	flower : iris
less intense and more intense	rich : opulent
part to whole	kernel : corn
whole to part	corn : kernel
age	cub : bear
gender	comedian : comedienne
	CONTINUED

worker and tool	butcher : cleaver
worker and product created	jeweler : ring
tool and associated action	saw : sever
scientist and object of study	podiatrist : feet
raw material and end product	clay : pot
person and associated quality	gymnast : athletic
symbol and what it stands for	chains : bondage

Answering Synonym and Antonym Questions

Synonym or antonym questions give you a word and ask you to select the word that has the same meaning (for a **synonym**) or the opposite meaning (for an **antonym**). You must select the best answer even if none is exactly correct. For this type of question, you should consider all the choices to see which is best. Always notice whether you are looking for a synonym or an antonym. You will usually find both among the answers. Think aloud with a partner about how to answer the following question:

Mark the letter of the word that is most nearly the OPPOSITE in meaning to the word in capital letters.

1. RESPLENDENT
    a. shiny
    b. dull
    c. bright
    d. crazed

THINK AND REFLECT

How would you select the correct answer to this antonym question? **(Apply)**

_____
_____
_____
_____
_____

Answering Sentence Completion Questions

Sentence completion questions present you with a sentence that has two words missing. You must select the pair of words that best completes the sentence. The key to this kind of question is to make sure that both parts of the answer you have selected work well in the sentence. Think aloud with a partner about how to complete the following sentence.

2. The _____ are people well versed in literature, while a _____ is somebody frightened by technology.
    a. literary . . . digiphobe
    b. literati . . . digiphobe
    c. academics . . . digiphone
    d. English teachers . . . digiphile

THINK AND REFLECT

How would you select the correct answer to the sentence completion question? **(Apply)**

_____
_____
_____
_____
_____

Answering Constructed-Response Questions

In addition to multiple-choice questions, many standardized tests include **constructed-response questions** that require you to write essay answers in the test booklet. Constructed-response questions might ask you to identify key ideas or examples from the text by writing a sentence about each. In other cases, you will be asked to write a paragraph in response to a question about the selection and to use specific details from the passage to support your answer. For example, the following prompt might occur after Walt Whitman's "Song of Myself," Unit 4, page 147.

> **Essay prompt:** What does the speaker of the poem think about death? Use details from the poem to support your answer.
>
> **Short response:** The speaker believes that death is actually regeneration. He says that those who have died "are alive and well somewhere, / The smallest sprout shows there is really no death." Instead, "[a]ll goes onward and outward, nothing collapses." In the poem, the leaves of grass are growing out of the ground in which the dead are buried, and in some ways, the grass speaks for the dead. These are the voices that the speaker longs to translate. In conclusion, the speaker believes that death is a happy transformation, not an end: "And to die is different from what any one supposed, and luckier."

Other constructed-response questions ask you to apply information or ideas from a text in a new way. For example, imagine that you have just read the excerpt from "Self-Reliance" (Unit 7, page 286 on a standardized test. This essay explores the nature of individuality. One question might ask you what Emerson might think of school dress codes. Another question might ask you to imagine that you are Emerson and that you have been asked to speak to a group of twenty-first-century high school students about how they should live. What would Emerson say to those students? As you answer these questions, remember that you are being evaluated based on your understanding of the text. Although these questions offer opportunities to be creative, you should still include ideas, details, and examples from the passage you have just read.

NOTE THE FACTS

What is a constructed-response question?

_____
_____
_____
_____

NOTE THE FACTS

How are constructed-response questions evaluated? What should you be sure to include?

_____
_____
_____

Reading STRATEGY REVIEW

VISUALIZE. Draw a picture of what your test booklet would look like if you followed the process at the right.

The following tips will help you answer constructed-response questions effectively.

Tips for Answering Constructed-Response Questions

- ❑ **Skim the questions first.** Predict what the passage will be about.
- ❑ **Use reading strategies** as you read. Underline information that relates to the questions and make notes. After you have finished reading, you can decide which of the details you have gathered to use in your answers.
- ❑ **List the most important points** to include in each answer. Use the margins of your test booklet or a piece of scrap paper.
- ❑ **Number the points** you have listed to show the order in which they should be included.
- ❑ **Draft your answer to fit** in the space provided. Include as much detail as possible in the space you have.
- ❑ **Revise and proofread** your answers as you have time.

Unit 10 Test-Taking Review

Choose and Use Test-Taking Strategies

Before answering the sample test questions below, review with a partner how to use each of these test-taking strategies.

GENERAL STRATEGIES
- ❏ Know what will be on the test
- ❏ Make a study plan
- ❏ Review the subject matter
- ❏ Make lists
- ❏ Try to predict questions
- ❏ Preview the passage and questions
- ❏ Plan your time
- ❏ Use reading strategies to read the passage
- ❏ Come back later to questions that seem too difficult
- ❏ Save time for reviewing answers

STRATEGIES FOR OBJECTIVE TESTS
- ❏ Read each question carefully
- ❏ Read all answer choices before selecting one
- ❏ Scan the passage again if you are uncertain of the answer
- ❏ Rule out some choices
- ❏ Beware of distractors
- ❏ Understand how to answer analogy questions
- ❏ Understand how to answer synonym and antonym questions
- ❏ Understand how to answer sentence completion questions
- ❏ Fill in circles completely

STRATEGIES FOR ESSAY TESTS
- ❏ Understand how to answer constructed-response questions
- ❏ Analyze the question
- ❏ Plan your answer
- ❏ Write your answer
- ❏ Revise your answer

Now read "Modern American Drama" below and answer the questions that follow. Use the strategies from this unit to complete this practice test.

Although mainstream American literature found a voice uniquely its own in the period surrounding the Civil War, serious American drama lagged behind for more than a half-century. Not until after World War I, in the works of Eugene O'Neill, did American drama begin to assert importance in world literature.

Through the 1920s and into the 1950s, O'Neill (1888–1953) dominated the American stage with such plays as *Beyond the*

Horizon, Anna Christie, Strange Interlude, The Emperor Jones, The Hairy Ape, The Iceman Cometh, A Moon for the Misbegotten, and *Long Day's Journey into Night.* Known for their brooding realism, his plays explore motifs of love, death, frustration, illusion, and fate. O'Neill also experimented with symbolic Expressionism, a twentieth-century literary movement that reacted against Realism by exaggerating elements of the artistic medium in an attempt to express feelings or ideas. In an Expressionist work, the author transforms reality rather than imitates it. For example, in *The Emperor Jones*, characters appear spotlighted on an otherwise dark background, and a strong drumbeat creates an atmosphere of dread. A four-time winner of the Pulitzer Prize for drama, O'Neill received the Nobel Prize for literature in 1936.

During the Depression of the 1930s came plays of social protest, many of them critical of the excesses of American capitalism and of the international growth of fascism. Representative playwrights of the decade were Clifford Odets, Sidney Kingsley, Robert Sherwood, Lillian Hellman, and Maxwell Anderson.

Immediately following World War II, two American playwrights, Arthur Miller (1915–) and Tennessee Williams (1911–1983), skyrocketed to prominence. In 1947 Miller's *All My Sons* appeared on Broadway, followed by *Death of a Salesman* (1949), *The Crucible* (1953), *A View from the Bridge* (1955), and *After the Fall* (1964). Frequently revived since their initial productions, Miller's plays are noted for fusing Naturalism—a literary movement that showed actions and events as resulting inevitably from biological, environmental, or natural forces—and symbolism into psychodramas of illusion and betrayal. His landmark play *Death of a Salesman* tells the story of a common man, Willy Loman, who searches for some value in himself despite his failures.

Tennessee Williams's plays deal with troubled, emotionally intense social misfits and are often set in the post-Civil War South. Because of the intensity of emotion in these plays and because of their powerfully evocative settings, they are often referred to as examples of Southern Gothic. Williams was also an Expressionist, using lighting, sound, and props as symbols. After *The Glass Menagerie* (1945), regarded as "a memory play," opened in New York, Williams went on to write numerous Naturalistic dramas famed for their lyricism, sexuality, and violence. These include *A Streetcar Named Desire, Cat on a Hot Tin Roof, Suddenly Last Summer*, and *The Night of the Iguana.*

Bridging the pre- and post-World War II period was the work of Thornton Wilder (1897–1975), whose plays, rooted in commonplace human realities, continue to delight audiences: *Our Town*, which opened on Broadway in 1938, elevates the small details of everyday life to a position of highest importance. *Our Town* was followed by *The Skin of Our Teeth* (1942) and *The Matchmaker* (1956).

Later, Edward Albee (1928–) would write dramas marked by allegorical confrontations and surrealistic techniques, among them *The Zoo Story* (1958), *Who's Afraid of Virginia Woolf?* (1962), *Tiny Alice* (1965), and *A Delicate Balance* (1966).

In recent decades, a number of American playwrights—David Rabe, Sam Shepard, August Wilson, Arthur Kopit, Le Roi Jones [Imamu Amiri Baraka], Ed Bullins, David Mamet, Christopher Durang, Marsha Norman, Ntozake Shange, and Wendy Wasserstein—in their plays have dealt with such contemporary American problems as rootlessness, violence, and sexism, or with the realities of the African-American urban experience. Because of rising production costs, the work of these playwrights has often been staged off Broadway or even off off Broadway.

At the beginning of the new millennium, the strength and vitality of American drama seems ensured, thanks to a backlog of enduring plays, to the growth and energy of community and regional theaters, to experimental theaters off Broadway, and to the extraordinary talent of numerous young playwrights.

____ 1. Which of the following details about *The Glass Menagerie* would best support an argument that it is an example of Expressionism?
   a. One character is nicknamed Blue Roses.
   b. It is considered a "memory play."
   c. One character is based on Williams's sister Rose, to whom Williams was very close as a child.
   d. The outside of the building is represented by a gauzy curtain that suggests the action takes place in memory.

____ 2. According to this article, American drama seems to have followed a progression
   a. from Realism to Expressionism to Naturalism.
   b. from Surrealism to Realism to Expressionism.
   c. from Realism and Naturalism to Expressionism to Realism again.
   d. from Expressionism to Realism to Expressionism again.

_____ 3. Which of the following best describes contemporary drama?
   a. concerned with social problems
   b. unrelentingly violent
   c. heavily influenced by Expressionism
   d. unrealistic and escapist

4. Which of the plays described in this article would you choose to be performed at your school, and why? Use details from the article to explain why your choice would be appropriate to your school and community.

_____
_____
_____
_____

_____ 5. O'NEILL : EXPRESSIONISM :: ALBEE :
   a. REALISM
   b. SURREALISM
   c. NATURALISM
   d. MEMORY PLAYS

On Your Own

FLUENTLY SPEAKING. Review this unit and make a list of thirty key words about test taking. Use a word processor to key your words so that they are easy to read or use the Word Recognition Skills: Word Race form in Appendix A, page A-4. Then exchange lists with a partner. While your partner listens and times you with a stopwatch, read the list of words your partner gave you as quickly as you can without making errors. Then have your partner read the list of words you made while you time him or her. Practice reading the words until you can do it with no errors, and try to beat your partner's time.

PICTURE THIS. Find an informational article on a topic that interests you. After reading the article, come up with two essay questions. Practice planning answers for essay questions by constructing a graphic organizer that will help you organize your answer for each question. For more practice on planning responses to essay questions, exchange essay questions with a partner, and plan your answer for your partner's questions.

PUT IT IN WRITING. Find and read an informational article on any topic that interests you. After you have read the article, write three multiple-choice and two constructed-response questions that test reading comprehension. As models, use the sample questions in this unit as well as those in the Reading Skills and Test Practice section that follows every literature selection in this book. Finally, exchange your passage and questions with a partner, and take one another's tests.

Appendix A:
Building Reading Fluency

WORD RECOGNITION SKILLS
INCREASE YOUR AUTOMATICITY, A-2
Crossword Puzzle, A-3
Word Race, A-4
Word Matrix, A-5

SILENT READING SKILLS
INCREASE THE AMOUNT YOU READ, A-6
How Much Can You Learn in 10 Minutes?, A-6
Free Reading Log, A-7
Pages-per-Minute Graph, A-8
Minutes-per-Section Graph, A-8

ORAL READING SKILLS
PERFORM REREADING ACTIVITIES, A-9
Repeated Reading Exercise, A-11
Repeated Reading Record, A-12
Passages for Fluency Practice, A-13

WORD RECOGNITION SKILLS: INCREASE YOUR AUTOMATICITY

WHAT ARE WORD RECOGNITION SKILLS? Word recognition skills are skills that help you recognize and decipher words. Learning how to read increasingly more words with faster recognition leads to **automaticity,** the ability to recognize words quickly and automatically. The activities below develop word recognition skills.

1 **CREATE A CROSSWORD PUZZLE.** Put together a crossword puzzle that includes clues for words you are studying and clues for facts everyone should know. Look at puzzles in the newspaper or a puzzle book to learn how to number your clues and add blank spaces. Here is how you might set up a puzzle.

2 **CREATE A WORD RACE.** Make a list of 20 words you have studied. Practice reading the words aloud. Have a classmate keep track of how many seconds it takes you to read the entire list. Have another person keep track of the words you mispronounce. Have teams compete to see which team pronounces the same list of words the fastest with the fewest errors.

3 **CREATE A WORD MATRIX.** Choose vocabulary words that you find difficult to pronounce and place them in a chart. Add the same words to each row of your chart, but add the words to each row in a different order. Practice reading the words until you are comfortable pronouncing them. Have a partner time how many words in your chart you can read in 1 minute.

Word Recognition Skills: Crossword Puzzle

In a small group, list words to include in a crossword puzzle. Your list should contain 10 vocabulary words and 10 words that refer to facts that everyone knows. For instance, if the word *Washington* is on your "facts" list, add a CLUE ACROSS that says, *Our nation's first president.* Your first word down can come from one of the letters in *Washington*. For instance, the vocabulary word *wallow* can use the *w* in *Washington* with a CLUE DOWN that says, *Indulge oneself immoderately.* Use as many of the words on your list as you can (you may not be able to use all of them). Use your own paper for the CLUES ACROSS and CLUES DOWN. After you fill in your puzzle and finish your clues, make another blank, numbered puzzle. Exchange blank puzzles and clues with another group. See which group can solve their puzzle the fastest.

1. washington
a
l
l
o
w

WORD RECOGNITION SKILLS: WORD RACE

Create a list of 20 vocabulary words you have studied. Practice reading the list aloud. Have someone keep track of how many seconds it takes you to read the entire list. Have another person keep track of the words you mispronounce. After you have practiced the list, create teams. Have the team compete to see which team can pronounce the list the fastest with the fewest errors.

1.	11.
2.	12.
3.	13.
4.	14.
5.	15.
6.	16.
7.	17.
8.	18.
9.	19.
10.	20.

Keep track of the following data for each team member.

Number of seconds it took to read the list:
Number of words mispronounced:

WORD RECOGNITION SKILLS: WORD MATRIX

Choose 5 words that you find difficult to pronounce, and place them in the matrix below. Add the same words to each row, but use the words in a different order in each row. After a brief practice run-through, have a classmate use a clock or timer to see how many times you can make it through the chart in 1 minute. Have another classmate circle or check words you pronounce correctly. Use the second matrix below to run through your words a second time. Try to increase the number of words spoken correctly on your second reading.

Number of words correct in 1 minute: _____

Number of words correct in 1 minute: _____

SILENT READING SKILLS: INCREASE THE AMOUNT YOU READ

WHAT ARE SILENT READING SKILLS? **Silent reading skills** are skills you use as you read a text to yourself. Fluent silent readers can read a text quickly, easily, and smoothly. To build **silent reading fluency**, set aside time each day to read parts of a long selection or book. Most often, choose selections you consider easy and interesting. Vary the subject matter of selections you choose and, over time, include selections from several different genres—fiction, nonfiction, drama, short stories, poems, and informational and visual media. Use the charts below to keep track of your silent reading activity.

1 **FILL IN A FREE READING LOG.** Read silently for a sustained period several times a week. Write down what you read, the number of minutes you read, the number of pages you read, and your thoughts and reactions. Selections you read may be easy, moderate, or challenging.

2 **USE A PAGES-PER-MINUTE GRAPH.** Chart the number of pages you read in a 30-minute reading session. Try to increase the number of pages you read in each session. Be sure the selections you use for this activity are easy to read.

3 **USE A MINUTES-PER-SECTION GRAPH.** Each reading session, chart the time it takes you to read 5 pages of a selection. Try to decrease the number of minutes it takes to read 5 pages. Be sure the selections you use for this activity are easy to read.

SILENT READING SKILLS: HOW MUCH CAN YOU LEARN IN 10 MINUTES?

READING RATE. Pay attention to your silent reading rate. Do you vary your rate as you read? Do you slow down for difficult vocabulary and long sentences? Do you speed up when the ideas are easy to understand? Learn to use different reading rates with different tasks. Here are three methods to try.

Scan	Skim	Read Closely
To locate particular information (to find a quotation, verify a statement, locate a word, or answer a question)	To get the overall picture (to preview or to review)	To absorb the meaning of a book you're reading for fun or a textbook on which you'll be tested (to read with understanding the first time)

Practice using different reading rates as you read silently for 10 minutes. How much can you learn in 10 minutes? Write what you learn below.

SILENT READING SKILLS: FREE READING LOG

Develop your silent reading fluency by reading silently for a sustained period several times a week. Keep track of what you read each day. List your reactions and thoughts about what you read.

Week of _____

Date/ Minutes Read	Title/Author	Pages Read From/To	Reactions/Thoughts

Total number of pages read this week:

Total number of minutes read this week:

Genres read this week: (circle)
Fiction   Nonfiction   Poetry   Drama   Informational or Visual Media   Other _____

SILENT READING SKILLS: PAGES-PER-MINUTE GRAPH

Choose an easy and interesting book. Read for 30 minutes, and count the number of pages you read. Record the number in the chart below. Try to read more pages in each practice session.

Over 10 pages										
9 pages										
8 pages										
7 pages										
6 pages										
5 pages										
4 pages										
3 pages										
2 pages										
1 page										
Practice Number	1	2	3	4	5	6	7	8	9	10
Number of Pages Read										

SILENT READING SKILLS: MINUTES-PER-SECTION GRAPH

Choose an easy and interesting book. Record in the chart below the time it takes you to read 5 pages of the book. Try to decrease the time it takes you to read 5 pages each time you read. You can time several 5-page sections in one reading by placing paper clips at 5-page intervals. Each time you reach a paper-clipped page, stop to record the time it took you to reach that page.

10 minutes										
9 minutes										
8 minutes										
7 minutes										
6 minutes										
5 minutes										
4 minutes										
3 minutes										
2 minutes										
1 minute										
Practice Number	1	2	3	4	5	6	7	8	9	10
Number of Minutes Read										

Oral Reading Skills: Perform Rereading Activities

WHAT ARE ORAL READING SKILLS? **Oral reading skills** are skills you use when you read aloud. Have you ever noticed how radio and television reporters read a news report? They do not read every word at the same speed and volume. They emphasize important points by putting more stress on some words. They use facial expressions and the tone of their voice to convey what words mean. They add pauses to give listeners time to think about what is being said. These news reporters exhibit **oral reading fluency**, the ability to read aloud smoothly and easily.

HOW CAN YOU BUILD ORAL READING SKILLS? To demonstrate that you are a fluent oral reader, you do not have to read fast without mistakes. Even the best news reporters mispronounce words or stumble over unfamiliar phrases. Good news reporters, however, use strategies that make the oral reading task easier. They read and reread material before they go on the air, and they vary their speed and vocal expression. The rereading activities below build oral reading skills.

1. **PREPARE A REPEATED READING EXERCISE.** Choose a 100–150-word passage that you consider difficult to read. With a partner, use the passage to prepare a repeated reading exercise. Read the passage aloud to your partner. Have your partner record the time it takes you to read the passage and the number of errors you make. Then have your partner read the passage to you while you record the time and number of errors. On your second reading see if you both can improve your initial time and error rate, and include more vocal expression. Reread the passage a third time, working to decrease your time and error rate and trying to increase your vocal expression.

2. **PERFORM A CHORAL READING.** Find a poem, song, or part of a story that would be fun for a group to read aloud. Practice reading the piece aloud. Everyone in the group should use the same phrasing and speed. Have group members add notes to the text that help them pronounce the words and pause at appropriate times. Poems such as "Because I could not stop for Death—" on page 131 and "I, too, sing America" on page 166 work well as choral readings.

3. **THINK ALOUD.** Read a selection aloud with a partner. As you read, discuss thoughts you have about what you are reading. Ask questions, make connections and predictions, and respond to the ideas in the selection. When you are finished with your oral reading, reread the selection again, either orally or silently.

4. **PERFORM A PLAY.** Read aloud a play you have previously read silently. Assign parts. In small groups, have each speaker rehearse his/her part several times. Present the play to an audience. Use props and costumes, if possible.

5. **WRITE YOUR OWN PLAY.** Rewrite a prose selection, or a part of a prose selection, as a play. Assign parts. In small groups, have each speaker rehearse his/her part several times. Present the play to an audience. Use props and costumes, if possible.

6. **MAKE A RECORDING.** Read a 100–150-word passage into a tape recorder or DVD player. Listen to your recording. Keep track of errors you make: mispronouncing a word, leaving a word out, or adding a word that is not there. Rerecord the passage. Try to decrease the number of errors you make, and increase the smoothness with which you read the passage. Rerecord the passage until you can read it smoothly without error.

7 Memorize a Passage. Memorize a 100–150-word passage from a selection you have read. Have a partner help you memorize the passage by chunking it. Memorize short sections at a time, and work up to repeating the entire passage from memory. Possible passages to memorize include lines from a speech, poem, or song, such as "The Raven" by Edgar Allan Poe on page 137 or scenes from a short story or play such as *The Glass Menagerie* by Thornton Wilder on page 235.

8 Make a Video. Reread a selection with a partner. Prepare a video script that retells the selection. Record the retelling. Show the video retelling to an audience.

9 Experiment with Speed and Expression. Read a section of a selection silently. Reread the section aloud to a partner. Experiment with your speed and expression by rereading the section aloud in several different ways. Discuss which speed and means of expression work best.

10 Read with a Mask. Read silently, pretending that you are a character or the speaker in a selection. Reread aloud using a character or speaker mask that you hold in front of your face or wearing a costume that the character or speaker might wear.

11 View and Reenact. Watch a dramatic version of a selection on video. Read the print version, and reenact part of the selection.

ORAL READING SKILLS: REPEATED READING EXERCISE

❏ Choose a 100–150-word passage that you consider difficult to read. With a partner, use the passage to prepare a repeated reading exercise.

❏ Use a computer or a copier to make 6 copies of the passage: 3 for yourself and 3 for your partner.

❏ Read the passage aloud to your partner. Have your partner record the time you start reading, errors you make while reading, and the time you stop reading. Add this information to your Repeated Reading Record on page A-12.

❏ Have your partner read the passage to you. As your partner reads, record the time he/she starts reading, errors he/she makes, and the time he/she stops reading. See if your partner can improve your time and error rate. Record this information in your partner's Repeated Reading Record.

❏ Read the passage again. This time, work on varying your speed and vocal expression. Record the start/stop times and the number of errors you make, but this time your partner should listen for the meaning your words communicate. Have your partner comment on your speed and expression. For instance, your partner might note that "you read the first line too slow," "you had excellent pauses in the 2nd paragraph," or that you should "show more anger in the last line."

❏ Have your partner read the passage again. Record your partner's start/stop times and errors. Write down ways that your partner can vary his/her speed and vocal expression.

❏ You and your partner should reread the passage one more time. Continue to work on varying your speed and expression, and try to decrease your time and your number of errors. Record the information in your Repeated Reading Record.

ORAL READING SKILLS: REPEATED READING RECORD

Name: _____

Text Read: _____

Date	Evaluator	Errors	Time	Speed/Expression

ORAL READING SKILLS: REPEATED READING RECORD

Name: _____

Text Read: _____

Date	Evaluator	Errors	Time	Speed/Expression

ORAL READING SKILLS: PASSAGE FOR FLUENCY PRACTICE

from "An Occurrence at Owl Creek Bridge" by Ambrose Bierce, page 42

> Peyton Farquhar was a well-to-do planter, of an old and highly respected Alabama family. Being a slave owner and like other slave owners a politician he was naturally an original secessionist and ardently devoted to the Southern cause. Circumstances of an imperious nature, which it is unnecessary to relate here, had prevented him from taking service with the gallant army that had fought the disastrous campaigns ending with the fall of Corinth, and he chafed under the inglorious restraint, longing for the release of his energies, the larger life of the soldier, the opportunity for distinction. That opportunity, he felt, would come, as it comes to all in war time. Meanwhile he did what he could. No service was too humble for him to perform in aid of the South, no adventure too perilous for him to undertake if consistent with the character of a civilian who was at heart a soldier, and who in good faith and without too much qualification assented to at least a part of the frankly villainous dictum that all is fair in love and war.

Time started:_____   Number of errors:_____   Time stopped:_____
Comments about speed and expression:

> Peyton Farquhar was a well-to-do planter, of an old and highly respected Alabama family. Being a slave owner and like other slave owners a politician he was naturally an original secessionist and ardently devoted to the Southern cause. Circumstances of an imperious nature, which it is unnecessary to relate here, had prevented him from taking service with the gallant army that had fought the disastrous campaigns ending with the fall of Corinth, and he chafed under the inglorious restraint, longing for the release of his energies, the larger life of the soldier, the opportunity for distinction. That opportunity, he felt, would come, as it comes to all in war time. Meanwhile he did what he could. No service was too humble for him to perform in aid of the South, no adventure too perilous for him to undertake if consistent with the character of a civilian who was at heart a soldier, and who in good faith and without too much qualification assented to at least a part of the frankly villainous dictum that all is fair in love and war.

Time started:_____   Number of errors:_____   Time stopped:_____
Comments about speed and expression:

ORAL READING SKILLS: PASSAGE FOR FLUENCY PRACTICE

from Speech in the Virginia Convention by Patrick Henry, page 278

> Mr. President:[1] No man thinks more highly than I do of the patriotism, as well as abilities, of the very worthy gentlemen who have just addressed the house. But different men often see the same subject in different lights: and, therefore, I hope it will not be thought disrespectful to those gentlemen, if, entertaining, as I do, opinions of a character very opposite to theirs, I shall speak forth my sentiments freely and without reserve. This is no time for ceremony. The question before the house is one of awful moment to this country. For my own part, I consider it as nothing less than a question of freedom or slavery. And in proportion to the magnitude of the subject ought to be the freedom of the debate. It is only in this way that we can hope to arrive at truth, and fulfill the great responsibility which we hold to God and our country. Should I keep back my opinions at such a time, through fear of giving offense, I should consider myself as guilty of treason toward my country, and of an act of disloyalty toward the Majesty of Heaven, which I revere above all earthly kings.

Time started:_____   Number of errors:_____   Time stopped:_____
Comments about speed and expression:

> Mr. President:[1] No man thinks more highly than I do of the patriotism, as well as abilities, of the very worthy gentlemen who have just addressed the house. But different men often see the same subject in different lights: and, therefore, I hope it will not be thought disrespectful to those gentlemen, if, entertaining, as I do, opinions of a character very opposite to theirs, I shall speak forth my sentiments freely and without reserve. This is no time for ceremony. The question before the house is one of awful moment to this country. For my own part, I consider it as nothing less than a question of freedom or slavery. And in proportion to the magnitude of the subject ought to be the freedom of the debate. It is only in this way that we can hope to arrive at truth, and fulfill the great responsibility which we hold to God and our country. Should I keep back my opinions at such a time, through fear of giving offense, I should consider myself as guilty of treason toward my country, and of an act of disloyalty toward the Majesty of Heaven, which I revere above all earthly kings.

Time started:_____   Number of errors:_____   Time stopped:_____
Comments about speed and expression:

Appendix B:
Graphic Organizers for Reading Strategies

READING STRATEGIES CHECKLIST, B-2

READ WITH A PURPOSE
Author's Purpose Chart, B-3
Reader's Purpose Chart, B-4

CONNECT TO PRIOR KNOWLEDGE
K-W-L Chart, B-5
Reactions Chart, B-5

WRITE THINGS DOWN
Note Taking Chart, B-6
Pro and Con Chart, B-6
Venn Diagram, B-7
Cluster Chart, B-7

MAKE PREDICTIONS
Prediction Chart, B-8
Character Chart, B-8

VISUALIZE
Sensory Details Chart, B-9
Figurative Language Chart, B-9

USE TEXT ORGANIZATION
Story Strip, B-10
Time Line, B-10
Plot Diagram, B-11
Cause-and-Effect Chart, B-12
Summary Chart, B-12
Drawing Conclusions Log, B-13
Main Idea Map, B-13

TACKLE DIFFICULT VOCABULARY
Word Sort, B-14
Word Study Notebook, B-14
Word Map, B-15

MONITOR YOUR READING PROGRESS
Fix-Up Ideas Log, B-16
Your Own Graphic Organizer, B-16

Reading Strategies Checklist

Use at least one before-, during-, or after-reading strategy listed below.

Reading Strategy	Before Reading	During Reading	After Reading
READ WITH A PURPOSE	___ I write down my reason for reading. ___ I write down the author's purpose for writing.	___ I read with a purpose in mind.	___ I reflect upon my purpose for reading.
CONNECT TO PRIOR KNOWLEDGE	___ I write down what I know about a topic.	___ I use what I know. ___ I add to what I know.	___ I think about what I learned.
WRITE THINGS DOWN	___ I have the materials I need for writing things down.	___ I mark key points. ___ I use sticky notes. ___ I take notes. ___ I highlight. ___ I react to text.	___ I summarize.
MAKE PREDICTIONS	___ I preview. ___ I guess.	___ I gather more information. ___ I guess again.	___ I analyze my predictions.
VISUALIZE	___ I picture the topic.	___ I make a mind movie. ___ I continue my mind movie.	___ I sketch or summarize my mind movie.
USE TEXT ORGANIZATION	___ I skim the text.	___ I read sections or stanzas. ___ I pay attention to introductions and conclusions. ___ I use headings and signal words. ___ I read charts and graphic aids. ___ I study the pictures. ___ I follow familiar plot, themes, and hidden outlines.	___ I use the organization to review the text.
TACKLE DIFFICULT WORDS	___ I study words beforehand.	___ I use context clues. ___ I look at prefixes and suffixes. ___ I consult a dictionary. ___ I ask a teacher or friend for help.	___ I use the words and add them to my working vocabulary.
MONITOR YOUR READING PROGRESS		**Fix-Up Ideas** ___ I reread. ___ I ask questions. ___ I read in shorter chunks. ___ I read aloud. ___ I take time to refocus. ___ I unlock difficult words. ___ I change my reading rate. ___ I create a mnemonic device.	

Read with a Purpose: Author's Purpose Chart

An author may write with the following purposes in mind:
- ❑ to inform (expository/informative writing)
- ❑ to entertain, enrich, enlighten, and/or use an artistic medium such as fiction or poetry to share a perspective (imaginative/descriptive writing)
- ❑ to make a point by sharing a story about an event (narrative writing)
- ❑ to reflect (personal/expressive writing)
- ❑ to persuade readers or listeners to respond in some way, such as to agree with a position, change a view on an issue, reach an agreement, or perform an action (persuasive/argumentative writing)

The following types of writing reflect these purposes:
- ❑ Expository/informative: news article, research report
- ❑ Imaginative/descriptive: poem, short story
- ❑ Narrative: biography, family history
- ❑ Personal/expressive: diary entry, personal letter
- ❑ Persuasive/argumentative: editorial, petition

Before Reading
Identify the author's purpose, the type of writing he or she uses, and the ideas he or she wants to communicate.

During Reading
Gather ideas that the author communicates to readers.

After Reading
Summarize the ideas the author communicates. Explain how these ideas help fulfill the author's purpose.

Read with a Purpose: Reader's Purpose Chart

Fill in the Reader's Purpose Chart at each stage of reading to set a purpose for reading and to help you attain it.

Before Reading
Set a purpose for reading. *(Example: I am going to determine the overall mood of this poem.)*

During Reading
Take notes on what you learn. *(Example: mournful owl—sounds sad)*

After Reading
Reflect on your purpose and what you learned. *(Example: I wanted to find the overall mood of this poem. From the notes that I took, I believe the mood is melancholy and sad.)*

CONNECT TO PRIOR KNOWLEDGE: K-W-L CHART

Connect to what you know and what you want to know by filling in the first two columns before you read. Fill in the last column after you read.

What I *Know*	What I *Want* to Learn	What I Have *Learned*

CONNECT TO PRIOR KNOWLEDGE: REACTIONS CHART

Since you cannot write in, mark up, or highlight text in a textbook or library book, use this chart to record your thoughts and reactions. As you read, ask yourself questions, make predictions, react to ideas, identify key points, and/or write down unfamiliar words.

Page #	Questions, Predictions, Reactions, Key Points, and Unfamiliar Words

WRITE THINGS DOWN: NOTE TAKING CHART

Take notes in the chart below as you read nonfiction or informational selections.

Section or Page	Main Ideas	My Reactions

Summary of My Notes

WRITE THINGS DOWN: PRO AND CON CHART

As you read a persuasive or argumentative selection, take notes on both sides of each argument.

Arguments in Favor (Pro)	Arguments Against (Con)
Argument 1: Support:	Argument 1: Support:
Argument 2: Support:	Argument 2: Support:

APPENDIX B

WRITE THINGS DOWN: VENN DIAGRAM

Use a Venn diagram to compare and contrast ideas in one selection or to compare two selections.

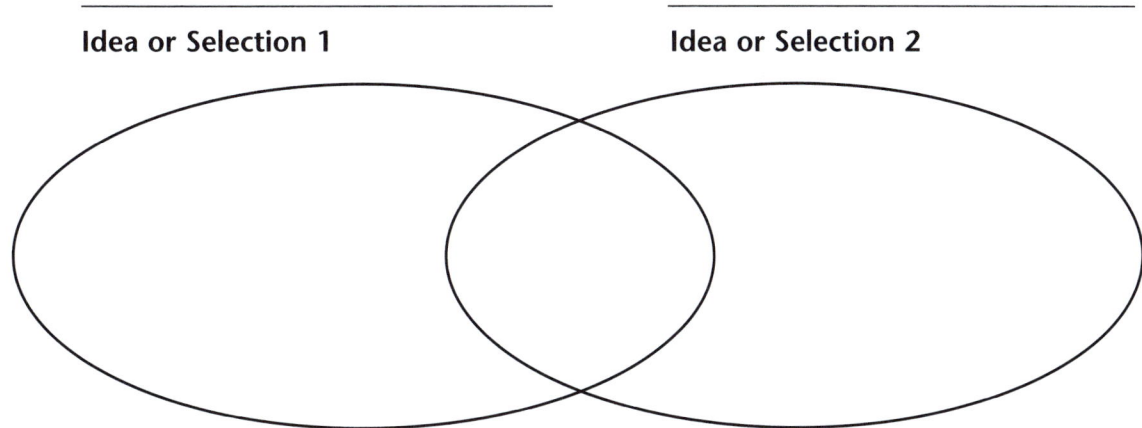

WRITE THINGS DOWN: CLUSTER CHART

Fill in the cluster chart below to keep track of character traits or main ideas. In the center circle, write the name of the character or topic. In the circles branching out from the center, write details about the character or topic.

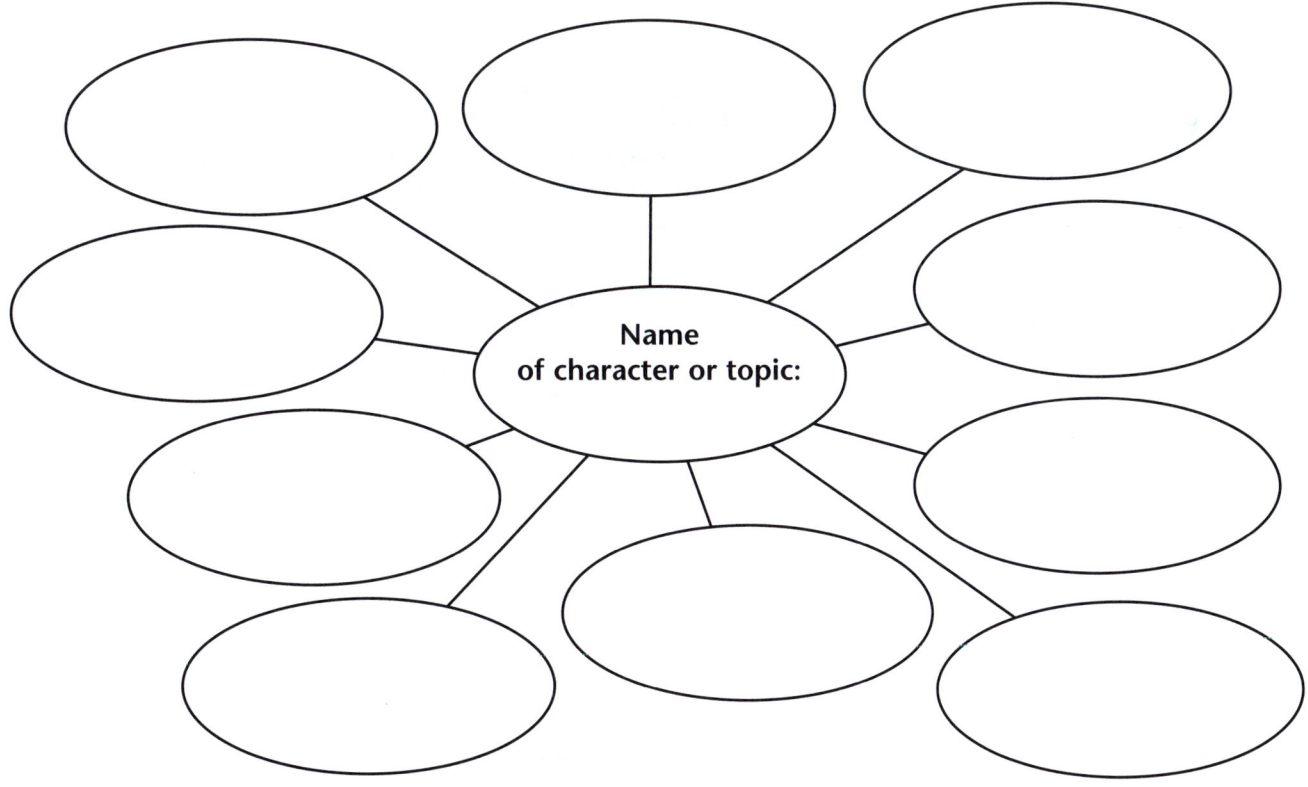

MAKE PREDICTIONS: PREDICTION CHART

Gather information before and during reading that helps you make predictions about a literature selection. Write your predictions in the "Guesses" column. Write reasons for your guesses in the "Reasons" column. As you read, gather evidence that either supports or disproves your predictions. Change your predictions and add new ones as you learn more about the selection.

Guesses	Reasons	Evidence

MAKE PREDICTIONS: CHARACTER CHART

A **character** is a person (or sometimes an animal) who figures in the action of a literary work. Choose one character from the selection and fill in the chart below based on what you learn about the character as you read.

Character's Name:	Physical Appearance	Habits/ Mannerisms/ Behaviors	Relationships with Other People	Other Characteristics
Your description of the character at the beginning of the story				
Your predictions for this character				
Your analysis of the character at the end of the story				

Visualize: Sensory Details Chart

As you read, identify images or words and phrases that contain sensory details. Write each sensory detail beneath the sense to which it appeals.

Sight	Sound	Touch	Taste	Smell

Visualize: Figurative Language Chart

As you read, identify examples of figurative language. Write down examples of figurative language in the first column below. In the second column, write down the comparison being made by the figurative language, and in the third column, describe what the figurative language makes you envision.

Example of Figurative Language	What Is Compared	What You Envision

APPENDIX B

USE TEXT ORGANIZATION: STORY STRIP

Draw pictures that represent key events in a selection. Then write a caption under each box that explains each event. Draw the events in the order in which they occurred.

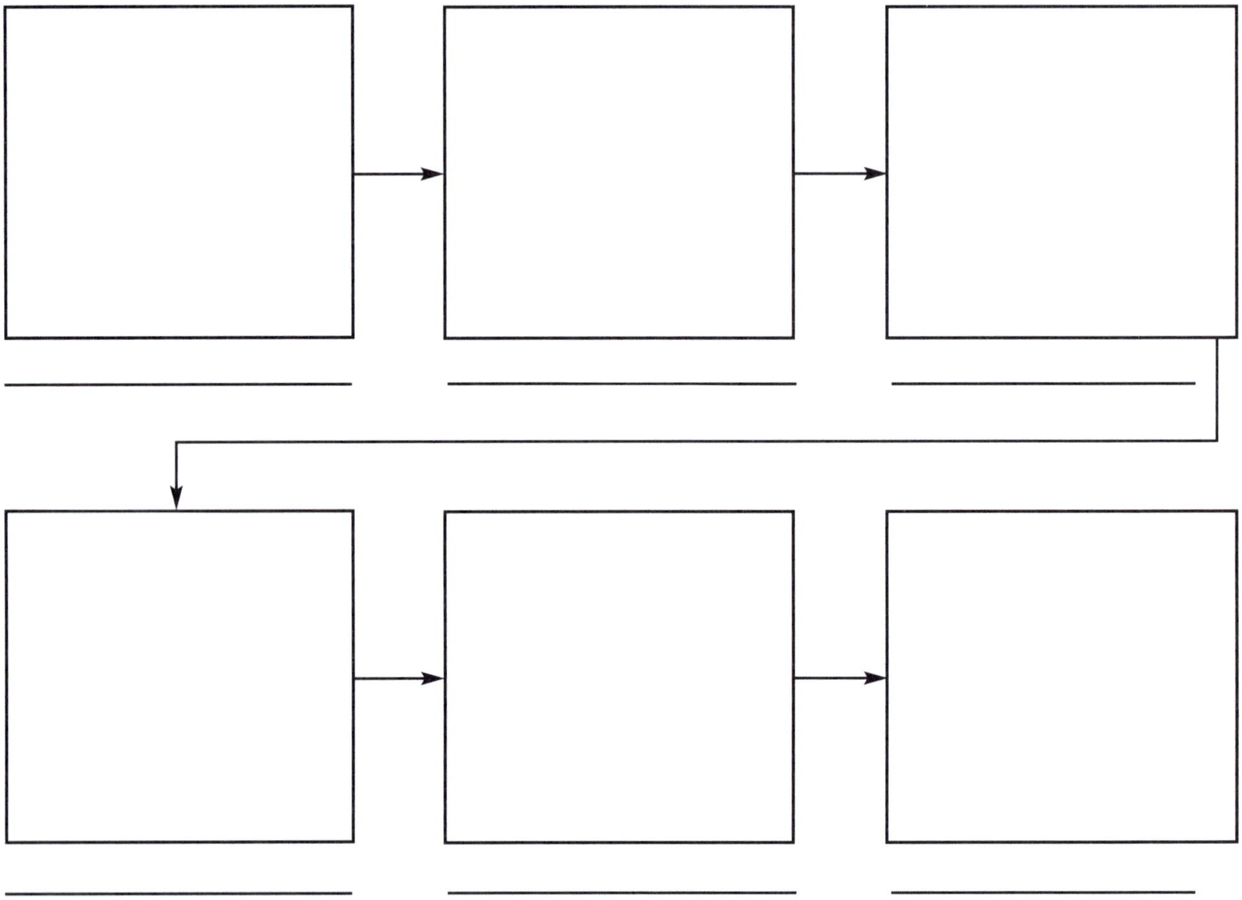

USE TEXT ORGANIZATION: TIME LINE

Use a time line to keep track of important events in a literature selection.

Dates:

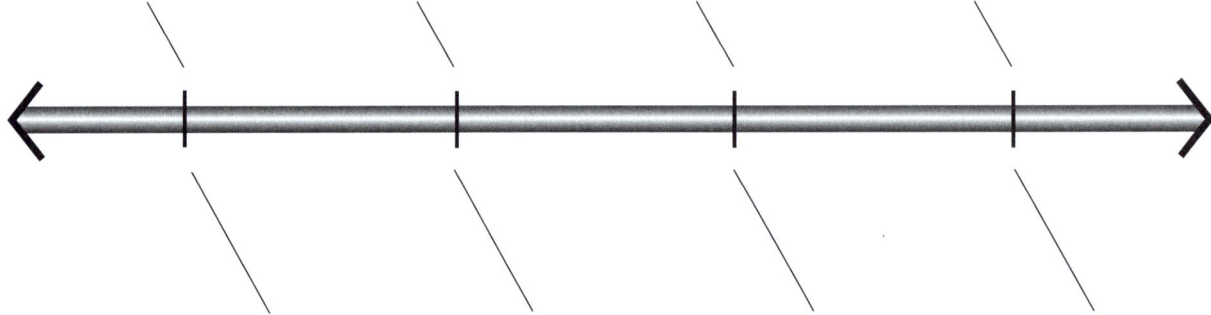

Events:

USE TEXT ORGANIZATION: PLOT DIAGRAM

Use the plot diagram below to chart the plot of a literature selection. In the spaces provided, describe the exposition, inciting incident, rising and falling action, climax, resolution, and dénouement. Be sure to include in the rising action the key events that build toward the climax of the selection.

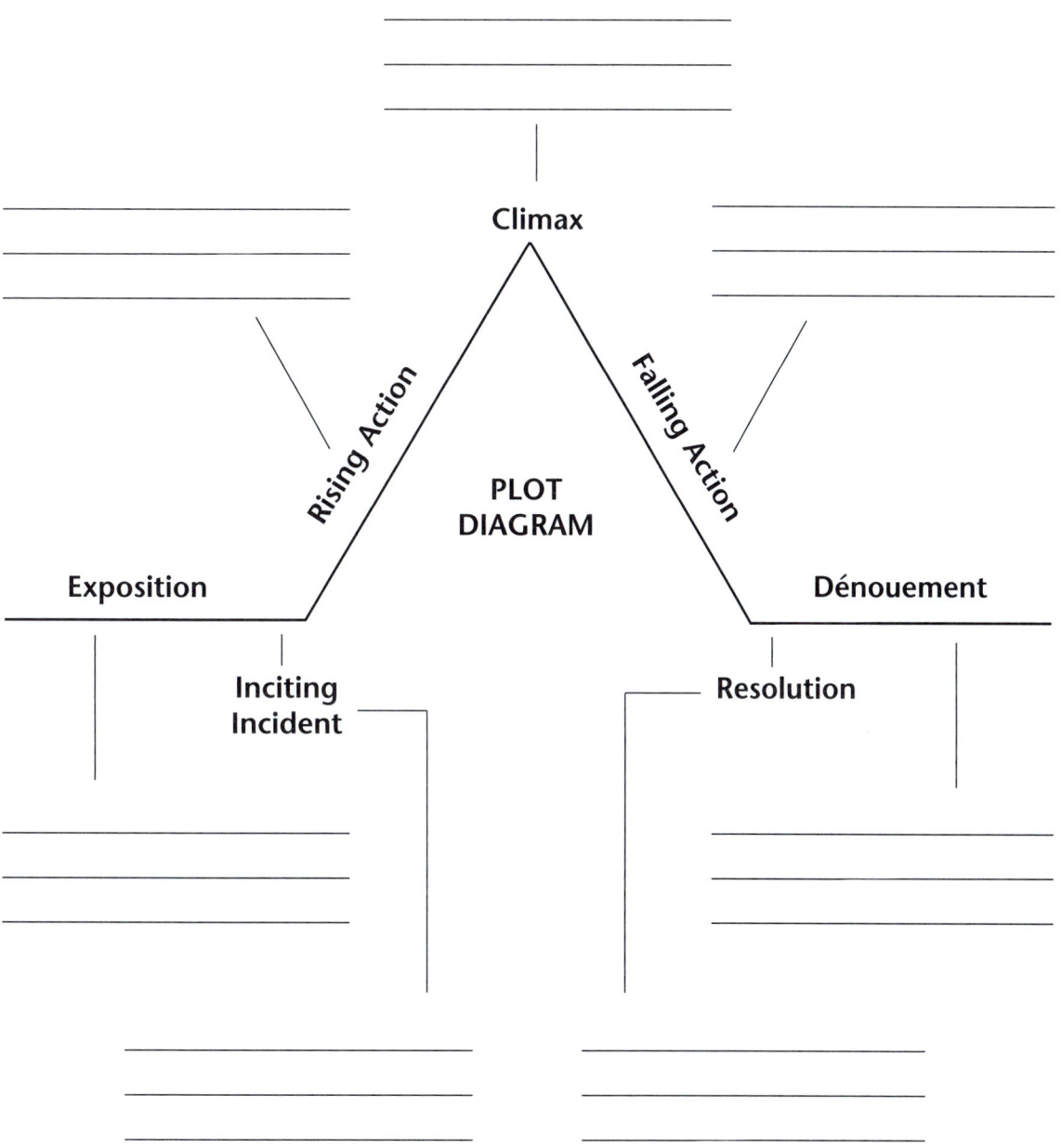

USE TEXT ORGANIZATION: CAUSE-AND-EFFECT CHART

Keep track of what happens in a story and why in the chart below. Use cause-and-effect signal words to help you identify causes and their effects. (Examples of cause-and-effect words: *as a result, because, if/then, since, therefore, this led to*.)

Cause →→→→→→→→→→→ Effect

_____   _____

_____   _____

↓
↓

Summary statement of what happened
in the selection and why:

_____

_____

USE TEXT ORGANIZATION: SUMMARY CHART

Read and summarize short sections of a selection at a time. Then write a summary of the entire work.

| Summary of Section 1: |
| Summary of Section 2: |
| Summary of Section 3: |
| Summary of the Selection: |

USE TEXT ORGANIZATION: DRAWING CONCLUSIONS LOG

Draw conclusions about a selection by gathering supporting points for key ideas. Reread the supporting points and key ideas and draw a conclusion about the main or overall message of the selection.

Key Idea: Supporting Points:	Key Idea: Supporting Points:	Key Idea: Supporting Points:
Conclusion about Overall Message:		

USE TEXT ORGANIZATION: MAIN IDEA MAP

To find the main or overall message of a whole selection or a part of the selection, gather important details into a Main Idea Map. Use the details to determine the main or overall message. Note: In fiction, the main idea is also known as the theme.

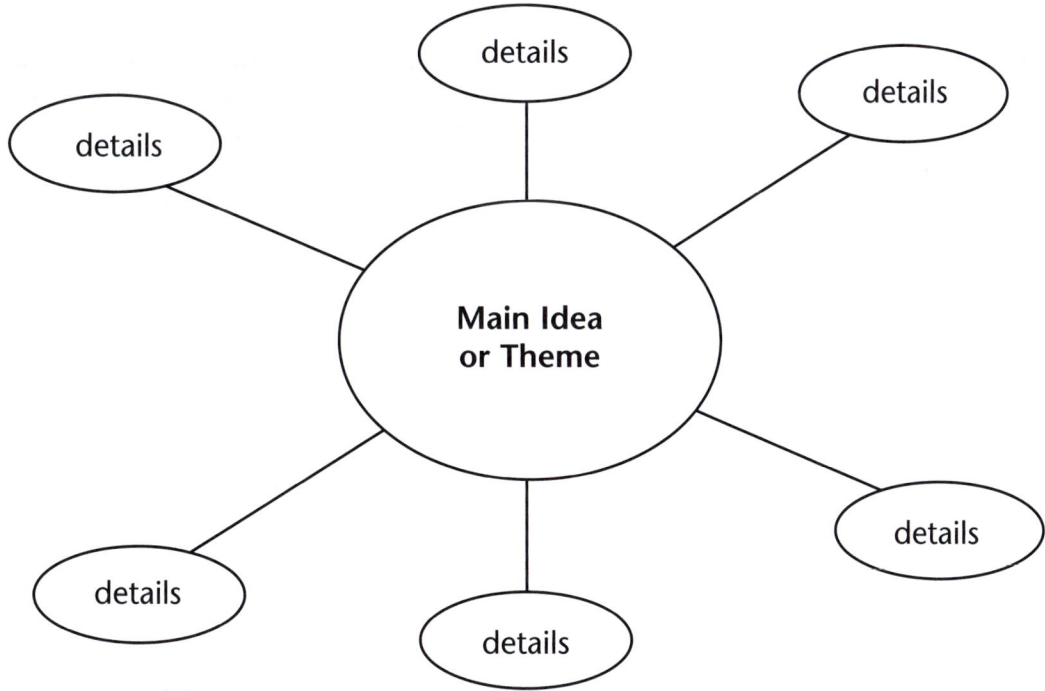

APPENDIX B   B-13

TACKLE DIFFICULT VOCABULARY: WORD SORT

Write one challenging word or phrase in each of the boxes below, along with its definition and part of speech. Cut the boxes apart. Then sort the words using one of the following methods.

- Same parts of speech
- Words with similar or opposite meanings
- Words with prefixes and suffixes
- Words that relate to each other or that can be used together
- My own sorting method: _____

Word:	Word:	Word:
Definition:	Definition:	Definition:
Part of Speech:	Part of Speech:	Part of Speech:

Word:	Word:	Word:
Definition:	Definition:	Definition:
Part of Speech:	Part of Speech:	Part of Speech:

TACKLE DIFFICULT VOCABULARY: WORD STUDY NOTEBOOK

Keeping a word study notebook is a convenient way to log new words, their meanings and their spelling, as well as prefixes, suffixes, word roots, and other concepts. When you record a new word, include its definition, pronunciation, and origins, along with an example sentence and a drawing to help you remember it.

Word: _____

Pronunciation: _____

Origins: _____

Definition: _____

Sentence: _____

Drawing:

TACKLE DIFFICULT VOCABULARY: WORD MAP

Write a challenging word or phrase in the first box below. Beneath the word or phrase, include its definition, word parts you recognize, and several synonyms. In the two boxes at the bottom, write a sentence that uses the word or phrase and create a drawing that helps you remember it.

A Challenging Word or Phrase

Definition

Word Parts I Recognize

Synonyms

A Sentence That Contains the Word or Phrase

A Picture That Illustrates the Word or Phrase

MONITOR YOUR READING PROGRESS: FIX-UP IDEAS LOG

Recognizing that you don't understand something is as important as knowing that you do understand it. Sometimes you may find yourself just reading the words but not actually comprehending or getting the meaning of what you are reading. If you are having trouble comprehending something you are reading, try using some of the fix-up ideas listed below to get back on track.

- Reread
- Ask a question
- Read in shorter chunks
- Read aloud
- Retell
- Work with a partner
- Unlock difficult words
- Change your reading rate
- Choose a new strategy
- Create a mnemonic device

Problems I Encountered while Reading	Fix-Up-Ideas I Used

MONITOR YOUR READING PROGRESS: YOUR OWN GRAPHIC ORGANIZER

Graphic organizers help you understand and remember information. Use your imagination to modify a graphic organizer in this appendix, or invent a new one. Use your graphic organizer to arrange ideas as you read and to guide your discussion and writing actions after you read. Graphic organizer possibilities are endless!

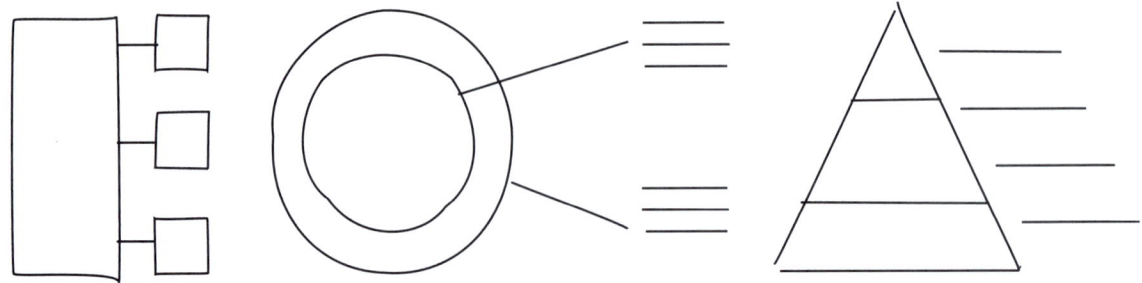

Appendix C: *Acknowledgments*

LITERARY ACKNOWLEDGMENTS

Georges Borchardt, Inc. From *The Glass Menagerie* by Tennessee Williams. Copyright © 1945 The University of the South. Reprinted by permission of Georges Borchardt, Inc. for the Tennessee Williams Estate.

The Continuum International Publishing Group. From *The Very Brief Relation of the Devastation of the Indies* by Bartolomé de las Casas. Copyright © 1992 by Continuum Publishing Company. Reprinted by permission of The Continuum International Publishing Group.

Lucy Dos Passos Coggin. "Newsreel LXVIII" from *The Big Money* by John Dos Passos. Copyright © 1936 J. Dos Passos, renewed 1964 John Dos Passos. Reprinted with permission granted by Lucy Dos Passos Coggin.

Harcourt, Inc. "The Jilting of Granny Weatherall" from *Flowering Judas and Other Stories* by Katherine Anne Porter. Copyright © 1930 and renewed 1958 by Katherine Anne Porter, reprinted by permission of Harcourt, Inc. "A Worn Path" from *A Curtain of Green and Other Stories* by Eudora Welty. Copyright © 1941 and renewed 1969 by Eudora Welty, reprinted by permission of Harcourt, Inc.

Harvard University Press. "Because I could not stop for Death—", "I heard a Fly buzz—when I died—" from *The Poems of Emily Dickinson*, Thomas H. Johnson, ed. Copyright © 1951, 1955, 1979, 1983 by the President and Fellows of Harvard College. Reprinted by permission of the publishers and the Trustees of Amherst College, Cambridge, Mass.: The Belknap Press of Harvard University Press.

Henry Holt and Company. "Mending Wall" from *The Poetry of Robert Frost* edited by Edward Connery Lathem. Copyright © 1930, 1939, 1969 by Henry Holt and Company, © 1967 by Lesley Frost Ballantine, © 1958 by Robert Frost. Reprinted by permission of Henry Holt and Company, LLC.

Houghton Mifflin Company. "Ambush" from *The Things They Carried* by Tim O'Brien. Copyright © 1990 by Tim O'Brien. Reprinted by permission of Houghton Mifflin Company. All rights reserved.

Liveright Publishing Corporation. "anyone lived in a pretty how town" from *Complete Poems*: 1904-1962 by E. E. Cummings, edited by George J. Firmage. Copyright © 1940, 1968, 1991 by the Trustees for the E. E. Cummings Trust. Reprinted by permission of Liveright Publishing Corporation. "somewhere i have never travelled,gladly beyond" from *Complete Poems*: 1904-1962 by E. E. Cummings, edited by George J. Firmage. Copyright © 1931, copyright © 1959, 1991 by the Trustees for the E. E. Cummings Trust. Copyright © 1979 by George James Firmage. Reprinted by permission of Liveright Publishing Corporation.

Penguin Group (USA) Inc. From *The Crucible* by Arthur Miller. Copyright © 1952, 1953, 1954, renewed © 1980, 1981, 1982 by Arthur Miller. Used by permission of Viking Penguin, a division of Penguin Group (USA) Inc.

Random House, Inc. "I, too, sing America," "The Negro Speaks of Rivers" from *The Collected Poems of Langston Hughes* by Langston Hughes. Copyright © 1994 by The Estate of Langston Hughes. Used by permission of Alfred A. Knopf, a division of Random House, Inc. "A Noiseless Flash" from *Hiroshoma* by John Hersey. Copyright © 1946 and renewed 1974 by John Hersey. Used by permission of Alfred A. Knopf, a division of Random House, Inc.

Sunstone Press. "Song of the Sky Loom" from *Songs of the Tewa* by Herbert Spinden appears courtesy of Sunstone Press, Box 2321, Santa Fe, NM 87504-2321, USA.

Yale University Press. From "Sinners in the Hands of an Angry God" by Jonathan Edwards from *Images or Shadows of Divine Things* (The Works of Jonathan Edwards). Reprinted by permission of Yale University Press.

ART ACKNOWLEDGMENTS

Cover Illustration Works; **43** © Library of Congress; **58** © CORBIS/Bettmann; **107** © Photodisc; **187** © David Ryan; **203** © CORBIS; **226** © CORBIS/Hulton-Deutsh Collection; **294** © David Benoit; **302** © David Benoit; **313** © Library of Congress; **323** © CORBIS; **353** © CORBIS; **370** © SuperStock.